THE HR TOOLKIT

AN INDISPENSABLE RESOURCE FOR BEING A CREDIBLE ACTIVIST

DENISE A. ROMANO

McGraw Hill

New York   Chicago   San Francisco   Lisbon   London   Madrid
Mexico City   Milan   New Delhi   San Juan   Seoul
Singapore   Sydney   Toronto

The **McGraw·Hill** Companies

1 2 3 4 5 6 7 8 9 0   DOC/DOC   1 5 4 3 2 1 0

ISBN   978-0-07-170081-8
MHID 0-07-170081-1

Product or brand names used in this book may be trade names or trademarks. Where we believe that there may be proprietary claims to such trade names or trademarks, the name has been used with an initial capital or it has been capitalized in the style used by the name claimant. Regardless of the capitalization used, all such names have been used in an editorial manner without any intent to convey endorsement of or other affiliation with the name claimant. Neither the author nor the publisher intends to express any judgment as to the validity or legal status of any such proprietary claims.

This publication is designed to provide accurate and authoritative information in regard to the subject matter covered. It is sold with the understanding that neither the author nor the publisher is engaged in rendering legal, accounting, futures/securities trading, or other professional service. If legal advice or other expert assistance is required, the services of a competent professional person should be sought.

—From a Declaration of Principles jointly adopted
by a Committee of the American Bar Association
and a Committee of Publishers

McGraw-Hill books are available at special quantity discounts to use as premiums and sales promotions, or for use in corporate training programs. To contact a representative, please e-mail us at bulksales@mcgraw-hill.com.

This book is printed on acid-free paper.

Library of Congress Cataloging-in-Publication Data

Romano, Denise A.
  The HR toolkit: an indispensable resource for being a credible activist / Denise A. Romano.
      p. cm.
  Includes bibliographical references.
  ISBN-13: 978-0-07-170081-8
  ISBN-10: 0-07-170081-1
  1. Personnel management. 2. Labor laws and legislation. I. Title.
  HF5549.R62117 2010
  658.3—dc22
                                                        2009052632

Dedicated to

Credible Activists everywhere—

those HR professionals, organizational development professionals,

consultants, coaches, emotional intelligence researchers

and practitioners, and others at every level who courageously

educate multidirectionally within companies in support of

"competitive corporate governance," which is based on

continual learning and sound, ethical, and lawful processes

and practices while clearly and firmly opposing practices

and processes that are arbitrary, inconsistent,

unethical, retaliatory, and unlawful and significantly

impact individuals, workgroups, safety, health, reputations,

families, communities, the environment, product quality,

investors, profits, and whole economies.

—Denise A. Romano, M.A., Ed.M.

CONTENTS

ACKNOWLEDGMENTS

Many thanks to my wonderful and witty agents Janet Rosen and Sheree Bykofsky, and to my helpful and kind editors, Michele Wells, Ron Martirano and Maureen Dennehy. Also, thanks to Nina Levy Girand, the freelance proofreader, for her contributions.

For those friends who gave me valuable assistance through this process: James Gomez, Don Osterweil, and Gregg Bowen.

For loving friendship during the best and worst of times, enormous thanks to my true sisters: Kim Bridgewood, Marcia Osgood, Alyssa Bonilla, Carolynn Regan, Diana Angell, Selma Karaca, Vicki Beltz, Aldijana Sabovic, Lisa Colon, and Joanna Foley.

For true friendship, laughter, and love: Don Scime, Dave Burke, Adam Holland, Steve Bonadonna, Linda Martino, Anthony Buczko, Connie Halporn, Mike Schlicht, Tom Witt, LisaJo Landsberg, Micki Wesson, John Wright, John Campbell, Barbara Fae Feldstein, Phil Saltzman, and Bob Wong.

For valiant efforts and intelligent teamwork, enormous thanks to: Tim McInnis, Rich Bernstein, Phil Michael, Christina Bost-Seaton, Laura Conway-Fried, Eric Unis, Amos Alter, and Seanna Brown.

With gratitude to the most skillful and inspiring trainers from whom I've had the privilege of learning: Bernadette Poole-Tracy, Ed.D.; Thom Bond; Steve Stein, Ph.D.; David Caruso, Ph.D.; Shakil Choudoury; Anaheed Dashtgard; Emily Menn, J.D.; Mark Slaski, Ph.D.; Heather Anderson; Tim Turner, Ph.D.; Peter Papadogiannis, Ph.D.; Derek Mann, Ph.D.; Wendy Gordon; Chaya Cohen; Henry "Dick" Thompson, Ph.D.; Allan H. Church, Ph.D.; Janine Waclawski, Ph.D.; Alison Ritchie; Janice Marie Johnson; KC Wagner; and Rick Ulfick.

For keeping me healthy: Dr. Richard Mueller, Dr. Peter Dicpingaitis, Andrea Beaman, Alexa Brill, Dr. Raj Singla, Dr. Mark Stein, Dr. Alex Meneshian, and Dr. Geoffrey Pollack.

With appreciation to the emotionally intelligent bosses I've had: Sister Elizabeth Myles; Vince Butler; Kate Boland; Joanna Foley, LCSW; Sandy Yanai; and Joe Drogo.

With appreciation to the other bosses I've had for inspiring me to be a credible activist.

With deep appreciation for those who have helped with technical issues over the years: Richard Vargas; Julian Birnbaum, J.D.; Leo Lewkowitz; S.A. Janet Briscoe; and The Honorable Jaclyn Brilling, J.D.

With thanks to my wonderful, caring neighbors: Amy Lopez-Cepeda, Dave Poster, Susan Weinstein, Glenn Berman, Carl Ferrando, and the late Jim Sneed.

With gratitude to my first-grade teacher, Mrs. Cohen, who gave me a composition book and told me to write down all of my feelings. With love and appreciation for A.G.'s generous teaching, encouragement, presence, friendship, and affection.

For my uncle, Philip F. O'Mara, Ph.D., and to the memory of my Aunt Joan O'Mara, Ph.D., who both taught me to love art and Manhattan.

Thanks to the Avett Brothers for their great music, which got me through the formatting of this book.

For my grandparents, Myra Regina O'Mara, Philip Joseph O'Mara, and Sadie (Kaufer) Romano, and for my wonderful brother, John E. Romano, who have loved me unconditionally and have demonstrated this love powerfully through both words and actions.

PROLOGUE

My hope is that this book will ultimately be helpful to Human Resources (HR) and Organizational Development (OD) professionals, consultants, coaches, and trainers at any level and in any industry. Please remember that city, state, and federal employment laws are almost constantly changing. Different states have different laws. What is unlawful harassment or wrongful termination in one city or state is perfectly legal in another. Use these tools prudently, and always research any applicable laws in your city or state regarding whatever situation you must address. Utilize the free government technical assistance links and other information provided here for the most current information regarding any situation that you want to address. Always do credible research before taking any action at work to address workplace issues.

My recommendation for using this book is to begin at the beginning. Start with the first chapter so you have a clear understanding of the importance of, and rationale for, HR/OD professionals being credible activists in their workplaces. I encourage you to research any laws you are looking for information on with a current source on the Web or with the Society for Human Resource Management (SHRM) in the event there have been changes since this book has been published. The HR world is always growing, developing, and changing.

INTRODUCTION

On any given day, millions of Human Resources professionals encounter unpleasant workplace experiences ranging from mild annoyance to potentially costly lawsuits. Unfortunately, most of these professionals' recommendations to deal with these experiences are either ignored or dismissed by their leadership, resulting in unnecessary problems for the company. The Society for Human Resource Management (SHRM) has identified being a "credible activist" as one the six most important skills an HR professional must have to succeed. However, there don't seem to be any courses on how to become a skilled credible activist. It isn't taught in graduate school, and it can't be faked.

Many popular magazine articles, news features, Web sites, and e-zines about how to cope with various types of workplace dysfunction often advise HR professionals and other employees who suffer at work to simply get another job. This is frequently not an ideal or even realistic solution, particularly during a recession. HR professionals know there are better solutions. They know there are greater employment lawsuits during economic downturns, and whether they know it or not, in most states, they are in a unique position of having advantages that most employees don't.

A 2008 survey of HR professionals asked, "Do you trust and respect your company's senior management team?" Of the nearly 300 respondents who replied, the results were as follows:

Yes: 38 percent
No: 53 percent
Not sure: 9 percent

Many non-HR employees might be surprised to see these results, thinking that just because HR professionals are part of "management," there is always agreement among them. The average HR professional, however, wouldn't be surprised at the results, as most within the field agree that no matter how many academic degrees, professional certifications, or additional training they have, management often considers HR to be unimportant fluff rather than the essential strategists they are. Additionally, HR professionals are well aware that while they are part of management, they are also employees reporting to that management, who are often reluctant to value what HR has to offer at critical moments or to take seriously the employment laws in the realm of the HR discipline.

These results indicate a crisis in corporate governance, which is not surprising given the current global recession. When companies function in full legal compliance while using competitive management methods, their businesses are more profitable and experience far fewer lawsuits and regulatory fines. Many workplaces fail to handle employee complaints about harassment, discrimination, retaliation, or ethical concerns appropriately. Many don't appropriately handle issues relating to safety, violence in the workplace, or the consistent application of policies. Most organizations also have severe problems relating to issues that are more common, yet harder for most employees to articulate, such as unfair performance evaluation systems, abusive managers, confusion about how roles are defined, how to make legitimate complaints, retaining incompetent people in powerful positions, and more.

In these challenging times, HR professionals and other managers need to know how to strategically position themselves to be of the most value to their companies. To survive now and remain sustainably competitive, business leaders need to look beyond the seemingly obvious cost-cutting measures of the past. The world has changed. The organizational Development (OD) field has taught us a great deal over the last several decades that serves us well now.

When HR professionals' recommendations are dismissed, vetoed, or marginalized even in the face of serious consequences resulting from poor corporate governance, there is an important opportunity available. The HR professional has an opportunity to be a credible activist, gain the respect of leadership, positively influence the culture and governance practices of the company, and protect him- or herself in the process of saying what needs to be said in a diplomatic and professional manner.

Implementing crucial changes in operations to ensure safety, legal compliance, efficiency, competence, and improved processes will save money and increase profit and productivity. The credible activist HR professional can skillfully recommend a number of changes that will benefit the company and its employees. In doing so, the credible activist also benefits him- or herself.

This book will help you identify and address workplace dysfunction, recommend improvements for the workplace, and remain within ethical and legal parameters valued by HR/OD professionals. It will give every HR professional—no matter their position or educational level—the tools to articulate his or her concerns to the right people in management in a way that increases the likelihood of a positive outcome. This book will also help you discern the best ways to spend your company's training allowance or your own professional training, if you are lucky enough to have that benefit. I encourage emotional intelligence (EI) assessment and skill development for every HR/OD professional, corporate leader, consultant, coach, and trainer. It will only make you even better at what you do than you already are.

If you are an organizational leader reading this book, welcome aboard! Please know all of the work herein is to support you, the company's mission and goals, and to do so in a manner that is legally compliant and ethical. HR also strive to do so in a way that makes work efficient, profitable, pleasurable, and physically, psychologically, and emotionally healthy. I trust and hope you fully support us in meeting these goals.

This book will also cover some common pitfalls any of us can encounter, and I encourage you to keep the book nearby, as you never know when one of these situations will pop up. As we who work in HR/OD know, this field is never dull. I also hope you will check out the LinkedIn Group I created for credible activists and join us in our quest for legally and ethically compliant corporate governance. As of this writing, the hype keeps growing! I hope you will read on and choose to join us in our quest for legally and ethically compliant corporate governance.

There are six parts to this book. Sample memos, letters, templates and checklists can be found at the end of each chapter in the HR Tools section.

Part One of this book helps HR professionals and managers understand foundational traits needed to practice HR/OD and handle serious problems in the workplace. Sample memos, templates, and checklists are included here. Part One also helps HR/OD professionals assess their own EI skills and technical skills, while also assisting with assessments of

HR/OD positions and prospective companies—keeping in mind what aspects of corporate culture must be in place to support ethical and excellent HR practices.

Part Two addresses the alphabet soup of employment laws HR professionals must understand. Workplaces in the United States have a legal responsibility to *prevent* violations of these employment laws, and the HR role is central in preventing such violations as well as providing multidirectional education within the company to ensure all staff are working and interacting within legal and ethical compliance. Unfortunately, many companies do not accomplish this well, or at all. To address these challenges, this section includes sample memos, templates, and checklists designed specifically to assist and support the HR professional.

Part Three helps HR professionals and managers monitor themselves and their own professional behavior to ensure that they are not contributing to the problems and dysfunctions found in many workplaces. HR professionals (like business leaders and lawyers) are held to a higher standard; self-awareness regarding workplace behavior is enormously important and affects credibility. The more individual improvement there is among higher-level employees, the more group and workplace improvement there will be. Very often people think everyone else is problematic, unprofessional, difficult, or impossible, but that they themselves are none of those things. This section will help HR professionals review their own workplace behaviors and reactions to ensure they are not unwittingly contributing to workplace dysfunction and to help them adjust their behavior if needed. This section will also help readers develop into the kinds of professionals who are more likely to be successful credible activists in their HR and/or management roles. In addition, this section will help the credible activist HR professional address behavioral problems in other employees at any level. This section includes sample memos, templates, and checklists.

Part Four helps the credible activist add value to his or her company by using OD knowledge that ties directly to sound internal corporate governance and profitability. The credible activist has more credibility when he or she is able to recommend efficiency-building processes that both prevent unnecessary costs and improve internal systems and processes. This section includes sample memos, templates, and checklists.

Part Five helps HR professionals and managers recommend workplace improvements to make workplaces more pleasant in general and improve talent retention, particularly during a recession, when employees are often asked to give more time and effort for less compensation or scaled-back benefits. This section includes sample memos, templates, and checklists.

Part Six includes resources to help HR professionals and managers find information, get support, obtain answers to legal questions, connect with others in similar situations, improve their marketability, improve job search strategies, and make good use of being unemployed, should they find themselves without a job at some point. Every HR professional has had an unpleasant if not nightmarish workplace experience he or she still recalls and occasionally ponders. Given the increasing number of lawsuits, regulatory violations, workplace violence incidents, and fraud scandals, there is a great deal of work to do, so let's get out there and do it well!

PART ONE

FOUNDATIONAL ISSUES FOR HR CREDIBLE ACTIVISTS

"All truth passes through three stages.
First, it is ridiculed.
Second, it is violently opposed.
Third, it is accepted as being self-evident."

—Arthur Schopenhauer

CHAPTER 1

WHY CREDIBLE ACTIVISM?

HOUSTON FIRM TO PAY $21 MILLION
IN IMMIGRATION CASE

OSHA FINES BP $21 MILLION FOR
FATAL TEXAS CITY, TX EXPLOSION

Sidley Austin Law Firm to Pay $27.5 Million
to Resolve Landmark Age Discrimination Case

When you read these recent headlines from across the United States, ask yourself: Can my company afford risking convictions in civil court, criminal court, and/or the court of public opinion? Which employees and internal processes might be putting my company at risk? A 2007 article in the CPA Journal cites these statistics from the Association of Certified Fraud Examiners' 2006 "Report to the Nation on Occupational Fraud and Abuse":

- More than $600 billion in annual losses is attributed to fraud.
- Tips from employees, customers, vendors, and anonymous sources account for:
  - 34 percent of the detection of all fraudulent activity
  - 34 percent of the detection of fraudulent activity for not-for-profit companies
  - 39.7 percent of the detection of fraudulent activity for government agencies
  - 48 percent of the detection of owner/executive fraud schemes
- Anonymous reporting mechanisms are the antifraud measure with the greatest impact on reducing losses:
  - Companies with anonymous reporting mechanisms reported median losses of $100,000, while those without these mechanisms reported median losses of $200,000.[1]
  - BNET Business Network reports that shareholder litigation accounts for 47 percent of all directors' and officers' liability cases filed against executives of for-profit

companies, 16 percent against executives of privately held companies, and 1 percent against executives of not-for-profit companies in the United States.[2]

Add to these trends a responsive trend among directors' and officers' liability insurance providers to put forth exclusions in company policies for sexual harassment claims, fraud litigation, dishonesty, and other sources of cost that are considered entirely preventable. The clear message even from liability coverage firms to all types of workplaces is "Really? You were stupid enough to allow *that* to happen? Don't look at us to help you with this one!"

You don't want your company to be the next Enron. There is no room or reason for costly, preventable errors. Compliance violations, safety violations, harassment and discrimination lawsuits, fraudulent activity, false claims cases, accounting scandals, and financial mismanagement are all extremely costly, but most importantly, they are also all preventable. Well-informed HR professionals who position themselves as credible activists and find the courage to professionally and graciously address serious workplace problems are ahead of the competition in every way.

BASIC HR CONCEPTS

A surprising number of HR professionals and managers don't have the necessary skills to write an effective memo to the appropriate person in the workplace in order to have a serious issue addressed or resolved well. Many also don't have sufficient interpersonal skills to handle conflict, recognize significant diversity issues, or address problematic gaps between policy and practice. Even higher-level managers often lack these skills because they are deficient in technical HR compliance knowledge.

However, most HR professionals know when they find themselves in the midst of a seemingly impossible situation and/or are put in the position of violating professional ethics codes.

Most HR professionals put in a position like the one described wish they could have done something about these situations to either help themselves or help someone who was treated unfairly, unethically, or unlawfully. However, most HR professionals and managers do not have the skills, knowledge, or abilities to know how to effectively address situations in which they must educate and disagree with those above them. Countless HR professionals are regularly ignored, excluded from decision-making processes, dismissed as fluff peddlers, and not listened to when their expertise could prevent costly lawsuits and scandals.

As mentioned in the Introduction, SHRM encourages HR/OD professionals to be credible activists in their workplaces and agents of ethical strategic change while remaining allied with corporate business interests. A new reality includes HR and OD professionals as credible activists. Additionally, many HR professionals are unaware that when they advocate for certain Equal Employment Opportunity (EEO) and Americans with Disabilities Act (ADA) rights of others in the workplace, they become protected from retaliation as well. This is a key ingredient in many of the relevant memos, which serves as a protective factor for HR professionals using these memos to improve their workplaces and thus their work and personal lives.

RETALIATION AS DEFINED BY THE EEOC

Per the Equal Employment Opportunity Commission (EEOC),

> An employer may not fire, demote, harass or otherwise 'retaliate' against an individual for filing a charge of discrimination, participating in a discrimination proceeding, or otherwise opposing discrimination. The same laws that prohibit discrimination based on race, color, sex, religion, national origin, age, and disability, as well as wage differences between men and women performing substantially equal work, also prohibit retaliation against individuals who oppose unlawful discrimination or participate in an employment discrimination proceeding.

In addition to the protections against retaliation that are included in all of the laws enforced by EEOC, the ADA also protects individuals from coercion, intimidation, threat, harassment, or interference in their exercise of their own rights or their encouragement of someone else's exercise of rights granted by the ADA, now the ADAAA (Americans with Disability Act Amendments Act.

Three main terms are used to describe retaliation. Retaliation occurs when an employer, employment agency, or labor company takes an *adverse action* against a *covered individual* because he or she engaged in a *protected activity*. These three terms are described in the following as per the EEOC.

> **Adverse action**. An adverse action is an action taken to try to keep someone from opposing a discriminatory practice, or from participating in an employment discrimination proceeding. Examples of adverse actions include employment actions such as termination, refusal to hire, and denial of promotion; other actions affecting employment such as threats; unjustified negative evaluations, or references; or increased surveillance. Additionally, any other action such as an assault or unfounded civil or criminal charges that are likely to deter reasonable people from pursuing their rights would be classified as an adverse action. Adverse actions do not include petty slights and annoyances, such as stray negative comments in an otherwise positive or neutral evaluation, "snubbing" a colleague, or negative comments that are justified by an employee's poor work performance or history.
>
> Even if the prior protected activity alleged wrongdoing by a different employer, retaliatory adverse actions are unlawful. For example, it is unlawful for a worker's current employer to retaliate against him or her for pursuing an EEO charge against a former employer.
>
> Of course, employees are not excused from continuing to perform their jobs or follow their company's legitimate workplace rules just because they have filed a complaint with the EEOC or opposed discrimination.
>
> **Covered individuals**. Covered individuals are people who have opposed unlawful practices, participated in proceedings, or requested accommodations related to

employment discrimination based on race, color, sex, religion, national origin, age, or disability. Individuals who have a close association with someone who has engaged in such protected activity also are covered individuals. For example, it is illegal to terminate an employee because his spouse participated in employment discrimination litigation.

Individuals who have brought attention to violations of law other than employment discrimination are *not* covered individuals for purposes of antidiscrimination retaliation laws. For example, "whistleblowers" who raise ethical, financial, or other concerns unrelated to employment discrimination are not protected by the EEOC-enforced laws.

Protected activities. Protected activities include the *opposition to a practice believed to be unlawful discrimination.* Opposition is informing an employer that you believe that he or she is engaging in prohibited discrimination. It is protected from retaliation as long as it is based on a reasonable, good-faith belief that the practice in question violates antidiscrimination law and the manner of the opposition is reasonable.

Examples of protected opposition include the following:

- Threatening to file a charge of discrimination
- Picketing in opposition to discrimination
- Refusing to obey an order reasonably believed to be discriminatory

Examples of activities that are *not* protected opposition include the following:

- Actions that interfere with job performance so as to render the employee ineffective
- Unlawful activities such as acts or threats of violence

• • •

A protected activity can also include requesting a reasonable accommodation based on religion or disability. For more information about Protected Activities, see EEOC's *Compliance Manual*, Section 8, *Chapter II, Part B: Opposition* and *Part C: Participation.*[3]

In fiscal year (FY) 2008, the EEOC received 32,690 charges of retaliation discrimination based on all statutes enforced by the EEOC. The EEOC resolved 25,999 retaliation charges in 2008, and recovered more than $111 million in monetary benefits for charging parties and other aggrieved individuals (not including monetary benefits obtained through litigation).[4]

What it comes down to is this: If you are an HR professional and you realize your company has made inadvertent errors, is handling certain things improperly, or is somehow failing to prevent harassment, discrimination, and retaliation, and/or is looking the other way while certain employees engage in unlawful or unallowable behavior, you have a number of choices:

- You can leave and say nothing.
- You can leave and truthfully let the company know why you are leaving verbally.
- You can leave and truthfully let the company know why you are leaving, in writing.
- You can leave and do any of the above while also reporting any wrongdoing that concerned you in writing to the relevant authorities.

- You can remain and try to graciously, directly, and professionally address the wrongdoing in the spirit of being a chief learning officer and a chief compliance officer as well as the HR professional you are.
- You can approach what you see needs to be remediated in a careful, diplomatic, and direct manner. This approach will only add to your professionalism and credibility as an HR professional who is concerned with the company operating within legal compliance and who is concerned with being part of a lawful, respectable operation.

Here is why the disclaimer at the beginning of this book is necessary: most people do not like to be told they're mistaken. This, of course, circles back to emotional intelligence, communication, and conflict resolution skills, but we'll get to that later. There is a *Seinfeld* episode in which Jerry says that the only difference between lawyers and everyone else is that they've read the entire inside top of the Monopoly box and know all the rules, while the rest of us haven't. Oprah frequently says, "Knowledge is power"; she is correct. The knowledge is there for us all. We can choose to learn whatever we need to; we can choose to know and practice our compliance responsibilities in order to abide by them. So what's the problem?

"Role confusion" and "ego" get in the way. If you're reporting to or working alongside executives who don't have this technical knowledge and who assume that HR is meaningless fluff that anyone can do, they'll often assume they know as much as you do—or more than you do—even if they don't. If you're reporting to or working alongside executives who don't care to know what their compliance responsibilities are, your memos telling them what the inside of the Monopoly box top says might not be welcome. And it may not even be because they're bad people, because they don't respect the laws, or because they have an unconscious desire to be sued for millions of dollars. They just don't want to be wrong. They don't want to be "not right."

You report to them, you may be younger than they are, you may have less workplace experience, and you probably earn less money than they do. It sounds ridiculous, *and it really is ridiculous*, but instead of the grateful response of, "Thank you for doing your job properly, for letting us know this, and for helping to save us costly regulatory fines and lawsuits!" what may happen instead is that you may be met with retaliatory anger that you read the inside of the top of the Monopoly box and had the nerve to point it out to them. Some people will react this way. This book will help you deal with such people, should you be unfortunate enough to encounter and report to them. In addition, it bears pointing out that there are those executives to whom you may compose the most perfectly worded and informative memo ever written who will still react as though you had just committed murder.

However, let's be optimistic for now. For a sample form you may use to truly invite and welcome any kind of employee feedback, including complaints about unlawful harassment and discrimination, please see the HR Tool entitled "Sample Feedback Report to HR/OD," at the end of the chapter, on pages 10–11. Feel free to customize this form for your own company.

)) CORPORATE GOVERNANCE

What is organizational development and how does it relate to corporate governance? How is it different from HR, and why should HR professionals and leaders care? Here are three definitions from pioneers in the OD field, which were given in a Multi-Rater Feedback graduate class that was taught by Allan Church and Janine Waclawski.

Richard Beckhard defines organizational development as a planned, top-down, company-wide effort to increase the company's effectiveness and health. OD is achieved through interventions in the company's "processes," using behavioral science knowledge.·

Warren Bennis defines OD as "a complex strategy intended to change the beliefs, attitudes, values, and structure of companies so that they can better adapt to new technologies, markets, and challenges."

Warner Burke emphasizes that OD is not just "anything done to better an organization"; it is a particular kind of change process designed to bring about a particular kind of end result. OD involves company reflection, system improvement, planning, and self-analysis.

The OD field has learned a great deal about what makes any kind of company succeed or fail and why. This book will spare you the boring case studies and endless research and present what has proven to work and what will provide you with a competitive edge via cost-saving governance practices that can be influenced, recommended, and implemented by the credible activist HR/OD professional who wishes to improve his or her workplace and do his or her job ethically and with excellence.

What the HR/OD professional must always remember is that the HR/OD department, no matter how large or small, *is* the government of an organization, and the employee handbook is the constitution. Whether the HR/OD professional reading this book has the authority of the executive, legislative, or judicial power in the company, or some combination of those, depends on the company, its culture, and its leadership. The HR/OD professional must clearly understand his or her role in the company in order to be effective and credible, and, frankly, to remain personally calm.

The new world is flat—and apparently hot and crowded, too. In the not-so-distant past, discussion of wages could get an employee fired; nepotism ran rampant; people took care of "their own"; racial and gender ceilings were impenetrable; there was no recourse for harassment or discrimination and retaliation; and all of this was completely allowable under the law. The world has changed, and employment laws are ever changing. A growing global middle class, increased educational opportunities, global markets, and technological advances have eliminated almost all commerce and communication barriers, resulting in increased competition not only for the best jobs but also for the best employees.

The existence of various "corporate governance indices" illustrates that the direct relationship between profitability and OD principles *is* what I call "competitive corporate governance." HR/OD professionals can and must influence ethical and legally compliant competitive corporate governance. HR/OD professionals have the benefit of being able to stand on the shoulders of countless scholars, researchers, and successful business leaders who came before them.

Even nonprofits and government entities must use every dollar as efficiently as possible. Several corporate governance indices have been developed to rate publicly traded companies in terms of the quality of their corporate governance so investors have information they need to make determinations. Would you invest in a company that had no written EEO policies? Would you invest in a company that had policies but didn't follow them consistently? Would you invest in a company that hired only family members and close friends who weren't properly trained for crucial positions such as chief executive officer (CEO), chief financial officer (CFO), internal controls officer, ethics officer, chief of staff, or chief compliance officer? If investors would not, then taxpayers and donors will not either.

Factors used in most corporate governance indices include ratings of risk in various areas including accounting, regulatory, legal, reputation, environmental and social, compliance, portfolio, credit, and market. Investors seeking to hold shares in a company for the long term will typically be concerned about the quality of their company's corporate governance, as research has shown that a high quality of corporate governance typically leads to enhanced shareholder returns. Prudent investors look to these measures to determine whether to invest in various companies. Investment research has come to include many OD principles in the evaluation of a company's competitiveness and predicted profitability. Even if a company is not publicly traded, leadership and HR/OD will want to ensure that what I call "competitive corporate governance" is in place to both boost profits and prevent unnecessary risk. The chapters that follow will explore how an HR/OD professional or any corporate leader with influence, authority, and determination can do this from an OD perspective, which unsurprisingly mirrors those areas that are now scrutinized by the most prudent institutional and individual investors.

Many of us have seen or heard interviews with Warren Buffett and have learned how he personally visits and researches companies before investing in them, as well as maintains both a balance of personal relationship and trusting autonomy with business leaders in whom he chooses to invest. He is only able to trust them because he has researched his own sense of competitive corporate governance, and he knows what he requires in a business in order for it to be worth his financial backing.

Although HR/OD professionals still often struggle for the respect their colleagues with MBAs and law degrees get in the C-suite, the most crucial linchpins of competitive corporate governance are rooted in OD knowledge and will determine whether a company survives and thrives, or fails. Even HR/OD professionals who don't have the influence, authority, or experience they wish they did will be able to find many ways to apply what we have learned in the OD field about why these linchpins have proven to contribute to corporate success and increased profitability. See the HR Tool entitled "Competitive Corporate Governance Implementation," on pages 11–12.

WHAT IS A "CREDIBLE ACTIVIST" AND WHY IS IT IMPORTANT?

Being a credible activist is the most challenging of the six critical skills any HR/OD professional must have, according to SHRM. Many helpful articles and white papers are available on www.SHRM.org regarding the importance of being a credible activist. A credible activist is someone who backs up his or her positions and recommendations with credible research, who takes a strong stand on certain points, who is respected, and who accomplishes organizational improvement in doing these things. Credible activism has also been called "HR with guts" or "HR with sharp elbows."

The HR/OD field has evolved significantly from the "personnel departments" from decades ago and from out-of-touch HR professionals who give HR/OD a bad name. One man in Annabel Gurwitch's film *FIRED!* describes how, as a former HR professional, he would betray the confidences of employees to their managers while claiming that was his job and referring to HR as "the dark arts."[5] This is unethical and not at all consistent with the new HR/OD professional of today. While it has historically been true that HR has been mistrusted by employees and inaccurately regarded as valueless fluff by executive management, HR has emerged as a prominent and valuable aspect of OD that directly connects profitability to governance.

)) CREDIBLE ACTIVISM

SHRM encourages HR/OD professionals to be credible activists in their workplaces and agents of ethical strategic change while remaining allied with corporate business interests. This new reality of HR and OD professionals as credible activists is extremely different than the former perception of HR practicing the "dark arts."

Most HR/OD professionals have encountered company and corporate leaders who don't understand what HR/OD is, what HR/OD can be, or how crucial the practice of ethical, legally compliant HR/OD is to competitive corporate governance and efficient and profitable operations. They mistakenly think that HR is all about health benefits and facilitating the firing of employees when necessary. Yet this could not be further from the truth. We in HR know that much more is involved with our roles. In addition, we know that unless there is a separate OD department in your company, adding OD to the HR title is now necessary, not optional icing on the cake. We need all the knowledge and awareness we can get to support our leaders and companies in order to be as competitive and robust as possible.

Imagine an HR/OD credible activist working for Enron who notices that something is not quite right. Let's say this ardent, earnest HR/OD professional says, "Excuse me, boss, but Joe from accounting just came to me and asked me to relay to you that there are some serious issues that need to be discussed." What does the boss say or do? Does the boss say, "Thank you, credible activist! You've helped us avoid disaster. We will investigate, change how we do things if necessary, and you and Joe in accounting are getting promotions and raises for having pointed this out!" Or does the boss suddenly decide that the credible activist's and Joe's job performance are not quite what they needs to be and that they have also been interpersonally "difficult" and have used "poor judgment." Perhaps after giving them poor performance evaluations, he puts them on probation, until it is time to terminate them.

We know this happens in the real world. We know that protections from retaliation and whistleblower laws don't always work to protect well-meaning employees and HR professionals who speak up about anything that is not being done ethically or lawfully.

So, what is a credible activist to do? This book addresses all of the issues involved. But for now, your job as a credible activist is to keep your résumé up-to-date, continue cultivating current and new professional contacts, assess your life now and what you can risk, and assess how receptive your current workplace is to your being a credible activist. You will learn to predict your leadership's responses to your credible activist role. You will need to keep all of your ducks in a row, always do credible research, and further develop and practice every communication, conflict resolution, and EI (emotional intelligence) skill you have.

HR TOOLS

SAMPLE FEEDBACK REPORT TO HR/OD
(Suggestions and Requests for Intervention)

> __ **This IS Confidential**
>
> __ This is NOT Confidential

> **IMPORTANT:** In the case of concerns, complaints, information, or feedback that has to do with any issue involving discrimination, harassment, retaliation, accidents, injury, threats, or violence, great care will be taken to protect confidentiality. However, because (Company) takes these issues seriously, discussion with others will be necessary but will be limited only to those who absolutely must be involved in order for (Company) to conduct a thorough, prompt, and sound investigation.

To: _____, HR

From:

Date:

Level of Urgency:

    URGENT!

    Request response by:_____

    Not at all Urgent

Type of Feedback Report:

    Complaint

    Request for Intervention/Mediation

    Suggestion

    Policy Question

    Assistance Needed

    Other: _____

Re:

Step 1: Improve the situation on your own by discussing it with your direct supervisor.

Step 2: If you still need/want assistance from HR, please use this form to give full details and to help HR understand and prioritize.

Problem:

(Source of Frustration, Confusion, or Obstacle preventing excellence):

Suggested Solution/Intervention Requested/General Suggestion:

Please feel free to use additional space or paper. Your feedback is valued.

Either you may fax this to HR at _____ or you may e-mail this to HR at _____

Of course, you are always welcome to call or visit HR.

However, it does help if you present the issue, its urgency, and what you have already tried to resolve it.

Please understand that the HR/OD department handles multiple priorities.

Certainly if you have an emergency, a response will be as immediate as possible.

However, at times responses cannot be immediate and/or require consultation.

Your patience and understanding are appreciated. Your feedback is extremely valued.

COMPETITIVE CORPORATE GOVERNANCE IMPLEMENTATION

The costs and benefits involved (**in terms of time and effort**) in implementing competitive corporate governance can include:

- ☐ The time you invest in reading this book and noting your current corporate governance practices to see how competitive they are and what needs improvement
- ☐ Revising your employee handbook to clearly implement improved culture, internal complaint and investigation procedures, policies, performance management, and other changes as needed
- ☐ Feedback mechanism implementation and/or revision
- ☐ Training for you, your executives, your managers, and ultimately your entire staff
- ☐ Conflict Resolution training for you and your entire staff
- ☐ Emotional Intelligence (EI) and Nonviolent Communication (NVC) training for you and your entire staff
- ☐ Job description revisions for you and your entire staff

- ☐ The careful and lawful termination of employees who don't add value to your competitive goals
- ☐ The further training and development of employees who do add value to your competitive goals
- ☐ Your own continued professional and leadership development

By not implementing the crucial linchpins of competitive corporate governance, a company exposes itself to the following costs and liabilities:

- ☐ Costly turnover
- ☐ Costly external complaints and lawsuits
- ☐ Costly regulatory fines
- ☐ Negative publicity
- ☐ Declining stock prices, profits, or other forms of financial mismanagement
- ☐ Unmotivated employees without good citizenship behaviors
- ☐ Catastrophic Leadership Failure™ (a concept created by Henry L. Thompson, Ph.D.)[6]
- ☐ Loss of motivated, innovative, critically thinking, emotionally intelligent employees
- ☐ Keeping employees who are "yes-people," lazy, unmotivated, not innovative, and not critical thinkers
- ☐ Poor employee behavior modeled after poor leadership behavior

CHAPTER 2

THE IMPORTANCE OF EMOTIONAL INTELLIGENCE FOR THE CREDIBLE ACTIVIST

If you do a Web search on "emotional intelligence," you will probably get at least a couple million hits. For the purposes of this book, the working definition of emotional intelligence is one constructed by John D. Mayer, Ph.D., and Peter Salovey, Ph.D., in 1990:

> The ability to monitor one's own and other's feelings and emotions, to discriminate among them and to use this information to guide one's thinking and actions.[1]

Upon hearing this definition, many people may quickly respond, "Oh, yeah! I do that all the time!" And they may. However, it is a very good idea to find out for sure where your skill levels are. The fantastic news is that almost anyone can improve their EI skills if they are open to doing so, if they practice, and if they make it a priority. This is even better news for all of us when we consider that research shows us that humans have much more control over changing their EI than changing their IQ. This news becomes even better when we look at research that repeatedly indicates that EI is much more important to workplace and interpersonal success than IQ is.

Henry L. "Dick" Thompson, Ph.D., has done important and revealing research into what he calls "Catastrophic Leadership Failure™." Dr. Thompson has found direct relationships between EI and Catastrophic Leadership Failure, but what does this mean for HR/OD professionals, and what, if anything, can we do about this when we encounter it?

Thompson argues that stress and its impact on cognitive and emotional abilities may provide at least a partial explanation for the degree of failure that lets an Enron, a WorldCom, a Tyco, or a Katrina happen. His research on leadership, stress, IQ, and EI showed that over the last 25 years, "when a leader's stress level is sufficiently elevated—whether on the front line of a manufacturing process, in the emergency room, the Boardroom or on the battlefield—his/her ability to fully and effectively use IQ and EI in tandem to make timely and effective decisions is significantly impaired. This impairment often leads to catastrophic results. A war for talent is underway. Finding, recruiting, and hiring talented leaders with high IQ and EI are only the first battle of the war. The war will be won or lost by those who are able to control stress at the individual and company levels. Stress negates talent, IQ and EI."

Thompson goes on to say that "EI involves managing/controlling the Awareness and Appraisal of emotions and the resulting action in a manner that produces successful outcomes, whether in the presence or absence of others."[2] This has great significance for decision making, performance evaluation, how a leader responds to diversity issues, how a leader responds to legal compliance issues, how a leader experiences and uses his or her authority, and whether or not a leader wants to know if he or she has spinach in his or her teeth, as theorist Heather Anderson describes it.[3]

What can we learn from Thompson's important research for ourselves, to better understand and assist our leadership, and to better understand the entire workforce? Many important things. The implications of this research extend far beyond Catastrophic Leadership Failure. The issues of stress and health are very relevant for HR/OD credible activists, as well as any employees, and these will be expanded upon in all parts of this book.

Change is hard. People—any of us—can be resistant or defensive to it. However, we can also be *resilient* and bring awareness to ourselves; we can ask what about our EI—and lives—we want to be different and better. We can explore what is in our power to adjust, change, and improve. We can make changes. We can define what our goals are and plan to meet them. When we consider how far we have come from the time of cave dwellers until now, we realize just how much change, growth, and development is possible for human beings.

There will be those leaders who don't want to hear Thompson's cautionary message on Catastrophic Leadership Failure and who don't want to understand how it is they wound up in the news media, in court, or having bankrupted millions of stakeholders. There will be those business leaders who are too frightened or ashamed to acknowledge that they have mishandled something important. They will keep it a secret. They will view all those around them who try to do things differently than them as their enemies. There will be those leaders who don't understand that employees who are hardworking, innovative, creative, and ethical, but who aren't "yes-men" or "yes-women" will either grow bored and leave or might even be lost via unwise corporate termination decisions. This points to another form of leadership failure—firing the wrong people and retaining the wrong people.

Leaders who fail will exclude quality staff from meetings, decisions, and processes because they don't want to share power, to share success or to share failure—they don't want to share learning. They may continue to make quite bad decisions and not even be aware they are violating the law or creating more and more serious problems for themselves because they only want to be surrounded by those who agree with them—or because they will only accept disagreement and critical thinking from a select few.

This is another area where diversity and emotion, largely happening in the unconscious, must be noticed, acknowledged, and addressed. Catastrophic Leadership Failure can be a downward spiral. The refusal to share power is crucial.

When the HR credible activist steps up and says, "I think we need to do something different," he or she is asserting him- or herself in a way that may not be welcome. He or she may not be welcome to do this on certain issues or may be welcome to do this under one boss but not under another. These permissions are sometimes made clear and defined in professional roles and sometimes are not.

You may find yourself in a meeting during which nobody speaks to you, looks at you, asks you what you think, or allows you to speak without being spoken over or interrupted. This means you are invisible, you are not welcome, your feedback is not welcome, your thoughts are not welcome, and you have no power; there is an unwillingness to share power with you. For whatever reasons, your skills, knowledge, and abilities are unwelcome and there is a preference that you remain quiet and not rock any boats. This is a particularly interesting dynamic when leadership will accept boat rocking from others on staff—but not from HR, or not from you.

Someone once said "A boat that cannot rock, also cannot sail." Credible activists are only "rocking the boat" if there is some issue in the company—and this exists in many companies—wherein the credible activist's input is unwelcome because the company's leadership does not want to know they've got spinach in their teeth. This can be a corporate response whether the activist is credible or not. Those who don't want to allow others into an in-group (that, for whatever reason, needs an out-group) wind up cutting themselves off from valuable resources in their own midst—on their own teams. However, leaders who fail don't see those who think critically of their decisions as team members but only as enemies and threats.

EMOTIONAL INTELLIGENCE IS A HARD SKILL

EI is far from a "soft skill" or a fun and fluffy diversion from work; it is a hard skill.[4] Development of EI is the work in every moment, in every decision, and in every interaction or noninteraction. It is the work in performance evaluation, hiring, promoting, retaining, and terminating, and HR/OD must help leadership understand this if they are not already aware. Rater-bias is a significant problem in companies whose leaders are in a downward spiral of failure and who are not bringing critical awareness to decisions, processes, systems, and their own emotional and thought processes, which are intertwined.

Many scholars, researchers, and practitioners point out that we make decisions based on emotions. What kinds of emotions happen at work? How many of us have been taught that emotions don't belong in the workplace? How many of us have been taught or told outright we should be unemotional or less emotional in the workplace? In fact, who among us has not been told we're either "too emotional" or "too aloof" for the workplace?

Rank and gender issues are very salient aspects of such conclusions, whether consciously or not. Anger, for example, has often been accepted in the workplace from certain employees, depending on who they are, what their position is, and, unfortunately, what their gender is. That is a serious problem. Similarly, whereas anger from certain employees is accepted, sadness may or may not be, again depending on rank, gender, or other identity characteristics. Disgust, fear, and anger, when in existence yet unexamined and/or unallowed, can easily lead to harassment, discrimination, retaliation, and/or workplace violence. Yet emotions are as much a part of human beings as are our respiratory systems. Emotions are a part of the human condition. If humans belong in the workplace, so do emotions. (See the HR Tool entitled "Sample Memo on Addressing Emotions in the Workplace," at the end of the chapter, on pages 19–20.

What is needed in the workplace is more emotional intelligence, skillful communication training, and conflict resolution skills training. How is employee A thought of, and how is employee B thought of? And why? What are the criteria? What are the standards? Are any issues of conflict of interest and/or personal relationships, cronyism, or nepotism involved? Are there ethical issues to be addressed? What are the emotions and thoughts that are affecting these performance evaluations and why? When HR/OD notices troubling systemic patterns, such as everyone in one department is of one race yet the city where the company is located is very diverse, it is important to raise these concerns with leadership. Or, when some employees' errors or violations of policy are overlooked, not acknowledged, or minimized yet those same violations of policy or similar errors of other employees are documented, disciplined, or used as reasons for termination, HR professionals must take note and find a way to discuss these inconsistencies with their leadership and their legal departments.

This is also true of assessing whether an applicant is an appropriate hire for the company and whether the applicant has proven to be an appropriate hire during the usual three- to six-month introductory period. (See the HR Tool entitled "Sample Interview Questions," on pages 21–22)

You will need to develop your own EI so that you can monitor how your credible activist role is affecting your leadership, your company, your own position, your colleagues, your stress levels, your health, and your life. You will learn to observe and measure these to see if your actions are welcome or not. Are you being valued or devalued? Are your efforts appreciated as the loyalty to and concern for the company that they are, or are your efforts considered annoyances and/or personally embarrassing for those with whom you raise these issues because they may fear this represents some failure on their part for not having noticed or acted?

You'll need to learn to measure these responses to your actions and determine how far you want to go with certain things. Do your credible research and present it in a brief format with citations ready for those who don't have much time to be persuaded by you that another course of action would be better. You will need to learn whether presenting the business case, the ethics case, or both to your leadership will be the most effective manner of persuading them on any given issue.

You will want to use all of your emotional intelligence skills when communicating verbally and in writing with your corporate leadership regarding any suggestions you hope to put forth. Even if you are being excluded from meetings and processes and even if you are being treated badly, you will want to remain as professional and pleasant as possible. Frequently, not only are credible activists whose input is unwelcome in the workplace excluded from any power-sharing, but they are also actively devalued in the following ways: ridiculed for any reason at all, marginalized in various ways, excluded from information and processes, slandered, and discredited personally and/or professionally without reason.

This requires an enormous amount of emotional and psychological resilience as well as well-developed emotional intelligence to endure. You will also need a good support system in your life, perhaps a good therapist, and you will need to take excellent care of yourself physically, emotionally, and psychologically. If you have a spiritual practice, that can help and be a source of strength for you as well. Being part of a community of even one or two other HR professionals who fully understand this kind of experience will also be enormously helpful.

If it helps you to understand why adults with whom you work, whom you believed were mature professionals, and whom you may have even considered friends would behave in ways that are childish, cruel, irrational, and destructive to themselves and to the corporate culture—or why your corporate culture seems to sanction the ridicule of some employees but not others—be sure to do additional reading regarding group dynamics, power sharing, emotional intelligence, and the primal brain. A brief explanation is shown in the HR Tool entitled "Checklist of Behaviors," on pages 20–21.

Credible activists are *not* the enemy. You are committed to performing your HR/OD job according to an ethical code of standards and within legal compliance. It takes a strong sense of self, strong professional ethics, and good external support to know this and remain strong in the face of irrational attacks from people who don't want to know what the dysfunctions in the workplace are.

HIRING

If you have any input into hiring, you will want to consciously look for signs of robust emotional intelligence, rational decision-making abilities, and integrity. You will want to ask questions, such as those shown in the HR Tool entitled, "Sample Interview Questions" on pages 21–22.

PERFORMANCE EVALUATIONS

If you are involved in performance evaluations, you will want to ensure that the same form of fight/flight response that you yourself might experience is not happening to any other employee who may be speaking up in his or her own way and in his or her own work realm. Have qualified HR staff review all performance evaluations with supervisors before they are presented to employees, if possible. Alternatively, ensure that all supervisors have evaluation skills that make them aware of avoiding rater-bias, attribution error, and conflicts of interest. Welcome employee concerns and complaints, and take them seriously. Ensure that the workplace culture supports all employees' right to bring any concerns to HR; this should be made clear repeatedly by leadership and all managers as well as by HR.

Discuss problematic managers with leadership. Offer these managers training and improvement or different responsibilities. Examine workplace culture and take the collective pulse of the staff with annual or semiannual anonymous surveys.

COMPANY ASSESSMENT

Use this book to do whatever you can to address and eliminate any dysfunction and implement corporate culture linchpins that ensure a healthy workplace. Every good HR professional understands that there are significant connections between EI, conflict resolution skills, effective feedback delivery, diversity issues, communication skills, and whether or not the company is functioning optimally.

Bernadette Poole-Tracy, Ed.D., created a simple company assessment that HR professionals can use to get a sense of where their company is currently with some of the core principles every HR credible activist must examine. Poole-Tracy's assessment appears in the HR Tool entitled "Company Assessment Tool: Conflict Resolution Climate, Dimensions and Scope," on pages 22–23, but it can only be used on a corporate-wide level with written permission from her. The assessment is usually distributed anonymously and companywide to all employees. The assessment will help you take the temperature of the staff for one of the most important diagnoses that can be made about a workplace.

›› FEEDBACK DELIVERY

Having a feedback delivery policy and training for a workplace that is not used to these concepts is necessary. The HR Tools entitled "Sample Feedback Delivery Policy for the Management Team" and the "Sample Feedback Guidelines," on pages 23–24, are two helpful samples that you can easily customize for your workplace. Be sure to have an hour-long training session with groups of approximately 20 people to roll out this initiative. Of course, any initiative is most successful with leadership demonstrating full support to all staff and visibly participating. Feel free to customize and change these to suit your workplace culture as needed.

›› THE IMPORTANCE OF CRITICAL THINKING ABILITIES, LOGIC, AND BEING A "REASONABLE PERSON"

As an HR/OD professional, you must be able to think critically, compare options rationally, and be a "reasonable person." At this point, you probably know that in the legal world there is the "Reasonable Person Standard." One source defines a reasonable person as an

> Ordinary, prudent person who normally exercises due care while avoiding extremes of both audacity and caution. Used as a test of liability in cases of negligence, this standard is not applied uniformly on all persons because varying degrees of reasonableness may be expected from a minor (infant), an adult, an unskilled person, or a professional such as a doctor.[5]

Another source defines "reasonable person standard" as

> *A phrase frequently used in TORT and Criminal Law to denote a hypothetical person in society who exercises average care, skill, and judgment in conduct and who serves as a comparative standard for determining liability.* The decision whether an accused is guilty of a given offense might involve the application of an objective test in which the conduct of the accused is compared to that of a reasonable person under similar circumstances. In most cases, persons with greater than average skills, or with special duties to society, are held to a higher standard of care. For example, a physician who aids a person in distress is held to a higher standard of care than is an ordinary person.[6]

The point is, you as an HR/OD professional must be reasonable, logical, and able to think rationally and critically. The last HR Tool in this chapter, entitled "Sample Critical Thinking Quiz for HR/OD Professionals," on pages 24–26, is a short but important test for you to take right now in order to help you assess your own "reasonableness."

HR TOOLS

SAMPLE MEMO ON ADDRESSING EMOTIONS IN THE WORKPLACE

On letterhead, in interoffice memo format, or via e-mail

To: Your Supervisor (Include any others on this list to whom this memo should be addressed.)

From: Your Name

Date:

Re.:   Addressing Emotions in the Workplace Culture at (Company)

I want to make several suggestions regarding addressing emotions in the workplace that I believe we should remain aware of.

I am concerned about how the recent situation with (employee's name) is being handled. Unless I am unaware of additional information or documentation related to this matter, my concern is that by (employee)'s supervisor telling her/him that she/he may not express any negative emotion in any way either verbally or nonverbally, that a grave mistake is being made. I do believe this requires immediate remediation.

Moving forward, I recommend that the/an HR Director must review all written directives to employees before they are given to employees to avoid the communication of inappropriate directives such as in this example. Additionally, I recommend that all (Company) management employees who supervise employees attend formal trainings on discipline, communication, emotional intelligence, and sound management skills for handling challenging situations.

I will follow this memo up with a list of quality upcoming available trainings in our area or via webinar, and/or I can create a training on my own that will cover the necessary topics.

We share a collective responsibility to ensure (Company)'s compliance with EEO laws. I know we share a commitment to prevent liability exposure for (Company) as well as personal liability exposure.

Specifically my concerns about this directive to this employee are:

Emotions are part of being human; therefore, this request is unrealistic and unreasonable.

This directive is not being given to other employees that I am aware of, and could be an example of disparate and inconsistent treatment.

The directive may appear to be gender discrimination and/or harassment since it has not been given to members of the opposite gender. Many other employees have cursed, yelled, slammed doors, raised their voices, or hung up on other employees during moments of anger; yet those employees have not been given such a directive, so there is a consistency issue.

The reasons for this employee's anger must be explored, considered, addressed, and resolved.

This could easily appear to be an example of disparate treatment for any reason including related to personal conflicts of interests. I am unaware of this employee ever engaging in behavior that has been characterized as threatening or violent, and I see no reason for such a directive to be given to this or any employee.

CHECKLIST OF BEHAVIORS

Those who feel they are being attacked at work may respond with one of two general sets of behaviors that can take many forms, either fight (attack) or flight (retreat):

FIGHT RESPONSES

☐ You may be bullied.

☐ You may be ridiculed.

☐ You may be excluded from meetings, processes, decisions, trainings, consultant meetings, etc.

☐ You may be subjected to further exclusion than existed before.

☐ There may be secrecy around information you would normally or should have access to.

☐ You may be put on probation, given a poor performance evaluation, or fired.

☐ You may have rumors started about you.

☐ You may be slandered.

☐ You may be harassed.

☐ You may be retaliated against.

☐ Your harassment and/or retaliation may be ignored if known about, not acted upon properly when observed by others, and/or not taken seriously.

☐ There may be conflicts started with you more often—or when they weren't previously—and won't be handled with sound conflict resolution methods.

☐ You may be accused of "causing problems" or "starting problems" if you attempt to raise real issues or resolve a conflict using sound conflict resolution methods.

☐ You may be characterized as "litigious" or not trusted as a valuable team member; a background check may even be conducted on you to see what your history in any lawsuits has been.

☐ There may be a general devaluing of the HR field as though it is valueless fluff.

☐ There may be a general devaluing of your education, training, skills, and abilities.

- ☐ There may be a subtle shift of certain responsibilities away from you and to others and similarly, you may be forced to take on busy-work that is not appropriate for your position and is designed to demean and anger you.

- ☐ People whom you have helped with things or with whom you have never had a problem may suddenly gang up on you with others who are discrediting you— "Groupthink" can happen and individual rational thought can be overtaken in some people.

FLIGHT RESPONSES

- ☐ They may retreat, reluctantly go with your recommendations, yet resent you for it.

- ☐ They may ignore you, and exclude you from meetings, processes, decisions, trainings, consultant meetings, etc.

- ☐ There may be further exclusion than existed before.

- ☐ Any issues you raise may just be avoided instead of resolved and you may later be blamed for having raised them, even though it is your job to do so.

- ☐ Any conflicts with you will be avoided rather than used as opportunities for resolution, learning, and development for all involved.

- ☐ There may be a subtle shift of certain responsibilities away from you and to others— or there may be a shift of certain responsibilities to you and away from others; either of these is a communication to you about your status in the workgroup.

- ☐ Any harassment or retaliation against you may be ignored and/or not taken seriously.

- ☐ People with whom you have had good rapport or even friendships may become reluctant to talk to you or be seen with you.

- ☐ In short, you are viewed as "the enemy" even though you are not the enemy.

SAMPLE INTERVIEW QUESTIONS:

- ☐ How do you respond to misunderstandings between you and a colleague? You and your supervisor?

- ☐ On a scale of 1 to 10, how punctual are you?

- ☐ On a scale of 1 to 10, how likely are you to directly discuss a conflict you might be having with someone at work?

- ☐ On a scale of 1 to 10, how likely are you to avoid a conflict you're having with someone at work?

- ☐ On a scale of 1 to 10, how aware of your emotions would you say you are?

- ☐ On a scale of 1 to 10, how would you rate your verbal and/or written skills while you're having a very frustrating day?

- ☐ What kinds of things do you do to alleviate stress while at work?

☐ On a scale of 1 to 10, how likely are you to make a suggestion regarding workplace improvements you might imagine?

☐ On a scale of 1 to 10, how would you rate each of these skills of yours?

    A. Conflict resolution?

    B. Communication?

    C. Self-awareness in general?

COMPANY ASSESSMENT TOOL: CONFLICT RESOLUTION CLIMATE, DIMENSIONS AND SCOPE

For each item below, give (Company)'s score:

Strongly Agree (4), Agree (3), Disagree (2), Strongly Disagree (1)

1. People clearly understand the results they are expected to achieve and are empowered to act to achieve them. _____

2. Functional and personal boundaries of responsibility and accountability are negotiated and clear. _____

3. People can accomplish their task objectives without unnecessary rules or procedures getting in the way. _____

4. People have the skills, resources, and tools to do their work well, individually or in teams. _____

5. People are appropriately involved in decisions that affect them, especially ones that modify their roles. _____

6. People feel free to take informed risks to achieve their job objectives. They also understand boundaries and consequences. _____

7. Our company has systems and procedures in place to resolve workplace conflict in a fair and equitable way. _____

8. All employees know where to go if they are having a conflict with another employee or with their supervisor/manager. _____

9. All managers know about and how to use the internal mechanisms to resolve workplace conflicts. _____

10. Supervisors, managers, and employee relations staff are free to enlist the services of external ADR consultants and encouraged to do so as appropriate. _____

11. Our company has clearly defined its Employee Relations policies, practices, and expectations, and communicates them to employees at every level. _____

12. Managers' and employees' use of the conflict resolution resources available to them is optimal and incorporated in most departments' daily operations. _____

13. Conflict is usually on a personal one-to-one basis. _____

14. Conflict often involves multiple parties. _____

15. Conflict tends to be contained within one departmental unit. _____

16. Conflict often spills over into other departments. _____

17. Our company conflicts rarely involve customers. _____

18. Our company conflicts rarely involve vendors or external contractors. _____

SAMPLE FEEDBACK DELIVERY POLICY FOR THE MANAGEMENT TEAM

Feedback: Communicating with someone about your experience of them—how they speak, behave, communicate, or do something.

This policy exists to help keep feedback about employees' job performance moving appropriately. This does not mean that managers and employees should feel disempowered to resolve their own conflicts.

Certainly, we should all feel empowered to resolve our own conflicts as they happen in the course of our regular work contact. However, it is important to remember that feedback coming from a person with greater authority is *always* experienced as a formal evaluation—whether that feedback is meant as such or not.

Ideally, feedback should only come at a time when it is scheduled, requested, and given regularly, and is from a person who has daily work contact with an employee. If feedback is delivered unexpectedly or by someone who does not have daily work contact with an employee, the feedback will only create anxiety, stress, and fear in employees. It is VERY important that feedback be delivered at the appropriate time, in an appropriate manner, and by the appropriate person in order for it to be most effective.

Therefore, as members of the Management Team and the Executive Management Team, we must all exercise the use of feedback delivery with care, discipline, and with the use of Sample Feedback Guidelines.

SAMPLE FEEDBACK GUIDELINES

☐ ANY employee of (Company) regardless of title or reporting structure may give POSITIVE Feedback to any employee at ANY time. In fact, this is encouraged.

- ☐ Negative/Constructive/Critical Feedback regarding any employee's job performance may ONLY be given by that employee's direct supervisor either during regularly scheduled meetings, scheduled employment reviews, or when feedback is requested by the employee.

- ☐ Feedback Delivery by someone other than an employee's Direct Supervisor should be in WRITTEN FORM and given directly to HR and the employee's supervisor, not to the employee. This is the ONLY appropriate way for a nonsupervisor to contribute feedback about another employee's job performance. HR and the employee's supervisor will determine whether or not the feedback is credible and should be discussed. (As a work group becomes more and more skilled in giving and receiving feedback, some of these guidelines can be relaxed and/or eliminated, and employees of all levels can give feedback to each other without involving others, but they should always have the option of involving HR or another third party should they feel the need to do so.)

- ☐ All Managers, Directors, and Executive Management need to be trained in Effective Feedback Delivery by HR. Training will include Effective Feedback Delivery methods, Effective timing, Effective manner, and the use of Feedback as a Coaching and/or Disciplinary tool.

- ☐ Feedback given to HR will be assessed before it is made official and filed or used in a performance evaluation.

- ☐ Feedback Delivery is different from Conflict Resolution and Mediation Methods, which are available at any time to any employee via HR. If any employee wishes to schedule a Conflict Resolution and/or Mediation session with HR, they may do so by simply requesting one.

- ☐ Only one person needs to request such a session, and it will be granted at a scheduled time convenient for all involved. All company employees are invited to engage in conflict resolution sessions with openness, honesty, and a commitment to resolving the conflict using sound conflict resolution and communication procedures from our mandatory conflict resolution, nonviolent communication (NVC—which will be described in detail on pages 100–101), and emotional intelligence trainings.

SAMPLE CRITICAL THINKING QUIZ FOR HR/OD PROFESSIONALS

1. A candidate does not show up for an interview and does not call to say s/he won't be coming. What happened is:

   A. S/he is irresponsible.

   B. S/he encountered some unknown problem that prevented her/him from arriving and from calling.

   C. S/he got another job and did not bother to call us.

D. S/he did not like us on the phone, and chose not to attend the interview.

E. We simply don't know; it could be any of these or any other reason.

2. An employee sleeps a lot at her desk. We can assume:

   A. She is lazy.

   B. She is sick.

   C. She has a new baby at home that keeps her up at night.

   D. She has another job at night.

   E. We simply don't know; it could be any of these or any other reason.

3. An employee, Rosie, is unable to attend a workplace party for another coworker, Susan, that is taking place after work hours and is optional. Rosie has done a great deal to help Susan and has been very close to Susan in the past ten years. It can be assumed that:

   A. Rosie is jealous of Susan.

   B. Rosie has a schedule conflict and was not told about the party in time to rearrange her schedule or is unable to rearrange her schedule.

   C. Rosie is ill or has a sick child or other family member to care for.

   D. Rosie intends to sabotage and ruin the party by not attending.

   E. We simply don't know; we would have to ask. However, in this instance, given Rosie's past behavior, the most logical and reasonable answer is B.

4. A company is newly implementing the use of vending machines that will distribute basic over-the-counter headache and other medicines for a nominal fee. The company takes a survey of employees to ask what they think about this versus asking the HR/OD VP for headache medicine or Band-Aids when needed. Another option presented was that employees could bring their own supplies to work and make sure they have enough of what they need, but the problem was that many employees kept forgetting to do this so the company wanted to have supplies on hand. However, when they were just free in a supply kit, they would often all be taken and none would be left. Some of the employee responses are below. Given that there has been a problem of supplies being stolen, choose the most reasonable and the least reasonable response.

   A. I don't want to have to go get them from someone, because then my headache is not private and other people know I'm not feeling well. But I always forget to bring my own medicine, and I don't always have change.

   B. I like the vending machine; everyone is responsible for himself or herself and it's refilled regularly. It's fair.

   C. I think we should keep the free first aid kit and put a camera on it to see who is stealing all the supplies.

   D. I don't think we should have a first aid kit at all; if someone gets hurt, it's his or her own fault.

E. We should have both a first aid kit for emergencies only that only managers have access to in case there is an injury, and we should have a vending machine for non-emergency supplies for all staff to use as needed for non-emergency situations.

5. An employee breaks her arm during the winter. There is ice all over the roads and sidewalks. Her doctor advises her to work from home because if she slips again, she won't be able to balance herself and could become even more seriously injured. Her manager knows this and gives her permission to work from home but then still becomes angry with her because she doesn't attend the office holiday party. The manager thinks about this for a while and can say any of these responses below. Which is reasonable and why? Which are unreasonable and why?

A. I was disappointed that she couldn't attend, but I know it's not reasonable to be angry with her. It's a health issue and she's following doctor's orders.

B. I cannot believe how irresponsible she is! She only thinks of herself! She knows how important this party is to me!

C. Maybe I should discipline her for this; she knows that our holiday party is important to everyone. She should have gotten special permission to miss it.

D. She has always hated the holiday party and now she's making it clear to everyone. The only reason she isn't going is to make me angry and upset everyone else.

Hopefully, you chose these answers as those of a reasonable person:

1. E.
2. E.
3. E.
4. E is most reasonable; A is least reasonable.
5. A is most reasonable.

CHAPTER 3

THE CREDIBLE ACTIVIST AT WORK

WHEN HR PROFESSIONALS INTERVIEW FOR HR POSITIONS

When you are interviewing for HR positions of any kind, there are several questions you should ask, and you must remember that you are interviewing the company just as much as they are interviewing you. This is extremely important and not just some hyped-up job-hunting sound bite. Because HR professionals can be held personally liable and sued by current and former employees for their role in certain employment decisions, this is a very real issue.

Do take notes on the answers to your questions, and do note the demeanor and apparent emotional intelligence of those whom you encounter during your recruitment process. Your asking these questions may make the company decide that you are not the kind of HR professional it wants, and if that is the case, it is good news for everyone. Consider it a first date in which you are both spared months or years of misery, because you saw early on that you just weren't compatible.

You will also want to be able to meet the person to whom you will be reporting. This is very important. You need to know who this person is, what he or she is like, what his or her qualifications are, what his or her understanding of HR is, and whether or not you feel you could report to this person. Having an informational interview by discussing previous situations you have handled or that have come up at the company or in his or her career is one good way to do this. Just get a feel for how this person communicates, how the person responds to being asked questions, and how comfortable you feel with him or her. Always have all of your typed references with complete contact information including full name, address, phone numbers, e-mail address, references' relationships to you, and positions you both held as well as several copies of your résumé available at your interviews.

You don't want to wind up in a situation where you work for a company that is employing illegal aliens, engaging in fraud, or otherwise placing you and every other stakeholder in a precarious position. You don't want to be in a situation where sexual harassment is allowed to run rampant without appropriate complaint mechanisms and investigative procedures. You don't want to work for a company that has high injury rates because workplace safety laws are considered optional.

You want to ensure you join a company that understands what HR is, values HR, and includes you in processes as is appropriate. You want to make sure there are codes of conduct regarding behavior and that policies and procedures apply to all employees consistently, including leadership.

You also want to be sure you clearly understand what the HR role at that particular company is and is not. HR's role will be very different in different companies depending on company size, industry, mission, geographical area, and whether it is privately held or publicly held, nonprofit or for-profit. Once you understand all of this, you can determine whether or not your skills, knowledge, and abilities will be a good fit for that HR position in that company. You must also consider the corporate culture and whether or not you will be personally and professionally fulfilled, sufficiently challenged, and in agreement with the extent to which the company is an optimally functioning legally and ethically compliant workplace. In addition, if the company does *not* appear to be an optimally functioning legally and ethically compliant workplace, are those interviewing you aware of and openly stating that as a serious problem while interviewing you? Is their intention to have HR be a strategic part of the solution, or are they not naming these serious problems and expecting you to silently be absorbed into and support a culture of corporate governance resulting in Catastrophic Leadership Failure?[1] Alternatively, is the state of the company something in between these two?

When you are interviewing for HR positions, it can be difficult to read the actual culture of the company, as that takes time. However, you can get a sense when you are there just by observing and communicating with any employees you meet and observing the workplace itself. Still, you must be sure of what you may be getting into professionally, and you'll want to review with your interviewers not only the job posting to which you've responded but also your goals for your role in your next HR position and how you approach, view, and practice HR. The HR Tool entitled "Sample Outline of What HR Can Be: Focus of HR," at the end of the chapter, on pages 32–33, includes a description of HR, that you can customize to reflect your own experience, as well as your HR career hopes. In reviewing this model with your interviewers and in asking the recommended questions in HR Tool entitled "Checklist of Job Interview Questions for the Credible Activist to Ask the Company," on pages 33–35, you will have a better sense of whether or not the position is a good fit for you. You won't want to ask all of them, but choosing 10 or 15 is fine.

HR professionals should have awareness of the SHRM Code of Ethics whether they are SHRM members or not. The sad truth is that many HR executives do raise these issues with their leadership and are not taken seriously, are ignored, and/or are overruled in their recommendations. The SHRM Code of Ethics appears in the HR Tool entitled, "SHRM Code of Ethical and Professional Standards in HR Management," on pages 35–39.

EMPLOYEE ASSESSMENT

See the HR Tool entitled, "Sample New Employee Assessment," on pages 39–40. Please note that new employees should also be invited to provide feedback on their supervisors.

SKILLS THE HR CREDIBLE ACTIVIST WILL BENEFIT FROM CULTIVATING

There are a number of core competencies that are critical for any HR/OD professional to cultivate. When an HR professional endeavors to take the credible activist path, these skills become even more crucial and useful.

1. Continuous emotional intelligence skill development
2. Continuous coaching core-competency skill development
3. Solid technical HR knowledge (including frequently changing employment laws) and use of credible HR/OD research sources
4. Continuous learning and self-awareness concerning diversity issues
5. The best communication skills you can deliver
6. OD knowledge as available to you and as applicable
7. The ability to take excellent care of yourself, your health, and your stress levels, and to have reliable and healthy support systems
8. A clear vision of your personal and professional goals

It is a good idea to define these skills with the understanding that they may change for you over time. Cultivating coaching skills is also extremely helpful for HR credible activists. These skills can help in assessing oneself, as well as in assessing others. Visit the many coaching schools' Web sites and see if gaining a certification would be helpful to you in your position.

THE BUSINESS CASE, THE ETHICS CASE, OR BOTH

There are many ways to try to persuade corporate leaders that HR professionals possess valuable skills, knowledge, and abilities that absolutely influence the bottom line and/or the efficiency of the business operation. Some approaches work better than others with certain people.

Hopefully your company has an HR/OD professional in the C-suite with any number of additional duties (if not accompanying titles) such as chief compliance officer, chief learning officer, chief privacy officer, and/or chief ethics officer. Hopefully you are that person or you work closely with that person. However, many HR professionals don't have a title or a position of prominence and must use the opportunities for access to the decision makers wisely and carefully. The truth is, you may not get much time, and you will want to be prepared with your strategic approach.

In many ways, when you have one of these meetings you're essentially acting out the adult version of an old *Sesame Street* short in which consequences are explored. In the cartoon, a young girl would ask herself aloud, "What would happen if I took this pin and popped this balloon?" She would then imagine what would happen. She would then imagine further: "What would happen if I took this pin and popped this balloon and woke up my baby brother?" Then, she takes her inquiry further, "What would happen, if I took this pin and popped this balloon and woke up my baby brother and he began to cry?" And so on. The bad decisions that are made in companies are often comprised of several smaller bad decisions, and HR professionals need to be on the lookout for these and need to be ready to speak up if they see them about to be made or being made, as bad decisions can be reversed, corrected, learned from, and understood.

Depending on the personality of the person you are trying to persuade and depending on the issue, you may or may not be able to discern which approach will be most effective.

If you have no idea what will work, I recommend you stick to one of the perspectives (or both) shown in the HR Tool "Recommended Approaches to Influence Leadership on HR Issues," on pages 40–41.

One way to prepare for such a meeting is to check in with yourself personally and professionally. Use the list shown in the "Checklist of Questions Credible Activists Ask Themselves," on pages 41–42, in the HR Tools section to confirm your readiness.

WHAT PRO-COMPLIANCE, PRO-HR LEADERSHIP CAN LOOK LIKE

Pro-compliance is pro-HR. Leaders who understand this carefully and consciously set a tone for the companies they lead. They might send a letter like the one in the HR Tool "Sample Letter from Company Leadership Introducing New HR Leader," on pages 44–45, to introduce a new HR director or VP to the whole staff and to set a tone for a culture change in a positive new direction. Even if you are not new in your HR position, you can meet with your leadership and ask that they review this book with you, support you in your efforts to positively transform your corporate culture, implement the linchpins of competitive corporate governance, and improve legal and ethical compliance. Let your leadership know that you cannot do this without their full support.

The template in the HR Tool "Sample Teambuilding Exercise," on pages 42–43, can be combined with any number of items to create a team-building exercise among any small group of employees—5 to 15 employees in a group works well. You can use this before going over new policies, processes, procedures, roles, job descriptions, codes of conduct, or employee handbook, or to introduce key staff.

The group dynamics model explains to the group what often happens in work groups at different stages, and this can help people be more patient with each other as they go through the earlier stages. If we anticipate the bumps, we can handle them better. If we are instructed specifically in how to respond to them, the bumps will hardly be noticed. If we begin by labeling the bumps as necessary to a growth process for a developing company, we can accept them more readily and understand that they are part of a group process. We will then be less likely to fall into the unfortunate trap of attempting to place blame on one or a few individuals when really the issue is how the entire group works together as a whole. Scapegoating one or a few people when a group is growing and developing is hardly ever an effective solution for what is really going on, and the scapegoats are rarely the actual cause for what is happening.

An example of leaders who don't support compliance or HR will often completely misunderstand not only HR's crucial role in the company but also their own individual and professional compliance responsibilities. These are the leaders who tend to consider legal and ethical compliance to be optional, to be something that is not taken seriously, and to erroneously consider any HR professional who advocates for legal and ethical compliance to be "radical," "inappropriate," or "not on the side of the company," even though these are not accurate characterizations at all. Persons who think in this way need to be reminded that when they chose to do business in the United States, they agreed to abide by all employment laws. HR's advocacy for legal and ethical compliance with all relevant city, state, and federal laws is an important compliance position that corporate leadership is expected to share and value along with HR; in that way, the company and employees are both protected, as the law intended them to be. The HR Tools entitled "Sample HR Flyer for New Staff, New HR, or Implementation of New HR Practices," on pages 43–44, is an information sheet to introduce new HR staff to employees, which can be customizable to cover whatever that particular HR person will be responsible for in the HR department.

HR TOOLS

SAMPLE OUTLINE OF WHAT HR CAN BE: FOCUS OF HR

STAFFING

☐ Recruiting/Selection/Placement

☐ Corporate Change and HR Planning

☐ Job Design

REWARDS AND RECOGNITION

☐ Compensation

☐ Benefits

☐ Benefits Comparison

☐ Benefits Enhancements

☐ Company Program Development

☐ Strategic Staffing

COMMUNICATION

☐ Policies and Procedures

☐ Safety and Health

☐ Conflict Resolution and Mediation

☐ Facilitating Self-Awareness

☐ Training Manuals

☐ Company Change

PERFORMANCE MANAGEMENT

☐ Performance Evaluation

☐ Facilitating Self-Evaluation

☐ Managerial Self-Awareness

☐ Coaching/Empowering Staff

☐ Process Flow Improvements

TRAINING AND DEVELOPMENT

☐ HR as a Strategic Company Resource

☐ Conflict Resolution and Mediation

☐ Effective Communication

☐ Corporate Citizenship

CHECKLIST OF JOB INTERVIEW QUESTIONS FOR THE CREDIBLE ACTIVIST TO ASK THE COMPANY

QUESTIONS *YOU* WANT TO ASK PROSPECTIVE EMPLOYERS

1. Does the HR position have a private office?

2. Does the company have a Chief Compliance Officer? If that is someone other than the HR Director or VP, who is that person, and what is the relationship between the head of HR and the Chief Compliance Officer? Is there a Privacy Officer? Who is that?

3. Does the company have written policies in the form of a clear and up-to-date employee handbook that has been reviewed by attorneys?

4. Does the company truly support policies regarding preventing and responding promptly and soundly to any EEO or other Employee Relations complaints?

5. Does the company truly welcome complaints and want to know what is going on in the workplace so it can be aware of, address, and prevent future incidents?

6. Does the company have a workplace violence prevention policy that it also takes seriously? Is HR responsible for this?

7. Does the company have an investigation policy?

8. Who will conduct investigations? Does whoever conducts investigations have training in conducting sound unbiased investigations that avoid any conflicts of interest?

9. Are there procedures in place for having third-party external experienced consultants conduct investigations in the event that there would be a conflict of interest in having internal attorneys or HR personnel conduct an investigation? Is there a realistic budget for this?

10. Is there a lawyer in the HR department? If so, what is that person's role?

11. Is there a General Counsel for the company? If so, what is that person's role?

12. Is the General Counsel someone with employment law experience?

13. If not, is the General Counsel someone with HR experience or any SHRM or other HR training?

14. Is the General Counsel's role to ensure that the company is compliant with all relevant city, state, and federal employment laws or is the General Counsel's role to cover up any possible complaints and protect the company at all costs?

15. What kind of HR training does the General Counsel have?

16. How does the HR role you are interviewing for intersect with the roles of any others who may be involved in employee complaints of any kind, investigations, and employment decisions?

17. Does the company have a decision-making protocol in place for personnel decisions and who is involved in those? If so, what is HR's role in this process?

18. Do all of those involved in any employment decisions have relevant SHRM-approved training in conflict resolution, mediation, rater-bias, conflict of interest, and/or legal or SHRM codes of ethics and sound employment investigation methods?

19. Does the company have in place policies designed to prevent any conflicts of interest in the case of employment decisions of any kind including transfer, promotions, raises, demotions, terminations, hiring, approval of Family and Medical Leave Act (FMLA) and/or maternity leaves, approval of flex or comp time, and any other benefits available to employees?

20. Does the company have in place a culture that truly welcomes employees to come forward with complaints or concerns about inappropriate behavior? Are employees very clear on who receives complaints and in what manner? Are there several people to whom employees may go with their complaints?

21. Are those who receive employee complaints fully trained in how to properly receive and process them?

22. Are there annual EEO and Sexual Harassment Prevention (SHP) trainings for all employees? Are these trainings required? Are mandatory trainings made up if they are missed?

23. Is there a sense that all employees are responsible for appropriate workplace behavior—not just managers or HR staff?

24. How have previous employee complaints been handled? Have there been any lawsuits resulting from EEO complaints against this company? If so, how many and when were they?

25. Will there be a delineation of autonomy for this HR position (bring and show them the sample from this book), and if there isn't one, may I make one for approval so I am very clear on what I am authorized to do and what I'm not authorized to do?

26. How are conflicts among staff generally handled?

27. Is there mandatory conflict resolution training for all staff? If not, would you consider this?

28. Is there a behavioral code of conduct for all staff? If so, is this consistently enforced? If not, would you consider implementing one?

29. Are all policies and procedures applied consistently to all staff? If not, what would be an explanation for that?

30. What are three words that would describe this workplace culture?

31. Would most employees agree with that if I asked them?

32. What would happen if I made a recommendation regarding an employment decision and I was overruled on that decision? Would my disagreement or attempts to persuade corporate leadership be welcome or unwelcome?

33. For the HR person and/or Executives and/or anyone you may report to: Have you read any of these books?

    ☐ *The Thin Book of Naming Elephants: How to Surface Undiscussables for Greater Organizational Success Naming Elephants* by Sue Annis Hammond and Andrea B. Mayfield

    ☐ *The Seven Habits of Highly Successful People* by Steven Covey

    ☐ *The EQ Edge* by Steven J. Stein, Ph.D., and Howard Book, Ph.D.

    ☐ *The Emotionally Intelligent Manager* by David Caruso, Ph.D.

    ☐ *Make Your Workplace Great: The Seven Keys to an Emotionally Intelligent Company* by Steven J. Stein, Ph.D.

    ☐ *Designing and Using Company Surveys: A Seven-Step Process* by Allan H. Church, Janine Waclawski, and Allen I. Kraut

34. Has there ever been an HR Director/VP/etc. here before and if so, why is this position now vacant?

35. Will the company pay for my SHRM membership?

36. Will the corporate leadership support me in practicing HR in alignment with SHRM Code of Ethics? (Have the code ready there with you to review.)

SHRM CODE OF ETHICAL AND PROFESSIONAL STANDARDS IN HR MANAGEMENT (11/16/2007)

CORE PRINCIPLE

As HR professionals, we are responsible for adding value to the companies we serve and contributing to the ethical success of those companies. We accept professional responsibility for our individual decisions and actions. We are also advocates for the profession by engaging in activities that enhance its credibility and value.

INTENT

☐ To build respect, credibility, and strategic importance for the HR profession within our companies, the business community, and the communities in which we work.

☐ To assist the companies we serve in achieving their objectives and goals.

☐ To inform and educate current and future practitioners, the companies we serve, and the general public about principles and practices that help the profession.

- ☐ To positively influence workplace and recruitment practices.
- ☐ To encourage professional decision making and responsibility.
- ☐ To encourage social responsibility.

GUIDELINES

- ☐ Adhere to the highest standards of ethical and professional behavior.
- ☐ Measure the effectiveness of HR in contributing to or achieving company goals.
- ☐ Comply with the law.
- ☐ Work consistent with the values of the profession.
- ☐ Strive to achieve the highest levels of service, performance, and social responsibility.
- ☐ Advocate for the appropriate use and appreciation of human beings as employees.
- ☐ Advocate openly and within the established forums for debate in order to influence decision making and results.

PROFESSIONAL DEVELOPMENT

CORE PRINCIPLE

As HR professionals, we must strive to meet the highest standards of competence and commit to strengthen our competencies on a continuous basis.

INTENT

- ☐ To expand our knowledge of HR management to further our understanding of how our companies function.
- ☐ To advance our understanding of how companies work ("the business of the business")

GUIDELINES

- ☐ Pursue formal academic opportunities.
- ☐ Commit to continuous learning, skills development, and application of new knowledge related to both HR management and the companies we serve.
- ☐ Contribute to the body of knowledge, the evolution of the profession and the growth of individuals through teaching, research, and dissemination of knowledge.
- ☐ Pursue certification such as Certified Compensation Professional (CCP), Certified Employee Benefit Specialist (CEBS), Professional in Human Resources (PHR), Senior Professional in Human Resources (SPHR), etc. where available, or comparable measures of competencies and knowledge.

ETHICAL LEADERSHIP

CORE PRINCIPLE

As HR professionals, we are expected to exhibit individual leadership as role models for maintaining the highest standards of ethical conduct.

INTENT

- ☐ To set the standard and be an example for others.
- ☐ To earn individual respect and increase our credibility with those we serve.

GUIDELINES

- ☐ Be ethical; act ethically in every professional interaction.
- ☐ Question pending individual and group actions when necessary to ensure that decisions are ethical and are implemented in an ethical manner.
- ☐ Seek expert guidance if ever in doubt about the ethical propriety of a situation.
- ☐ Through teaching and mentoring, champion the development of others as ethical leaders in the profession and in companies.

FAIRNESS AND JUSTICE

CORE PRINCIPLE

As HR professionals, we are ethically responsible for promoting and fostering fairness and justice for all employees and their companies.

INTENT

- ☐ To create and sustain an environment that encourages all individuals and the company to reach their fullest potential in a positive and productive manner.

GUIDELINES

- ☐ Respect the uniqueness and intrinsic worth of every individual.
- ☐ Treat people with dignity, respect, and compassion to foster a trusting work environment free of harassment, intimidation, and unlawful discrimination.
- ☐ Ensure that everyone has the opportunity to develop his or her skills and new competencies.
- ☐ Assure an environment of inclusiveness and a commitment to diversity in the companies we serve.
- ☐ Develop, administer and advocate policies and procedures that foster fair, consistent, and equitable treatment for all.

- ☐ Regardless of personal interests, support decisions made by our companies that are both ethical and legal.
- ☐ Act in a responsible manner and practice sound management in the country(ies) in which the companies we serve operate.

CONFLICTS OF INTEREST

CORE PRINCIPLE

As HR professionals, we must maintain a high level of trust with our stakeholders. We must protect the interests of our stakeholders as well as our professional integrity and should not engage in activities that create actual, apparent, or potential conflicts of interest.

INTENT

- ☐ To avoid activities that are in conflict or may appear to be in conflict with any of the provisions of this Code of Ethical and Professional Standards in HR Management or with one's responsibilities and duties as a member of the HR profession and/or as an employee of any company.

GUIDELINES

- ☐ Adhere to and advocate the use of published policies on conflicts of interest within your company.
- ☐ Refrain from using your position for personal, material, or financial gain or the appearance of such.
- ☐ Refrain from giving or seeking preferential treatment in the HR processes.
- ☐ Prioritize your obligations to identify conflicts of interest or the appearance thereof; when conflicts arise, disclose them to relevant stakeholders.

USE OF INFORMATION

CORE PRINCIPLE

As HR professionals, we must consider and protect the rights of individuals, especially in the acquisition and dissemination of information while ensuring truthful communications and facilitating informed decision making.

INTENT

- ☐ To build trust among all company constituents by maximizing the open exchange of information, while eliminating anxieties about inappropriate and/or inaccurate acquisition and sharing of information.

GUIDELINES

☐ Acquire and disseminate information through ethical and responsible means.

☐ Ensure only appropriate information is used in decisions affecting the employment relationship.

☐ Investigate the accuracy and source of information before allowing it to be used in employment-related decisions.

☐ Maintain current and accurate HR information.

☐ Safeguard restricted or confidential information.

☐ Take appropriate steps to ensure the accuracy and completeness of all communicated information about HR policies and practices.

☐ Take appropriate steps to ensure the accuracy and completeness of all communicated information used in HR-related training.[2]

SAMPLE NEW EMPLOYEE ASSESSMENT

The following should be observed and noted on a weekly basis as the new employee progresses. Reporting should begin when employment starts and should be observed fairly and documented for the first 12 weeks of an employee's job. At the end of 12 weeks, these forms should be used for a detailed report about the employee with a recommendation to continue or discontinue employment. Ideally, the new employee will be given this same form to do a self-assessment, and then the supervisor's and employee's assessments of the new employee will be compared. Any gaps in ranking should be discussed with a posture of curiosity and learning and an aim toward understanding. Similarly, this form can and should be adapted for the new employee to also rate the supervisor, and those two ratings should be discussed in the same open manner to build understanding and a positive working relationship in which both employee and supervisor are held to the same standards around what this form measures.

Employee: _____

Date:_____

Please rate each quality with a number from 1–10 (10 is excellent) and provide commentary:

Attendance	1	2	3	4	5	6	7	8	9	10
Punctuality	1	2	3	4	5	6	7	8	9	10
Cooperation/Teamwork	1	2	3	4	5	6	7	8	9	10
Taking Initiative	1	2	3	4	5	6	7	8	9	10
Following Through	1	2	3	4	5	6	7	8	9	10

Respectfulness	1	2	3	4	5	6	7	8	9	10
Shows Good Judgment	1	2	3	4	5	6	7	8	9	10
Asks Appropriate Questions	1	2	3	4	5	6	7	8	9	10
Knowledge matches résumé and interview	1	2	3	4	5	6	7	8	9	10
Skills match résumé and interview	1	2	3	4	5	6	7	8	9	10
Abilities match résumé and interview	1	2	3	4	5	6	7	8	9	10
Abides by company policies	1	2	3	4	5	6	7	8	9	10
Uses rational decision-making processes	1	2	3	4	5	6	7	8	9	10
Uses investigational problem-solving skills	1	2	3	4	5	6	7	8	9	10

Overall Rating   1   2   3   4   5   6   7   8   9   10

Low   High

Recommendation(s)

Supervisor: _____ Dept: _____

Has this been discussed with the employee?

Would you like HR to discuss anything with this employee with or without you?

RECOMMENDED APPROACHES TO INFLUENCE LEADERSHIP ON HR ISSUES

THE BUSINESS CASE

☐ What are the dollar-amount, PR possibilities, and legal non-compliance possibilities for the options related to legal non-compliance with relevant city, state, and federal employment laws?

☐ How can we establish a sound decision-making process for various issues to avoid these problems?

THE ETHICS CASE

☐ What are the legal noncompliance possibilities for the options related to a certain situation, and why were issues such as this made into laws? Are there ethical codes of conduct for the HR professional, the corporate officers, and any others that would be violated by a certain decision? What might the consequences of that be?

☐ How can we establish a sound decision-making process for various issues to avoid these problems?

BOTH

☐ Start with the business case and finish with the ethics case.

CHECKLIST OF QUESTIONS CREDIBLE ACTIVISTS ASK THEMSELVES

☐ Am I certain there is something wrong here?

☐ Whom can I talk to with sufficient technical knowledge to check my perceptions?

☐ What will happen to the people I leave behind if I leave and say nothing?

☐ Why didn't the people before me say or do anything before they left? Can I find out by talking to them or are my options to guess, keeping in mind that my guesses may be correct or incorrect?

☐ Who else here can I trust to also speak up so we are stronger in what we are saying and less afraid?

☐ What authorities, if any, can I go to for guidance, assistance, and protection with the information and proof that I have?

☐ How many people at Enron knew what was going on and chose to not speak up? How might things be different for all those people who lost their savings if someone had spoken up?

☐ Have I done an honest and accurate cost/benefit analysis for my own career, life, and family regarding speaking up versus not speaking up? Have I spoken to my spouse or partner about this?

☐ Do I have enough good support if I choose to speak up?

☐ If I leave quietly and safely land somewhere else, what are my professional, legal, and ethical obligations to speaking up to help those who have been left behind where there is wrongdoing happening?

☐ What authorities can I go to for assistance, guidance, and protection in that case?

☐ How will I sleep at night knowing that I could contribute to putting a stop to wrongdoing and enormous human suffering if I don't say anything?

☐ What kind of professional am I if I stay and don't say anything?

☐ What would I want someone else to do if I were left behind in an organization that was legally non-compliant, unethical, or engaging in fraud?

☐ If I have already left the company, who else am I still in contact with who is also a person of principle and would be willing to speak up about wrongdoing at the former company? How might I help them by also saying what I know on the record to a trusted authority?

☐ What does my religious tradition or understanding of professional ethics tell me I am responsible for doing in this situation?

☐ Do I have documentation and/or any other kind of proof for what I believe is wrongdoing happening at the company?

SAMPLE TEAM-BUILDING EXERCISE

Bruce Tuckman's Group Formation Theory: Forming/Storming/Norming/Performing/Transforming[3]

Characterized by:

Forming. Learning about each other as people and professionals

Storming. Misunderstandings, competition, defining roles, defining protocols, experimenting with processes and procedures, defining values

Norming. Accepting roles and personalities, lack of competition, more cooperation, fewer misunderstandings

Performing. A well-oiled machine, personalities responsive to feedback, strong performance in roles, excellent cooperation, strong productivity, corporate culture established

Transforming. Innovation, risk-taking, learning organization culture, open systems, sound conflict resolution as part of culture, high emotional intelligence skills of employees, employee relations and compliance high priorities so the BUSINESS can be focused on

1. Joking

   The Line:

   Watch EEO boundaries.

   Avoid mean-spirited ridicule or any form of bullying.

   If someone lets you know not to tease about something, don't.

2. Conflict Resolution

   Conflict communication, interactions, and resolutions are generally characterized by AEIOU:

   A Attacking—Yelling, sarcasm, name-calling, passive-aggression.

   E Evading—Avoidance (warranted and useful if serving as a cooling-off period; otherwise not).

   I Informing—"I" statements, sharing information, communicating openly and willingly.

O Opening—Think of a can-opener: asking questions to open up discussion about a situation and better understand it and the other person's position.

U Unifying.—"I'm sure there is a solution we can find together."

"I'm sure we can try to come to an agreement."

"Let's find a solution we're both comfortable with."

Avoid AE; use IOU.

3. *Game*: Two truths and a lie

This is an information game to help us learn more about each other, what we have in common, and what differences we have. As the name suggests, each person tells two truths and one lie. Everyone else has to guess which the lie is.

SAMPLE HR FLYER FOR NEW STAFF, NEW HR, OR IMPLEMENTATION OF NEW HR PRACTICES

HR—Name, title, direct phone, e-mail, work cell phone

My Role: **I work with:**

Staffing

Job design/Process flow (How do we do our jobs? Can we do them differently/better/more safely?)

Recruiting/Selection/Placement (Getting the right person for the job!)

Company change and planning (Helping all of us adjust to change when it occurs.)

Rewards and Recognition:

Compensations

Benefits

Benefits Enhancements

Company Program Development (Give me your ideas!)

Strategic Staffing (Are we fully utilizing the many strengths we have on this staff?)

Communication:

Troubleshooting

Policies and Procedures

Safety and Health

Conflict Resolution (How can we conduct ourselves so that we decrease the likelihood of conflict?)

Facilitating Self-awareness (Do we know how we affect those with whom we work? Can we improve this?)

Training Manuals and Materials

Company Change Initiatives and Programs

Performance Management:

Coaching for improved performance (This can be a pleasant and educational experience)

Facilitating Self-Evaluation

Leader Self-Awareness

Managerial Self-Awareness

Coworker Self-Awareness

Training and Development:

Conflict Resolution and Mediation (conflict is normal—and we CAN resolve it skillfully and fairly)

Effective Communication

Corporate Citizenship

Other specific training needs detailing with communication, getting along, delegating, conflict resolution, coaching, motivating, problem-solving, speaking and behaving within legal compliance, awkward workplace situations, etc.

SAMPLE LETTER FROM COMPANY LEADERSHIP INTRODUCING NEW HR LEADER

On letterhead, in interoffice memo format, or via e-mail

Date

Dear (Company) Staff,

By now, all of you have met _____, our HR Director, and most of you have had brief meetings with her/him to learn more about what HR is all about out. If you have not yet attended this meeting, you will have an opportunity to do so in the next week or two.

I want to encourage you all to discuss with _____ any concerns you have about your job, and s/he will do what s/he can to help you find a solution.

_____ will maintain confidentiality, unless you give her/him permission to address a situation and intervene in order to resolve a conflict or difficult situation. Other exceptions to confidentiality are if you discuss illegal activities or issues pertaining to harassment, discrimination, threats, violence, or injury; then s/he must discuss those issues with me or _____.

(Company) staff won't experience reprisals or retaliation if they choose in good faith to bring concerns to the attention of HR. You can even bring concerns to her/him about me, and I will do my best to adjust my own management and communication styles if it is brought to my attention that these can be improved.

The best thing that can happen in any workplace is that everyone on staff really wants to know how they can adjust how they relate to their coworkers and to their work. Once we all really *want* to know these things, then we become more receptive to ideas about what to adjust and how to adjust it.

_____ is trained to give feedback in a way that is respectful, fair, and clear and to train others in doing the same. So, if you are asked to consider an observation about your relationships to your coworkers or to your work, please view this as an opportunity for you to improve professionally and to positively contribute to your work environment.

Part of what we will all be working on together includes trainings both individually and in groups focused on improving communication skills, emotional intelligence, and conflict resolution skills. If you are invited to an individual or group training with _____, or, if you are involved in a problem-solving session with other coworkers, your only job is to attend with an open mind and be willing to make changes in how you relate to your coworkers and how you relate to your work, as suggested.

Please give _____ your full support and cooperation.

Thank you,

President of (Company)

PART TWO

LEGAL ISSUES

"What is right is often forgotten by what is convenient."

—Bodie Thoene, Warsaw Requiem

CHAPTER 4

LEGAL ISSUES FOR CREDIBLE ACTIVISTS

This chapter includes legal noncompliance issues the American employer has a responsibility to *prevent* and the employee has every right to raise until noncompliance is eliminated. The HR professional has an ethical and professional responsibility to raise these as well once he or she becomes aware of them; the HR professional is also an employee and thus has all employee rights. Brief and clear explanations, sample memos, and risk assessments for raising these issues will be provided to the HR professional for various situations and violations. Information on governmental agencies from which to seek recourse and information will also be provided.

EMPLOYMENT AT-WILL

Employment at-will means that the employer and the employee are free to terminate the employment relationship at any time for any reason unless there is an employment contract with other terms in it. While the law differs in every state, there are three major exceptions to employment at-will that you may encounter, depending upon your region:

- The prevention of terminations for reasons that violate a state's public policy.
- The prohibition of terminations after an implied contract for employment has been established; such a contract can be created through employer representations of continued employment, in the form of either verbal assurances or expectations created by employer handbooks, policies, or other written assurances.
- The prevention of terminations when there is an implied covenant of good faith and fair dealing in the employment relationship.

In some states, none of these are in effect. You'll want to look up your state in the HR Tool "Recognition of Employment-at-Will Exceptions, by State, as of October 1, 2000," at the end of the chapter, on pages 58–59. As a result of employment-at-will and the exceptions to it, most employee handbooks will explicitly state that the handbook is not an employment contract and that employment is at-will. Handbooks that do not explicitly state this can be argued as evidence that an employment contract existed when it actually was not meant to have existed.

ADDRESSING EEO COMPLIANCE ISSUES

HR professionals are sometimes present for discussions about decisions concerning employment or continued employment of someone, which include comments that show that someone with the authority to hire or fire or make recommendations around hiring or firing someone is discriminating against someone. This is a very troubling situation. All HR professionals must be aware that when anyone advocates for someone else's rights under EEO or ADA laws, the person advocating is also protected from retaliation. If more HR professionals had the courage to document when this happens and then advocate for EEO and ADA laws, it might begin to happen less. Before moving forward, however, be prudent and check your state public policy exceptions under employment at-will laws and learn whether those trump the EEOC's prohibitions against retaliation for advocating for others. Never assume; always research!

One frustrating thing for an HR professional to overhear is, "Well, I'm not a member of a protected group." We are *all* members of protected groups. If a man of a particular ethnicity and color works in a factory and every other employee and manager there is also a male of that color and ethnicity, but this particular man is offended by racist or sexist jokes, he may file a legitimate complaint if such behavior is displayed in his presence. Legitimate complaints are about the behavior that is in violation of civil rights employment laws—not necessarily about the identity of the person complaining. You never know whom someone is dating, married to, cousins with, adopted by, whom they've adopted, and so on. Do not assume that someone's entire family is of the same ethnicity or color as they are.

Similarly, if an employee observes or overhears other employees harassing or discriminating against someone at work, and the subject of the negative behavior does not complain for whatever reason, any employee who in any way witnesses or somehow becomes aware of this behavior may also file a legitimate complaint with the company and subsequently with the EEOC, the state's Division of Human Rights, and/or the city's Division of Human Rights, if there is one.

)) RETALIATION

A newly added protection to EEOC guidelines includes protection from retaliation for anyone who participates in an investigation into an EEO or ADA complaint. Discrimination or retaliation based on any of the above actions is unlawful in all states in the United States. Hundreds of thousands of EEO charges are brought by employees and former employees each year to the EEOC, State Divisions of Human Rights, and City Commissions on Human Rights. Employees usually bear the burden of proof and have varying amounts of success in proving allegations of unlawful discrimination and harassment depending on whether or not they have proof. Proof can be in the form of written materials by those harassing or discriminating against them or others, signed statements from witnesses, several people making the same complaints and bearing witness for one another, employees making audio or video recordings of actual harassment (recording is only legal in certain states), or rare confessions of those who engaged in the unlawful harassment, discrimination, or retaliation.

In fiscal year 2008, the EEOC received 32,690 charges of retaliation discrimination based on all statutes enforced by EEOC. The EEOC resolved 25,999 retaliation charges in 2008, and recovered more than $111 million in monetary benefits for charging parties and other aggrieved individuals (not including monetary benefits obtained through litigation).[1]

You may at times have to educate colleagues and others in the company at various levels about this concept. In addition, you might need to ask your company to make it clear to supervisors what retaliation is and is not; and you personally may have to be the person to design and present such a training. A good idea is to implement protective measures so that HR approves all discipline to ensure that HR is a firewall preventing any retaliatory discipline and using those near misses as opportunities to educate angry supervisors who are tempted to retaliate as to why it is unwise and potentially costly to do so. You should inform supervisors that retaliation charges and lawsuits can be successful for plaintiffs even if the original complaint was untrue or unfounded. Retaliation awards to plaintiffs and punitive damages for employers who are found guilty of this are often greater than awards or punitive damages for initial complaints of harassment or discrimination if those are found to have occurred.

COMPLIANCE

As a credible activist, you will want to ensure that your workplace genuinely intends to be compliant with EEO laws and all other employment laws; otherwise, you will have a very difficult time doing your job ethically and well. Most HR professionals have as part of their job description to "ensure that the company is compliant with all relevant employment laws." However, if your leadership is not really on board with this and is only paying lip service to these laws, that will be communicated to the staff in various ways and there will be unlawful behavior, which you will wind up either learning of and handling, or not learning of for various reasons.

In companies wherein these laws are not taken seriously, this unfortunate condition can emerge in several ways. Unlawful harassment and discrimination may run rampant, employees may be too fearful to make complaints to those who are charged with receiving them, or employees may make complaints thinking their complaints will be properly and thoroughly investigated only to learn that they are not and are promptly ignored, not taken seriously, or otherwise not handled properly.

The HR credible activist finds him- or herself in a difficult position if it becomes obvious that he or she is working in an organization or company that does not take EEO and other employment laws seriously. The credible activist may decide to simply look for another job and then give a polite and untrue reason for resigning, he or she may tell the company truthfully why he or she is resigning, or he or she may remain there and do his or her best to educate others about the company's legal compliance responsibilities as well as the personal liability to which certain leadership and HR professionals are exposed if not in compliance with various employment laws. (Sample memos in HR Tools at the end of this chapter, on pages 60–69, address some ways to communicate about personal and company liability to a leadership who does not take EEO and other employment laws seriously.)

The HR employee who chooses to silently collude with a leadership that does not take seriously EEO and other employment laws is taking very serious risks in terms of personal liability, abandonment of professional ethics, abuse of employee trust, and company liability. The unfortunate reality is that HR employees who fail to live up to their ethical obligations may do so out of fear of the repercussions they might face if they were to speak up:

retaliation, job loss, hostile work environment, and so on. This is a difficult argument to reasonably make, even in a difficult world economy.

HR professionals can and must use the knowledge and leverage they have to find ways to diplomatically, graciously, professionally, and directly address issues of legal noncompliance with their leadership. However, depending on the company values, the HR professional who writes a perfect memo addressing legal noncompliance may still find him- or herself out of a job. There are still a shocking number of companies that don't take EEO and other employment laws seriously, and there are a shocking number of HR professionals who practice the HR profession in a seriously unethical manner. This practice gives HR a bad name as a profession causing employees not to trust HR professionals. If HR is to be a true partner with actual significant responsibilities in the company, then HR must not be silenced, vetoed, or overruled when it raises very serious concerns about legal noncompliance.

Too many HR professionals, however, *are* silenced, ignored, vetoed, and overruled. Many HR professionals at HR expos, training seminars, and conferences will report the same. They are often at a loss as to how to handle this. They don't want to lose their jobs (the majority of which are in employment at-will states), they don't want to betray the trust of employees, they don't want to expose themselves to personal liability, they don't want to add to the company's liability, and they don't want to participate in unethical behavior. Surprisingly, many HR professionals are unaware of their unique position and ability to address these situations.

Given that HR professionals also have personal liability exposure if EEO and other employment laws are handled improperly, they can simply address the issue beginning with concern about both company and personal liability while also being protected from retaliation for (as per the EEOC) "protected activity," which includes the following:[2]

Opposition to a practice believed to be unlawful discrimination. Opposition is informing an employer that you believe that he/she is engaging in prohibited discrimination. Opposition is protected from retaliation as long as it is based on a reasonable, good-faith belief that the complained of practice violates anti-discrimination law; and the manner of the opposition is reasonable.

Regardless of your initial response to a situation, some leaders may be harder than others to convince to take proper action. Some may have strong emotional reactions to the HR professional attempting to address this issue. They may use what I call the "Jedi Mind Trick Approach" to respond to any serious concern raised with them. The way this works is that anyone in the company raises a concern with the leadership about how something is not being handled as well as it could or should be, and the leadership will say something like, "It is being handled exactly as it should be. It is being handled within legal compliance," as though saying something untrue once or even several times will make it true.

You may recall the *Star Wars* scene in which storm troopers, searching for Luke Skywalker's droids, encounter Obi-Wan Kenobi—a Jedi master who waves his hand slowly in front of the storm troopers and says, "These aren't the droids you're looking for." The storm troopers agree, reinforcing the lie in their own words by responding that "these aren't the droids we're looking for"—even though they *are*. And it *works*.

Jedi Mind Tricks don't have actual power in real life. Lying is usually eventually seen through, as we have observed in the media with the exposure of Ponzi schemes and the disintegration of poorly governed companies. We regularly read about huge judgments and penalties in cases involving unsafe work conditions, harassment and discrimination, various forms of fraud, and retaliation. Eventually, it comes out. HR professionals need to ask themselves which role they are going to play in the story of what happened once everything settles. Will they be the person who courageously wrote a memo both protecting him- or herself from personal liability and nobly warning the company of its risky and unlawful practices, or will he or she silently cooperate and enable unlawful practices for whatever reason while doing grave harm to the entire company?

When EEO and other employment laws are not complied with or taken seriously, everyone suffers. Employees who experience unlawful harassment and discrimination obviously suffer, but so do employees who merely observe this and feel powerless and/or afraid to address these issues. Even employees who engage in unlawful harassment and discrimination suffer, as they work in an environment that allows them to behave in reprehensible ways, which diminishes them personally and professionally as well as takes time away from important work that could be being done instead.

⟩⟩ DOCUMENTATION

By addressing your concerns in a memo, the leadership to whom this memo will be addressed will also be aware that the HR person is intentionally documenting this concern and is probably aware of instances, which have not been properly handled. These two things alone may be enough to compel an organization to begin to handle EEO and other employment laws with the seriousness and procedural propriety that is necessary. A simple formula to follow when considering the correct course of action in responding to questionable situations is shown in the HR Tool entitled "PACE Memo-Writing Formula," on page 60.

After adding credible research, this approach will guide the HR professional credible activist in every situation and in each memo. Why memos? Why put yourself on the line like that? There are several reasons. You must protect yourself. HR professionals can have exposure to personal liability, and you want to have it on record that you did the necessary research and that you made recommendations based on that research. You will not always have control over important decisions, and this can be frustrating. You must keep a record of your recommendations in case there are consequences for the company when your recommendations are or are not followed. You will want to keep citations for the research you did to back up your recommendations as well. SHRM (Society for HR Management) is an excellent source of current, credible information. Membership in SHRM is crucial for any HR professional.

You want to have a record of your initiative and contributions to the company. Having a file of these memos as well as the citations for your research will provide this. Whether you need to use these in a self-evaluation to showcase the valuable work you've done or whether you need to remind someone of a recommendation you made that was not taken and should have been, this will become one of your most important files, which you should keep both at work and at home in duplicate.

This file will also come in handy when interviewing for HR leadership positions. You want to always remember that you are interviewing the company just as much as it is interviewing you. This is even more important for HR professionals who are credible activists. Why? Because you want to be sure that the company is aligned with your HR credible activist commitment. You don't want to wind up working at a company that will react badly to your implementation of the PACE strategy. You don't want to work for a company that does not intend to adhere to relevant laws and policies, that does not apply relevant laws and policies consistently, or that will ignore, veto, or override your recommendations because it has no intention of handling HR matters properly, lawfully, ethically, or consistently. See HR Tools entitled "Sample Memo Regarding EEO Compliance Concerns," "Sample EEO Training Aid," and "Sample Memo Cautioning against Unlawful Retaliation," on pages 60–63, for examples.

ADDRESSING OSHA COMPLIANCE

In 2008, the Occupational Safety and Health Administration (OSHA) conducted 77,179 total inspections in response to over 6,696 complaints from employees and as a result of their own inspection plans regarding unsafe working conditions. In 2008, there were over 87,687 violations and over 956 fatalities due to workplace injury or illness nationwide.[3] Historically, OSHA has often been understaffed and underfunded given the number of complaints it receives, which translates into fewer complaints being investigated or less thorough investigations of complaints, or both.

Just as with EEO laws, HR professionals have an ethical duty and a professional responsibility to address issues of unsafe working conditions. There are many ways to raise this including a cost/benefit approach that may work best with a leadership who considers safety laws to be unnecessary and costly inconveniences.

Making the business case for adhering to safety laws, providing safety trainings, and implementing strong accident-prevention educational programs and procedures often comes down to numbers and publicity. Just as with EEO laws, even if a company leader believes that OSHA safety regulations are unnecessary and costly inconveniences, he or she will likely not say so publicly. Executives, shareholders, and other company stakeholders and leaders do care about publicity given that it does affect profits and reputation even if not immediately.

There may be times when an employer will reasonably question whether an employee's claim of having sustained a workplace injury or illness is legitimate. Workers' compensation fraud is real. In these instances, you'll want to follow your state's guidelines for controverting any such claims and be aware of all paperwork and deadlines necessary for doing so properly. You will also want to be aware of your workers' compensation insurance carrier's procedures for doing so.

Comparisons between injury rates within an industry are very telling, as are the rising workers' compensation insurance rates a company with many injuries will experience. Presenting it as purely a financial issue is one approach if that is the message that will get through to the recipient. You know best what will or won't work, given to whom your memo has to be presented and who the ultimate decision makers will be.

Your job is to influence your company's decision makers to choose to operate within legal compliance. This is your job because you are a credible activist, which means you take employment laws seriously, you intend to abide by them, you want to work for a company that abides by them and takes them seriously, and you want to minimize your own personal liability as well as any liability exposure for the company.

As with business leaders who are not impressed with concerns about personal or company liability, you may need to present the sobering data on injuries that include permanent disabilities and deaths as well as multimillion-dollar fines given to various companies by OSHA each year. OSHA, National Institute of Occupational Safety and Health (NIOSH), and state Division of Safety and Health (DOSH) offices often have compelling educational materials, which may help make your case. You may also visit their Web sites to see what can be downloaded or requested via the mail.

Another excellent resource for HR professionals is the Job Accommodation Network (JAN) at http://www.jan.wvu.edu/.[4] There is a great deal of information about the free technical assistance JAN provides to employers of every type regarding every possible issue related to ADA: accommodation, avoiding retaliation, cost/benefit analyses, and specific information on every type of disability covered by the ADA. JAN's Web site is extremely comprehensive, with accommodation ideas for nearly every disability, and is organized in a completely user-friendly manner. You can search by disability or by profession, and go to many other options for resource information from consultants who help with devices as accommodations to support groups to other relevant laws for persons with disabilities. You will notice that their informational material is so well cross-referenced that it may seem repetitive as you go through it. This is intentional, as the purpose is to make the material as easily accessible as possible.

When you are presenting information to your executive leadership and/or other decision makers and you know you have limited time during which to be persuasive or influential, you will want to provide them with information that is extremely user-friendly, gets to the point, and is sufficiently persuasive. Similarly, JAN, SHRM, and companies that provide important information for HR professionals know that your time is often limited and you often need the same kind of user-friendly convenience.

If an employee raises a safety concern and is then retaliated against, that employee may file an OSHA 11c retaliation complaint against the company, which OSHA will then investigate. The HR Tool entitled "Sample Memo Concerning OSHA's Prohibition against Retaliation," at the end of the chapter, on pages 63–64, is an example of how to address possible retaliation under OSHA.

ADDRESSING ADA AND ADAAA COMPLIANCE

As with EEO and workplace safety laws, some business leaders are simply unaware of the personal liability exposure they have if they don't take these laws seriously, while others stubbornly resist these laws for misguided personal and/or financial reasons. An example of how to handle this situation is shown in the HR Tool entitled "Sample Memo Concerning Compliance with the Americans with Disabilities Act," on pages 65–66. Also, the ADA, in light of recent changes, is now called the ADAAA: Americans with Disabilities

Act Amendment Act. (For our purposes, we will continue to refer to it as the ADA throughout the book.)

As one of the final acts of his presidency, President Bush expanded the ADA to include protection from retaliation for anyone who advocates for anyone else to have their ADA rights addressed and met. Per the EEOC, the Act, effective as of January 1, 2009, "makes important changes to the definition of the term 'disability' by rejecting the holdings in several Supreme Court decisions and portions of EEOC's ADA regulations. The effect of these changes is to make it easier for an individual seeking protection under the ADA to establish that he or she has a disability within the meaning of the ADA. The Act retains the ADA's basic definition of 'disability' as an impairment that substantially limits one or more major life activities, a record of such an impairment, or being regarded as having such an impairment. However, it changes the way that these statutory terms should be interpreted in several ways.

"Most significantly, the Act directs EEOC to revise that portion of its regulations defining the term 'substantially limits', and expands the definition of 'major life activities' by including two non-exhaustive lists. The first list includes many activities that the EEOC has recognized (e.g., walking) as well as activities that EEOC has not specifically recognized (e.g., reading, bending, and communicating). The second list includes major bodily functions (e.g., functions of the immune system, normal cell growth, digestive, bowel, bladder, neurological, brain, respiratory, circulatory, endocrine, and reproductive functions)."[5]

Per the EEOC, the amendment also:

- States that mitigating measures other than "ordinary eyeglasses or contact lenses" shall not be considered in assessing whether an individual has a disability.
- Clarifies that an impairment that is episodic or in remission is a disability if it would substantially limit a major life activity when active.
- Changes the definition of "regarded as" so that it no longer requires a showing that the employer perceived the individual to be substantially limited in a major life activity, and instead says that an applicant or employee is "regarded as" disabled if he or she is subject to an action prohibited by the ADA (e.g., failure to hire or termination) based on an impairment that is not transitory and minor.
- Provides that individuals covered only under the "regarded as" prong are not entitled to reasonable accommodation."[6]

As we have learned, sometimes employers misguidedly engage in unlawful retaliation. HR Tool entitled "Sample Memo Concerning/Alleging Retaliation for Advocating for the ADA/ ADAAA," on pages 66–67, shows an example of how to respond to such a situation. Another HR Tool entitled "Sample Memo Addressing Workplace Safety Concerns," on pages 67–69, shows how one might respond to questions about a company's compliance with both OSHA workplace safety regulations and ADA/ADAAA.

》 JAN'S ACCOMMODATION AND COMPLIANCE SERIES

JAN's Accommodation and Compliance Series (http://www.jan.wvu.edu/bulletins/adaaa1 .htm) is designed to help employers determine effective accommodations and comply with

Title I of the Americans with Disabilities Act (ADA). The following Web sites are resources that will help you navigate through ADA-related situations:

- Employees' Practical Guide to Requesting and Negotiating Reasonable Accommodations under the Americans with Disabilities Act (ADA) at http://www.jan.wvu.edu/EeGuide/
- Employers' Practical Guide to Reasonable Accommodation under the Americans with Disabilities Act (ADA) at http://www.jan.wvu.edu/Erguide/
- Medical Inquiry in Response to an Accommodation Request at http://www.jan.wvu.edu/media/Medical.htm

)) JAN'S FACT SHEET SERIES

JAN's Fact Sheet Series on the ADA and related laws is designed to provide readers with a quick overview of legal issues related to the employment of people with disabilities:

- Pre-Offer, Disability-Related Questions: Dos and Don'ts at http://www.jan.wvu.edu/media/preofferfact.doc
- Sample Reasonable Accommodation Request Form for Employers at http://www.jan.wvu.edu/media/raemployersform.htm
- Title III Checklist at http://www.jan.wvu.edu/media/IIIChecklist.html

)) CONSULTANTS' CORNER AND SEARCHABLE ONLINE ACCOMMODATION RESOURCE

JAN offers two online publications: Consultants' Corner and Searchable Online Accommodation Resource (SOAR). Consultants' Corner is a resource written by experienced JAN consultants to provide helpful hints, techie tips, and innovative ideas regarding various topics. SOAR is designed to let users explore various accommodation options and legal issues for people with disabilities in work and educational settings.

)) ADDITIONAL JAN RESOURCES

Following are additional resources available at the JAN Web site:[7]

- Accommodations, ADA, and Light Duty at http://www.jan.wvu.edu/corner/vol03iss05.htm
- Ideas for Writing an Accommodation Request Letter at http://www.jan.wvu.edu/media/accommrequestltr.htm
- Making the On-Line Application Process Accessible under the Americans with Disabilities Act (ADA) at http://www.jan.wvu.edu/corner/vol02iss05.htm
- How to Determine Whether a Person Has a Disability under the Americans with Disabilities Act (ADA) at http://www.jan.wvu.edu/corner/vol02iss04.htm
- *California AB 2222 v. the ADA* at http://www.jan.wvu.edu/corner/vol01iss08.htm
- The Garrett Decision at http://www.jan.wvu.edu/corner/vol01iss03.htm

- Parking and the ADA, Act I at http://www.jan.wvu.edu/corner/vol01iss14.htm
- Parking and the ADA, Act II at http://www.jan.wvu.edu/corner/vol03iss01.htm
- Requesting and Negotiating a Reasonable Accommodation at http://www.jan.wvu.edu/corner/vol03iss04.htm
- Job Accommodation Network Whitepapers. Universal Design and Assistive Technology as Workplace Accommodations: An Exploratory White Paper on Implementation and Outcome at http://www.jan.wvu.edu/research/JANUDATWhitePaper.doc

These resources can also be found in Spanish at http://www.jan.wvu.edu/espanol.

JAN's resources can easily become the new best friend of the credible activist. Use them often and publicize their resources to other HR professionals, to the managers with whom you work, and to employees who may find the information helpful.

Disability can happen to anyone. It can happen to workplace leaders, workplace lawyers, to HR staff, and to any employee. Additionally, there are now hundreds of thousands of newly disabled veterans, many of whom are still able to work as long as they have reasonable accommodations for their disabilities. It's time to stop thinking about employees as "them" and as certain management employees as "us." We are all "us," and we are all entitled to the same rights, protections, and accommodations under the laws that govern our workplaces.

An earlier chapter referred to a joke on *Seinfeld* that only lawyers read the inside top of the Monopoly box. Although this is a funny joke, it makes an essential point that fuels many HR credible activists: We're all playing the same game, and we have all supposedly agreed to understand and follow all the rules. If there is a small group of people (whether lawyers or anyone else) who can find loopholes around the rules to which everyone else has agreed in good faith, what is the point of playing with those people? Why don't they simply play by the rules instead of putting so much time, effort, and money into looking for ways that they can get around those rules? Therefore, information that assists and empowers employees—whether how to write an accommodation request letter, how to request mediation, how to file a complaint with an external regulatory agency, or how to maximize use of their medical benefits—is for everyone in the workplace, and there should be nothing "radical" about this concept.

We also have a responsibility to assist the entire workplace with becoming more comfortable with persons with disabilities by using emotional intelligence-based diversity trainings. We've all seen a young child of five or six react in horror at seeing a disabled person. Sometimes, adults have the same reactions, despite knowing better. We can openly explore the primal brain feelings of fear, anger, and disgust with employees in response to persons who are different from them, whether disabled or not. This is an excellent way to train all staff in diversity knowledge that is both experiential and sustainable.

More and more workplaces consider the mediation services provided by the EEOC to be preferable to lawsuits. For more information on the EEOC's mediation program, visit: http://www.eeoc.gov/mediate/index.html. Workplaces that make this kind of information available to all employees do so because they know their corporate culture demands of them a level of performance that welcomes employees' internal feedback, concerns, complaints, and questions. This kind of open system is the modern healthy workplace system, toward which all workplaces need to strive. Why? Because it's healthier for all employees emotionally, psychologically, and physically, and, ultimately, less costly.

RECOGNITION OF EMPLOYMENT-AT-WILL EXCEPTIONS, BY STATE, AS OF OCTOBER 1, 2000

	State Public Policy Exception	Implied-Contract Exception	Covenant of Good Faith and Fair Dealing
Total	43	38	11
Alabama	No	Yes	Yes
Alaska	Yes	Yes	Yes
Arizona	Yes	Yes	Yes
Arkansas	Yes	Yes	No
California	Yes	Yes	Yes
Colorado	Yes	Yes	No
Connecticut	Yes	Yes	No
Delaware	Yes	No	Yes
District of Columbia	Yes	Yes	No
Florida	No	No	No
Georgia	No	No	No
Hawaii	Yes	Yes	No
Idaho	Yes	Yes	Yes
Illinois	Yes	Yes	No
Indiana	Yes	No	No
Iowa	Yes	Yes	No
Kansas	Yes	Yes*	No
Kentucky	Yes	Yes	No
Louisiana	No	No	No
Maine	No	Yes	No
Maryland	Yes	Yes	No
Massachusetts	Yes	No	Yes
Michigan	Yes	Yes	No
Minnesota	Yes	Yes	No

	State Public Policy Exception	Implied-Contract Exception	Covenant of Good Faith and Fair Dealing
Mississippi	Yes*	Yes	No
Missouri	Yes	No*	No
Montana	Yes	No	Yes
Nebraska	No	Yes	No
Nevada	Yes	Yes	Yes
New Hampshire	Yes	Yes	No*
New Jersey	Yes	Yes	No
New Mexico	Yes	Yes	No
New York	No	Yes	No
North Carolina	Yes	No	No
North Dakota	Yes	Yes	No
Ohio	Yes*	Yes	No
Oklahoma	Yes	Yes	No
Oregon	Yes	Yes	No
Pennsylvania	Yes	No	No
Rhode Island	No	No	No
South Carolina	Yes	Yes	No
South Dakota	Yes	Yes	No
Tennessee	Yes	Yes	No
Texas	Yes	No	No
Utah	Yes	Yes	Yes
Vermont	Yes	Yes	No
Virginia	Yes	No	No
Washington	Yes	Yes	No
West Virginia	Yes	Yes	No
Wisconsin	Yes	Yes	No
Wyoming	Yes	Yes	Yes

* Overturned previous decision that was contrary to current doctrine.

Source: David J. Walsh and Joshua L. Schwarz, "State Common Law Wrongful Discharge Doctrines: Up-date, Refinement, and Rationals," American Business Law Journal, 645 (Summer 1996). Case law was shepardized (verified) to update the recognition of exceptions through October 1, 2000. Used with permission.

PACE MEMO-WRITING FORMULA

P. Posture you are taking in this memo: Are you educating, reminding, citing policy, citing precedent, citing a law, concerned, reminding a second time, citing ethical codes, or pointing to something else? You may be doing more than one of these in your memo, but you should be clear on which of these you are doing and why, so you choose the right words and keep the memo targeted and brief.

A. Awareness regarding whether or not there are legal compliance issues involved with the matter. Conduct necessary research with credible sources, and document your research, including names and titles of technical assistance persons and/or government sources spoken to and any case law or white papers.

C. Commitment to consistent application of all relevant laws and company policies related to the matter.

E. Execution of relevant policies and procedures in a consistent manner for all employees related to the matter with awareness of precedent and addressing any grey areas or different circumstances that may exist.

SAMPLE MEMO REGARDING EEO COMPLIANCE CONCERNS

On letterhead, in interoffice memo format, or via e-mail

CONFIDENTIAL

To: Your Supervisor
(Include any others on this list to whom this memo should be addressed.)

From: Your Name

Date:

Re.: Concerns about (Company)'s Compliance with EEO Laws

I am compelled to express concern about how we at (Company) handle issues related to EEO and Sexual Harassment Prevention laws.

As you know, the EEOC has determined that if a workplace environment is such that employees are afraid to make complaints; this environment can contribute substantially to a viable retaliation claim. Additionally, now any employee who participates in an investigation is also protected from retaliation. Additionally, we have a responsibility to investigate complaints promptly, thoroughly, and soundly. Just as important, we have a legal responsibility to *prevent* any harassment, discrimination, and/or retaliation based on any category protected by our city, state, and federal laws.

I am concerned about how the recent situation with (employee's name or complaint) is being handled. Unless I am unaware of additional information or documentation related to this matter, I recommend that we revisit this situation and seek technical EEO and Sexual Harassment Prevention (SHP) assistance to ensure that we at (Company) have not made any errors in violation of any aspect of EEO law.

If we learn that any errors have been or are being made, I recommend that we remediate those as soon as possible. Moving forward, I recommend that we consider implementing a decision-making protocol that will include technical assistance consultation from no-cost government or SHRM resources to prevent errors in the future. Additionally, I recommend that all persons involved in EEO complaint-receipt, investigations, or determinations attend formal training on EEO and SHP compliance issues. I will follow this memo up with a list of quality upcoming available trainings in our area or via webinar.

We share a collective responsibility to ensure (Company)'s compliance with EEO laws and training requirements. I know we share a commitment to prevent liability exposure for (Company) as well as personal liability exposure.

The resources below are free and available to us to use at any time. My membership in SHRM provides free information, white papers, case-law information, and cutting-edge research capabilities along with toolkits for how to best handle EEO and SHP-related issues. I recommend that we use these resources in the future to ensure legally compliant decision-making processes related to EEO and SHP issues.

http://www.eeotraining.eeoc.gov/viewpage.aspx?ID=030b9cb8-8e56-433c-a410-cc94ccb64b3a

http://www.eeoc.gov/outreach/index.htm

http://www.shrm.org

http://www.workplacefairness.org/resources

I know we share a strong commitment to the consistent application of all (Company)'s policies as well as legal compliance with all relevant city, state, and federal laws related to EEO laws.

Additionally, I know we share an awareness of the importance of precedent in our decision-making processes and our handling of EEO issues in a legally compliant manner.

SAMPLE EEO TRAINING AID

WHAT "THE WORKPLACE" MEANS WITHIN (COMPANY)'S HARASSMENT POLICY

☐ The office

☐ Client locations

- ☐ Other (Company) locations
- ☐ The parking lot
- ☐ The company garage
- ☐ In company vehicles
- ☐ Your lunch hour with coworkers
- ☐ A bar or club after work with coworkers and friends
- ☐ Dealing with vendors, clients, trustees, consultants, board members, interns, contractors, customers, etc.
- ☐ Board meetings
- ☐ Workplace committee meetings
- ☐ Union meetings
- ☐ Traveling for work, to and from home, meetings, trainings, conferences, seminars, etc.
- ☐ Any place where you are working, for work purposes, or with coworkers

SAMPLE MEMO CAUTIONING AGAINST UNLAWFUL RETALIATION

On letterhead, in interoffice memo format, or via e-mail

CONFIDENTIAL

To: Your Supervisor
(Include any others on this list to whom this memo should be addressed.)

From: Your Name

Date:

Re.:   Concerns about (Company) Engaging in Actions That Could Be Characterized as Retaliatory

I am compelled to express concern about how we at (Company) handle issues related to unlawful retaliation under EEO and other laws.

I am concerned about how the recent situation with (employee's name) is being handled. Unless I am unaware of additional information or documentation related to this matter, I recommend that we revisit this situation and seek technical assistance to ensure that we at (Company) have not made any errors in violation of laws that prohibit unlawful retaliation.

If we learn that any errors have been made, I recommend that we remediate those as soon as possible. Moving forward, I recommend that we consider implementing a decision-making protocol that will include technical assistance consultation from no-cost government or SHRM resources to prevent errors in the future. Additionally, I recommend that all persons involved in any employment decision or action that could be characterized as unlawfully retaliatory attend formal training on these important compliance issues in order to prevent costly errors and noncompliance. I will follow this memo up with a list of quality upcoming available trainings in our area or via webinar.

We share a collective responsibility to ensure (Company)'s compliance with laws governing issues related to unlawful retaliation. I know we share a commitment to prevent liability exposure for (Company) as well as personal liability exposure.

The resources below are free and available to us to use at any time. My membership in SHRM provides free information, white papers, case-law information, and research capabilities along with toolkits for how to best handle issues that could be characterized as unlawfully retaliatory. I recommend that we use these resources in the future to ensure legally compliant decision-making processes likely to assist us in avoiding any actual or appearance of unlawful retaliation.

http://www.eeoc.gov/types/retaliation.htm

http://www.eeoc.gov/policy/docs/retal.htm

http://moss07.shrm.org/hrdisciplines/employeerelations/Pages/retaliation.aspx

http://www.shrm.org

http://www.jan.wvu.edu/

http://www.workplacefairness.org/resources

I know we share a strong commitment to consistent application of all (Company)'s policies regarding zero tolerance for unlawful retaliation as well as compliance with all relevant city, state, and federal laws.

Additionally, I know we share an awareness of the importance of precedent in our decision-making processes and our handling of issues that could be characterized as retaliatory in a legally compliant and ethically sound manner.

SAMPLE MEMO CONCERNING OSHA'S PROHIBITION AGAINST RETALIATION

On letterhead, in interoffice memo format, or via e-mail

CONFIDENTIAL

To: Your Supervisor
(Include any others on this list to whom this memo should be addressed.)

From: Your Name

Date:

Re.: Concerns about (Company)'s Compliance with OSHA Prohibitions against Retaliation

I am compelled to express concern about how we at (Company) handle issues related to Occupational and Safety and Health Administration's (OSHA) prohibition against retaliation against an employee for raising concerns about workplace safety issues.

I am concerned about how the recent situation with (employee's name) is being handled. Unless I am unaware of additional information or documentation related to this matter, I recommend that we revisit this situation and seek technical OSHA assistance to ensure that we at (Company) have not made any errors in violation of OSHA regulations.

If we learn that any errors were made, I recommend that we remediate those as soon as possible. Moving forward, I recommend that we consider implementing a decision-making protocol that will include technical assistance consultation from no-cost government or SHRM resources to prevent errors in the future. Additionally, I recommend that all persons involved in workplace safety, performance evaluation, discipline, and related decisions attend formal training on OSHA compliance issues. I will follow this memo up with a list of quality upcoming available trainings in our area or via webinar.

We share a collective responsibility to ensure (Company)'s compliance with OSHA regulations. I know we share a commitment to prevent liability exposure for (Company) as well as personal liability exposure.

The resources below are free and available to us to use at any time. My membership in SHRM provides free information, white papers, case-law information, and research capabilities along with toolkits for how to best handle workplace safety and retaliation-prevention issues. I recommend that we use these resources in the future to ensure legally compliant decision-making processes related to OSHA and retaliation-prevention issues.

http://www.osha.gov/pls/oshaweb/owadisp.show_document?p_table=FEDERAL_REGISTER&p_id=19814

http://www.osha.gov/pls/oshaweb/owadisp.show_document?p_table=DIRECTIVES&p_id=1830

http://www.shrm.org

http://www.jan.wvu.edu/

http://www.workplacefairness.org/resources

I know we share a strong commitment to the consistent application of all (Company)'s policies as well as compliance with all relevant city, state, and federal laws related to workplace safety and prohibitions against unlawful retaliation under OSHA.

Additionally, I know we share an awareness of the importance of precedent in our decision-making processes and our handling of workplace safety issues in a legally compliant manner.

SAMPLE MEMO CONCERNING COMPLIANCE WITH THE AMERICANS WITH DISABILITIES ACT

On letterhead, in interoffice memo format, or via e-mail

CONFIDENTIAL

To: Your Supervisor
(Include any others on this list to whom this memo should be addressed.)

From: Your Name

Date:

Re.:   Concerns about (Company)'s Compliance with the Americans with Disabilities Act (ADA) and ADAAA

I am compelled to express concern about how we at (Company) handle issues related to the Americans with Disabilities Act (ADA) and ADAAA.

As you know, the ADA was recently changed and made more robust. I am concerned about how the recent situation with (employee's name) is being handled. Unless I am unaware of additional information or documentation related to this matter, I recommend that we revisit this situation and seek technical ADA assistance to ensure that we at (Company) have not made any errors in violation of the ADA/ADAAA.

If we learn that any errors were made, I recommend that we remediate those as soon as possible. Moving forward, I recommend that we consider implementing a decision-making protocol that will include technical assistance consultation from no-cost government or SHRM resources to prevent errors in the future. Additionally, I recommend that all persons involved in ADA decisions, contributing to job descriptions, and involved in interviewing and hiring decisions attend formal training on ADA/ADAAA compliance issues. I will follow this memo up with a list of quality upcoming available trainings in our area or via webinar.

We share a collective responsibility to ensure (Company)'s compliance with ADA and ADAAA. I know we share a commitment to prevent liability exposure for (Company) as well as personal liability exposure.

The resources below are free and available to us to use at any time. My membership in SHRM provides free information, white papers, case-law information, and research capabilities along with toolkits for how to best handle the ADA and related issues. I recommend that we use these resources in the future to ensure legally compliant decision-making processes related to ADA/ADAAA issues.

http://www.ada.gov/   http://www.shrm.org

http://www.jan.wvu.edu/media/   http://www.workplacefairness.org/
accessibilityfact.doc   resources

I know we share a strong commitment to the consistent application of all (Company)'s policies as well as compliance with all relevant city, state, and federal laws related to the ADA and ADAAA.

Additionally, I know we share an awareness of the importance of precedent in our decision-making processes and our handling of ADA issues in a legally compliant manner.

SAMPLE MEMO CONCERNING/ALLEGING RETALIATION FOR ADVOCATING FOR THE ADA/ADAAA

On letterhead, in interoffice memo, or via e-mail

CONFIDENTIAL

To: Your Supervisor
(Include any others on this list to whom this memo should be addressed.)

From: Your Name

Date:

Re.: Concerns about (Company's) Compliance with ADA, the ADAAA, and Retaliation

I am compelled to express concern about the response to my memo regarding how we at (Company) handle issues related to the Americans with Disabilities Act (ADA and ADAAA).

The ADA protects against retaliation any employee who advocates for the ADA to be properly administered, even if that employee is advocating for another employee's disability or is ultimately mistaken in his or her recommendations.

I documented my concern about how the recent situation with (employee's name) was handled, and since then, I have experienced greater scrutiny of my job performance. I have also experienced disparate treatment of any ordinary minor errors I have made both as compared to those of my colleagues and as compared to treatment given to minor errors I may have made prior to my having raised my ADA concerns.

These instances fit the definition of retaliation against me under the ADA. I request and recommend that we address these issues with an experienced, impartial external mediator and/or investigator who is knowledgeable about ADA law, retaliation, and sound conflict resolution methods. The EEOC has an excellent mediation program.

I recommend again that we consider implementing a decision-making protocol that will include technical assistance consultation from no-cost government or SHRM resources to prevent errors around retaliation in the future. Additionally, I again recommend that all persons involved in decisions that have salience under ADA as stated in my previous memo attend formal training on ADA prohibitions against retaliation and related compliance issues.

I did send a list of quality upcoming available trainings in our area or via webinar to you on (date). I recommend that we all attend the same training and/or webinar so we are all on the same page regarding our understanding of our shared compliance responsibilities under the ADA, including those prohibiting retaliation. I would be more than happy to arrange our attendance at any of these available trainings; please let me know if you have any thoughts on which trainings we might attend either separately or together, and I would be more than happy to make all registration arrangements. If you would like to meet to discuss these trainings, I would be happy to do that as well.

We share a collective responsibility to ensure (Company)'s compliance with ADA and ADAAA. I know that we also share a commitment to prevent liability exposure for (Company) as well as personal liability exposure. I know that we also share a commitment for zero tolerance for retaliation against anyone who raises ADA concerns.

Again, the resources below are free and available to us to use at any time. My membership in SHRM provides free information, white papers, case law information, and research capabilities along with toolkits for how to best handle the ADA and related issues. I again recommend that we use these resources in the future to ensure legally compliant decision-making processes related to ADA issues.

http://www.ada.gov/

http://www.shrm.org/

http://www.jan.wvu.edu/links/adasummary.htm

http://www.workplacefairness.org/resources

It is my hope that we share a strong commitment to the consistent application of all (Company)'s policies as well as compliance with all relevant city, state, and federal laws related to the ADA, which includes zero tolerance for retaliation against any employee who raises an ADA concern, as I did on (date).

Additionally, I hope we share an awareness of the importance of precedent in our decision-making processes and our handling of ADA issues in a legally compliant manner, including refraining from any form of retaliation against any employee who raises ADA concerns.

SAMPLE MEMO ADDRESSING WORKPLACE SAFETY CONCERNS

On letterhead, in interoffice memo format, or via e-mail

CONFIDENTIAL

To: Your Supervisor
      (Include any others on this list to whom this memo should be addressed.)

From: Your Name

Date:

Re.: Concerns about (Company)'s Compliance with OSHA Workplace Safety Regulations and ADA/ADAAA Compliance

I am compelled to express concern about how we at (Company) handle issues related to workplace safety compliance combined with ADA/ADAAA issues.

I am specifically concerned about how the recent situation with (employee's name) is being handled. Unless I am unaware of additional information or documentation related to this matter, I recommend that we revisit this situation and seek technical workplace safety assistance to ensure that we at (Company) have not made any errors in violation of OSHA or the ADAAA.

As you are aware, workplace safety issues also have relevance for our workers' compensation (WC) employee injury and illness records as well as our WC insurance rates.

If we learn that any errors were made, I recommend that we remediate those as soon as possible. Moving forward, I recommend that we consider implementing a decision-making protocol that will include technical assistance consultation from no-cost government or SHRM resources to prevent errors in the future. Additionally, I recommend that all persons involved in workplace safety decisions attend formal training on workplace safety compliance issues. I will follow this memo up with a list of quality upcoming available trainings in our area or via webinar.

We share a collective responsibility to ensure (Company)'s compliance with OSHA rules and regulations. I know we share a commitment to prevent liability exposure for (Company) as well as personal liability exposure.

The resources below are free and available to us to use at any time. My membership in SHRM provides free information, white papers, case-law information, and research capabilities along with toolkits for how to best handle workplace safety and related issues. I recommend that we use these resources in the future to ensure legally compliant decision-making processes related to job descriptions, job hazard analysis, personal protective equipment, record-keeping requirements, ADA accommodations for injured employees, WC law for our state, and all other relevant supervisory and policy issues that relate to workplace safety. Additionally, there are OSHA programs and DOL-DOSH programs that provide free safety trainings, which I will research and report on.

http://www.osha.gov/

http://www.shrm.org

http://www.dol.gov/dol/topic/workcomp/index.htm

http://www.jan.wvu.edu/

http://www.workplacefairness.org/resources

I know we share a strong commitment to consistent application of all (Company)'s policies as well as compliance with all relevant city, state, and federal laws related to workplace safety laws.

Additionally, I know we share an awareness of the importance of precedent in our decision-making processes and our handling of workplace safety issues in a legally compliant manner.

I have attached information from the Job Accommodation Network's (JAN's) Web site that I believe will assist us in ensuring that our corporate governance practices around ADA (and ADAAA) and related issues are handled in a legally compliant manner.

Please review the attached when you have time or visit the Web site at: http://www.jan.wvu.edu/. I am also including information from JAN on recommended formats for employees requesting accommodations. This will ensure that we are prepared to respond appropriately and proactively provide forms for employees who may require reasonable accommodations and continue to provide excellent internal HR customer service to (Company)'s employees while also remaining in compliance with ADA and related laws.

CHAPTER 5

LEGAL ISSUES CONCERNING COMPENSATION, INSURANCE, LEAVE, AND OVERTIME

WORKERS' COMPENSATION

Different states have different workers' compensation (WC) laws that often change. Both JAN at http://www.jan.wvu.edu/ and DOL at www.dol.gov have the updated information you need to know. Find out what deadlines apply to your state for submitting workplace illness and injury paperwork to your WC insurance carrier.

》 HELPFUL TIPS

1. Make laminated business cards for every employee with the following information to keep in their wallets, at home, and at their desk. An example is shown in the HR Tool entitled "Sample WC Card," at the end of the chapter, on page 75.

   Provide employees with at least three cards, and remind them periodically via monthly themes on workplace safety and how WC works that they use *these* cards for workplace injuries, *not* their private health insurance.

2. Have self-inking stamps made of the following:
   - Your company's full address
   - The full address of the nearest medical provider/hospital/ER that provides medical care for WC injuries and illnesses
   - The full address of your WC carrier

   You will be stamping this information on many forms, letters, and slips of paper for WC paperwork and confused employees. You will also need to learn how your short-term and long-term disability carrier policy addresses workplace injuries and illnesses and if it does at all. You will also need to keep very careful records of any workplace injury both on the form OSHA requires you to post annually (in a place where employees can see it) listing every workplace injury or illness for that year, as well as on copies of the injury report forms required by your WC carrier and anyone else in your organization (legal department, supervisors, safety committee, employee files). These forms contain confidential information such as social security numbers, so you must consider them confidential and treat them accordingly.

3. You will also want to cultivate an excellent relationship with the various representatives of your WC carrier, who may call you with questions about injuries if your descriptions on the forms are not accurate enough. They will also call you (or not) to schedule safety examination site visits of your offices and operations. If you have a

good relationship with your carrier's reps and have high injury rates, you will likely receive notice, which should prompt you to notify certain colleagues: building staff, leadership, legal, any department head whose staff have high injury rates, and so on. You should also keep accurate records of all internal and external safety training your staff has attended, including dated sign-in sheets that indicate the training topic, location, trainer, and length of training.

The HR Tool entitled "Sample Letter to Medical Providers Who Erroneously Bill Employees or Company for Workers' Compensation Bills," on pages 75–76, shows how the situation of erroneous WC billing might be handled.

DISABILITY INSURANCE

Be sure that you understand your disability insurance carrier's policy regarding employees on FMLA leave or leave without pay; they may refuse to cover the employee under the disability policy, stating that the employee was not "actively" employed. Be aware of waiting periods before employees are paid their disability benefits under certain circumstances, and learn all you can about this and other aspects of your policy by interviewing your policy representative. The details are often not indicated in your policy. Do not promise employees coverage, as the STD/LTD (for short-term disability/long-term disability) company will make decisions on their claims based on what their physician certifies on the necessary forms. Also, be aware that statutory disability benefits vary by state, and if you have employees working in different states, you will need to understand those details so you can explain them to employees.

You may want to consider a company leave donation program to allow employees to help each other out when they are very ill and run out of sick time. The HR Tool outlining the policy entitled "Sample Memo: Leave Donation Policy," is on page 76.

FAMILY MEDICAL LEAVE ACT COMPLIANCE

The FMLA requires private employers with 50 or more employees and public agencies, including all state, local, and federal government employers regardless of the number of employees, to provide covered employees with up to 12 workweeks of unpaid, job-protected leave a year. It also requires these employers to maintain group health benefits during the leave as if employees continued to work instead of taking leave. To be covered by the FMLA, an employee must (1) have been employed by the employer for at least 12 months, (2) have been employed for at least 1,250 hours of service during the 12-month period immediately preceding the commencement of the leave, and (3) be employed at a worksite where 50 or more employees are employed by the employer within 75 miles of that worksite.

For more information regarding the FMLA, visit JAN's FMLA Library or contact the U.S. Department of Labor, Wage and Hour Division, at (866) 487-9243. To find your nearest office, check your local phone directory under U.S. Government, Department of Labor. For a list of state Wage and Hour offices, visit http://www.dol.gov/esa/contacts/state_of.htm.[1]

Your FMLA policy may allow these 12 weeks by calendar year or by rolling year. This means that if you allow 12 weeks per calendar year and you have an employee who begins an FMLA leave on November 1 and is out on FMLA for all of November and all of December, that employee has not used up the entire 12 weeks. If that employee continues to be out after January 1 of the following year, your calendar year policy now allows that employee to be out another full 12 weeks as of January 1. If your FMLA policy only allows for FMLA on a rolling-year basis, that employee would only have FMLA leave for the remaining unused time of a maximum of 12 weeks from when the employee's FMLA leave began on November 1 of the previous year.

Your company's FMLA policy may or may not require employees to use their paid time off concurrently with the use of their FMLA. There are also protections for certain caregivers under FMLA. See the following page for information on this from the EEOC.

The FMLA was recently changed to include the Final Regulations, which implement two important new military family leave entitlements for eligible specified family members:

1. Up to 12 weeks of leave for certain qualifying exigencies arising out of a covered military member's active-duty status, or notification of an impending call or order to active-duty status, in support of a contingency operation, and
2. Up to 26 weeks of leave in a single 12-month period to care for a covered service member recovering from a serious injury or illness incurred in the line of duty on active duty. Eligible employees are entitled to a combined total of up to 26 weeks of all types of FMLA leave during the single 12-month period. The Final Regulations became effective on January 16, 2009.

)) EEO AND CAREGIVERS

The EEOC has issued a document entitled "Enforcement Guidance: Unlawful Disparate Treatment of Workers with Caregiving Responsibilities." This document illustrates circumstances under which discrimination against a working parent or other caregiver constitutes unlawful disparate treatment under the federal EEO statutes.

Changing workplace demographics, including women's increased participation in the labor force, have created the potential for greater discrimination against working parents and others with caregiving responsibilities. The new guidance is intended to assist employers, employees, and Commission staff in determining whether discrimination against persons with caregiving responsibilities constitutes unlawful disparate treatment under federal EEO law.

The federal EEO statutes do not prohibit discrimination based solely on parental or other caregiver status. Under the federal EEO laws, discrimination must be based on a protected characteristic such as sex or race. However, some state or local laws may provide broader protections for caregivers. A particular caregiver also may have certain rights under other federal laws, including the Family and Medical Leave Act.

Unlawful disparate treatment arises where a worker with caregiving responsibilities is subjected to discrimination based on a protected characteristic under federal EEO law. Generally, this means that, under Title VII of the Civil Rights Act of 1964, unlawful disparate treatment arises where a caregiver is subjected to discrimination based on sex and/or race.

Unlawful disparate treatment of a caregiver also can arise under the Americans with Disabilities Act of 1990 where an employer discriminates against a worker based on his or her association with an individual with a disability.

The new enforcement guidance illustrates various circumstances under which discrimination against a caregiver might violate federal EEO law. Examples include the following:

- Treating male caregivers more favorably than female caregivers
- Denying women with young children an employment opportunity that is available to men with young children
- Reassigning a woman to less desirable projects based on the assumption that, as a new mother, she will be less committed to her job
- Reducing a female employee's workload after she assumes full-time care of her niece and nephew based on the assumption that, as a female caregiver, she won't want to work overtime
- Subjective decision-making: Lowering subjective evaluations of a female employee's work performance after she becomes the primary caregiver of her grandchildren, despite the absence of an actual decline in work performance
- Making assumptions about pregnant workers: Limiting a pregnant worker's job duties based on pregnancy-related stereotypes
- Discriminating against working fathers: Denying a male caregiver leave to care for an infant under circumstances where such leave would be granted to a female caregiver
- Discriminating against women of color: Reassigning a Latina worker to a lower-paying position after she becomes pregnant
- Stereotyping based on association with an individual with a disability
- Refusing to hire a worker who is a single parent of a child with a disability based on the assumption that caregiving responsibilities will make the worker unreliable
- Subjecting a female worker to severe or pervasive harassment because she is a mother with young children
- Subjecting a female worker to severe or pervasive harassment because she is pregnant or has taken maternity leave
- Subjecting a worker to severe or pervasive harassment *because his wife has a disability*[2]

FMLA abuse by employees is also a very serious issue and can take many forms. Some employees fill out FMLA medical certification forms themselves. Some employees fake illnesses and convince medical doctors to fill out forms for them. There are even some medical providers who will certify that an employee or an employee's close family member has a serious illness when that is in fact untrue. These situations present unique challenges that require delicate handling. HR professionals who suspect that any of this may be happening are advised to consult with their internal or external labor counsel, their own supervisor(s), and the supervisor of the employee presenting the FMLA forms.

Another form of FMLA abuse is the employee who refuses to provide a clear schedule to his or her supervisor and HR. There are situations that truly do make this difficult or impossible—for example, the care of an Alzheimer's patient who frequently goes missing or has another serious illness that is truly fraught with elements of unpredictability. However, if the FMLA leave is, for example, to allow the employee to be present with a family member who has a serious illness and who is in the care of a hospital, hospice, or with other family members, this employee should be able to present a clear schedule and adhere to it, barring the occasional emergency.

Unfortunately, there are employees who will abuse their FMLA leave by refusing to provide a schedule, adhere to a provided schedule, or claim repeatedly that he or she simply does not understand his or her responsibilities under FMLA. In this case, HR professionals are advised to meet with the employee in the presence of his or her supervisor or another manager, explain the FMLA policy, ask the employee if he or she has any questions, provide the employee with four written copies of the policy to keep at home, to share with family members, to keep at work, and to have an extra just in case. It is then advised to e-mail the employee after the meeting and request that the employee either ask any questions he or she has or acknowledge that he or she understands the FMLA policy. It is also advised that the employee be instructed in writing and preferably via e-mail that if he or she subsequently has any questions whatsoever about his or her responsibilities regarding FMLA leave, he or she is instructed to contact HR immediately.

There are times when non-HR executive staff and other managers don't understand the intricacies of FMLA law and don't understand that FMLA abuse is happening. The HR Tool entitled "Sample Memo Regarding FMLA Compliance Concerns," on pages 77–78, shows how you can customize for your needs.

CONCERNS ABOUT FLSA STATUS: KNOWING WHO MUST BE PAID OVERTIME AND WHEN

The FLSA's basic requirements are payment of the minimum wage, overtime pay for time worked over 40 hours in a workweek, restrictions on the employment of children, and record keeping. There are a number of employment practices that the FLSA does not regulate. For example, the FLSA does not require (1) vacation, holiday, severance, or sick pay; (2) meal or rest periods, holidays off, or vacations; (3) premium pay for weekend or holiday work; (4) pay raises or fringe benefits; (5) a discharge notice, reason for discharge, or immediate payment of final wages to terminated employees; and (6) pay stubs or W-2s.

In addition, the FLSA does not limit the number of hours in a day, or days in a week, an employee may be required or scheduled to work, including overtime hours, if the employee is at least 16 years old. However, some states have laws covering some of these issues, such as meal or rest periods, or discharge notices. For a list of state labor offices, visit http://www.dol.gov/esa/contacts/state_of.htm. For more information regarding the FLSA, contact your nearest Department of Labor Wage and Hour District Office. To find your nearest office, check your local phone directory under U.S. Government, Department of Labor.[3] The HR Tool entitled "Sample Memo Regarding FLSA Concerns," on page 78, is an example of how FLSA issues might be addressed.

HR TOOLS

SAMPLE WC CARD

Workers' Comp (WC) Policy Number

A sentence that says "Send all bills to: Workers' Comp (Carrier Company Name), Phone, Address, and Contact info for billing inquires at the WC Insurance Carrier

Your Company's FEIN (Federal Employer Identification Number) and UI (Unemployment Insurance) Reg. Number

A sentence that says: "I am an injured employee of (Company). Provide address, phone number, and an e-mail contact if possible."

SAMPLE LETTER TO MEDICAL PROVIDERS WHO ERRONEOUSLY BILL EMPLOYEES OR COMPANY FOR WORKERS' COMPENSATION BILLS

On letterhead, via postal mail, fax, or e-mail

Date

To Whom It May Concern:

The bill we are sending to you was erroneously sent to either an employee or this workplace. This bill relates to a workers' compensation injury; therefore, only the workers' compensation (WC) carrier listed below should be billed by any medical provider related to this case.

All of (Company)'s employees present a card to any WC medical provider, which includes all of the necessary WC billing information needed by the medical provider.

In case you no longer have that information, I have provided it for you below:

Name and full address and contact info for (Company)'s WC Insurance carrier:

(Company)'s WC Policy Number:

(Company)'s FEIN (Federal Employer Identification Number):

Our UI (Unemployment Insurance) Reg. Number:

The State in which this employee works:

For any billing inquiries related to this or any other workplace injury related to (Company), please call: _____ (phone number for Company's WC carrier)

Thank you,

Your Full Name

Full Contact Information

Company Web site

CC: Injured Employee

          Injured Employee's file

SAMPLE MEMO: LEAVE DONATION POLICY

On letterhead, in interoffice memo format, or via e-mail

Date

Dear Staff,

(Company) has a leave donation program for staff members who are out due to injury or illness and have run out of paid time off. _____ **has requested leave donation.** She is expected to be absent until further notice. She does not have sufficient leave accruals to cover her expected time out of work.

This program allows staff to voluntarily donate vacation, sick, and personal leave accruals to employees who are on medical or disability leave and don't have enough leave accruals to cover their salary. Your donated leave is used to cover the recipient's salary during their waiting period for disability and/or to delay the use of disability benefits, which pay only partial salary.

This is voluntary.

Eligibility to Donate:

In order to donate you must:

☐ be an employee of (Company);

☐ have a minimum of 1 weeks' paid time off vacation leave after the donation; and

☐ make donations in 8-hour units

If you wish to donate unused vacation, sick, or personal leave accruals, please let me know by responding to this message. The identity of donors remains confidential and is only disclosed to certain members of HR and Finance for tracking purposes.

To review this policy, please review the Employee Handbook. Please let me know if you have any questions.

Thank you,

HR Name, Title

SAMPLE MEMO REGARDING FMLA COMPLIANCE CONCERNS

On letterhead, in interoffice memo format, or via e-mail

To: Your Supervisor (also include the supervisor of an employee, or any others on this list to whom this memo should be addressed)

From: Your Name

Date:

Re.:   Concerns about (Company)'s Compliance with FMLA

I am compelled to express concern about how we at (Company) handle issues related to the Family Medical Leave Act (FMLA).

I am concerned about how the recent situation with (employee's name) is being handled. Unless I am unaware of additional information or documentation related to this matter, I recommend that we revisit this situation and seek technical FMLA assistance to ensure that we at (Company) have not made any errors in violation of the FMLA. There are times when FMLA issues include ADA and EEO issues, and I have included a link to the EEOC's guidance on this below as well as other informational links that relate to my concerns about the situation involving (employee's name). There is also an informational link to Company's obligations to provide reasonable accommodations under ADA.

If we learn that any errors have been made, I recommend that we remediate those as soon as possible. Moving forward, I recommend that we consider implementing a decision-making protocol that will include technical assistance consultation from no-cost government or SHRM resources to prevent errors in the future. Additionally, I recommend that all persons involved in FMLA decisions attend formal training on FMLA compliance issues. I will follow this memo up with a list of quality upcoming available trainings in our area or via webinar.

We share a collective responsibility to ensure (Company)'s compliance with FMLA. We also share a commitment to prevent liability exposure for (Company) as well as personal liability exposure.

The resources below are free and available to us to use at any time. My membership in SHRM provides free information, white papers, case-law information, and research capabilities along with toolkits for how to best handle the FMLA and related issues. I recommend that we use these resources in the future to ensure legally compliant decision-making processes related to FMLA issues.

http://www.eeoc.gov/policy/docs/fmlaada.htm

http://www.dol.gov/esa/whd/fmla/

http://www.shrm.org/

http://www.jan.wvu.edu/Erguide/Three.htm

http://www.workplacefairness.org/resources

I know we share a strong commitment to consistent application of all (Company)'s policies to all employees as well as compliance with all relevant city, state, and federal laws related to the FMLA.

Additionally, I know we share an awareness of the importance of precedent in our decision-making processes and our handling of FMLA issues in a legally compliant manner.

SAMPLE MEMO REGARDING FLSA CONCERNS

On letterhead, in interoffice memo format, or via e-mail

CONFIDENTIAL

To: President of (Company) (also include your supervisor, Legal, Finance, payroll)

From: Your Name

Date:

Re.:   (Company)'s Compliance with FLSA

I am recommending that my attached audit dated _____ be used to change the FLSA status of the attached list of employees so that (Company) avoids FLSA penalty fines from the DOL, lawsuits from those who have not been compensated properly according to FLSA laws, the possibility of angry employees voting to bring a union to (Company), and negative publicity for (Company).

I have reviewed all up-to-date job descriptions for these employees, have confirmed with their supervisors that they are accurate, and have reviewed their job duties with the most recent FLSA training and guidance information available from the DOL. (If true: I have cultivated an excellent working relationship with _____ at the DOL, who has given me guidance regarding any of the job descriptions that may land in an FLSA-status that is unclear.

I also recommend that (Company) acknowledge previous misclassification of those employees listed with an asterisk next to their name, apologize for the error, and reimburse them for any unpaid wages plus interest going back to whatever date is necessary. This will demonstrate (Company)'s good will and commitment to remaining legally compliant with all relevant labor laws, and will serve to help keep (Company) union-free.

CHAPTER 6

LEGAL ISSUES CONCERNING PUBLIC SAFETY AND FRAUD

KNOWLEDGE OF THREATS TO PUBLIC SAFETY BECAUSE OF SOMETHING THE COMPANY IS DOING OR PRODUCING

On August 14, 2008, Section 219 of the Consumer Product Safety Improvement Act (CPSIA) was enacted, establishing new retaliation protections for employees in the consumer product industry. In general, covered employers under the CPSIA include manufacturers, importers, private labelers (owners of a brand or trademark on the private label of a consumer product), distributors, and retailers.

Under the CPSIA,

a covered employer may not discharge or in any other manner retaliate against you because you provided, caused to be provided or are about to provide or cause to be provided to the employer, the federal government, or the attorney general of a state information you reasonably believed related to any violation of, or any act or omission the employee reasonably believes to be a violation of the Consumer Product Safety Act (CPSA) or any other Act enforced by the Consumer Product Safety Commission (CPSC), or any order, rule, regulation, standard or ban under any such Acts.

In general, under the CPSA, a 'consumer product' means any article, or component part thereof, produced or distributed: (i) for sale to a consumer for use in or around a permanent or temporary household or residence, a school, in recreation, or otherwise, or (ii) for the personal use, consumption or enjoyment of a consumer in or around a permanent or temporary household or residence, a school, in recreation, or otherwise. Under the CPSA, the CPSC regulates about 15,000 types of consumer products used in the home, schools, and recreation; but does not regulate on-road motor vehicles, boats, aircraft, food, drugs, cosmetics, pesticides, alcohol, tobacco, firearms, and medical devices. Other Acts enforced by the CPSC include the Federal Hazardous Substances Act, the Flammable Fabrics Act, the Poison Prevention Packaging Act and the Refrigerator Safety Act. Further information about the laws and related requirements enforced by the CPSC can be found on the CPSC's Web site at: http://www.cpsc.gov/businfo/businfo.html.

In addition, under the CPSIA, your employer may not discharge or in any manner retaliate against you because you participated in or assisted in a proceeding under the laws, orders, rules, regulations, standards or bans enforced by the CPSC. Also, your employer may not discharge or in any manner retaliate against you because you objected to, or refused to participate in, any activity, policy, practice, or assigned task that you reasonably believed to be in violation of any provision of the CPSA or any other act enforced by the CPSC, or any order, rule, regulation, standard or ban under any such acts.

Your employer may be found to have violated this statute if your protected activity was a contributing factor in its decision to take unfavorable personnel action against you. Such actions may include:

- Firing or laying off
- Blacklisting
- Demoting
- Denying overtime or promotion
- Disciplining
- Denying benefits
- Failing to hire or rehire
- Intimidation
- Reassignment affecting promotion prospects
- Reducing pay or hours

Complaints must be filed within 180 days after the alleged unfavorable personnel action occurs (that is, when you become aware of the retaliatory action).[1]

The HR Tool entitled "Sample Memo Regarding Knowledge of Threats to Public Safety under CPSC," at the end of the chapter, on pages 85–86, illustrates one way to address CPSC issues.

If you experience or observe retaliation for having raised the public safety concerns, reference the HR Tool entitled "Sample Memo Regarding Concerns about Retaliation against Employee for Raising Public/Product Safety Concerns," on pages 86–87.

KNOWLEDGE OF FINANCIAL FRAUD OR OF YOUR COMPANY DEFRAUDING THE U.S. GOVERNMENT

If you have knowledge of employees at any level of your company financially defrauding the federal government, you are in a very difficult (yet interesting) position. This is also true if you live in a city and/or a state that also has a False Claims Act case. You have a number of choices. You can pretend you don't know, which may or may not come back to haunt you. You can ask yourself to what extent you have been involved in the fraud, meaning, are you merely aware of it or were you required to be a part of it in some way such as preparing research or documents or signing something related to the fraud? Is your name listed on anything related to the fraud? What kind of direct contact have you had with the proof?

The False Claims Act (FCA) is also known as Lincoln's Law, as it was implemented during Lincoln's presidency as a way for the U.S. federal government to prevent being defrauded by citizens or companies. It also provided the government the opportunity to recoup any monies of which it had been defrauded. The Act allowed ordinary citizens who had proof of fraud to come forward with the information under seal to the appropriate federal agency and to receive a share of the recouped funds. This reward is often hard-earned given the stress generally experienced. Another name for these kinds of cases is *qui tam*, or "he who comes forth on behalf of the king," as this comes from English law. Many U.S. states and cities now have their own FCA laws allowing persons who are aware of anyone or any entity defrauding that city or state to come forward with knowledge and proof.

Of course, you want to be sure there is actual fraud before taking any action. One way to help you determine whether there is fraud happening is to contact someone at either Taxpayers Against Fraud (www.taf.org) or the Government Accountability Project (www.whistleblower.org). Please see additional resources in Part Six of this book. You can confidentially describe your concerns to an experienced FCA or qui tam attorney, who can then advise you on whether or not your concerns have any relevance to the FCA laws in existence where you work. Coming forward with a qui tam case at the federal level requires that you be represented by an attorney and such a case is filed under seal, meaning that those who come forward are prohibited from allowing anyone other than their attorney to know they've done so.

There is always the possibility that what you think is fraud is simply an honest mistake, and there are ways to check that out; however, you need to be prepared for the possibility of an unpleasant response if there is, in fact, fraud happening. Your attempt to learn whether it is fraudulent or not by pointing out that a mistake may have been made can expose you to anger and retaliation if, for example, your company is fearful of getting caught and suspects you may someday cause it to get caught.

Here is an easy metaphor for what you can expect while trying to ascertain if your company or someone at your company is engaging in fraud. Suppose you are in an airport. You see someone litter, intentionally, and this bothers you. However, you want to give the person the chance to do the right thing, and you also want the person to know that littering is socially unacceptable. So you say as nicely as you possibly can, "Excuse me, I think you dropped something."

There are a number of responses to this scenario. A completely innocent person will generally be glad that you pointed this out because he would never want to litter and only did so unintentionally and, most importantly, will be eager to correct this mistake and pick up the litter. On the other hand, a guilty person—someone who littered intentionally and is angry that he got caught—might respond with anger toward you, perhaps deny that he dropped the litter, may not want to pick it up because he will be so ashamed and angry, and may even go further with his anger and begin to berate you that you should mind your own business.

To translate this reaction to a workplace fraud situation, if you point this out and there really is fraud going on, you must realize that you may be jeopardizing the scammers' plan to obtain funds they know they are not entitled to receive. Therefore, even if you give them a face-saving option by saying, "I think an error has been made here," you might not be merely pointing out an embarrassment-inducing error; you might be getting in the way of a money-making scheme. In this case, you are going to be seen as a problem. If it's an honest mistake, you will be met with gratitude and praise for having helped the company avert wrongdoing and very possibly more serious and perhaps costly problems in the future.

A company or person whose plans for funds have been foiled because you pointed out this error will be angry and may try to lie and say it is not an error. They might say that your judgment is faulty and that the information you raise is false. You may even be told that you are inappropriately overstepping the boundaries of your position in the company. Some companies and fraudsters are better at hiding their anger than others. Some will try the previously mentioned "Jedi Mind Trick" on you and simply thank you graciously for having raised your concerns and then assure you that there is no error or wrongdoing. The question is this: Do they go into detail about why there is no error or wrongdoing to an extent that satisfies your concerns while also allowing you to engage freely in a conversation exploring why you are concerned, given the information you have related to the issues? Or do they simply say, "There is no wrongdoing here" and leave it at that? It would be wise to be suspicious of the latter response.

A variation on the angry response is what I call "preemptive retaliation." In this case, you may have had to unwittingly supply some of the information needed for the scheme. Of course, you haven't been told, "this is a scheme; make sure the information says this on it." Therefore, you provide the information as requested. Then, because the information you supply is problematic, someone with authority over you may actually chastise, discipline, or otherwise criticize your work as sloppy, incorrect, or of poor quality. This enables the person to revise your information or construct his or her own false information, which is needed in order for the fraudulent claim to be successful and profitable. If you are sure that your original information was true and that the information that has instead been used on an official city, state, or government claim for funds of any kind is false, you most certainly need to consult with a FCA or qui tam attorney.

This kind of angry response is tricky. Not only is your concern being discounted and the information you carefully prepared being ignored, but your work is being revised into something you know is false and you are now being discredited. This is preemptive in that should you bring a claim in the future regarding this issue, your employer has already laid the groundwork to say officially, "Oh that person? That person's work was incorrect and, in fact, we were so troubled that we disciplined her for that bad information she gave us."

This might make it harder for you to prove that your information was correct—but it might not. It all depends on what other proof you have. If you have access to other records that prove your information is correct and their information is knowingly and intentionally doctored, you will want to make sure you have copies of that proof at home just in case your giving them a chance to correct any fraud results in your immediate termination. (This is one reason to keep a printed file of significant e-mails at your home.) Although this reaction would be unusual, it cannot be ignored as a possibility. If your proof is solid and incontrovertible, your employer's discipline of you will only make the employer look even guiltier and the attempt to cover tracks preemptively will most likely be seen for what it was.

It isn't always easy to do the right thing. There is certainly stress that comes with it when you're working with others, particularly working *for* others, who consider anyone questioning them or ensuring that things are done properly as an inconvenience or a blow to their own egos, which they find intolerable. Leaders who want to comply with employment and other relevant laws will graciously thank you when errors are pointed out. When your conscientiousness is responded to with anger, annoyance, disdain, or criticism of your work, this is a serious sign that either your leadership doesn't want to know they're making errors or that they have a problem with you pointing errors out. When your conscientiousness and observations are unwelcome, it is an indication of a toxic workplace that does not value integrity or the credible activist.

There are several ways to respond to such a workplace. You may decide you don't have room in your life for stress right now and so may choose to remain in that position and keep your mouth shut about any errors you observe, as it has been made very clear to you that you are not welcome to point these out. What you will have to do in order to protect yourself, however, is document that you were told not to give input or correct errors and ideally have this in writing from someone who has authority over you. This will prevent anyone from blaming you for any problems related to wrongdoing that may emerge in the future. However, this is not in actuality a stress-free option, as looking the other way and simply "following orders" may still bother any person of principle and conscience.

Another option is to find another job. If you feel this is the best option for you, you still have a decision to make. Will you move on quietly and not burn any bridges? Or will the reason you felt compelled to move on bother you enough to report any wrongdoing, unethical behavior, or possible fraud to the authorities or relevant governmental agencies so that the company learns a lesson and the wrongdoing is stopped? Do bear in mind that in FCA cases, former employees are often subpoenaed to testify, even long after they have left the company. So even if you choose not to report the company or take any action concerning their poor decisions, you will want to keep the proof of your innocence in any fraudulent activity or other wrongdoing in a very safe place forever, just in case you need it if you are called to testify in a future trial.

Another option is to remain in your job and also address the wrongdoing or possible fraud. If you choose this option, be prepared for a possible roller coaster of events. Depending on your current standing in the company, how well liked and well respected you are (or not), and how you raise the issue, any number of things may happen. There may be the preemptive retaliatory response, you may be fired, you may be told there is nothing to be concerned about, you may be given the courtesy of an honest discussion of your concerns as well as the paperwork in question, and you may be thanked for pointing out the error and see the error changed. Quite a spectrum of possibilities! You must be prepared for any of these if you choose to remain there and also come forward. This is not an easy thing to do.

It makes perfect sense to feel afraid, mistrustful, and concerned. You will want to make sure you have a backup plan, should you lose your job over this. In at-will states, an employee can be fired for any reason or for no reason as long as that reason is not a violation of law. Check Chapter 4 for information about at-will states to see if your state protects you for coming forward with knowledge of public policy violations. If you are in fact fired because they become angry you raised these issues, that is retaliation in many *but not all* states, and it would be an unlawful firing. Also, check to see if your city or state has an FCA law or if your action is covered under federal FCA laws; then speak to an FCA attorney to clarify which laws supersede which and to what extent you are theoretically protected. Depending on the situation, it can sometimes be difficult in proving that a termination was retaliatory. This is why it is so important for you to be able to accurately read the climate and your standing with those who might make such a decision before you decide how to respond.

Alternatively, if you don't mind losing your job and see this as an adventure and an experience to be had, go for it, but still be careful. You want to have good form. Be mindful of being discreet as you gather the evidence that may either protect you or prove your case at some point in the future. Be careful about calling attorneys, TAF, or GAP for advice from your work phone. Don't discuss your suspicions with anyone unless the lawyer who specializes in qui tam cases advises you to do so.

As mentioned, qui tam cases are filed under seal, and a significant part of winning such a claim is that you are the first source who brings the possible fraud to the attention of the government. It may be stressful to keep such information to yourself, and so you will need a well-qualified qui tam attorney with whom you can speak about your concerns and stresses as you go through this process, which can also take time. It can take months for the government entity that is being defrauded to respond to the attorney's papers alleging fraud under the FCA. Frequently there are complex internal processes involving a number of decision makers in government who jointly decide whether to take on the case. If they do so, there is a very good chance that your employer (or former employer) will settle with the government and avoid the public scandal of going to court. Frequently, companies are allowed to admit no guilt but still settle out of court for an amount decided by the government, either the U.S. Attorney's Office (USAO) or the city or state attorney general's office. As the "relator," or, more commonly, "whistleblower, in the case, you will receive a share of the total amount the company is fined. This "relator's share" is often calculated by the FBI and/or state or city authorities based on how helpful you have been during their investigation and how much risk you were exposed to or chose to take.

One experienced qui tam attorney very aptly said, "Whistleblowers *earn* their share." This is very true. The stress alone can cause sleepless nights, irregular eating habits, worry, fear, isolation, irritability, weight gain or loss, panic attacks, heart palpitations, asthma attacks, headaches, and difficulty concentrating. This path is not for everyone, but it is one option for the credible activist. One successful whistleblower in a federal qui tam case said that gathering evidence, meeting with the FBI, meeting with the USAO, and knowledge of what was happening did not frighten her. What did frighten her was when she had to officially and formally let her employer know that she knew what was going on. This is often referred to as "blowing the whistle internally," and depending on the workplace culture, whether the company has a tendency to unlawfully retaliate against employees who make legitimate complaints, and other factors, the response can be anything from nothing to full-blown fright-inducing retaliation. See the HR Tool entitled "Sample False Claims Act 'Blowing the Whistle Internally' Fraud-Prevention Memo," on pages 87–88.

You will want to consult with an FCA attorney before writing and delivering a memo to your workplace. Additionally, if your workplace demands that you meet with them regarding your memo, which they inevitably will, you will want to demand that your attorney be present with you at this meeting. If you experience retaliation for raising these issues, you may want to speak with your attorney about presenting a memo like the one shown in the HR Tool entitled "Sample Memo Asserting Retaliation for Having Raised Concerns about Fraud or Possible Fraud," on page 88.

HR TOOLS

SAMPLE MEMO REGARDING KNOWLEDGE OF THREATS TO PUBLIC SAFETY UNDER CPSC

CONFIDENTIAL

On letterhead, in interoffice memo format, or via e-mail

To: Your Supervisor (Include any others on this list to whom this memo should be addressed.)

From: Your Name

Date:

Re.:   Concerns about (Company)'s Compliance with Public Safety Standards

I am compelled to express concern about how we at (Company) handle issues related to public safety.

I am concerned about how the recent situation with (product or employee) was handled. Unless I am unaware of additional information or documentation related to this matter, I recommend that we revisit this situation and that we seek technical product and public safety assistance to ensure that we at (Company) have not made any errors in violation of product and public safety laws.

If we learn that any errors have been made, I recommend that we remediate those as soon as possible. Moving forward, I recommend that we consider implementing a decision-making protocol that will include technical assistance consultation from no-cost government or SHRM resources to prevent errors in the future. Additionally, I recommend that all persons involved in issues related to product and public safety decisions attend formal training on prevention and compliance issues. I will follow this memo up with a list of quality upcoming available trainings in our area or via webinar.

We share a collective responsibility to ensure (Company)'s compliance with product and public safety laws. We also share a commitment to prevent liability exposure for (Company) as well as personal liability exposure.

The resources below are free and available to us to use at any time. My membership in SHRM provides free information, white papers, case-law information, and research capabilities along with toolkits for how to best handle product and public safety-related issues. I recommend that we use these resources in the future to ensure legally compliant decision-making processes related to issues concerning product and public safety.

http://www.ojp.usdoj.gov/odp/training_other.htm

http://www.ehso.com/oshaguidance.php#P

http://www.business.gov/business-law/contacts/federal/cpsc/

http://www.shrm.org/

http://www.workplacefairness.org/resources

I know we share a strong commitment to the consistent application of all (Company)'s policies to all employees and situations as well as compliance with all relevant city, state, and federal laws related to product and public safety.

Additionally, I know we share an awareness of the importance of precedent in our decision-making processes and our handling of product and public safety issues in a legally compliant manner.

SAMPLE MEMO REGARDING CONCERNS ABOUT RETALIATION AGAINST EMPLOYEE FOR RAISING PUBLIC/PRODUCT SAFETY CONCERNS

On letterhead, in interoffice memo format, or via e-mail

CONFIDENTIAL

To: Your Supervisor (Include any others on this list to whom this memo should be addressed.)

From: Your Name

Date:

Re.:   Concerns about (Company)'s Compliance with Public/Product Safety and Whistleblower Protection Laws and Prohibitions against Retaliation

I am compelled to express concern about how we at (Company) handle issues related to Public/Product Safety, prohibitions against unlawful retaliation, and Whistleblower Protection Laws.

Additionally, we have a responsibility to investigate concerns about public safety or product safety promptly, thoroughly, and soundly. Just as importantly, we have a legal responsibility to prevent retaliation against any employee who comes forward with such concerns.

I am concerned about how the recent situation with (employee's name or complaint) was handled. Unless I am unaware of additional information or documentation related to this matter, I recommend that we revisit this situation and seek technical _____ assistance to ensure that we at (Company) have not made any errors in violation of any aspect of any law.

If we learn that any errors have been or are being made, I recommend that we remediate those as soon as possible. Moving forward, I recommend that we consider implementing a decision-making protocol that will include technical assistance consultation from no-cost government or SHRM resources to prevent errors in the future. Additionally, I recommend that all persons involved in public and/or product-safety concerns or complaint-receipts, investigations, or determinations attend formal training on these technical compliance issues. I will follow this memo up with a list of quality upcoming available trainings in our area or via webinar.

We share a collective responsibility to ensure (Company)'s compliance with public and product safety laws as well as with laws that prohibit retaliation against any employee who raises concerns about public or product safety. I know we share a commitment to prevent liability exposure for (Company) as well as personal liability exposure.

The resources below are free and available to us for use at any time. My membership in SHRM provides free information, white papers, case-law information, and research capabilities along with toolkits for how to best handle issues concerning the prevention of inadvertent or intentional retaliation. I recommend that we use these resources in the future to ensure legally compliant decision-making processes related to these issues.

http://www.osha.gov/dep/oia/whistleblower/index.html

http://www.shrm.org/

http://www.dol.gov/compliance/guide/whistle.htm

http://www.dol.gov/compliance/laws/comp-whistleblower.htm

http://www.workplacefairness.org/resources

I know we share a strong commitment to the consistent application of all (Company)'s policies as well as compliance with all relevant city, state, and federal laws related to these important issues around safety.

Additionally, I know we share an awareness of the importance of precedent in our decision-making processes and our handling of these issues in a legally compliant manner.

SAMPLE FALSE CLAIMS ACT "BLOWING THE WHISTLE INTERNALLY" FRAUD-PREVENTION MEMO

On letterhead, in interoffice memo format, or via e-mail

CONFIDENTIAL

To: Whom It May Concern:

From: Your Full Name

Date:

Re.: Concerns about (Company)'s Fraudulent Activity Re.: _____

I am concerned that (Company)'s current practice of _____ might be fraudulent.

My specific concerns are:

[List Concerns]

SAMPLE MEMO ASSERTING RETALIATION FOR HAVING RAISED CONCERNS ABOUT FRAUD OR POSSIBLE FRAUD

On letterhead, in interoffice memo format, or via e-mail

(You may also want to have your attorney write a companion letter on his or her letterhead for you from him or her alleging the same things.)

CONFIDENTIAL

To: Whom It May Concern

From: Your Name

Date:

Re.:   Allegation of Retaliation for Having Raised Concerns about Possible Fraudulent Activity at (Company)

I believe I am being unlawfully retaliated against for having raised my concerns about practices at (Company) that seem to result in fraud.

Ever since I sent my memo dated _____, my job performance has been scrutinized much more than it was before I sent that memo, and my job performance is currently most certainly being scrutinized much more than that of my colleagues. My job performance is also being much more harshly evaluated than ever before. I believe I am being treated in disparate ways from my colleagues who have not raised such issues.

I am asking that our non-retaliation policies be reviewed, that my concerns noted in my previous memo dated _____ as well as in this memo be reviewed, and that all previous retaliatory actions against me be corrected and stop immediately. I also request that you review all federal, state, and city laws addressing prohibitions against unlawful retaliation with which (Company) is required to comply.

CHAPTER 7

DEALING WITH INCONSISTENT APPLICATION OF POLICIES AND DISPARATE TREATMENT

HR professionals have a professional and ethical responsibility to speak up if they believe their company is not following relevant labor laws and if employees' rights are being violated. HR professionals are also encouraged to follow SHRM's Code of Ethics.

Many employees incorrectly assume that either HR cannot be trusted or is only on the side of management. Although this is unfortunately true in some companies, a more common problem is that many HR professionals are ignored or overruled by their leadership and/or their corporate legal counsel when they raise concerns. In addition, these HR professionals need and want to keep their jobs. So, what is an ethical HR professional to do? At the end of this chapter is a sample memo that an HR professional can customize to his or her situation and send to leadership if necessary.

Many HR professionals forget that they and other executives can be personally named in lawsuits brought by employees if the employee believes that the HR professional allowed harassment or discrimination to occur and did not respond to it as is required. This is only one important reason why an HR professional might want to remind his or her leadership of their shared liabilities and of the HR professional's responsibilities under the SHRM Code of Conduct.

This kind of memo serves more than one purpose. It asks the company to change how they are doing things, it creates evidence that the sender attempted to address these issues, and it theoretically (remember the disclaimer!) protects the sender from being retaliated against for having raised these issues. There is risk involved in sending a memo. An employer may just not care if you sue them for retaliating against you; the employer may be unaware that they aren't permitted to retaliate against you for writing such a memo; they may make up some other reason to fire you and say it has nothing to do with this memo; they may eliminate your position and say it has nothing to do with this memo; or they may not care if they are dragged into court for retaliating against you—as long as they have gotten rid of you. Only you can estimate the likelihood of any of these outcomes knowing your company.

The HR Tool "Sample Memo Addressing Inconsistent Policy Application," on pages 95–99, is the longest sample memo in this book only because it addresses multiple (and sadly typical) issues of having to educate one's leadership around shared liability. It is best to keep memos as short as possible, but when multiple issues are being raised and examples are given, length can be a challenge. It is not recommended that you use the memo on pages 95–99 unless you are an HR professional. All memos (even resignation memos) should be written in a diplomatic manner that will allow a positive relationship to continue, even if the subject matter is difficult.

It is always important to think carefully through all of the possible outcomes before sending memos such as these, including any of the sample memos in this book. The possibility of being retaliated against is always there, especially in at-will states, which includes most states, as the employer can make it appear as though you have been fired for something having nothing to do with your memo. Employers are well aware that it is costly to retain an employment lawyer and that most employees cannot afford to do so; this is why so many employers do get away with unlawful harassment, discrimination, retaliation, and wrongful termination.

However, there is strength in numbers and there are no-cost complaint methods available to employees with their city and state Human Rights Commissions as well as with the EEOC. Sadly, however, these agencies tend to be overwhelmed with the number of employee complaints they receive, as well as understaffed and underfunded, which can significantly affect the attention given to employee complaints as well as the quality of the handling of those complaints. Assessing your risk for being unlawfully retaliated against or wrongfully terminated is not always as easy as it sounds. Anytime you assess your risk for being fired for raising any of these issues at work, you must look honestly at your own performance evaluation history and ask yourself if there is anything that might justify having your employment terminated. You must be sure to double-check your state's particular laws and what might—or might not—exist to protect you in each and every situation you raise in this way. You can use SHRM's updated information to clarify what laws may or may not exist in your state that relate to your concerns. Another excellent source of information is Workplace Fairness at http://www.workplacefairness. org/resources.[1]

Additionally, it is difficult to determine how others may respond to your perfectly good intentions to protect the company, others, and yourself from liability exposure. If there is other wrongdoing happening at the company that you are not aware of or if there is not but those to whom you write respond with defensiveness, competitiveness, or anger, the response to your having raised serious concerns can cost you your job. You must know this before you take any action, and you must assess your own life and discuss a plan with your family, significant other, or other support network in the event that your well-intentioned and completely justifiable actions do backfire.

Speaking up at work does take courage; however, it becomes easier to know what to do once you have clarity about the possible risks involved and your many options for making sure the issues are raised. You want to be sure to think very carefully through any decisions you make to speak up and then always make sure to consider all the possible outcomes. You want to be sure that you have accurate information about risks and whether or not you will have any recourse should your employer take adverse action against you. You will want to prepare for the worst by carefully documenting all conversations, dates, times, and meetings and who is present at them, should they relate to the serious concerns you intend to raise. As mentioned in a previous chapter, you will also want to print out and keep at home any important e-mails that could serve as evidence of your concerns just in case those e-mails mysteriously disappear from the company's servers. You will also want to keep copies of any other non-e-mail documentation that could serve as evidence of your concerns. This may include voice mail messages, copies of memos or reports, or anything else to which you normally have access. An attorney would probably advise you to not use anything to which you would normally not have access.

You know that waging a formal complaint or lawsuit against an employer can take months or years and can be very costly and stressful on an individual and an entire family. These warnings are not given to dissuade you from speaking up but merely to ensure that you clearly understand what you may be up against. Even if your concerns are ultimately proven to be true and your memos and other communications that raise these issues during your tenure at the company are perfectly diplomatic, emotionally intelligent, and perfectly worded, do not have a blameful tone, and have the full intention of responsibly and ethically partnering with your corporate leadership, you may still be unlawfully retaliated against and wrongfully terminated.

However, as the HR professional in the company, you must realize that you do have certain advantages. You presumably have a global view of inconsistent policy application resulting in disparate treatment to which other employees are not privy. You also know your rights under the employment laws of your city, state, and country. You also know your company policies and know what your employee handbook says, and hopefully you have been carefully documenting anything that is of concern to you from the moment you first became concerned. Although a negative, retaliatory response to your well-intentioned communications to your leadership does not bode well for your continued employment at that company, you can still prepare yourself for the many possible outcomes of your courageous and ethical actions. It is possible that if you complain and present compelling evidence to the appropriate authorities, that your job will be safe and your company's noncompliance will be remediated. At the first sign of any retaliation against you for having performed your job ethically, professionally, and well, you are advised to consider which of the steps listed in the HR Tool entitled "Personal Protective Steps to Take at the First Sign of Retaliation," on pages 99–100, might benefit you in your situation.

If you have experienced unlawful harassment, discrimination, or retaliation, document it as accurately, thoroughly, and succinctly as you can and call either your city or state Human Rights Commission or the EEOC to consult with their staff on whether you are at a point that warrants filing a formal charge against your company. Try to document this on your own time at a computer other than your workplace computer.

You will want to think very carefully about whom you can trust at work, if anyone. Remember, when people become afraid of losing their jobs, their income, and their health benefits for themselves and their families, their loyalties can easily shift out of fear, or they can just become extremely self-protective. They may not want to be seen with you, may not want to be associated with you, and may not be willing to themselves make anonymous complaints even if they have knowledge and/or proof of wrongdoing.

You will need to be sure that you are ready for whatever happens, and remain as composed and centered as you possibly can at work. The last thing you will want to do is have a very bad day and then blow up or send an ill-advised e-mail without thinking through all the wording and possible consequences very carefully. If you are going to speak up at work, you need to do so with as much accurate information in front of you as possible, having thought carefully about all the risks, and having considered what you will do if it does not have the outcome for which you had hoped.

The very good news is that there are whistleblower protections for employees and there is recourse for wrongly terminated employees. The bad news is you need to see which, if any, of these apply to your state. There are no guarantees. You may have a case, but you may be told by an attorney that it is weak. Even having a good case does not mean that every investigator, judge, jury, or decision-making panel will make a decision in your favor. Unfortunately, even with a good amount of evidence, the outcomes of these things are often a gamble.

Speaking up at work is something that must always be handled with diplomacy, intelligence, and emotional intelligence. You know when you are being marginalized at work. You know when you have made an important recommendation to address some form of workplace dysfunction or noncompliance and it has been ignored, dismissed, or vetoed.

Sometimes this experience can happen at a workplace when it previously had not happened to you in that same workplace for years prior. There is always a reason for this type of exclusionary refusal to share power with someone, no matter who it is. This is where your use of emotional intelligence and your own resilience will become very important yet again. You will have to try to figure out why this is happening. Did you provide incorrect information regarding an issue and affect your credibility? Did you do, say, or e-mail something inappropriate? It is always a good idea to consider realistically what you may have done, if anything, to contribute to such a situation.

However, the reason for this kind of significant shift from HR professionals being respected, valued, included, and invited to share power to a new dynamic in which one or more persons at the workplace will begin to disrespect, devalue, exclude, and refuse to share power with the HR professional is usually due to a leadership change of some kind. It may be obvious, such as a new leader for the entire company, or it might be as subtle such as a new VP of another department. Moreover, it may not happen immediately but very gradually, even over months or years. In fact, usually this experience of being disrespected, devalued, excluded, and not invited to share company power does happen gradually. It can easily begin with one influential person disliking that you know something they don't (remember the inside top of the Monopoly box?) and then spread in any direction, depending upon who the person is and how much company power he or she has. It can take the form of being ignored by one or more persons, not having your e-mails or voice mails responded to, or even being excluded from processes in which you would normally have a role. It can also take the form of outright hostility, which once realized, will probably shed some light on why this is happening at all. For example, if there is someone who routinely challenges whether your well-researched recommendations are correct or who frequently assumes that you've recommended something incorrect or improper, you can probably correctly assume that this person feels competitive with you for whatever reason. Often it is impossible to learn the truth about why this might be happening and why people are behaving as they are.

The use of Nonviolent Communication (NVC), EI, and conflict resolution skills will serve you well in such a situation. While being disrespected, devalued, excluded, and not invited (or uninvited) to share organizational power can be enormously stressful and difficult, it is also an opportunity to do any or all on the checklist, to follow.

More in-depth NVC training will be described in Part Six of this book, but for now, it will be helpful for you to learn the absolute basics of NVC by reviewing the lists of feelings and needs (and values) in the HR Tools "Things You Can Do to Turn Being/Feeling Devalued as HR into a Learning Experience" and "Nonviolent Communication Skills," on pages 100–101.

The best way to use the list now is to simply help yourself identify how you are feeling in any given moment and then try to relate that to any needs you have that either are being met or that are not being met. Being able to clearly identify your feelings and needs is the first step to self-awareness in emotional intelligence as well as a very helpful skill to have when communicating at work and during any conflict resolution situations.

In order to hone your EI skills, you will need to be aware of and improve each of the following:

Self-regard. Check in with yourself to see how you feel in this work environment, if you've always felt this way in this work environment, and if you think there is any hope for you to feel valued, respected, included, and to be welcomed to share company power in this company at this time or in the near future.

Emotional self-awareness. Check in with yourself to measure what you feel about yourself, your actions taken thus far, those with whom you must deal at work, your supervisor, any colleagues, and other aspects of your life.

Assertiveness. Assess your comfort level as to whether you feel safe and comfortable enough in order to assertively communicate what you feel certain of and feel strongly about, verbally or via carefully worded memos.

Independence. Check in with yourself to measure whether you feel independent in this situation or completely alone. You will need support as you endure this kind of marginalization, and you will be able to cope better if you have a clear awareness of how you are experiencing these dynamics.

Self-actualization. Check in with yourself to ascertain what your goals for yourself in your life at this time and in the long term are. Our goals for our lives do change, and this kind of situation is one during which you will fare better if you are clear on your goals. You may be very close to retirement and not feel safe risking anything at work at this time. You may be considering moving to another state and have the support of your spouse or partner, which may give you courage you would not otherwise have. You may realize that you would rather work in another form of HR, another company, or another industry or field altogether. You may wish to remain in this job, but you should still address these issues as much as you possibly can. Your goal may even be to internally or externally blow the whistle on your company regardless of the outcome. "Winning" looks like something different to every person. Know what "winning" means to you right now in this situation.

Empathy. Do your best to be aware of how others are experiencing you, especially if you are having a difficult and stressful time, which you very likely are. You will need to make efforts to get the support you need in whatever ways available to you so that you will still be able to be concerned with employees' needs for your assistance.

Social responsibility. Be aware of how much of yourself you have in reserve to give while you are going through a difficult and stressful time. This awareness will prevent you from promising anything you are not able to deliver, with ease and without causing more stress in your life.

Interpersonal relationship skills. Manage these very carefully. Tension at work may be subtle or unbearable. Do your best to put your best face on when at work. Do what you can to manage your time and work with as little stress as possible.

Stress tolerance. Do whatever you can to manage stress well. Know what all of your options are for stress release both at work and at home. Let your support system know that you may need them more than usual now.

Impulse control. This is very important right now, especially if your baseline scores in impulse control are among your lowest. Practice various methods of improving impulse control by counting to five before responding, waiting several hours before sending e-mails (if possible), and having trusted confidants read any memos before you send them.

Reality testing. This is important for stressful times. It can become too easy to jump to conclusions without having complete information. Don't get all worked up over something that may be nothing. Try not to react to incomplete information unless you're relatively certain what it means.

Problem-solving abilities. Practice problem-solving within your situation. Look for credible training seminars, research, articles, books, studies, support groups, listserves, Web sites, and so on that address what you're going through. You may find some good ideas for your situation from these sources, so use them!

Optimism. It is important that optimism be grounded in reality; otherwise, it's just delusion. Try to look at your situation as clearly and realistically as possible. Make a list of all of your options. Consider that there may be unknown silver linings to any outcome whether you're aware of what those are now or not.

Happiness. Know your baseline score for happiness so you can gauge whether or not you're getting depressed and need more help than usual. Therapists can be extremely helpful during times like these, as can coaches and NVC practice groups and classes.

It is completely natural to feel fear (or even dread) before raising compliance issues at work, and that is why at times it makes sense to have as many people as possible write and sign the same or similar memos. There is strength in numbers. There is also enormous strength in researching all of your options, double-checking your facts, getting support from credible resources, and putting forth your recommendations for remediating serious non-compliance issues. You may or may not wind up on the cover of *Time* magazine for having averted a crisis for your company and you may or may not be named Employee of the Month; however, you will be able to sleep better at night knowing you did your job ethically and properly. Moreover, you may gain more respect from your leadership and/or your colleagues in having addressed serious issues in a professional, gracious, and direct manner.

HR TOOLS

SAMPLE MEMO ADDRESSING INCONSISTENT POLICY APPLICATION

On letterhead, in interoffice memo format, or via e-mail

CONFIDENTIAL

To: Leadership (by name) (Include any others on this list to whom this memo should be addressed.)

From: HR Professional's Full Name

Date:

Re.:   Concerns about Individual and Company Liability at Company

I have concerns about personal liability and liability for (Company) due to:

Inconsistent application of (Company) policies to staff seemingly driven by conflicts of interest issues in application of policies that result in disparate treatment of staff.

Lack of leadership and legal's technical compliance knowledge, which I believe explains inadvertent errors that have been made as (Company) grows. I recommend that we review, note, and learn from these errors and in some cases revisit and correct them.

I have a responsibility to adhere to SHRM code of professional conduct and our legal staff has an obligation to adhere to their own code of professional responsibility. We are all responsible for complying with city, state, and federal laws.

I believe we will realize we all have the same goals once more clarity is gained regarding technical compliance knowledge and once the codes of conduct mentioned above are reviewed. I have made several recommendations throughout this memo because the SHRM Code of Ethical and Professional Standards require me to address these issues and because I value (Company).

I have a responsibility under SHRM Code of Ethical and Professional Standards to, among other things:

Comply with the law.

Advocate openly and within the established forums for debate in order to influence decision making and results.

Question pending individual and group actions when necessary to ensure that decisions are ethical and are implemented in an ethical manner.

Seek expert guidance if ever in doubt about the ethical propriety of a situation.

Treat people with dignity, respect, and compassion to foster a trusting work environment free of harassment, intimidation, and unlawful discrimination.

Ensure an environment of inclusiveness and a commitment to diversity in the company.

Develop, administer, and advocate policies and procedures that foster fair, consistent, and equitable treatment for all.

Adhere to and advocate the use of published policies on conflicts of interest within the company.

Prioritize obligations to identify conflicts of interests or the appearance thereof; when conflicts arise, disclose them to relevant stakeholders.

Acquire and disseminate information through ethical and responsible means.

Ensure only appropriate information is used in decisions affecting the employment relationship.

Investigate the accuracy and source of information before allowing it to be used in employment-related decisions.

I recommend that leadership and HR review SHRM's Code of Ethical and Professional Standards as well as develop sufficient technical knowledge of ADA, EEO, State Human Rights laws, and other laws, so there is clarity regarding how these must inform our compliance roles and responsibilities at (Company).

I recommend that we create a structure for rational, informed, respectful discussion of all employment decisions to ensure that we are acting consistently, ethically, and in compliance with laws and policies. I also recommend that those included in these discussions be encouraged to contribute their knowledge, research, questions, and concerns and that we consider who, if anyone, should recuse themselves from involvement in the decision-making process. I again recommend that we take full advantage of technical assistance resources available to us when there is disagreement among us, including the following:

☐ ADA and ADAAA Technical Assistance

☐ EEOC Technical Assistance

☐ State Division of Human Rights Technical Assistance

☐ City Commission on Human Rights

☐ OSHA Technical Assistance

☐ DOL DOSH Technical Assistance

☐ FLSA Technical Assistance

☐ FMLA Technical Assistance

☐ JAN Technical Assistance

☐ DOL Technical Assistance

☐ Others, as needed

INCONSISTENT APPLICATION OF POLICIES

There are significant inconsistencies that are liability risks in terms of disparate policy application to different employees without justification. It is my observation that several instances of policy interpretation and application have been made based on personal relationships and personal conflicts of interest and not according to actual policy, to previous interpretations and applications of policy. This has happened with no attention to precedent and no attention to the spirit of the policy.

I have observed, as have other employees who have raised these issues with me, that this positive bias extends to performance evaluations, promotions, raises, tolerance of unacceptable behavior, company influence allowed, hiring decisions allowed, allowance of several policy violations, and various other inconsistencies that are problematic.

I have also observed, as have other employees who have raised these issues with me, that this positive bias also extends to whether or not problematic job performance is noted, addressed sufficiently, documented, or acknowledged at all.

There have been inconsistent responses to different employees regarding certain policy infractions. I recommend that we apply responses to policy infractions consistently to all employees. There are staff members at (Company) who have not received any response to policy infractions despite engaging in problematic behaviors regularly, even daily. There are other employees who don't enjoy the privilege of personal relationships that have the outcome of protecting them from the consequences of policy violations who have been disciplined and/or terminated for the very same or even lesser policy infractions.

There are also several examples of staff members who have regularly and repeatedly engaged in policy infractions yet have been given raises, promotions, public praise, and extremely unusual privileges without having their regular policy infractions addressed at all. If these policy infractions have been addressed, I have no documentation of these for these employees' personnel files and have not been made aware of any documentation or actions taken.

When our policies are not consistently applied, it becomes extremely difficult for me to perform my job ethically or well. I can almost never predict how a policy will be interpreted or implemented because of these inconsistencies. Furthermore, this inconsistent application of policies creates a serious morale problem among staff, who notice this disparate treatment, discuss it amongst themselves, and now experience diminished trust in both HR and (Company).

I recommend that conducting sound staff performance evaluations be made mandatory, that those supervisors not conducting them have this noted in their own performance evaluations, and that new firm deadlines be given to those supervisors. I also recommend that all management (including leadership) be trained in effectively evaluating staff without personal bias or attribution error and in preparing and giving feedback soundly. I recommend that HR and/or leadership review all performance evaluations before they are presented to employees to ensure they are sound and free of rater-bias and attribution error.

I recommend actively preventing rater-bias companywide by ensuring that all those who supervise others have sufficient competencies in communication, investigative problem solving, conflict resolution, collaboration, evaluation, reality-testing, and supervisory skills. I recommend that training be provided regularly and when necessary and that supervisors be coached on these skills in their annual performance evaluations. HR can provide internal low-cost training in all of these areas to supervisors. However, if performance evaluation and multi-rater feedback were to rate staff on these skills, they would be practiced and used more than they currently are; there needs to be accountability for using these skills and improving them.

I recommend that all performance evaluations be based on each employee's job description as well as on a universally enforced behavioral code of conduct. I recommend that management and other supervisory positions also be rated on necessary core competencies such as constructive conflict resolution skills, collaborative skills, communication skills, project management skills, harassment awareness, policy awareness, performance management skills, ethics, reality testing, prevention of rater-bias, and prevention of attribution errors. I recommend using a 360-feedback format so that all (Company) employees rate all other (Company) employees with whom they have contact. Multi-rater feedback provides robust results that are more accurate than feedback from only an employee's supervisor. Therefore, multi-rater feedback can prevent disparate treatment due to rater-bias and attribution errors that are driven by personal relationships and other conflicts of interest.

I recommend that (Company) create an ethical code of conduct regarding interactions with others, behavior, and rational, policy-based decision-making for all staff. I would be happy to research options for this and present what I find.

COMPLIANCE ISSUES

It is in (Company)'s best interests to take all EEO and ADA complaints seriously and have mandatory regular trainings on these issues. If one of our supervisors were to engage in unacceptable behavior, we can say that we have trained them and we can then respond as necessary according to our policies and the incident. If we fail to train employees regularly, we are then responsible as an organization and as individuals with compliance responsibilities for not having prevented their harassing, discriminatory, and/or retaliatory behavior. Each of us can personally be named in lawsuits brought by employees alleging noncompliance with our shared legal responsibility to prevent harassment, discrimination, and retaliation. Most directors' and officers' liability policies will not cover sexual harassment lawsuits and other lawsuits if any of us is found to have been negligent in following our own policies.

It has been my experience that I am regarded negatively when I attempt to raise these topics and be persuasive on them. I hope to advocate for more compliance-related technical knowledge training for leadership so that we can more easily reach consensus in an informed manner regarding employment decisions. However, I don't want these attempts to be inaccurately viewed as problematic job performance.

The ADA, EEO laws, State Human Rights laws, FMLA, disability insurance and coverage, and (Company) policies **must** apply consistently to all employees. However, it is my observation that this does not happen in practice. It does not matter if an employee is liked or disliked, has real or perceived performance deficiencies, has been at (Company) for many years, or is friendly or not friendly with various key employees; all employees are still entitled to have our policies and relevant laws consistently applied to them as our policies are applied to all other employees. I recommend that we create an investigation policy to prevent conflicts of interest and to ensure fairness and sound, impartial investigation practices prior to any discipline or termination and in response to all complaints regarding violations of law we receive.

I recommend that all management staff (and eventually all staff) be regularly trained in sound conflict resolution procedures. I believe this will have enormous positive effects on staff interaction, on company functioning, and on conflict in general, which is inevitable and which can ultimately improve company functioning when handled productively.

I believe that leadership and HR have the same compliance goals and will more easily reach consensus once we all have the same technical knowledge regarding these important issues. I also believe that work relationships are dynamic and can be improved when there is willingness, effort, and a clear understanding of compliance responsibilities. I attach a copy of SHRM code of ethics for your review, and I look forward to your response.

PERSONAL PROTECTIVE STEPS TO TAKE AT THE FIRST SIGN OF RETALIATION

- ☐ Delete all personal e-mails you may have sent, even if the company allows use of personal e-mail.

- ☐ Refrain from sending any personal e-mails from work, even if allowed and even if using personal e-mail accounts on a company computer.

- ☐ Gradually and inconspicuously bring home most personal items from your office, even if the company allows personal items at work.

- ☐ Research employment lawyers in your area and ask if any take cases on contingency. Ask for a free consultation so you don't spend hundreds of dollars interviewing lawyers before you find the right one. If you cannot get free consultations, ask them to review a one-page synopsis of your case before letting you know if they they're interested.

☐ Consider taking a personal day, vacation day, or lunch hour to meet with an employment lawyer or talk to one on the phone. You may want to fax, e-mail, or postal mail a description of your situation to the attorney first and ask that he or she discuss it with you over the phone to minimize your time away from the office.

THINGS YOU CAN DO TO TURN BEING/FEELING DEVALUED AS HR INTO A LEARNING EXPERIENCE

☐ Make a list of meetings, decisions, or trainings you have not been included in that you either normally would have been included in or that you believe you should have been included in based on your role, your written job description, and/or any recommendations or issues you may have made or raised.

☐ Try to learn why this is happening by talking to your supervisor or trusted colleagues and openly noting that you've observed that you've been or felt excluded and you are wondering why this might be.

☐ If you do get feedback from your supervisor or a colleague regarding something you did or said that might be contributing to this situation, meet with your supervisor and honestly discuss these issues and assertively state that you would like to know if there is anything he or she would like you to work on improving. Also, notice if anyone else's similar errors or actions are being responded to in this way or if you are receiving disparate treatment. If you are receiving disparate treatment, do try to learn why, document it, and address it in a memo.

☐ If your sense is that you find yourself in this situation not because of anything you have done but because of a leadership change or a colleague with more company power than you have (who either devalues HR in general or who has some personal issue with you), consider using as many diplomatic skills as you possibly can. Diplomacy skills for this situation include using NVC, EI, and sound conflict resolution skills.

Used with permission from Thom Bond of the New York Center for Nonviolent Communication[SM].

NONVIOLENT COMMUNICATION SKILLS

☐ Being able to check in with yourself and then give yourself "self-empathy" as well as get empathy and support as you go through this from good sources such as an NVC practice group, a good friend, a close family member, other HR professionals, or a therapist.

☐ Being able to focus on the other person's feelings and needs even if they are behaving with extreme unpleasantness towards you.

☐ Wanting to learn what the other person's feelings and needs are and being positively and empathically responsive to them as much as you are able.

☐ Understanding that you can make requests of this other person.

☐ Understanding that if they say "no" to a request you make, that should be viewed as a "yes to something else." Ask the appropriate person directly what that something else might be.

☐ Communicating calmly with the other person as best as you can to try to learn what that "something else" might be.

☐ Conducting yourself with the intention of having your needs met in the situation but not at the expense of anyone else's needs.

Used with permission from Thom Bond of the New York Center for Nonviolent Communication^{SM}.

CHAPTER 8

CONCERNS ABOUT WORKPLACE VIOLENCE, BULLYING, AND ENVIRONMENTS THAT DAMAGE EMPLOYEE HEALTH, EFFICIENCY, AND PROFITS

WORKPLACE VIOLENCE AND BULLYING

There are currently no specific OSHA standards for workplace violence. However, there are rules, proposed rules, notices, and standard interpretations related to workplace violence available at OSHA's Web site. Section 5(a)(1) and (2) of the OSH Act requires an employer to "furnish to each of his employees employment and a place of employment which are free from recognized hazards that are causing or are likely to cause death or serious physical harm to his employees" and requires employers to "comply with occupational safety and health standards promulgated under this Act." Twenty-four states, as well as Puerto Rico and the Virgin Islands, have OSHA-approved state plans and have adopted their own standards and enforcement policies. Most of these states adopted standards that are identical to federal OSHA standard.[1]

Each year from 1993 through 1999, "an average of 1.7 million people were victims of violent crime while working or on duty in the United States, according to a report published by the Bureau of Justice Statistics (BJS). An estimated 1.3 million (75 percent) of these incidents were simple assaults, while an additional 19 percent were aggravated assaults. Of the occupations examined, police officers, corrections officers, and taxi drivers were victimized at the highest rates. The Bureau of Labor Statistics' Census of Fatal Occupational Injuries (CFOI) reported 11,613 workplace homicide victims between 1992 and 2006. Averaging just under 800 homicides per year, the largest number of homicides in one year occurred in 1994, while the lowest number occurred in 2006.[2]

The FBI has available on its Web site the monograph, *Workplace Violence: Issues in Response,* which includes discussions from law enforcement and behavioral perspectives on interpersonal aspects of workplace violence issues.

The monograph highlights findings from the collaboration of experts who looked at the latest thinking in prevention, threat assessment and management, crisis management, critical incident response, research, and legislation. It also offers common-sense recommendations and is recommended to employers, employees, and labor unions; law enforcement agents; medical, mental health, and social service agencies; state and federal occupational safety and criminal justice agencies; and legislators, policymakers, and the legal community.[3]

The FBI also cites workplace bullying at least eight times in its report on workplace violence:

- "It is the threats, harassment, bullying, domestic violence, stalking, emotional abuse, intimidation, and other forms of behavior and physical violence that, if left unchecked, may result in more serious violent behavior."
- "A plan should take into account the workplace culture: work atmosphere, relationships, traditional management styles, etc. If there are elements in that culture that appear to foster a toxic climate—tolerance of bullying or intimidation; lack of trust among workers, between workers and management; high levels of stress, frustration and anger; poor communication; inconsistent discipline; and erratic enforcement of company policies—these should be called to the attention of top executives for remedial action."
- "In defining acts that will not be tolerated, the statement should make clear that not just physical violence but threats, bullying, harassment, and weapons possession are against company policy and are prohibited."[4]

)) WHAT IS WORKPLACE BULLYING AND WHO IS AFFECTED?

As per the NIOSH Web site,

Workplace bullying refers to *repeated,* unreasonable actions of individuals (or a group) directed toward an employee (or a group of employees), which is intended to intimidate and creates a risk to the health and safety of the employee(s). Workplace bullying often involves an abuse or misuse of power. Bullying includes behavior that intimidates, degrades, offends, or humiliates a worker, often in front of others. Bullying behavior creates feelings of defenselessness in the target and undermines an individual's right to dignity at work.

Bullying is different from aggression. Whereas aggression may involve a single act, bullying involves repeated attacks against the target, creating an *ongoing pattern* of behavior.

"Tough" or "demanding" bosses are not necessarily bullies, as long as their primary motivation is to obtain the best performance by setting high expectations. Many bullying situations involve employees bullying their peers, rather than a supervisor bullying an employee.

One study from the National Institute of Occupational Safety and Health (NIOSH) found that a quarter of the 516 private and public companies studied reported some occurrence of bullying in the preceding year.[5]

See the HR Tool entitled "Examples of Bullying" at the end of the chapter, on page 108, to help you identify bullying and the HR Tool entitled "Sample Memo Regarding Bullying and Workplace Violence," on pages 108–109, for an example of how it might be addressed in memo form. The example information about bullying in the HR Tool entitled "Examples of Bullying" on pages 108, is from the Washington State Department of Labor and Industries, one of the first American states to implement this important anti-workplace bullying policy.

The Washington State Department of Labor and Industries provides this helpful directive that any world-class workplace behavioral policy will include:

> If you are aware of bullying in the workplace and don't take action, then you are accepting a share of the responsibility for any future abuses. This means that witnesses of bullying behavior should be encouraged to report any such incidences. Individuals are less likely to engage in antisocial behavior when it is understood that the company does not tolerate such behavior and that the perpetrator is likely to be punished.[6]

Keep in mind that certain scenarios at companies can increase the likelihood of bullying. See the HR Tool entitled "Factors That May Increase the Risk for Bullying Behavior," on page 110. For the consequences of bullying on employees, see the HR Tool entitled "How Bullying Affects People," on page 110.

)) ADDRESSING BULLYING

Bullying is harassment, discrimination, and retaliation that is not based on any protected category such as race, color, religion, age, sex, gender, disability, or veteran status. It is legal in the United States, yet it is unlawful in most other first-world nations, which have recognized it as a form of workplace violence that harms people, companies, and profits.

Bullying is recognized by the FBI as a form of workplace violence. Smart companies will implement policies prohibiting workplace bullying before laws are passed in the United States. There are at least 13 states with legislative efforts working toward making workplace bullying unlawful.

The fascinating aspect of opposition to workplace bullying laws is that although the message is essentially that we find harassment, discrimination, and retaliation reprehensible as a society—and when it's because of these certain reasons, that makes it even worse, there is a willingness to overlook this otherwise reprehensible behavior when it is not based on a reason of outright discrimination. That is, when someone "just doesn't like someone" and decides to mistreat him or her, there is something happening there that is either not being honestly acknowledged or is not in conscious awareness. In other words, when people say "Oh, I just don't like him or her," they are either not aware of why they don't like the person or they are aware of why but are smart enough to not say why because it is very likely due to an unlawful reason such as race, gender, age, disability, color, national origin, etc. When people really do not like someone for a concrete reason that is not unlawful and that is also reasonable, they have no difficulty identifying why they don't like the person.

Does that matter to the person who is being harassed? No. He or she is still a person who is being harassed, which is reprehensible and which should not be allowed to continue. Yet it is a reminder that these important HR concepts really are very connected. If someone experiences the emotion of disgust toward someone but cannot understand or articulate why, should he or she be allowed to harass that person or treat the person badly? Frequently disgust is a response to diversity when the diversity is misunderstood or feared. Just because an EEO claim cannot be proven because it isn't spoken or people aren't conscious of it does not mean it isn't present. This is just another reason to make all harassment in the United States unlawful. Harassment is harassment regardless of what drives it.

The HR Tool entitled "Sample Memo Defining Bullying," on pages 110–111, shows an example of how an HR professional might address a bullying situation to a supervisor.

The Washington State Department of Labor and Industry has an excellent sample policy titled "Workplace Bullying: What Everyone Needs to Know,"[7] as cited and quoted from throughout this chapter. Additionally, the Workplace Bullying Institute has a plan called "The Namie Blueprint" for workplace bullying prevention as well as research, statistics, model policies, and information about workplace bullying in most other first-world nations.[8] There are other model policy options as well:

http://www.bullyfreeworkplace.org/
http://www.bullyonline.org/workbully/bully.htm
http://www.overcomebullying.org/workplace-bullying-stories.html

⟩⟩ WHAT IS CORPORATE/INSTITUTIONAL BULLYING?

Corporate/institutional bullying occurs when bullying is entrenched in an organization and becomes accepted as part of the workplace culture. Corporate/institutional bullying can manifest itself in different ways:

- Placing unreasonable expectations on employees, where failure to meet those expectations means making life unpleasant (or dismissing) anyone who objects
- Dismissing employees suffering from stress as "weak" while completely ignoring or denying potential work-related causes of the stress; and/or
- Encouraging employees to fabricate complaints about colleagues with promises of promotion or threats of discipline[9]

See the HR Tool entitled "Signs of Corporate and Institutional Bullying," on page 111, for an aid to help you identify bullying in a corporate setting.

As a credible activist, you will want to take the initiative in creating and maintaining a bully-free workplace. Gather documentary and other educational and training materials to help staff understand the harm done by bullying. Beverly Peterson is a filmmaker who produced the documentary, *There Oughta Be a Law:NoJobIsWorthThis.com*, which aims to educate employees, managers, leaders, HR professionals, legislators, and others about the harm done by bullying.[10] Having behavioral policies in place such as anti-bullying policies can also contribute to keeping unions away from industries that do not usually have union presences.

UNIONS AND NLRA COMPLIANCE

Companies must know where the line is with regard to when they are engaging in activities to prevent union membership. While most companies do want to prevent their employees from joining unions, there are companies that welcome unions and respect the employees' rights to organize.

Congress approved the *National Labor Relations Act* (NLRA) in 1935 to encourage a healthy relationship between private-sector workers and their employers. The NLRB.gov Web site explains that the NLRA was designed to curtail work stoppages, strikes, and general labor strife, which were viewed as harmful to the U.S. economy and general well-being. The NLRA extends many rights to workers who wish to form, join, or support unions; to workers who are already represented by unions; and to workers who join together as a group (two or more employees) without a union seeking to modify their wages or working conditions, which is known as "protected concerted activities."

The NLRA also extends rights to employers, protecting commercial interests against unfair actions committed by labor organizations, and extends rights to labor organizations, protecting organizational and collective-bargaining representative interests against unfair actions committed by employers.

The NLRB's *Basic Guide to the National Labor Relations Act* presents a summary of the Act in clear, easy-to-understand language. The Act outlines basic rights of employees as follows:

- To self-organization.
- To form, join, or assist labor organizations.
- To bargain collectively for wages and working conditions through representatives of their own choosing.
- To engage in other protected concerted activities with or without a union, which are usually group activities (two or more employees acting together) attempting to improve working conditions, such as wages and benefits.
- To refrain from any of these activities. (However, a union and employer may, in a State where such agreements are permitted, enter into a lawful union-security clause).[11]

At the SHRM Annual Conference held on June 29, 2009, the message to HR professionals from Michael Lotito, an attorney with Jackson Lewis in San Francisco, was as follows: "Now is the time for HR to start talking to supervisors and employers about making unions irrelevant."[12] There has been a clarion call to HR professionals who are credible activists regarding making unions "irrelevant"; yet how can HR accomplish this?

In our attempt to do so, we must first make it clear that this is not an anti-union stance. On the contrary, organized labor brings an important voice to the table by representing the workforce that companies depend upon for daily operations and overall success. Here, the phrase "making unions irrelevant" is interpreted by the author to mean strategically circumventing the battle of wills, which sometimes develops over time when labor feels as if their experiences and concerns are not being acknowledged or valued, by actively anticipating needs and seeking out engagement before problematic situations become unnecessarily adversarial. A list of issues to raise with your leadership, managers, and supervisors is provided in the HR Tool entitled "Checklist: Recommendations from HR to Leaders to Make Unions Irrelevant," on pages 111-113. For examples on how to handle an issue concerning the

NLRA, refer to the HR Tool entitled "Sample Memo Regarding (Company)'s Compliance with the NLRA," on pages 113-115.

Organized labor's presence also often serves as an incentive to ensure that competitive corporate governance (CCG) is practiced, which benefits all business stakeholders, as CCG prevents costly dysfunction and promotes profitable, efficient, compliant, and healthy workplaces. See the HR Tool entitled "Reasons Some Companies Embrace Unions," on page 115. For an example of how an NLRA issue might be addressed, see the HR Tool entitled "Sample Memo Regarding Concerns about Union Compliance with the NLRA," on pages 115-116.

HR TOOLS

EXAMPLES OF BULLYING

Unwarranted or invalid criticism

Blame without factual justification

Being treated differently than the rest of your work group

Being sworn at

Exclusion or social isolation

Being shouted at or being humiliated

Being the target of practical jokes

Excessive monitoring[13]

SAMPLE MEMO REGARDING BULLYING AND WORKPLACE VIOLENCE

On letterhead, in interoffice memo format, or via e-mail

CONFIDENTIAL

To: Your Supervisor
(Include any others on this list to whom this memo should be addressed.)

From: Your Name

Date:

Re.:   Recommendation to Implement a Workplace Violence Prevention Policy at (Company)

I am compelled to express concern about how we at (Company) might better handle issues related to risk factors for workplace violence.

As you know, there are no laws in the United States addressing workplace bullying. I am concerned about how the (topic, employee name, incident) matter is being handled, and I recommend that we revisit this situation and seek technical assistance to ensure that we at (Company) fully understand what workplace bullying is. I further recommend that we evaluate its presence, frequency, and severity at (Company) with the intention to both prevent workplace violence and to actively support the creation of a workplace that is psychologically, emotionally, and physically healthy for all employees of (Company).

Other risk factors for workplace violence include domestic violence issues our staff may have about which we may be unaware, poor conflict resolution skills of some staff, and any drug or alcohol abuse by any staff members while at work.

We can do more to prevent workplace violence. Moving forward, I recommend that we consider reading the FBI's report on workplace violence at http://www.fbi.gov/publications/violence.pdf and also consider technical assistance consultation from no-cost government or SHRM resources so that we remain appraised of and follow current best practices for workplace violence prevention and implement a policy.

Additionally, I recommend that all persons involved in decisions related to addressing possible complaints about workplace bullying or workplace violence attend formal training on these issues. I will follow this memo up with a list of quality upcoming available trainings in our area or via webinar.

We share a collective responsibility to ensure (Company)'s compliance with OSHA workplace safety regulations. We also share a commitment to prevent liability exposure for (Company) as well as personal liability exposure.

The resources below are free and available to us to use at any time. My membership in SHRM provides free information, white papers, case-law information, and research capabilities along with toolkits for how to best handle workplace bullying and workplace violence issues. I recommend that we use these resources in the future to ensure prudent and educated decision-making processes related to instances of workplace bullying and workplace violence.

http://www.fbi.gov/publications/violence.pdf

http://www.osha.gov/SLTC/workplaceviolence/index.htm

http://www.workplacebullying.org/

http://www.shrm.org/

http://www.bls.gov/iif/oshwc/osnr0026.pdf

http://NoJobIsWorthThis.com

I know we share a strong commitment to the consistent application of all (Company)'s policies as well as compliance with all relevant city, state, and federal laws related to workplace safety.

Additionally, I know we share an awareness of the importance of precedent in our decision-making processes and our handling of workplace safety issues in a prudent, responsible, and legally compliant manner.

FACTORS THAT MAY INCREASE THE RISK FOR BULLYING BEHAVIOR

☐ Significant company change, such as major internal restructuring or technological change

☐ Changes in workforce dynamics due to close personal relationships, fallout from formal complaints or investigations, fallout from previous harassment, discrimination, or retaliation, retention of employees who violate conduct rules or laws, disparate treatment of certain employees

☐ Inadequate information flow between company levels, lack of employee participation in decisions

☐ Lack of policies about behavior, high rate and intensity of work, staff shortages, interpersonal conflict, company constraints, role ambiguity, and role conflict

HOW BULLYING AFFECTS PEOPLE

Victims of bullying experience significant physical and mental health problems.

These may include the following:

☐ High stress; post-traumatic stress disorder (PTSD)

☐ Financial problems due to absence

☐ Reduced self-esteem

☐ Musculoskeletal problems

☐ Phobias

☐ Sleep disturbances

☐ Increased depression/self-blame

☐ Digestive problems[14]

SAMPLE MEMO DEFINING BULLYING

On letterhead, in interoffice memo format, or via e-mail

CONFIDENTIAL

To: Your Supervisor
(Include any others on this list to whom this memo should be addressed.)

From: Your Name

Date:

Re.:   Recommendation to Implement an Anti-Bullying Policy for (Company)

I would like to suggest that (Company) implement an Anti-Workplace Bullying policy.

It is my observation that (Company) does in fact have a workplace-bullying problem. The situations that occurred with (employees' names) are examples of bullying.

While workplace bullying is completely legal in the United States, it has been cited by the FBI as a precursor to and risk factor for workplace violence; for more information please see: http://www.fbi.gov/publications/violence.pdf. The National Institute for Occupational Safety and Health (NIOSH) recognizes bullying as a form of workplace violence: http://www.cdc.gov/niosh/updates/upd-07-28-04.html.

Unless you have an objection, I will draft a sample policy for your review.

SIGNS OF CORPORATE AND INSTITUTIONAL BULLYING

☐ Failure to meet company goals;

☐ Increased frequencies of grievances, resignations, and requests for transfers;

☐ Increased absence due to sickness; and

☐ Increased disciplinary actions.[15]

CHECKLIST: RECOMMENDATIONS FROM HR TO LEADERS TO MAKE UNIONS IRRELEVANT

☐ Ensure that all wage and hour (including FLSA) laws are properly complied with in all finance and payroll practices. Ensure that errors are handled with a high level of customer service directed at employees as internal customers and with the first consideration being that the customer may be correct about any error in his or her paycheck. If this requires finance and/or payroll staff to attend trainings, schedule these regularly and make them mandatory.

☐ Ensure that all safety regulations are properly complied with in all building, job description, policies, and practices. Ensure that errors are handled with a high level of customer service directed at employees as internal customers and with the first consideration being that the customer may be correct about any concern about workplace safety.

☐ Make the prevention of workplace injuries and illnesses a high priority, with an emphasis on mandatory credible trainings from your local DOSH department of labor, from OSHA, or from other credible industry safety trainers.

- ☐ Collaborate with your local OSHA offices to explore prevention, training, and recommended best practices to ensure safe workplaces for all employees.

- ☐ Ensure that all EEO, ADA, ADAAA, ADEA (Age Discrimination in Employment Act), ERISA (Employment Retirement Security Income Security Act), COBRA (Consolidated Omnibus Budget Reconciliation Act), Uniformed Services Employment and Reemployment Rights Act (USERRA), HIPAA (Health Insurance Portability and Accountability Act), NLRA, and other employment laws are properly complied with in all respects, and that all managers and supervisors with any oversight of any employee is fully trained in their roles regarding these. Quickly acknowledge and remediate any errors to show good-faith dealings with employees. Over-respond to management errors by ensuring necessary corrective training is provided promptly to prevent future errors.

- ☐ Ensure that errors are handled with a high level of customer service directed at employees as internal customers, with the first consideration being that the customer may be correct about any concern about any of these issues.

- ☐ When management, supervisors, leaders, or HR make errors, openly acknowledge them and promptly remediate them to create a culture of trust between management and employees as well as a learning organization that fosters an environment where errors, conflicts, and misunderstandings are opportunities for improvement, learning, and innovation.

- ☐ Provide the same quality and level of health, disability, death, dismemberment, dental, orthodontic, vision, chiropractic, mental health, substance abuse, and other benefits to all employees, regardless of job description, title, or level.

- ☐ Don't allow the highest salary in the company to be more than 5, 10, 15, 20, or 40 times that of the lowest-paid employee. Choose a number appropriate for your industry and commit to it. Don't get around this by using bonuses or other means to avoid this cap. Publicize this policy to all employees. Demonstrate that when company profits grow, employee salaries will grow; this is only one way to get loyalty and commitment from employees.

- ☐ Allow employee involvement in as many policy and practice issues as possible through the use of open-systems feedback solicitations. Take this feedback seriously, and consider every employee to be your corporate partner whose feedback has value, is considered, and is responded to with some form of change, whenever possible, practical, reasonable, and legal.

- ☐ Provide the same quality and level of training, recognition, and advancement opportunities to all employees regardless of job description.

- ☐ Implement sound internal conflict resolution procedures in which employees have significant involvement on decision-making committees composed of both management and employee-peers.

- ☐ Implement sound performance management procedures that include extensive, thorough, and semiannual training for all managers, supervisors, leadership, HR, and anyone else involved in performance management and decision making. This training will ideally include high-quality education regarding how to avoid negative and positive rater-bias, conflicts of interest, harassment, discrimination, retaliation, attribution error, NVC skills training and practice, sound conflict resolution training and practice, and the use of statistically valid emotional intelligence measures such as the EQi, the EQ360, the MSCEIT (http://www.eiskills.com/MSCEIT.html) , or the TESI (http://www.theemotionallyintelligentteam.com/tesi.asp), with accountability processes within the environment of a learning organization.

☐ Implement a zero-tolerance policy to address workplace bullying, and adopt a sound policy such as that used by the Washington State Department of Labor and Industries.

☐ Avoid employee layoffs at all costs. Instead of eliminating jobs, consider other measures such as instituting four-day workweeks, lowering executive pay, lowering the ratio of the highest paid employee to the lowest-paid employee, and examining other cost-cutting measures in process, in benefits, or in other ways. Solicit ideas from all employees to include them in these challenging decision-making processes.

☐ Allow employees to donate paid time off to other employees who are ill, awaiting disability benefits, awaiting maternity benefits, and out of their own sick time due to serious illness. A sample memo follows this page regarding such a policy.

Clearly post and abide by all mandated city, state, and federal employment laws. To see which your company is required to post, go to http://www.dol.gov/osbp/sbrefa/poster/matrix.htm.

SAMPLE MEMO REGARDING (COMPANY)'S COMPLIANCE WITH THE NLRA

On letterhead, in interoffice memo format, or via e-mail

CONFIDENTIAL

To: Your Supervisor
(Include any others on this list to whom this memo should be addressed.)

From: Your Name

Date:

Re.:   Concerns about (Company)'s Compliance with the NLRA

I am compelled to express concern about how we at (Company) handle issues related to employees' rights to organize.

As you know, employees do have a right to organize under the NLRA. I am concerned with how the recent situation with (employee's name or incident involving company response to know that union organizers are talking with employees) is being handled. Unless I am unaware of additional information or documentation related to this matter, I recommend that we revisit this situation and seek technical assistance to ensure that we at (Company) have not made any errors in violation of the NLRA.

If we learn that any errors were made, I recommend that we remediate those as soon as possible. Moving forward, I recommend that we consider implementing a decision-making protocol that will include technical assistance consultation from no-cost government or SHRM resources to prevent errors in the future. Additionally, I recommend that all persons involved in any action or official statement regarding issues concerning unions and employees' rights to organize be mandated to attend formal training on the relevant compliance issues. I will follow this memo up with a list of quality upcoming available trainings in our area or via webinar.

We share a collective responsibility to ensure (Company)'s compliance with the NLRA. I know we share a commitment to prevent liability exposure for (Company) as well as personal liability exposure. Some examples of employer conduct which violate the NLRA are:

- ☐ Threatening employees with loss of jobs or benefits if they join or vote for a union or engage in protected concerted activity.
- ☐ Threatening to close the plant if employees select a union to represent them.
- ☐ Questioning employees about their union sympathies or activities in circumstances that tend to interfere with, restrain or coerce employees in the exercise of their rights under the Act.
- ☐ Promising benefits to employees to discourage their union support.
- ☐ Transferring, laying off, terminating, assigning employees more difficult work tasks, or otherwise punishing employees because they engaged in union or protected concerted activity.
- ☐ Transferring, laying off, terminating, assigning employees more difficult work tasks, or otherwise punishing employees because they filed unfair labor practice charges or participated in an investigation conducted by NLRB.

The resources below are free and available to us to use at any time. My membership in SHRM provides free information, white papers, case-law information, and research capabilities along with toolkits for how to best handle union and related issues. I recommend that we use these resources in the future to ensure legally compliant decision-making processes related to union issues:

http://www.shrm.org/

http://www.nlrb.gov/Workplace_Rights/nlra_violations.aspx

I know we share a strong commitment to the consistent application of all (Company)'s policies as well as compliance with all relevant city, state, and federal laws related to employees' rights to organize and choose union membership.

Additionally, I know we share an awareness of the importance of precedent in our decision-making processes and our handling of union issues in a legally compliant manner.

REASONS SOME COMPANIES EMBRACE UNIONS

☐ Many matters that can be grey-area territory requiring more time, research, effort, and internal consultation with your legal department or leadership, may be simplified into very clear black and white issues.

☐ Exposure to negotiations over benefits and other compensation is excellent training, is very good for the résumé of the HR professional, and can work out very well for both the company and for employees.

☐ Employees who feel protected and know what to expect do work harder and well for the company because they also feel a strong sense of pride and ownership in their union and in their jobs.

☐ Relationships between industry and the workforce are stabilized.

☐ Work stoppages are less likely.

SAMPLE MEMO REGARDING CONCERNS ABOUT UNION COMPLIANCE WITH THE NLRA

On letterhead, in interoffice memo format, or via e-mail

CONFIDENTIAL

To: Your Supervisor (Include any others on this list to whom this memo should be addressed.)

From: Your Name

Date:

Re.:   Concerns about (Union) Compliance with NLRA

I am compelled to express concern about how [Name of Union(s)] at (Company) is operating.

I am concerned about how the recent situation with (employee's name or department or situation or contract negotiation) was handled. Unless I am unaware of additional information or documentation related to this matter, I recommend that we take appropriate and legally compliant action to formally address this concern with (Union)'s leadership.

Moving forward, I recommend that we consider implementing a decision-making protocol that will include technical assistance consultation from no-cost government or SHRM resources to prevent errors in the future. Additionally, I recommend that all (Company) employees involved in communications with (Union) attend formal training related compliance issues. I will follow this memo up with a list of quality upcoming available trainings in our area or via webinar.

We share a collective responsibility to ensure (Company)'s compliance with NLRA. I know we share a commitment to prevent liability exposure for (Company) as well as personal liability exposure. Briefly, examples of labor organization conduct which violate the NLRA are:

☐ Threats to employees that they will lose their jobs unless they support the union.

☐ Seeking the suspension, discharge or other punishment of an employee for not being a union member even if the employee has paid or offered to pay a lawful initiation fee and periodic fees thereafter.

☐ Refusing to process a grievance because an employee has criticized union officials or because an employee is not a member of the union in states where union security clauses are not permitted.

☐ Fining employees who have validly resigned from the union for engaging in protected concerted activities following their resignation or for crossing an unlawful picket line.

☐ Engaging in picket line misconduct, such as threatening, assaulting, or barring non-strikers from the employer's premises.

☐ Striking over issues unrelated to employment terms and conditions or coercively enmeshing neutrals into a labor dispute.

The resources below are free and available to us to use at any time. My membership in SHRM provides free information, white papers, case-law information, and research capabilities along with toolkits for how to best handle union-related issues. I recommend that we use these resources in the future to ensure legally compliant decision-making processes related to union-related concerns:

http://www.nlrb.gov/Workplace_Rights/nlra_violations.aspx

http://www.shrm.org /

I know we share a strong commitment to the consistent application of all (Company)'s policies as well as compliance with all relevant city, state, and federal laws related to the NLRA.

Additionally, I know we share an awareness of the importance of precedent in our decision-making processes and our handling of union-related issues in a legally compliant manner.

CHAPTER 9

ROUNDUP OF ADDITIONAL LEGAL ISSUES, PROCEDURES, AND OBLIGATIONS

COMMUNICATING WITH COLLEAGUES ABOUT COMPLIANCE CONCERNS OR CONFIDENTIAL ISSUES

HR professionals should be aware of the SHRM Code of Ethics whether they are SHRM members or not and should abide by it as well as instruct their staff and unpaid interns to abide by it. The sad truth is that many HR executives do follow this code of conduct with their leadership yet are not taken seriously, are ignored, and/or are overruled regarding compliance issues.

By now you've seen several sample memos and can draft one of your own in a similar structure to let your supervisor and/or leadership know that this is the SHRM Code of Ethics and you will abide by it. This is a good opportunity to check in with your supervisor and ask for feedback on your job performance with regard to the SHRM Code of Conduct. It's a very good idea to also ask him or her if he or she has any commentary on how your role in the company and your job description specifically relate or do not relate to the SHRM Code of Ethics. Ideally, you would review a job ad and/or job description against the SHRM Code of Conduct during your HR job interview before you even accept the position. However, if you find yourself already in the position or with a new boss, this is also a good time to make sure you're both on the same page.

If you suspect that you may get a competitive or angry reaction from your boss, or he or she may dismiss the SHRM Code of Ethics, saying it isn't the company's policy, or directing you to not follow it, it's a good idea to be prepared before you meet. Bring a list of all applicable city, state, and federal laws that would protect you from unlawful retaliation for raising concerns about noncompliance with relevant employment laws. Don't try to memorize the laws instead; there is no need to add stress to the situation.

Refer to the HR Tool entitled "Sample Memo Requesting (Company)-Sponsored SHRM Membership" at the end of the chapter, on page 128.

THE LILLY LEDBETTER FAIR PAY ACT

According to the U.S. Department of Labor,

> The Lilly Ledbetter Fair Pay Act amends the Civil Rights Act of 1964 and other anti-discrimination laws to clarify at which points in time discriminatory actions qualify as

an "unlawful employment practice." According to the legislation, unlawful conduct occurs when: "(1) a discriminatory compensation decision or other practice is adopted; (2) an individual becomes subject to the decision or practice; or (3) an individual is affected by application of the decision or practice, including each time compensation is paid." The law further states that individuals may receive back pay as compensation for discrimination that occurred up to two years preceding the filing of a charge. The Fair Pay Act also allows an employee to recover back pay for up to two years preceding the filing of a discrimination claim. The Fair Pay Act significantly extends the window of time during which an employee may file a wage discrimination claim. The changes of the Fair Pay Act also apply to claims filed under the Americans with Disabilities Act of 1990 (ADA) and the Rehabilitation Act of 1973.[1]

Being a member of SHRM will keep you updated on similar employment law changes via e-mail. (HR professionals will want to ask their leadership and legal colleagues if they would like them to forward these so all executives with legal and ethical compliance responsibilities remain sufficiently educated and informed.) The Obama administration and the current congress are expected to push through many new pieces of labor legislation, and in order to stay current on what might happen, SHRM is among the best resources to join.

HIRING VETERANS

Hiring veterans requires of an HR professional a greater vigilance of FMLA, disability, and EEO laws. There has been a large influx of disabled veterans into the workforce since the early 1990s, and this is expected to continue for several years. Adherence to FMLA laws is also required for any employee who is a caregiver for a veteran or disabled veteran. There are often recruitment efforts that focus primarily on assisting veterans in finding employment, and many corporations find this to be a meaningful and excellent source of good talent.

The unemployment rate for all veterans of the U.S. Armed Forces was 4.6 percent in 2008, according to the Bureau of Labor Statistics (BLS). The jobless rate for those who have served in the U.S. Armed Forces since September 2001 was 7.3 percent. In 2008, 22.4 million men and women in the civilian noninstitutional population, ages 18 and over, were veterans.

Approximately 30 percent of employed male veterans of Gulf War era II (defined by the BLS as September 2001 to the present) worked in management, professional, and related occupations, compared with approximately 34 percent of male nonveterans. Sales and office occupations; natural resources, construction, and maintenance occupations; and production, transportation, and material moving occupations each accounted for approximately 18 percent of employed male veterans and nonveterans. Among female veterans of Gulf War era II, 43 percent were employed in management, professional, and related occupations, and 32 percent held sales and office jobs.

Approximately 88 percent of Gulf War era I (defined as 1990 to August 2001) veterans were in the labor force in 2008, about the same as the rate for Gulf War era II veterans. The unemployment rate for Gulf War era I veterans (4 percent) was lower than the rate for Gulf

War era II veterans (7.3 percent). One-half of the female veterans of Gulf War era II were in management, professional, and related occupations, compared with 40 percent of female nonveterans.[2] See also the sections in this chapter entitled "Uniformed Services Employment and Reemployment Rights Act," on pages 122–123, and "Office of Federal Contract Compliance Programs," on pages 120–121. Chapter 5's discussion of FMLA, and Chapter 4's discussion of ADA/ADAAA.

WORKER ADJUSTMENT AND RETRAINING NOTIFICATION ACT COMPLIANCE

Compliance assistance for the Worker Adjustment and Retraining Notification Act (WARN) can be found at www.dol.gov/compliance/laws/comp-warn-regs.htm. The Employment and Training Administration of the Department of Labor is publishing a final regulation carrying out the provisions of WARN. WARN provides that, with certain exceptions, employers of 100 or more workers must give at least 60 days' advance notice of a plant closing or mass lay-off to affected workers or their representatives, to the state dislocated worker unit, and to the appropriate local government.[3]

AGE DISCRIMINATION ACT COMPLIANCE

According to the Job Accommodation Network, "The Age Discrimination Act (ADEA) protects individuals who are 40 years of age or older from employment discrimination based on age. The ADEA's protections apply to both employees and job applicants. The ADEA permits employers to favor older workers based on age even when doing so adversely affects a younger worker who is 40 or older" (but younger than the older worker). "It is also unlawful to retaliate against an individual for opposing employment practices that discriminate based on age or for filing an age discrimination charge, testifying, or participating in any way in an investigation, proceeding, or litigation under the ADEA. The ADEA applies to employers with 20 or more employees, including state and local governments. It also applies to employment agencies and labor companies, as well as to the federal government."[4]

COMPREHENSIVE OMNIBUS BUDGET RECONCILIATION ACT COMPLIANCE

According to the U.S. Department of Labor's Job Accommodation Network,

the Supreme Court has ruled that an employer cannot cancel a former employee's medical coverage under the Comprehensive Omnibus Budget Reconciliation Act (COBRA), even if the former worker is covered under a spouse's health plan when separated from employment. As a result of the holding, a former employee may choose to continue health-care coverage provided by his or her previous employer if coverage under the spouse's health plan was in effect before the decision to continue health-care coverage under COBRA is made.

COBRA requires employers to provide a "qualified beneficiary" (for example, an employee who was fired) with continuation of health-care coverage as good as the coverage the employee received while employed. The continuation of coverage can last up to 18 months; the former employee pays the health-care insurance premiums.

The statutory language of COBRA clearly indicates that a former employee ceases to be eligible for coverage under the Act if the employee becomes covered under a different plan *after* the election of COBRA benefits. Section 1162(2)(D)(i) states that an employee's COBRA insurance may be canceled on "the date on which the qualified beneficiary first becomes, *after the date of the election* [to continue coverage from a former employer], covered under any other group health plan which does not contain any exclusion or limitation with respect to any pre-existing conditions of such beneficiary . . . " However, the language does not directly address whether a former employee who was covered by another plan *before* electing to continue coverage from the former employer (that is, while the former employee was still employed) is ineligible for COBRA benefits.[5]

OFFICE OF FEDERAL CONTRACT COMPLIANCE PROGRAMS

The U.S. Department of Labor's Web site states that

the Office of Federal Contract Compliance Programs (OFCCP) administers and enforces three legal authorities that require equal employment opportunity: Executive Order 11246, as amended; Section 503 of the Rehabilitation Act of 1973, as amended; and the Rehabilitation Act of 1973. Taken together, these laws ban discrimination and require Federal contractors and subcontractors to take affirmative action to ensure that all individuals have an equal opportunity for employment, without regard to race, color, religion, sex, national origin, disability or status as a Vietnam era or special disabled veteran. This order, signed by President Lyndon B. Johnson in 1965, prohibits discrimination in hiring or employment decisions on the basis of race, color, gender, religion, and national origin. It applies to all nonexempt government contractors and subcontractors and federally assisted construction contracts and subcontracts in excess of $10,000.

Under the Executive Order, contractors and subcontractors with a federal contract of $50,000 or more, and 50 or more employees are required to develop a written affirmative action program that is designed to ensure equal employment opportunity, and sets forth specific and action-oriented programs to which a contractor commits itself to apply every good faith effort.

Section 503 of the Rehabilitation Act of 1973, as amended, prohibits discrimination and requires affirmative action in all personnel practices for qualified individuals with disabilities. It applies to all firms that have a nonexempt Government contract or subcontract in excess of $10,000. An affirmative action program is required.

The Vietnam Era Veterans' Readjustment Assistance Act of 1974 (VEVRAA) prohibits discrimination and requires affirmative action in all personnel practices for all veterans who served on active duty in the U.S. military, ground, naval, or air service who are special disabled veterans, Vietnam Era veterans, recently separated veterans, or veterans who served on active duty during a war or in a campaign or expedition for which a campaign badge has been authorized. It applies to all firms that have a nonexempt Government contract or subcontract of $25,000 or more. An affirmative action program is required.

In carrying out its responsibilities, the OFCCP uses the following enforcement procedures:

- Offers technical assistance to federal contractors and subcontractors to help them understand the regulatory requirements and review process.
- Conducts compliance evaluations and complaint investigations of federal contractors and subcontractors personnel policies and procedures.
- Obtains Conciliation Agreements from contractors and subcontractors who are in violation of regulatory requirements.
- Monitors contractors and subcontractors progress in fulfilling the terms of their agreements through periodic compliance reports.
- Forms linkage agreements between contractors and Labor Department job training programs to help employers identify and recruit qualified workers.
- Recommends enforcement actions to the Solicitor of Labor.
- The ultimate sanction for violations is debarment—the loss of a company's federal contracts. Other forms of relief to victims of discrimination may also be available, including back pay for lost wages.

The OFCCP has close working relationships with other Departmental agencies, such as: the Department of Justice, the Equal Employment Opportunity Commission and the DOL, the Office of the Solicitor, which advises on ethical, legal, and enforcement issues; the Women's Bureau, which emphasizes the needs of working women; the Bureau of Apprenticeship and Training, which establishes policies to promote equal opportunities in the recruitment and selection of apprentices; and the Employment and Training Administration, which administers Labor Department job training programs for current workforce needs.

OFCCP has a national network of six Regional Offices, each with District and Area Offices in Major Metropolitan Centers, and focuses its resources on finding and resolving systemic discrimination. The agency has adopted this strategy to: (1) prioritize enforcement resources by focusing on the worst offenders; (2) encourage employers to engage in self audits of their employment practices; and (3) achieve maximum leverage of resources to protect the greatest number of workers from discrimination.[6]

UNIFORMED SERVICES EMPLOYMENT AND REEMPLOYMENT RIGHTS ACT

According to the U.S. Department of Labor's Web site, Uniformed Services Employment and Reemployment Rights Act (USERRA)

was signed on October 13, 1994, and applies to persons who perform duty, voluntarily or involuntarily, in the "uniformed services," which include the Army, Navy, Marine Corps, Air Force, Coast Guard, and Public Health Service commissioned corps, as well as the reserve components of each of these services. Federal training or service in the Army National Guard and Air National Guard also gives rise to rights under USERRA. In addition, under the Public Health Security and Bioterrorism Response Act of 2002, certain disaster response work (and authorized training for such work) is considered "service in the uniformed services."

Uniformed service includes active duty, active duty for training, inactive duty training (such as drills), initial active duty training, and funeral honors duty performed by National Guard and reserve members, as well as the period for which a person is absent from a position of employment for the purpose of an examination to determine fitness to perform any such duty. USERRA covers nearly all employees, including part-time and probationary employees and applies to virtually all U.S. employers, regardless of size. The pre-service employer must reemploy service members returning from a period of service in the uniformed services if those service members meet five criteria:

- The person must have held a civilian job;
- The person must have given notice to the employer that he or she was leaving the job for service in the uniformed services, unless giving notice was precluded by military necessity or otherwise impossible or unreasonable;
- The cumulative period of service must not have exceeded five years;
- The person must not have been released from service under dishonorable or other punitive conditions; and
- The person must have reported back to the civilian job in a timely manner or have submitted a timely application for reemployment.

USERRA establishes a five-year cumulative total on military service with a single employer, with certain exceptions allowed for situations such as call-ups during emergencies, reserve drills, and annually scheduled active duty for training.

Employers are required to provide to persons entitled to the rights and benefits under USERRA a notice of the rights, benefits, and obligations of such persons and such employers under USERRA. USERRA also allows an employee to complete an initial period of active duty that exceeds five years (e.g., enlistees in the Navy's nuclear power program are required to serve six years).

Under USERRA, restoration rights are based on the duration of military service rather than the type of military duty performed (e.g., active duty for training or inactive duty), except for fitness-for-service examinations. The time limits for returning to work are as follows:

- *Less than 31 days service.* By the beginning of the first regularly scheduled work period after the end of the calendar day of duty, plus time required to return home safely and an eight-hour rest period. If this is impossible or unreasonable, then as soon as possible;
- *31 to 180 days.* The employee must apply for reemployment no later than 14 days after completion of military service. If this is impossible or unreasonable through no fault of the employee, then as soon as possible;
- *181 days or more.* The employee must apply for reemployment no later than 90 days after completion of military service;
- *Service-connected injury or illness.* Reporting or application deadlines are extended for up to two years for persons who are hospitalized or convalescing.

USERRA also guarantees pension plan benefits that accrued during military service, regardless of whether the plan is a defined benefit plan or a defined contribution plan. USERRA provides that service members activated for duty on or after December 10, 2004 may elect to extend their employer-sponsored health coverage for up to 24 months. Service members activated prior to 12/10/04 could elect to extend coverage for up to 18 months. Employers may require these individuals to pay up to 102 percent of total premiums for that elective coverage. In addition, USERRA prohibits employment discrimination against a person on the basis of past military service, current military obligations, or an intent to serve.

The Veterans' Employment and Training Service (VETS) enforces USERRA. However, the law also allows an employee to enforce his or her rights by filing a court action directly, without filing a complaint with VETS. Compliance assistance information is available on the VETS Web site: http://www.dol.gov/vets/. Specific compliance assistance materials available include: the DOL USERRA regulations (20 CFR Part 1002), which implement the law for non-Federal employers; a fact sheet (OASVET 97-3) about USERRA; the notice/poster to employees of their rights, benefits and obligations under USERRA; and a non-technical USERRA Guide that contains general information about the law. Copies of VETS' publications, or answers to questions about USERRA, may also be obtained from your local VETS office.

Another compliance assistance resource, the elaws USERRA Advisor, helps veterans understand employee eligibility and job entitlements, employer obligations, benefits, and remedies under the Act. For additional compliance assistance, contact the Department's Toll-Free Help Line at 1-866-4-USA-DOL. A court may order an employer to compensate a prevailing claimant for lost wages or benefits. USERRA allows for liquidated damages for "willful" violations, does not preempt state laws providing greater or additional rights, but it does preempt state laws providing lesser rights or imposing additional eligibility criteria.[7]

THE EMPLOYEE RETIREMENT INCOME SECURITY ACT OF 1974

The U.S. Department of Labor defines The Employee Retirement Income Security Act (ERISA) as

a federal law that sets minimum standards for pension plans in private industry. ERISA does not require any employer to establish a pension plan; it only requires that those who establish plans must meet certain minimum standards. The law generally does not specify how much money a participant must be paid as a benefit. ERISA requires plans to regularly provide participants with information about the plan including information about plan features and funding; sets minimum standards for participation, vesting, benefit accrual and funding; requires accountability of plan fiduciaries; and gives participants the right to sue for benefits and breaches of fiduciary duty.

ERISA also guarantees payment of certain benefits through the Pension Benefit Guaranty Company, a federally chartered company, if a defined plan is terminated. The Department of Labor's (DOL) Employee Benefits Security Administration (EBSA) enforces ERISA. The EBSA Compliance Assistance Portal assists employers and employee benefit plan officials in understanding and complying with the requirements of ERISA as it applies to the administration of employee pension and welfare benefit plans.

Under ERISA, COBRA Continuation Coverage and The American Recovery and Reinvestment Act of 2009 (ARRA) provide for premium reductions and additional election opportunities for health benefits under the Consolidated Omnibus Budget Reconciliation Act of 1985 (COBRA). The TAA Health Coverage Improvement Act of 2009, enacted as part of ARRA, also made changes with regard to COBRA continuation coverage.

The Employment Law Guide: Employee Benefit Plans provides a summary of the requirements for most private sector employee benefit plans under ERISA. *The Cash Balance Pension Plans Guide* provides general information on cash balance pension plans. The Division of Pensions Through Qualified Domestic Relations Orders (QDROs) are generally qualified domestic relations orders that create or recognize the existence of an alternate payee's right to receive, or assign to an alternate payee the right to receive, all or a portion of benefits payable with respect to a participant under a pension plan. The EBSA's Orphan Plan Project describes an enforcement project to locate pension plans, particularly 401(k) plans, which have been abandoned by fiduciaries through death, neglect, bankruptcy, or incarceration and to determine if a fiduciary could be located. Another guide, *Your Employer's Bankruptcy: How Will It Affect Your Employee Benefits?* provides information on bankruptcy's effect on pension plans and group health plans. FEAST is a computerized processing system that simplifies and expedites the receipt and processing of the Form 5500 and Form 5500-EZ.

E-TOOLS for ERISA are found at the "elaws Health Benefits Advisor," which helps workers and their families better understand employer and employee company (such as a union) provide group health benefits and the laws that govern them, especially when they experience changes in their life and work situations such as marriage, childbirth, job loss, or retirement. It also assists employers in understanding their responsibilities under the applicable laws. The "elaws Small Business Retirement Savings Advisor" provides information to help small business owners understand their retirement savings options and determine which program is most appropriate for their needs. Compliance assistance for employers regarding reporting and filing information can be obtained from EBSA.

ERISA sets uniform minimum standards to ensure that employee benefit plans are established and maintained in a fair and financially sound manner. In addition, employers have an obligation to provide promised benefits and satisfy ERISA's requirements for managing and administering private pension and welfare plans. The EBSA can be reached at 1-866-444-EBSA (3272) or TTY: 1-877-889-5627. Pursuant to the U.S. Department of Labor's Confidentiality Protocol for Compliance Assistance Inquiries, information provided by a phone caller will be kept confidential within the bounds of the law. Compliance assistance inquiries won't trigger an inspection, audit, investigation, etc.[8]

THE IMMIGRATION AND NATIONALITY ACT

The U.S. Department of Labor explains that

the Immigration and Nationality Act (INA) sets forth the conditions for the temporary and permanent employment of aliens in the United States and includes provisions that address employment eligibility and employment verification. These provisions apply to all employers. *The Employment Law Guide: Authorized Workers* describes what employers must do to verify the identity and employment eligibility of anyone to be hired, and the protections afforded to employees from discrimination in hiring or discharge on the basis of national origin and citizenship status. *The Employment Law Guide: Crewmembers (D-1 Visas)* describes the requirements of vessels/employers seeking to employ their nonimmigrant aliens as crewmembers to perform longshore work in U.S. ports under D-1 Visas. *The Employment Law Guide: Workers in Professional and Specialty Occupations (H-1B Visas)* describes the requirements on the part of employers seeking to hire nonimmigrant aliens as workers in specialty occupations or as fashion models using the H-1B and H-1B1 nonimmigrant visa classification. *The Employment Law Guide: Temporary Agricultural Workers (H-2A Visas)* describes the procedures for obtaining a labor certification and the contractual obligations of employers seeking to hire temporary agricultural workers under H-2A Visas. *The Employment Law Guide: Temporary Nonagricultural Workers (H-2B Visas)* describes the requirements on the part of employers seeking to obtain temporary nonagricultural labor certifications in order to import temporary nonagricultural workers to work in temporary jobs in the United States under H-2B visas. *The Employment Law Guide: Permanent Employment of Workers Based on Immigration* describes the requirements on the part of employers seeking to hire foreign workers immigrating to the United States for the purpose of employment, including the application process for employers to obtain a permanent alien employment certification.[9]

)) INA AVAILABLE FACT SHEETS

- The Publication of Final H-1B (Professional and Specialty Occupation Visas) Regulations
- Changes made by the H-1B Visa Reform Act of 2004
- H-2A (Temporary Agricultural Worker Visas)
- Application of U.S. Labor Laws to Immigrant Workers (In Korean—PDF) (En Español)
- Fair Labor Standards Act Application to Foreign Commercial Vehicle Operators (En Español)

)) RECORDKEEPING: DOCUMENTS AND FORMS

The U.S. Department of Labor's Web site has

links to the forms needed to obtain foreign labor certification under various programs, including the Application for H-1B and H-1B1 Non-immigrants (form ETA-9035), the Application for Permanent Employment Certification (form ETA-9089), the Application for Alien Employment Certification (form ETA-750A), and Part B of this application: Statement of Qualifications of the Alien (form ETA-750B), and the Application for Alien Employment Certification for Agricultural Services (form ETA-790). Please note that these forms are in PDF format and require the Adobe Acrobat Reader.

H-2A Visa Program. Employers certified for H-2A contracts must keep records of the hours each worker actually works. In addition, the employer must retain a record of time "offered" to the worker but which the worker "refused" to work. Each worker must receive a wage statement showing hours of work, hours refused, pay for each type of crop, the basis of pay (i.e., whether the worker is being paid by the hour, by the piece, "task" pay, etc.). The wage statement must indicate total earnings for the pay period and all deductions from wages (along with a statement as to why deductions were made). See 20 CFR 655.102(b)(7) for further information on recordkeeping requirements under the H-2A visa program.

H-1B and H-1B1 Visa Program. Employers using the H-1B or H-1B1 visa classifications to hire nonimmigrant foreign workers in specialty (professional) occupations are required to maintain documentation to meet their burden of proof with respect to the validity of the statements made in their Labor Condition Application (LCA) and the accuracy of the information provided. See 20 CFR 655.760 for regulations for employers of H-1B and H-1B1 classified specialty/professional nonimmigrant foreign workers.

H-2B Visa Program. Employers of temporary nonagricultural workers under the H-2B visa program are not subject to any post entry (H-2B) program specific recordkeeping/posting/notice requirements; however, the recordkeeping/posting/ notice requirements of any other laws applicable from DOL to the employment would apply.[10]

)) APPLICABLE INA LAWS AND REGULATIONS

The U.S. Department of Labor's Web site explains

20 CFR Part 655. Regulations implementing the INA regarding the temporary employment of aliens in the United States. Interim Final Rule, 20 CFR Part 655 Subparts H and I (PDF): Interim Final Rule implementing DOL's responsibilities regarding H-1B1 visas for professionals from Chile and Singapore.

29 CFR Part 501. Regulations implementing the INA regarding the enforcement of contractual obligations applicable to the temporary employment of foreign and other workers employed in agriculture.[11]

HR TOOL

SAMPLE MEMO REQUESTING (COMPANY)-SPONSORED SHRM MEMBERSHIP

On letterhead, in interoffice memo format, or via e-mail

To: Your Supervisor
(Include any others on this list to whom this memo should be addressed.)

From: Your Name

Date:

Re.: Request for company-sponsored SHRM membership for HR personnel

I would like (Company) to purchase a SHRM annual membership in my name so that I am able to remain as educated as possible regarding any HR issue and remain informed about changing legislation, high-profile case studies in the news, important research, and high-quality educational opportunities.

SHRM's annual membership is currently $160.00 per year. SHRM's more than 250,000 members come from all over the world and work in all disciplines of HR. I will have the ability to communicate with them and learn from them.

We share a collective responsibility to ensure (Company)'s compliance with all relevant employment laws, which frequently change. SHRM will help keep me and us credibly informed of any changes. I know we share a commitment to prevent liability exposure for (Company) as well as personal liability exposure.

My membership in SHRM will provide free access to information, white papers, case-law information, and research capabilities along with toolkits for how to best handle every HR issue. I recommend that we use these resources in the future to ensure legally compliant decision-making processes related to any matter for which we require technical assistance.

I know we share a strong commitment to consistent application of all (Company)'s policies as well as compliance with all relevant city, state, and federal laws.

I also wish to include for you the SHRM Code of Ethics, which I endeavor to follow in my role as (title) at (Company). Please let me know if you would like to discuss these as they relate to my role at (Company).

If you would like to review the Web site, the address is: http://www.shrm.org /

Thank you very much.

CHAPTER 10

CHECKLIST OF HEALTH INSURANCE TERMS HR PROFESSIONALS NEED TO KNOW

The U.S. Federal Bureau of Labor Statistics (BLS) indicates that "in February 2002, the Federal Government's Interdepartmental Committee on Employment-based Health Insurance Surveys approved the following set of definitions for use in Federal surveys collecting employer-based health insurance data. The BLS National Compensation Survey currently uses these definitions in its data collection procedures and publications. These definitions will be periodically reviewed and updated by the Committee." It is prudent for HR professionals to review these periodically and also to be aware of changes to these and any other laws and guidelines affecting employment whenever there is a new government administration seated. The following information is provided by the U.S. Federal Bureau of Labor Statistics:[1]

ASO (Administrative Services Only)—An arrangement in which an employer hires a third party to deliver administrative services to the employer such as claims processing and billing; the employer bears the risk for claims. This is common in self-insured health care plans.

Association Health Plans—This term is sometimes used loosely to refer to any health plan sponsored by an association. It also has a precise definition under the Health Insurance Portability and Accountability Act of 1996 that exempts from certain requirements insurers that sell insurance to small employers only through association health plans that meet the definition.

Coinsurance—A form of medical cost sharing in a health insurance plan that requires an insured person to pay a stated percentage of medical expenses after the deductible amount, if any, was paid. Once any deductible amount and coinsurance are paid, the insurer is responsible for the rest of the reimbursement for covered benefits up to allowed charges: the individual could also be responsible for any charges in excess of what the insurer determines to be "usual, customary and reasonable." Coinsurance rates may differ if services are received from an approved provider (i.e., a provider with whom the insurer has a contract or an agreement specifying payment levels and other contract requirements) or if received by providers not on the approved list. In addition to overall coinsurance rates, rates may also differ for different types of services.

Copayment—A form of medical cost sharing in a health insurance plan that requires an insured person to pay a fixed dollar amount when a medical service is received. The insurer is responsible for the rest of the reimbursement. There may be separate copayments for different services. Some plans require that a deductible first be met for some specific services before a copayment applies.

Deductible—A fixed dollar amount during the benefit period—usually a year—that an insured person pays before the insurer starts to make payments for covered medical services. Plans may have both per individual and family deductibles. Some plans may have separate deductibles for specific services. For example, a plan may have a hospitalization deductible per admission. Deductibles may differ if services are received from an approved provider or if received from providers not on the approved list.

Flexible benefits plan (Cafeteria plan) (IRS 125 Plan)—A benefit program under Section 125 of the Internal Revenue Code that offers employees a choice between permissible taxable benefits, including cash, and nontaxable benefits such as life and health insurance, vacations, retirement plans and child care. Although a common core of benefits may be required, the employee can determine how his or her remaining benefit dollars are to be allocated for each type of benefit from the total amount promised by the employer. Sometimes employee contributions may be made for additional coverage.

Flexible spending accounts or arrangements (FSA)—Accounts offered and administered by employers that provide a way for employees to set aside, out of their paycheck, pre-tax dollars to pay for the employee's share of insurance premiums or medical expenses not covered by the employer's health plan. The employer may also make contributions to a FSA. Typically, benefits or cash must be used within the given benefit year or the employee loses the money. Flexible spending accounts can also be provided to cover childcare expenses, but those accounts must be established separately from medical FSAs.

Fully insured plan—A plan where the employer contracts with another company to assume financial responsibility for the enrollees' medical claims and for all incurred administrative costs.

Gatekeeper—Under some health insurance arrangements, a gatekeeper is responsible for the administration of the patient's treatment; the gatekeeper coordinates and authorizes all medical services, laboratory studies, specialty referrals, and hospitalizations.

Group purchasing arrangement—Any of a wide array of arrangements in which two or more small employers purchase health insurance collectively, often through a common intermediary who acts on their collective behalf. Such arrangements may go by many different names, including cooperatives, alliances, or business groups on health. They differ from one another along a number of dimensions, including governance, functions and status under federal and state laws. Some are set up or chartered by states while others are entirely private enterprises. Some centralize more of the purchasing functions than others, including functions such as risk pooling, price negotiation, choice of health plans offered to employees, and various administrative tasks. Depending on their functions, they may be subject to different state and/or federal rules. For example, they may be regulated as Multiple Employer Welfare Arrangements (MEWAs).

Health Care Plans and Systems
- **Indemnity plan**—A type of medical plan that reimburses the patient and/or provider as expenses are incurred.

- **Conventional indemnity plan**—An indemnity that allows the participant the choice of any provider without effect on reimbursement. These plans reimburse the patient and/or provider as expenses are incurred.
- **Preferred provider company (PPO) plan**—An indemnity plan where coverage is provided to participants through a network of selected health care providers (such as hospitals and physicians). The enrollees may go outside the network, but would incur larger costs in the form of higher deductibles, higher coinsurance rates, or non-discounted charges from the providers.
- **Exclusive provider company (EPO) plan**—A more restrictive type of preferred provider company plan under which employees must use providers from the specified network of physicians and hospitals to receive coverage; there is no coverage for care received from a non-network provider except in an emergency situation.
- **Health maintenance company (HMO)**—A health care system that assumes both the financial risks associated with providing comprehensive medical services (insurance and service risk) and the responsibility for health care delivery in a particular geographic area to HMO members, usually in return for a fixed, prepaid fee. Financial risk may be shared with the providers participating in the HMO.
  - **Group Model HMO**—An HMO that contracts with a single multi-specialty medical group to provide care to the HMO's membership. The group practice may work exclusively with the HMO, or it may provide services to non-HMO patients as well. The HMO pays the medical group a negotiated, per capita rate, which the group distributes among its physicians, usually on a salaried basis.
  - **Staff Model HMO**—A type of closed-panel HMO (where patients can receive services only through a limited number of providers) in which physicians are employees of the HMO. The physicians see patients in the HMO's own facilities.
  - **Network Model HMO**—An HMO model that contracts with multiple physician groups to provide services to HMO members; may involve large single and multispecialty groups. The physician groups may provide services to both HMO and non-HMO plan participants.
  - **Individual Practice Association (IPA) HMO**—A type of health care provider company composed of a group of independent practicing physicians who maintain their own offices and band together for the purpose of contracting their services to HMOs. An IPA may contract with and provide services to both HMO and non-HMO plan participants.
- **Point-of-service (POS) plan**—A POS plan is an "HMO/PPO" hybrid; sometimes referred to as an "open-ended" HMO when offered by an HMO. POS plans resemble HMOs for in-network services. Services received outside of the network are usually reimbursed in a manner similar to conventional indemnity plans (e.g., provider reimbursement based on a fee schedule or usual, customary and reasonable charges).
- **Physician-hospital company (PHO)**—Alliances between physicians and hospitals to help providers attain market share, improve bargaining power and reduce administrative costs. These entities sell their services to managed care companies or directly to employers.

Managed care plans—Managed care plans generally provide comprehensive health care. Examples of managed care plans include:

- **Health maintenance companies (HMOs)**
- **Preferred provider companies (PPOs)**
- **Exclusive provider companies (EPOs)**
- **Point-of-service plans (POSs)**

Managed care provisions—Features within health plans that provide insurers with a way to manage the cost, use, and quality of health care services received by group members. Examples of managed care provisions include:

- **Preadmission certification**—An authorization for hospital admission given by a health care provider to a group member prior to their hospitalization. Failure to obtain a preadmission certification in non-emergency situations reduces or eliminates the health care provider's obligation to pay for services rendered.
- **Utilization review**—The process of reviewing the appropriateness and quality of care provided to patients. Utilization review may take place before, during, or after the services are rendered.
- **Preadmission testing**—A requirement designed to encourage patients to obtain necessary diagnostic services on an outpatient basis prior to non-emergency hospital admission. The testing is designed to reduce the length of a hospital stay.
- **Non-emergency weekend admission restriction**—A requirement that imposes limits on reimbursement to patients for non-emergency weekend hospital admissions.
- **Second surgical opinion**—A cost-management strategy that encourages or requires patients to obtain the opinion of another doctor after a physician has recommended that a non-emergency or elective surgery be performed. Programs may be voluntary or mandatory in that reimbursement is reduced or denied if the participant does not obtain the second opinion. Plans usually require that such opinions be obtained from board-certified specialists with no personal or financial interest in the outcome.

Maximum out-of-pocket expense—The maximum dollar amount a group member is required to pay out of pocket during a year. Until this maximum is met, the plan and group member shares in the cost of covered expenses. After the maximum is reached, the insurance carrier pays all covered expenses, often up to a lifetime maximum. (See "Maximum plan dollar limit.")

Maximum plan dollar limit—The maximum amount payable by the insurer for covered expenses for the insured and each covered dependent while covered under the health plan. Plans can have a yearly and/or a lifetime maximum dollar limit. The most typical of maximums is a lifetime amount of $1 million per individual.

Medical savings accounts (MSA)—Savings accounts designated for out-of-pocket medical expenses. In an MSA, employers and individuals are allowed to contribute to a savings account on a pre-tax basis and carry over the unused funds at the end of the year. One major difference between a Flexible Spending Account (FSA) and a Medical Savings Account (MSA) is the ability under an MSA to carry over the unused funds for use in a future year, instead of losing unused funds at the end of the year. Most MSAs allow unused balances and earnings to accumulate. Unlike FSAs, most MSAs are combined with a high deductible or catastrophic health insurance plan.

Minimum premium plan (MPP)—A plan where the employer and the insurer agree that the employer will be responsible for paying all claims up to an agreed-upon aggregate level, with the insurer responsible for the excess. The insurer usually is also responsible for processing claims and administrative services.

Multi-employer health plan—Generally, an employee health benefit plan maintained pursuant to a collective bargaining agreement that includes employees of two or more employers. These plans are also known as Taft-Hartley plans or jointly-administered plans. They are subject to federal but not state law (although states may regulate any insurance policies that they buy). They often self-insure.

Multiple Employer Welfare Arrangement (MEWA)—MEWA is a technical term under federal law that encompasses essentially any arrangement not maintained pursuant to a collective bargaining agreement (other than a state-licensed insurance company or HMO) that provides health insurance benefits to the employees of two or more private employers. Some MEWAs are sponsored by associations that are local, specific to a trade or industry, and exist for business purposes other than providing health insurance. Such MEWAs most often are regulated as employee health benefit plans under the Employee Retirement Income Security Act of 1974 (ERISA), although states generally also retain the right to regulate them, much the way states regulate insurance companies. They can be funded through tax-exempt trusts known as Voluntary Employees Beneficiary Associations (VEBAs) and they can and often do use these trusts to self-insure rather than to purchase insurance policies. Other MEWAs are sponsored by Chambers of Commerce or similar companies of relatively unrelated employers. These MEWAs are not considered to be health plans under ERISA. Instead, each participating employer's plan is regulated separately under ERISA. States are free to regulate the MEWAs themselves. These MEWAs tend to serve as vehicles for participating employers to buy insurance policies from state-licensed insurance companies or HMOs. They don't tend to self-insure.

Premium—Agreed upon fees paid for coverage of medical benefits for a defined benefit period. Premiums can be paid by employers, unions, employees, or shared by both the insured individual and the plan sponsor.

Premium equivalent—For self-insured plans, the cost per covered employee, or the amount the firm would expect to reflect the cost of claims paid, administrative costs, and stop-loss premiums.

Primary care physician (PCP)—A physician who serves as a group member's primary contact within the health plan. In a managed care plan, the primary care physician provides basic medical services, coordinates and, if required by the plan, authorizes referrals to specialists and hospitals.

Reinsurance—The acceptance by one or more insurers, called *reinsurers* or *assuming companies*, of a portion of the risk underwritten by another insurer that has contracted with an employer for the entire coverage.

Self-insured plan—A plan offered by employers who directly assume the major cost of health insurance for their employees. Some self-insured plans bear the entire risk. Other self-insured employers insure against large claims by purchasing stop-loss coverage. Some self-insured employers contract with insurance carriers or third party administrators for claims processing and other administrative services; other self-insured plans are self-administered. Minimum Premium Plans (MPP) are included in the self-insured health plan category. All types of plans (Conventional Indemnity, PPO, EPO, HMO, POS, and PHOs) can be financed on a self-insured basis. Employers may offer both self-insured and fully insured plans to their employees.

Stop-loss coverage—A form of reinsurance for self-insured employers that limits the amount the employers will have to pay for each person's health care (individual limit) or for the total expenses of the employer (group limit).

Third party administrator (TPA)—An individual or firm hired by an employer to handle claims processing, pay providers, and manage other functions related to the operation of health insurance. The TPA is not the policyholder or the insurer.

Types of Health Care Provider Arrangements
- **Exclusive providers**—Enrollees must go to providers associated with the plan for all non-emergency care in order for the costs to be covered.
- **Any providers**—Enrollees may go to providers of their choice with no cost incentives to use a particular subset of providers.
- **Mixture of providers**—Enrollees may go to any provider but there is a cost incentive to use a particular subset of providers.

Usual, customary, and reasonable (UCR) charges—Conventional indemnity plans operate based on usual, customary, and reasonable (UCR) charges. UCR charges mean that the charge is the provider's usual fee for a service that does not exceed the customary fee in that geographic area, and is reasonable based on the circumstances. Instead of UCR charges, PPO plans often operate based on a negotiated (fixed) schedule of fees that recognize charges for covered services up to a negotiated fixed dollar amount.

CHAPTER 11

DIFFERENT LAWS IN DIFFERENT STATES

Note: This chapter is excerpted from an article, "State labor legislation enacted in 2008" by John J. Fitzpatrick, Jr., James L. Perine, and Bridget Dutton in *Monthly Labor Review Online.* Excerpted with permission from the U.S. Bureau of Labor Statistics http://www.bls.gov/opub/mlr/2009/01/art1full.pdf. Several tables displaying information on State labor laws, including tables on current and historical minimum-wage rates and a table on State prevailing-wage laws, along with tables concerning child labor issues, are available on the Internet at the Employment Standards Administration's Web site, www.dol.gov/esa/programs/whd/state/ state.htm.[1]

I would refer to persons with disabilities as "persons with disabilities," however, this excerpt has been presented exactly as it was written, which is why there are references to "handicapped persons."

HR credible activists are encouraged to review all state employment laws and recommend those that do not exist in your own state to your employer as policy or to your state legislators as new law if you find they will improve employee health and well-being as well as employee and employer accountability towards improved and more functional workplace systems.

John J. Fitzpatrick, Jr., James L. Perine, and Bridget Dutton report in the *Monthly Labor Review Online*, January 2009, on State labor legislation enacted in 2008. The bills that were introduced and then enacted by the States were concerned with more than 30 categories of labor legislation that are tracked: agriculture, child labor, State departments of labor, employee discharge, drug and alcohol testing, equal employment opportunity, employment agency matters, employee leasing, family issues, garment activity, genetic testing, handicapped workers, hours worked, human trafficking, independent contractor issues, inmate labor, living wages, the minimum wage and tipped employees, miscellaneous or other categories, offsite work, overtime, plant closing and the displacement or replacement of workers, employers' preferences regarding employees, prevailing wages, right-to-work matters, time off from work, unfair labor practices, wages paid, whistleblowers, worker privacy, workplace security, and workplace violence.

The legislative areas of equal employment opportunity, immigration protections, the minimum wage, prevailing wages, time off, wages paid, and worker privacy were among the most active during the individual sessions of the State legislatures in 2008.

Equal employment opportunity. California now requires that all contractors and subcontractors engaged in construction provide equal opportunity for employment, without discrimination, under an expanded list of factors. The District of Columbia now requires employers to provide reasonable daily unpaid break periods and a sanitary location so that breast-feeding mothers are able to express milk for their children. The District also broadened the definition of "discrimination" by bringing within its scope the concept of a gender-related identity, appearance, expression, or behavior of an individual. Florida expanded the exemption regarding privacy of information contained in discrimination complaints from applying only to executive branch agencies to now include all State agencies and the times such data may become available to the public. The exemption applies until (1) a finding has been made relating to probable cause; (2) the complaint has become inactive; or (3) the complaint or other record is made part of the official record of any hearing or court proceeding. The Kansas Department of Labor is now permitted to establish the rules and regulations necessary to enforce State laws that prohibit employment discrimination relating to victims of domestic violence or sexual abuse. Louisiana added a section to its statutes that stipulates a 1-year prescriptive period for a discrimination case, but the period may be suspended if an administrative review or investigation of the claim conducted by the Federal Equal Employment Opportunity Commission on Human Rights is pending. In Maryland, if a civil action is filed no more than two years after the occurrence of an alleged act of discrimination, then the filing of the civil action shall serve to automatically terminate any proceeding before the State Human Relations Commission. New Jersey made it unlawful for employers to discriminate against employees because of religious practices.

Human trafficking. The California Civil Code was amended by the addition of a section that prohibits an employer from deducting from an employee's wages the employer's cost of helping the employee emigrate and transporting the employee to the United States. Hawaii statutes expanded the definition of "kidnapping" to include unlawfully obtaining the labor or services of a person, regardless of whether the action related to the collection of debt. Such activity by an employer results in the employer's committing extortion. Illinois enacted a new law that will assist victims of trafficking in the State by allowing Federal resources to be used to prosecute local offenders. The Maine Revised Statutes were amended to define a "human trafficking offense" as kidnapping or criminal restraint. Tennessee created the Class B felony "trafficking offense" for the activity wherein a person knowingly subjects or maintains another in labor servitude or sexual servitude. Utah statutes now state that an individual commits human trafficking for forced labor or forced sexual exploitation by recruiting, harboring, transporting, or obtaining a person through the use of force, fraud, or coercion by various means. Such action is considered a second-degree felony, except when it is judged to be aggravated in nature, in which case it is considered a first-degree felony.

Immigration protections. Arizona State or local agencies responsible for issuing licenses are now required to verify that the applicant is lawfully present in the United States. In addition, the State expanded the scope of the crime of identity theft to include knowingly accepting the identity of another person if, when hiring an employee, the person doing the hiring knowingly accepts any personal identifying information of another person from the prospective employee, knowing that the prospective employee is not the person identified, and if the person doing the hiring uses the said information for work authorization under Federal law. Prospective contractors in Colorado, prior to executing a contract for services with a State agency or a political subdivision thereof, shall certify that, at the time of certification, they are not knowingly employing or contracting with an illegal alien who will perform work under the contract for services. In addition, the Colorado Commission on Fire Protection Standards is required to implement a voluntary statewide certified volunteer firefighter identification program. The Minnesota Governor ordered the State to implement measures to ensure that all newly hired executive branch employees are legally eligible to work. Mississippi enacted the Mississippi Employment Protection Act, which requires employers in the State to hire only legal citizens or legal aliens of the United States. In South Carolina, legislation was enacted that requires every agency or political subdivision of the State to verify the lawful presence of any person 18 years or older who has applied for State or local public benefits or public employment. Utah now prohibits a public employer from entering into a contract with a contractor for the physical performance of services within the State, unless the contractor registers with, and participates in, the Status Verification System to verify the work eligibility status of the contractor's new employees who are employed within the State. Virginia now permits the State Corporation Commission to terminate the corporate existence of a corporation for actions of its officers and directors that constitute a pattern or practice of employing unauthorized aliens in the commonwealth.

Independent contractors. Connecticut established a joint employment commission, along with an advisory board that will advise the commission on employee misclassification in the construction industry within the State. In Idaho, key employees or key independent contractors may enter into written agreements or covenants that protect the employer's legitimate business interests and prohibit the key employee or key independent contractor from engaging in employment or a line of business that is in direct competition with the employer's business after termination of employment. Michigan has created an Interagency Task Force on Employee Misclassification as an advisory body responsible for examining and evaluating the existing employee misclassification enforcement mechanism in the State and for making recommendations for more efficient mechanisms. The Missouri attorney general is authorized to investigate any alleged or suspected violation of the law in which an employer knowingly misclassifies a worker and fails to claim that worker as an employee. In addition, the State attorney general may seek an injunction prohibiting an employer from engaging in such conduct, for which penalties assessed may reach $50,000. Utah has created the Independent Contractor Enforcement Council, which has been directed to design an independent-contractor database that may be accessed by one or more agencies, the attorney general, and the State Department of Public Safety. The database is to be used to identify when a person holds him- or herself out to be an independent contractor or when a person engages in the performance of work as an independent contractor who is not subject to the employer's control.

Minimum wage. Connecticut increased the amount of gratuities that it would recognize as part of the minimum fair wage for bartenders and others who are employed in the hotel and restaurant industry. In addition, the minimum wage in the State was increased to $8.00 per hour on January 1, 2009, and will increase to $8.25 per hour on January 1, 2010. Illinois camp counselors under the age of 18 and employed at a day camp are not subject to the State adult minimum wage if they are paid a stipend on a one-time or periodic basis and, for those who are minors, if their parent, guardian, or other custodian has consented in writing to the terms of payment before employment begins. With some exemptions, the Iowa minimum-wage requirements shall not apply to an enterprise whose annual gross volume of sales made or business done, exclusive of excise taxes at the retail level, which are separately stated, is less than $300,000. Maine increased its minimum hourly wage to $7.25 per hour on October 1, 2008. An additional increase, to $7.50 per hour, is scheduled for October 1, 2009. In an amendment to the New Mexico Minimum Wage Act, the definitions of "employer" and "employee" were changed to exclude State and political subdivisions from all parts of the Act except the section that sets the minimum wage. Illinois, Kentucky, Michigan, and West Virginia increased their required hourly minimum-wage rates on July 1, 2008. The Illinois rate was increased from $7.50 per hour to $7.75, Kentucky increased its rate from $5.85 per hour to $6.55, Michigan increased its required rate from $7.15 per hour to $7.40, and the West Virginia required rate was increased from $6.55 per hour to $7.25.

On July 24, 2008, the following jurisdictions increased their required minimum-wage rates:

Jurisdiction	Minimum wage	
	Old	New
District of Columbia	$7.00	$7.55
Idaho	5.85	6.55
Indiana	5.85	6.55
Maryland	6.15	6.55
Montana	6.25	6.55
Nebraska	5.85	6.55
North Carolina	6.15	6.55
North Dakota	5.85	6.55
Oklahoma	5.85	6.55
South Dakota	5.85	6.55
Texas	5.85	6.55
Utah	5.85	6.55
Virginia	5.85	6.55

On September 1, 2008, New Hampshire increased its required hourly minimum wage from $6.50 per hour to $7.25. Arizona, Colorado, Florida, Missouri, Montana, Ohio, Oregon, Vermont, and Washington increased their hourly required minimum wage rates on January 1, 2009, on the basis of language in previously passed legislation that contained required annual cost-of-living increases to be implemented in the State minimum wage.

Prevailing wages. California will continue to require a contractor or subcontractor charged with violating the laws regulating public-works contracts and the payment of prevailing wages to appear before a hearing officer for a hearing. After January 1, 2009, California won't require that the aforesaid hearing be held by an administrative law judge. Delaware has tied the prevailing wage in a trade or craft to the collectively bargained wage if the collectively bargained wage has prevailed for that trade or craft for two consecutive years. A revision of the Hawaii Revised Statutes authorizes the State Governor to suspend the prevailing wage on public projects during a national emergency declared by the President or Congress or during an emergency declared by the Governor. In addition, contractors who violate the prevailing wage on public contracts in the State by falsifying records or delaying or interfering with an investigation shall be suspended for a period of three years. New Jersey now requires that the prevailing-wage rate be paid to workers employed in the performance of any construction contract, including contracts for millwork fabrication under the authority of financial assistance by the State. New Jersey also redefined the term "construction of a public utility" to mean the construction, reconstruction, installation, demolition, restoration, or alteration of facilities of the public utility. The term shall not be construed to include operational work such as flagging, plowing snow, managing vegetation in and around utility rights-of-way, marking out boundaries on roads, performing janitorial services, surveying for landscaping leaks, performing meter work, and making miscellaneous repairs. New York amended State labor law and general municipal law in order to provide additional guarantees of payment of prevailing wages to workers of the State, despite misdemeanor violations committed by their employers. New York also amended its law so that employers who owe back wages on State government contracts are now guilty of misdemeanors or various classes of felonies, depending upon the total amount of back wages owed. Rhode Island now requires general contractors and subcontractors who perform work on any State public-works contract worth $1,000,000 or more to employ apprentices for the performance of the contract, while complying with the apprentice-to-journeyman ratio approved by the Apprenticeship Council of the State Department of Labor and Training.

Time off. Members of the Civil Air Patrol in Colorado are now permitted to take a leave of absence, during the period of a mission, for up to 15 days annually without loss of pay or other benefits. Persons in Connecticut shall be excused from jury service if, during the preceding 3 years, they appeared in court for jury service and weren't excused from such service. Such persons, however, may request to be summoned for jury service. The District of Columbia established various requirements for employers who employ various numbers of employees to provide a certain amount of leave time for certain amounts of hours worked. Employers in Florida are now permitted to grant an employee up to three working days of leave during a 12-month period if the employee or a family or household member of the employee is the victim of domestic violence or sexual abuse. Elected or appointed trustees of any fire protection district in Illinois are now entitled to absent themselves from work on the days and times of meetings of the board of trustees for the duration of the meeting and during any time necessary for traveling to and from the meeting. Iowa employers shall not discharge or take or fail to take action regarding an employee's promotion or proposed promotion, or penalize the employee in another manner, due to the service of the employee as a witness in a criminal proceeding or as a plaintiff, defendant, or witness in a civil proceeding. Employees in Nebraska acting as volunteer emergency responders shall make a reasonable effort to notify their employers that they may be absent from, or report late to, their place of employment. Employers in the State shall neither terminate nor take any other disciplinary action against any employee who is a voluntary emergency responder if such employee is absent or reports late to work because of responding to an emergency in his or her status as a voluntary emergency responder. Most New Jersey State government employees, along with employees of any county, municipality, school district, or other political sub-division, may not be laid off from their employment position if they have been on military leave of absence for active service in the Armed Forces of the United States in a time of war or emergency. Employers in New York are required, at their option, either to grant a 3-hour leave of absence every 12 months to an employee who seeks to donate blood or to allow their employees to donate blood during work hours at least two times per year, without using any accumulated leave time. Rhode Island employers of more than 50 employees are now required to provide up to 30 days of unpaid family military leave during the time Federal or State orders are in effect, as long as the employees meet certain requirements. The employee also must have exhausted all other types of leave, except for sick and disability leave. Employees in Vermont shall have the right to take unpaid leave from employment for the purpose of attending a town meeting, provided that they notify the employer at least 7 days prior to the date of the town meeting. In addition, employers in Vermont shall provide reasonable time, either compensated or uncompensated, throughout the day for employees who continue to express breast milk for a nursing child 3 years after the birth of the child. Employees of the State, county, city, or any other political subdivision of Washington shall be entitled to, and shall be granted, military leave of absence from such employment for a period not exceeding 21 days each year.

Wages paid. California has made it a misdemeanor for an employer to require an employee, as a condition of being paid, to execute a statement of the hours the employee may have worked during a pay period when the employer knows the statement to be false. Colorado established the following definition of "paycard": "an access device that employees use to receive their payroll funds from their employer." Employers must meet two conditions in order to utilize paycards. Persons in Florida who, because of financial hardship, cannot satisfy a civil penalty shall be allowed to satisfy the penalty by participating in community service and shall receive credit for their service at the hourly rate specified under the Federal Fair Labor Standards Act. Iowa law now states that, upon written request by an employee, an employer must send any wages due to the employee by mail. Employers in Maryland are required to give each employee, at the time of hiring, notice of the employee's rate of pay, the regular paydays set by the employer, and leave benefits. New Jersey law now states that when a contract between a principal and a sales representative to solicit orders is terminated, the commissions and other compensation earned as a result of the representative relationship, but remaining unpaid, shall become due and payable within 30 days of the date the contract is terminated or within 30 days of the date the commissions are due, whichever is later. Upon meeting certain requirements, employers in West Virginia are now permitted to pay the wages that are due employees via the utilization of a payroll card and a payroll card account.

Worker privacy. Connecticut expanded the list of public employees in the State whose residential addresses may not be released under the Freedom of Information Act. Colorado employers may no longer require, as a condition of employment, that employees not disclose their wages or require employees to sign a waiver or other document that purports to deny them the right to disclose information about their wages. Florida added a number of positions of employment to those categories, which are exempt from the State's public-records requirement. Among these positions are general and special magistrates, judges of compensation claims, administrative law judges of the Florida Division of Administrative Hearings, and child support enforcement-hearing officers. Florida also excluded the records and timesheets of employees who are victims of sexual violence from the State's public-records requirement. Legislation enacted in Hawaii now requires each State and county government agency to designate an agency employee to have policy and oversight responsibilities for the protection of personal information. Idaho employment security law was amended to provide that certain specified employment security information be exempt from disclosure, except that such information may be disclosed as necessary for the proper administration of employment security programs or, subject to certain restrictions and fees, may be made available to public officials for use in the performance of their official duties. Indiana expanded the types of public records that are exempt from public disclosure unless access to the records is specifically required by Federal or State statute or is ordered by a court under the rules of discovery. Maine expanded the protection provided for the personal-contact information of public employees; however, such protection is not extended to elected officials. Missouri prohibits employers from requiring personal identification microchips to be implanted into employees for any reason. New York employers may not publicly post or display an employee's Social Security number, visibly print a Social Security number in files with unrestricted access, or communicate an employee's personal identifying information to the general public. Tennessee now prohibits the disclosure of home addresses, phone numbers, dates of birth, Social Security numbers, and driver's license information of State and local government employees, including law enforcement officers and their family members. Utah amended the State Government Records Access and Management Act to add protected status to certain information if the information is properly classified by a government entity.

ARIZONA

Immigrant protections. The State Legal Workers Act was amended by modifying the crimes of (1) taking the identity of another person or entity and (2) trafficking in the identity of another person or entity. The Act, as amended, now requires any State or local agency issuing a license in the State to verify that the applicant is lawfully present in the United States. The Act also expanded the scope of the crime of identity theft to include knowingly accepting the identity of another person if, when hiring an employee, the person doing the hiring knowingly accepts any personal identifying information of another person from the prospective employee, knowing that the prospective employee is not the person identified, and if the person doing the hiring uses the said information for work authorization under Federal law. Accepting the identity of a person when one knows that the person is not the one identified is a Class 5 felony. The State Legal Workers Act also establishes the Voluntary Enhanced Employer Compliance Program, which allows employers to voluntarily comply with certain verification requirements in cooperation with the State attorney general's office. First violations shall subject the employer to a 3-year probationary period for the business location where the unauthorized alien performed work. For a second violation, the court shall order the appropriate agencies to permanently revoke all licenses held by the employer specific to the business where the unauthorized alien performed work. If the employer does not hold a license specific to the business location where the unauthorized alien performed work, but a license is necessary to operate the employer's business in general, the court shall order the appropriate agencies to permanently revoke all licenses that are held at the employer's primary place of business.

Minimum wage. As a result of previously enacted legislation in which the State minimum wage was indexed to inflation, the minimum wage in the State was increased to $7.25 per hour on January 1, 2009.

Miscellaneous. If an employer interviews a law enforcement or probation officer and reasonably believes that the interview could result in the dismissal, demotion, or suspension of the officer, the latter may request to have a representative present during the interview at no cost to the employer. Before the interview begins, the employer shall provide the officer with a written notice informing the officer of the specific nature of the investigation, of all known allegations of misconduct that are the reason for the interview, and of the officer's right to have a representative present. The employer may require the officer to submit to a polygraph examination if the officer makes a statement to the employer during the investigation that differs from other relevant information that is known to the employer and if reconciling that difference is necessary to complete the investigation. If a polygraph examination is administered, the employer or the person administering the examination shall make an audio recording of the complete procedure and provide a copy of the recording to the officer. The employer is not required to stop the interview to issue another notice for allegations based on information provided by the employee during the interview, nor is the employer required to disclose any fact to the employee or his or her representative that would impede the investigation. In any appeal of a disciplinary action (that is, a dismissal, demotion, or suspension for more than 24 hours) in which a single hearing officer or administrative law judge has been appointed to conduct the proceedings, the officer or the employer may request a different hearing official. In cases before the office of administrative hearings or when the employer is a county with a population of 250,000 or a city with a population of 65,000 or more, the first request for an appeal shall be granted. All other requests may be granted only upon showing that a fair and impartial hearing cannot be obtained due to the prejudice of the official who has been assigned. The burden of proof in an appeal of a disciplinary action by a law enforcement or probation officer shall be on the employer.

Worker privacy. Public bodies shall maintain all records that are reasonably necessary or appropriate to maintain an accurate knowledge of disciplinary actions involving public officers or other employees of the public body. The records shall be open to inspection and copying pursuant to State law, unless their inspection or disclosure is contrary to public law. The law does not require the disclosure of the home address, the home phone number, or a photograph of any person who is protected pursuant to State law. In any county, an eligible person may request that the general public be prohibited from accessing certain information maintained by the county recorder, county treasurer, or county assessor, including (1) the unique identifier and the recording date contained in indexes of recorded instruments maintained by the county recorder and (2) the voting precinct number, residential address, and phone number of the requestor. An eligible person is a peace officer, a justice, a judge, a commissioner, a public defender, a prosecutor, a code enforcement officer, an adult or juvenile corrections officer, a corrections support staff member, a probation officer, a member of the Board of Executive Clemency, a law enforcement support staff member, a National Guard member who is acting in support of a law enforcement agency, a person who is protected under an order of protection or an injunction against harassment, a firefighter assigned to the State Center in the State Department of Public Safety, or a victim of domestic violence or stalking who is protected under an order of protection or an injunction against harassment. The State Revised Statutes now require the county recorder to notify certain persons six months prior to the expiration of a court-ordered redaction of their personal information. The statutes also allow the Anti-Racketeering Revolving Fund to be used for the payment of relocation expenses of any law enforcement officer who is a victim of a bona fide threat.

CALIFORNIA

Equal employment opportunity. The State may direct a local agency to require that all contractors and subcontractors engaged in construction provide equal opportunity for employment, without discrimination, under an expanded list of factors that now covers marital status, race, national origin, age, sex, sexual orientation, color, medical condition, religious creed, ancestry, mental disability, and physical disability.

Human trafficking. The State Civil Code and the State Penal Code were amended by the addition of a section to each that relates to human trafficking. The new civil law prohibits an employer from deducting from an employee's wages the employer's cost of helping the employee emigrate and transporting the employee to the United States. Because the existing penal law provides jurisdiction over certain crimes committed in more than one county, this new legislation requires a local prosecutor to present evidence to the court and requires the court to hold a hearing to consider whether a matter involving human trafficking in multiple jurisdictions should proceed in the county of filing or whether one or more counts should be severed. Charges alleging multiple violations that involve the same victim or victims in multiple territorial jurisdictions shall be subject to judicial review to determine the location and complexity of the likely evidence, to identify where the majority of the offenses occurred, and to consider the convenience of, or hardship on, the victims and witnesses.

Overtime. The State has extended the exemption from overtime pay requirements under State law to computer professionals who earn no less than $75,000 per year for full-time employment and are paid at least once per month in an amount no less than $6,250 per month.

Plant closing. Under existing law, the State Department of Public Health is responsible for licensing and regulating health facilities, including hospitals, and requires a hospital that is planning to reduce or eliminate emergency medical services to notify various entities at least 90 days before it takes that action. Legislation was enacted that changes the required notification period to 30 days prior to closing a general acute-care or psychiatric hospital or relocating the provision of a supplemental service to a different campus. Notification should be made to the public and the applicable administering department. The facility shall provide public notice of the proposed closure, including a notice posted at the entrance to all affected facilities, and shall also notify the board of supervisors of the county in which the health facility is located. In addition, an impact statement reflecting the changes in the delivery of care to the community must (1) specify how the elimination of services will be met by other existing agencies and (2) describe the three nearest available comparable services in the community.

Prevailing wages. Under existing law, the State labor commissioner is required to issue civil wage and penalty assessments to a contractor, a subcontractor, or both if, after an investigation, it is determined that the contractor or subcontractor violated the laws regulating public-works contracts and the payment of prevailing wages. The affected contractor can obtain a review of a civil wage and penalty assessment by transmitting a written request for a hearing to the office of the State labor commissioner within 60 days after receiving the assessment. A hearing officer or an administrative law judge must then commence a hearing within 90 days of receipt of the request. This legislation continues to require a hearing officer to hold the hearings, but, after January 1, 2009, does not require that the hearing officer be an administrative law judge. Further, the contractor or subcontractor may deposit the full amount of the assessment with the State Department of Industrial Relations, for that agency to hold in escrow pending review by the office of the labor commissioner. The director of the Department of Industrial Relations is authorized to waive payment of liquidated damages, or any portion thereof, if the contractor demonstrates that there were substantial grounds for its appeal.

Wages paid. The State Labor Code was amended to require that employees of temporary-service employers be paid weekly or daily wages if an employee is assigned to a client. The code does not apply to employees who are assigned to a client for more than 90 consecutive days, unless the employer pays the employee weekly. The code applies civil and criminal penalties of $100 for an initial violation and $200, plus 25 percent of the amount unlawfully withheld, for each subsequent violation. An employer who fails to pay any wages of an employee who is discharged or who has quit the company will be required to continue to pay the regular wages of that employee until action is commenced as a penalty or for no more than 30 days. Employees who refuse to receive payment, including any penalty accrued, won't be entitled to receive any benefits under the bill. Salaries of executive, administrative, and professional employees of employers covered by the Fair Labor Standards Act may be paid once a month on or before the 26th day of the month during which the labor was performed if the entire month's salaries, including the unearned portion between the date of payment and the last day of the month, are paid at that time. Employees covered by collective-bargaining agreements will be paid according to their specified pay arrangements. It shall be considered a misdemeanor for an employer to require an employee, as a condition of being paid, to execute a statement of the hours the employee may have worked during a pay period when the employer knows the statement to be false. This statement, called an *execution of release*, is a way for the employer to have a record of paying the employee in advance for work not yet actually done. An employer shall not require any such execution of release unless the wages have been paid. A violation of this law shall render the execution of release null and void between the employer and the employee.

Agriculture. The State created the Non-immigrant Agricultural Seasonal Worker Pilot Program in the State Department of Labor and Employment in order to expedite the Federal H-2A visa certification process so that eligible workers might legally come to Colorado to meet the needs of State farmers and ranchers. The directors of three State agencies (the commissioner of the State Department of Agriculture, the director of the State Department of Labor and Employment, and the director of the State Governor's Office of Economic Development and International Trade) are required to seek agreements between the State and foreign countries to assist in the recruitment and selection of eligible H-2A workers. The State Department of Labor and Employment is authorized to establish offices in foreign countries and retain local agents to aid in prospective employees' application processes, medical screening, and travel, as well as in the documentation of employee returns to their countries of origin. The program is limited to 1,000 employees the first year, with increases of 1,000 employees annually for five years. Employers and employees each have multiple requirements concerning pay, transportation, housing, working conditions, meals, minimum hours of work, background checks, identity cards, withholding of wages, and employees' return to their country of origin that must be met in order to participate in the program. Citizenship and Immigration Services, to establish a timely, efficient, and effective process for incorporating workers into the State Non-immigrant Agricultural Seasonal Worker Pilot Program and guiding them through H-2A visa certification.

Employee leasing. The State statutes governing employee-leasing companies that have ongoing relationships with employers at the sites at which the leased employees work were amended. Such companies are now required to become annually certified with the State Department of Labor and Employment for a fee not to exceed $500 per year. Each leasing company shall pay wages and collect, report, and pay all payroll-related taxes from its own accounts for all covered employees. The executive director of the department is authorized to take disciplinary action against leasing companies that violate the State statutes regarding required actions of such companies. The disciplinary action taken may include penalties such as probation, financial penalties, and revocation of certification.

Disabled employees. Legislation was enacted that established an income tax credit for taxpayers who hire individuals with a developmental disability. The credit is to be awarded for qualified employees first hired on or after January 1, 2009, and is applicable for income years 2009 through 2011 only. A qualified employee must be (1) a person with a developmental disability, (2) employed at a workplace located in one of seven designated State counties, and (3) compensated in accordance with applicable minimum-wage laws.

The income tax credit shall equal 50 percent of gross wages paid to the employee in the first three months of employment and 30 percent of gross wages paid in the subsequent nine months.

Immigrant protections. The State statute concerning requirements relating to public contracts for services was amended. Prior to executing a contract for services with a State agency or a political subdivision thereof, prospective contractors shall certify that, (1) at the time of certification, they are not knowingly employing or contracting with an illegal alien who will perform work under the contract for services and (2) they will participate in the e-verify program, jointly administered by the U.S. Department of Homeland Security and the Social Security Administration, or in the State Department of Labor and Employment's employee verification program, in order to confirm the eligibility of all of their newly hired employees to perform work under the contract for services. In addition, prospective contractors shall include a provision stating that they have confirmed the eligibility of all of their newly hired employees to perform work under the contract for services through participation in either the e-verify program or the department program.

Minimum wage. Because of previously enacted legislation in which the State minimum wage was indexed to inflation, the minimum wage in the State was increased to $7.28 per hour on January 1, 2009.

Time off. The State Revised Statutes were amended to allow a public or private employee who is a member of the Civil Air Patrol and is called for duty in a patrol mission to take a leave of absence during the period of the mission, for up to 15 days annually, without loss of pay or other benefits. To obtain this leave, the member is required to return to his or her job immediately after being relieved of duty in the mission. After serving, the member is allowed to return to the same job position in the same location. An employer shall not discriminate against or discharge from employment any member of the Civil Air Patrol because of such membership and shall not hinder a member or prevent a member from performing his or her duty during any Civil Air Patrol mission for which the member is entitled to leave under State law. If an employer violates the provisions of the law, the member is allowed to bring a civil action for damages, equitable relief, or both. In such action, the court shall award reasonable attorneys' fees and costs to the prevailing party. Employers are not required to provide this leave when doing so would result in more than 20 percent of the employer's employees being on leave on any workday. In addition, employers are not required to provide such leave for any employee designated as an essential employee, defined as an employee whom the employer deems to be essential to the employer's daily enterprise and whose absence would likely cause the employer to suffer economic injury.

Wages paid. As the result of an amendment to the State Revised Statutes, the definition of "paycard" was established and employers may now deposit an employee's wages on a paycard as long as certain conditions are met. The term "paycard" is defined as an access device that an employee uses to receive his or her payroll funds from the employer. In order to be allowed to utilize paycards, the employer must (1) provide the employee free access to the entire amount of the net pay at least once per pay period and (2) permit the employee to choose other means for payment of wages as authorized by other sections of the State Revised Statutes.

Worker privacy. The State Revised Statute prohibiting action against an employee for sharing wage information was amended. It shall now be a discriminatory or unfair employment practice, unless otherwise permitted by Federal law, for an employer to discharge, discipline, discriminate against, coerce, intimidate, threaten, or interfere with any employee because the employee inquired about, disclosed, compared, or otherwise discussed his or her wages. It is also prohibited for an employer to require, as a condition of employment, that an employee not disclose his or her wages or that the employee sign a waiver or other document that purports to deny the employee the right to disclose his or her wages. These prohibitions don't apply to employers who are exempt from the provisions of the National Labor Relations Act.

Child labor. The State removed the sunset provision pertaining to conditions under which a 15-year-old minor can be employed in a mercantile establishment. Employers continue to be exempt from any fines for employing 15-year-olds after the September 30, 2007, sunset, provided that such employment is (1) limited to periods during which school is not in session for five or more consecutive days, except that any such minor employed in a retail food store may work on any Saturday during the year; (2) for not more than 40 hours in any week; (3) for not more than eight hours in any day; and (4) between the hours of 7:00 a.m. and 7:00 p.m., except that from July 1 to the first Monday in September in any year, any such minor may be employed until 9:00 p.m.

Labor department. The State Department of Labor and Employment, in its quarterly electronic publication distributed to employers, shall, at a minimum, notify every employer of the Federal law against hiring or continuing to employ an unauthorized alien. In addition, the notice shall include information about the e-verify program jointly administered by the U.S. Department of Homeland Security and the Social Security Administration. Notifications are required on a quarterly basis for two years and twice per year thereafter.

Employment agencies. State Public Act No. 08-105 was amended to better codify (1) the criteria and responsibilities for professional employer companies, (2) the steps for becoming registered within the State, and (3) all appropriate fiduciary responsibilities for the company. In addition, the State legislature established a joint enforcement commission on employee misclassification. The commission members will consist of the State commissioners for labor, revenue services, and workers' compensation; the attorney general; and the chief State's attorney—or their designees. The commission shall meet no fewer than five times each year and shall review the problem of employee misclassification by employers for the purpose of avoiding the employer's obligations under State and Federal labor, employment, and tax laws. The commission shall coordinate the civil prosecution of violations of State and Federal laws as a result of employee misclassification and shall report any suspected violation to the Chief State's Attorney or the State's Attorney serving the district in which the violation is alleged to have occurred. The commission shall report to the Governor and the relevant joint standing committee of the State General Assembly.

Independent contractor. Legislation was enacted that established a joint enforcement commission on employee misclassification and the State Employee Misclassification Advisory Board. Civil prosecution will be coordinated by the commission in the event that an employer is found to have violated State and Federal laws as a result of employee misclassification. Beginning in 2010, the commission is required to produce a yearly report that summarizes its actions for the preceding calendar year and includes recommendations for administrative or legislative action. The board will advise the commission on employee misclassification in the construction industry in the state, and the members of the board will consist of management and labor representatives in the construction industry.

Minimum wage. The hourly minimum-wage rate of pay required under state law was increased to $8.00 per hour, effective January 1, 2009. The rate on January 1, 2010, will again increase, this time to $8.25 per hour. State law requires that whenever the highest Federal minimum wage is increased, the State minimum wage shall be increased to the amount of the Federal minimum wage plus one-half of 1 percent more than said Federal rate, rounded to the nearest whole cent, effective on the same date as the increase in the highest Federal minimum wage. The rates for learners, beginners, and persons under 18 years shall be no less than 85 percent of the minimum fair wage for the first 200 hours of such employment and equal to the minimum wage thereafter, except for institutional training programs specifically exempted by the State commissioner of labor. On January 1, 2009, the State increased the amount of all gratuities that it shall recognize as part of the minimum fair wage. From that date, the State shall recognize gratuities in an amount (1) equal to 31 percent of the minimum fair wage per hour for persons, other than bartenders, who are employed in the hotel and restaurant industry, including a hotel restaurant, and who customarily and regularly receive gratuities; (2) equal to 11 percent of the minimum fair wage per hour for persons employed as bartenders who customarily and regularly receive gratuities, and (3) not to exceed 35 cents per hour in any other industry.

Time off. A person shall be excused from jury service if, during the preceding 3 jury years, such person appeared in court for jury service and was not excused from serving, except that the person may request to be summoned for jury service during such a 3-jury-year period in the same manner as persons are summoned who are not excused from jury service. Such request may be made at any time, written to the jury administrator. Any juror-employee who has served eight hours of jury duty in any one day shall be deemed to have worked a legal day's work, and an employer shall not require the juror-employee to work in excess of eight hours. Any employer who fails to compensate a juror-employee pursuant to the State General Statutes and who has not been excused from such duty to compensate the juror-employee pursuant to the 2008 supplement to the General Statutes shall be liable to the juror-employee for damages.

Wages paid. Legislation was enacted that amended the acceptable reasons for which an employer can withhold or divert any portion of an employee's wages by adding instances in which deductions are made for contributions attributable to automatic enrollment, as defined as a provision of an employee retirement plan, or any subsequent corresponding internal revenue code of the United States, as from time to time amended, as established by the employer. Employers that provide automatic enrollment are relieved of liability for the investment decisions they make on behalf of participating employees, provided that (1) the investment plan allows the participating employee at least quarterly opportunities to select among investment alternatives available under the plan that are to serve as the employee's contribution to the plan; (2) the employee is given (a) notice of the investment decisions that will be made in the absence of the employee's direction, (b) a description of all the investment alternatives available under the plan, and (c) a brief description of procedures available for the employee to change investments; and (3) the employee is given at least annual notice of the actual investments made on behalf of the employee under the company's automatic contribution arrangement. The employer's relief from liability extends to any other official of the plan who actually makes the investment decisions on behalf of participating employees under the aforesaid automatic contribution arrangement.

Worker privacy. The list of public employees in the State whose residential addresses may not be released under the Freedom of Information Act was amended. The residential address of an employee of the State Department of Mental Health and Addiction Services who provides direct care to patients was added to the list.

DELAWARE

Prevailing wage. The Division of Industrial Affairs of the State Department of Labor shall establish the prevailing wage for each craft or class of laborers and mechanics at the same rates established in collective-bargaining agreements between labor companies and their employers that govern work for those classes of laborers and mechanics for the county where the public-works contract will be performed if that particular labor company's collective-bargaining rate prevailed and the said labor company participated in the prevailing-wage survey for that particular trade or craft in that particular county for two consecutive years. The agreed-upon rate of pay will become the prevailing wage for a period of five years, and the raise will be determined on the basis of the collective-bargaining agreement rate at the time the survey is conducted for that craft, county, and year. If the prevailing wage cannot be reasonably and fairly determined in any locality because no agreements exist or the rate has not prevailed for two consecutive years, the Department shall use the rate established by the annual prevailing-wage survey. There will be a one-time challenge of the prevailing-wage rate per cycle as stated in departmental regulations.

DISTRICT OF COLUMBIA

Equal employment opportunity. The District's Human Rights Act of 1977 was amended (1) to prohibit discrimination against breast-feeding women, (2) to ensure a woman's right to breast-feed in any location, public or private, where she has the right to be with her child, (3) to require employers to provide reasonable daily unpaid break periods and a sanitary location so that breast-feeding mothers are able to express breast milk for their children, and (4) to require the District Department of Health to monitor both breast-feeding rates in the District and the number and nature of complaints received by the District Office of Human Rights regarding violations of the Act. The Prohibition of Discrimination on the Basis of Gender Identity and Expression Amendment Act of 2008 is an attempt by the District government to broaden the definitions by which discrimination is practiced. The District Office of Human Rights Establishment Act of 1999 was amended by striking the phrase "sexual orientation" and substituting the phrase "sexual orientation, gender identity or expression" in its place, thereby bringing into the arena the concept of "a gender-related identity, appearance, expression, or behavior of an individual, regardless of the individual's assigned sex at birth." As part of this broader definition as well, the Office of Human Rights uses the term "transgender" to refer to any individual whose identity or behavior differs from stereotypical or traditional gender expectations. The term now refers to transsexual individuals, cross-dressers, androgynous individuals, and others whose appearance or characteristics are perceived to be gender atypical. These newly expanded definitions shall be applicable in such areas as employment, renting or leasing of housing and commercial space, public accommodations, educational institutions, and agencies of the District government and its contractors.

Minimum wage. As a result of requirements that were included in previously enacted legislation, the minimum wage in the District was increased to $7.55 per hour on July 24, 2008.

Time off. An employer with 100 or more full-time-equivalent employees shall provide not less than 1 hour of paid leave for every 37 hours worked, not to exceed seven days per calendar year; an employer with at least 25, but not more than 99, full-time-equivalent employees shall provide 1 hour of paid leave for every 43 hours, not to exceed five days per calendar year; and an employer with 24 or fewer full-time-equivalent employees shall provide not less than 1 hour for every 87 hours worked, not to exceed three days per calendar year. Employees who are exempt from overtime payment under the Fair Labor Standards Act shall not accrue leave for hours worked beyond a 40-hour workweek. Paid leave shall accrue in accordance with the employer's established pay period, at the beginning of the employee's employment, and the employee may begin to access paid leave after 90 days of service. An employee's unused paid leave accrued during a 12-month period shall carry over annually, but the employee shall not be reimbursed for this leave upon termination or resignation. An employee who is discharged after the completion of a 90-day probationary period and is rehired within 12 months may access paid leave immediately. The employee shall make a reasonable effort to schedule paid leave in a manner that does not unduly disrupt the employer's operations. Paid leave requests, if foreseeable, should be provided at least ten days in advance or as early as possible, with reasonable certification, including a signed document by a health care provider, a police report, or a court order by a witness advocate or domestic violence counselor. This act does not prevent an employer from adopting or retaining a paid-leave policy more generous than the one herein required. Further, an employer shall in no manner discharge or discriminate against an employee who (1) opposes any practice by the employer pursuant or related to this act, (2) files a complaint, (3) facilitates the institution of a proceeding, or (4) gives any information or testimony in connection with a relevant inquiry.

Wages paid. The Minimum Wage Act Revision Act of 1992 was amended to establish minimum-compensation requirements for District security officers working in the metropolitan area. An employer shall pay a security officer working in an office building in the metropolitan area wages (or any combination of wages and benefits) that are no less than the combined amount of the minimum-wage and fringe-benefit rate for the Guard 1 position classification established by the U.S. Secretary of Labor pursuant to the Service Contract Act of 1965. The Minimum Wage Act Revision Act shall take effect following approval by the mayor after a 30-day period of congressional review pursuant to the State Home Rule Act and publication in the municipal register. (In the event of a veto by the mayor, the act shall take effect following an override of the veto by the council.)

FLORIDA

Minimum wage. As a result of legislation that was previously enacted in which the State minimum wage was indexed to inflation, the State minimum wage was increased to $7.21 on January 1, 2009.

Time off. The State permits an employer to grant an employee up to 3 working days of leave during a 12-month period if the employee or a family or household member is the victim of domestic or sexual violence. It will be at the discretion of the employer whether the leave will be with or without pay. Employees must use the leave from work to, among other things, (1) obtain medical care or mental health counseling; (2) seek legal assistance in addressing issues arising from the act of domestic or sexual violence; or (3) make the employees' homes secure from the perpetrator. Except in cases of imminent danger, employees must provide appropriate advance leave notice as required by the employer's policy, along with documentation of the act of domestic or sexual abuse. All personal identifying information documenting domestic or sexual violence in the workplace will be deemed confidential.

Wages paid. The maximum authorized amount of day-labor contracts was increased in the State's school districts to $280,000, an amount to be adjusted annually by the Consumer Price Index. The contracts affected include those for construction, renovation, remodeling, or maintenance of existing facilities. If a person has been ordered to pay a civil penalty for a noncriminal traffic infraction and the individual is unable to comply with the court's order due to certifiable financial hardship, the court shall allow the person to satisfy the civil penalty by participating in community service until the penalty is paid. The person shall then receive credit for the penalty at the hourly credit rate specified under the Federal Fair Labor Standards Act, and each hour of community service shall reduce the civil penalty by that amount. The specified hourly credit rate is the wage rate then in effect under the Act and that an employer subject to the Act's provisions must pay per hour to each employee. If the individual has a trade or profession for which there is a need, the specified credit rate for each hour of community service shall be the average prevailing wage for that particular trade or profession. The community service agency shall record the number of hours worked and the date the service is completed and shall submit the information to the clerk of the court on appropriate agency letterhead bearing an authorized signature. The letter shall certify that the hours completed by the individual equal the amount of the civil penalty and that the debt is paid in full. The legislation took effect on July 1, 2008.

Worker privacy. The home addresses, phone numbers, and addresses of places of employment of the spouses and children, and of the schools and daycare facilities attended by the children, of active or former law enforcement personnel, including correctional officers and correctional probation officers, personnel of the State Department of Children and Family Services who are involved in investigations, personnel of the State Department of Health whose duties support investigations, and personnel of the State Department of Revenue or of local governments whose responsibilities include revenue collection and enforcement, are currently exempt from the State's public-records requirements. Added to this exempt category are the following State employment positions: general and special magistrates, judges of compensation claims, administrative law judges of the Division of Administrative Hearings, and child support enforcement hearing officers. It is feared that the release of such identifying information might place these individuals and their family members in danger of physical and emotional harm from disgruntled criminal defendants or litigants. Therefore, the harm that might result from the release of the information outweighs any public benefit that could be derived from disclosure of the information. The State amended statutes concerning the expansion of exemptions from public-records requirements for records and timesheets of employees who are victims of sexual violence. The bill, which would extend future legislative review and repeal, revises a statement expressing the public necessity to make sure that an employee's request for leave is temporarily confidential and exempt from exposure until one year after the leave has been taken.

Worker privacy. All complaints, and other records in the custody of any agency regarding a complaint, of discrimination relating to race, color, religion, sex, national origin, age, handicap, or marital status in connection with hiring practices, position classifications, salary, benefits, discipline, discharge, employee performance, evaluation, or any related activities shall be confidential. Any Federal or State agency that is authorized to have access to such complaints or records shall be granted access in the furtherance of such agency's statutory duties. If the victim chooses not to file a complaint, he or she may request that records of the complaint remain confidential and exempt from relevant public-record requirements. The request is upheld until a finding is made relating to probable cause, the investigation of the complaint becomes inactive, or the complaint or other record is made part of the official record of any hearing or court proceeding. This exemption is necessary because the release of such information could be defamatory to an individual under investigation or could cause unwarranted damage to the good name or reputation of the complainant. Further, exclusion of the records is a public necessity in order that the investigation not be significantly impaired and that a secure environment be created for the conduct of the investigation.

GEORGIA

Unfair labor practice. Except for exclusions provided by State Code, no private or public employer, including the State and its subdivisions, shall condition employment upon any agreement by a prospective employee that prohibits the employee from entering the parking lot and from access thereto when the employee's privately owned motor vehicle contains a firearm that is locked out of sight within the trunk, glove box, or other enclosed compartment or area within such privately owned motor vehicle, provided that the employee possesses a State firearms license. In addition, except for exclusions provided by State Code, no private or public employer, including the State and its subdivisions, shall establish, maintain, or enforce any policy or rule that has the effect of allowing such employer or its agents to search any locked, privately owned vehicles of employees or invited guests on the employer's parking lot or to gain access thereto.

HAWAII

Human trafficking. The State Revised Statutes were amended in order to expand the definition of "kidnapping" to include unlawfully obtaining a person's labor or services, regardless of whether it is or is not related to the collection of debt. The statutes now specify that a person commits "extortion" if the person obtains, or exerts control over, the property, labor, or services of another with the intent to deprive that other person of property, labor, or services by threatening, by word or conduct, to destroy, conceal, remove, confiscate, or possess any actual or purported passport, any other actual or purported government identification document, or any immigration document of another person. Further, the legislation explains that a person commits the offense of promoting prostitution in the first degree if the person knowingly advances prostitution by compelling a person by force, threat, or intimidation to engage in prostitution, by profiting from such coercive conduct, or by advancing or profiting from prostitution of a person younger than 18 years.

Inmate labor. The State House of Representatives requested that the State Department of Land and Natural Resources, along with the State Department of Public Safety, develop a plan to establish a statewide Inmate Conservation Corps Pilot Program. The purpose of the program is to perform resource conservation projects, including forest fire prevention, forest and watershed management, maintenance of recreation areas, fish and game management, soil conservation, forest and watershed revegetation, preventive maintenance or reconstruction of levees, and any other work necessary to prevent flood damage.

Prevailing wage. The revision of the State Revised Statutes resulted in the state Governor's being authorized to suspend the prevailing wage on public projects during a national emergency declared by the President or Congress or a state of emergency declared by the Governor. Under State law, contractors can be suspended for failure to pay back wages and penalties. For a first or second violation in this area, if a person or firm fails to pay wages found due, any penalty assessed, or both, the person or firm shall be immediately suspended from doing any work on any public work of a governmental contracting agency until all wages and penalties are paid in full. For a third violation, the contractor shall immediately be suspended from doing any work on any public work of a governmental contracting agency for a mandatory 3-year period. If, after the 3-year suspension (also mandated for falsification of records or delay or interference with an investigation), wages or penalties remain unpaid, the suspension shall remain in force until payment in full is made. As amended, the law now authorizes the State Department of Labor and Industrial Relations to immediately suspend and begin debarment proceedings against contractors that purposely defraud the State on a public-works project or that delay or interfere with the department in determining whether there has been a violation of the prevailing-wage law.

Worker privacy. Legislation was passed that authorizes the State to protect the security of personal information collected and maintained by State and county government agencies by designating an agency employee to have policy and oversight responsibilities for the protection of personal information. The designated employee will (1) ensure and coordinate agency compliance; (2) assist individuals who have identity theft and privacy-related concerns; (3) provide agency staff with education and information on privacy and security issues; (4) coordinate with Federal, State, and county law enforcement agencies on identity theft investigations; and (5) recommend policies and practices to protect individual privacy rights relating to individuals' personal information. The legislation establishes an information privacy and security council within the Department of Accounting and General Services. The council will identify best practices to assist government agencies in improving security and privacy programs relating to personal information. Every State government agency maintaining one or more personal information systems will be required to submit an annual report to the council on the existence and character of each personal information system added or eliminated since that agency's previous annual report. Government agencies must develop a plan to protect and redact personal information—for example, Social Security numbers—contained in existing hardcopy documents prior to making the documents available for public inspection. State and county government agencies that have primary responsibility for HR functions shall develop and distribute, to the appropriate agencies, written guidelines detailing recommended practices to minimize unauthorized access to personal information and personal information systems relating to personal recruitment, background checks, testing, employee retirement and health benefits, and time-reporting and payroll issues. Notification policies dealing with security breaches also shall be developed by State agencies.

IDAHO

Independent contractor. Key employees and key independent contractors may enter into written agreements or covenants that protect the employer's legitimate business interests and prohibit the employee or independent contractor from engaging in employment or a line of business that is in direct competition with the employer's business after termination of employment. The agreement or covenant shall be enforceable if it is reasonable as to its duration, geographical area, type of employment, or line of business and does not impose a greater restraint than is reasonably necessary to protect the employer's legitimate business interests.

Minimum wage. As a result of requirements that were included in previously enacted legislation, the State minimum wage was increased to $6.55 per hour on July 24, 2008.

Miscellaneous. Both houses of the State legislature resolved by memorandum to urge that the U.S. Congress take action to help stop children and employees from accessing Internet pornography and that legislation be enacted to facilitate a technology-based solution that allows parents and employers to subscribe to Internet access services that exclude adult content.

Worker privacy. The State employment security law was amended to provide that certain specified employment security information is exempt from disclosure, except that such information may be disclosed as is necessary for the proper administration of employment security programs or may be made available to public officials for use in the performance of their official duties, both conditions subject to such restrictions and fees as determined by the director of employment security. If a determination finds that a person has made any unauthorized disclosure of employment security information in violation of State law or code, a penalty of $500 for each act of unauthorized disclosure shall be assessed against the person.

ILLINOIS

Genetic testing. Genetic testing and information derived from genetic testing are confidential and privileged and may be released only to the individual being tested or to persons specifically authorized by that individual to receive the information. The information may not be admissible as evidence or discoverable in any action of any kind in any court or before any tribunal, board, or agency. Though confidential, the information may be disclosed for purposes of criminal investigation or prosecution and is admissible in any actions alleging a violation of this legislation. An employer shall not directly or indirectly solicit, request, require, or purchase genetic-testing information from a person or from a family member as a condition of employment, pre-employment, labor company membership, or licensure; nor shall the employer terminate the employment of an individual as a result of genetic testing. Neither can genetic information be used in furtherance of a workplace wellness program benefiting employees, unless health or testing services are offered by the employer; only the employee or family member may receive testing services, and any individually identifiable information is available only for purposes of the service provided. Genetic testing may be used for genetic monitoring of the biological effects of toxic substances in the workplace. Any person aggrieved by a violation of this legislation shall have a right of action against any party for liquidated damages of $2,500 or actual damages, whichever is greater. In addition, any party that intentionally or recklessly violates this act can be liable for damages of up to $15,000 or actual damages, whichever is greater.

Human trafficking. The U.S. House of Representatives passed a legal framework for fighting trafficking by combining and streamlining efforts against the international and domestic sale of human beings. The State legislature has adopted a resolution supporting the adoption of this Federal legislation, known as HR 3887, and urging the U.S. Senators from the State to support the legislation as passed, without modification, and to support Federal anti-trafficking legislation in the U.S. Senate. The purpose of the resolution is to expand Federal anti-trafficking legislation so that it more accurately represents the experiences of victims in the State and expands the ability of Federal prosecutors to bring domestic traffickers to justice. The State General Assembly implemented Public Act 94–0009, the Trafficking of Persons and Involuntary Servitude Act, a powerful first step in the fight against sex trafficking. Many local traffickers are not held accountable and continue to prey upon victims due to a lack of resources for researching, uncovering, and prosecuting domestic trafficking cases. The new law will assist victims in the State by allowing Federal resources to be used to prosecute local offenders.

Independent contractor. The State now excludes an employee, independent contractor, or other agent of a telecommunications carrier, communications cooperative, or mobile radio service from its definition of "electronic and information technology worker."

Minimum wage. The minimum-wage law in the State was amended to prohibit a camp counselor under the age of 18 and employed at a day camp from being subject to the adult minimum wage if the camp counselor is paid a stipend on a one-time or periodic basis and, for a camp counselor who is a minor, if the minor's parent, guardian, or other custodian has consented in writing to the terms of payment before the employment begins. In the past, the State stipulated that a camp counselor who resided on the premises of a seasonal camp was subject to the adult minimum wage if the camp counselor worked more than 40 hours per week and received a total weekly salary of no less than the adult minimum wage for a 40-hour workweek. Under the law, counselors who worked less than 40 hours per week were paid the minimum hourly wage for each hour worked. Because of requirements included in previously enacted legislation, the State minimum wage was increased to $7.75 on July 1, 2008.

Time off. The legislation that amended the State Fire Protection District Act provides that elected or appointed trustees of a fire protection district will be entitled to absent themselves from work on the days and times of meetings of the board of trustees for the period of the meeting and for any time required to travel to and from the meeting. Employers can neither penalize nor discriminate against a trustee as a result of his or her absence. Employers won't be required to compensate the trustee for the time during which the trustee is absent.

INDIANA

Minimum wage. Because of requirements included in previously enacted legislation, the State minimum wage was increased to $6.55 per hour on July 24, 2008.

Worker privacy. New legislation expanded the listing of types of public records that are exempt from public disclosure unless access to the records is specifically required by State or Federal statute or is ordered by a court under the rules of discovery. Records requested by an offender (a person confined in a penal institution as the result of having been convicted of a crime) that contain information relating to (1) a correctional officer, (2) the victim of a crime, or (3) a family member of a correctional officer or the victim of a crime, or that concern or could affect the security of a jail or correctional facility, are now normally exempt from disclosure.

IOWA

Discharge. Legislation was enacted that prohibits employment discrimination in the State by an employer against an employee who serves as a witness in a criminal proceeding or as a plaintiff, defendant, or witness in a civil proceeding.

Minimum wage. With some exceptions, the Monthly State minimum-wage requirements shall no longer apply to an enterprise whose annual gross volume of sales made or business done, exclusive of excise taxes at the retail level, which are separately stated, is less than $300,000. The minimum-wage requirements now apply to an enterprise engaged in the business of laundering, cleaning, or repairing clothing or fabrics and also apply to an enterprise engaged in construction or reconstruction. In addition, the requirements apply to an enterprise engaged in the operation of a hospital, a preschool, an elementary or secondary school, and an institution of higher education. Finally, the requirements also apply to a public agency.

Time off. An employer shall not discharge an employee, or take or fail to take action regarding an employee's promotion or proposed promotion, or take action to reduce an employee's wages or benefits for actual time worked, due to the service of the employee as a witness in a criminal proceeding or as a plaintiff, defendant, or witness in a civil proceeding.

Wages paid. The State law requirement regarding an employer's payment of wages to employees was amended. Henceforth, upon written request by an employee, employers must send any wages due to the employee by mail. The employer shall maintain a copy of the request for as long as it is effective and for two years thereafter. If an employer fails to pay an employee's wages on or by the regular payday, the employer is liable for the amount of any overdraft charge if the overdraft is created on the employee's account because of the employer's failure to pay the wages on or by the regular payday.

KANSAS

Discharge. Employers are now prohibited from terminating any employee because the employee serves as a volunteer firefighter, volunteer certified emergency medical services attendant, volunteer reserve law enforcement officer, or volunteer part-time law enforcement officer. The protection does not apply to full-time firefighters or law enforcement officers who volunteer as emergency medical services attendants, to firefighters, or to law enforcement officers.

Equal employment opportunity. An amendment of the State Age Discrimination in Employment Act increased the age of protection from 18 years to 40 years.

KENTUCKY

Immigrant protections. The State Commission on Fire Protection Personnel Standards is required to implement a voluntary statewide certified volunteer firefighter identification program. The program shall issue a color photo non-driver's identification card to all certified volunteer firefighters. Applicants for the card shall provide proof that they are citizens of the United States, permanent residents of the United States, or otherwise lawfully present in the United States. The commission is to promulgate administrative regulations to establish the standards of proof for citizenship or legal status of an applicant.

Minimum wage. Because of requirements included in legislation that was previously enacted, the State minimum wage was increased to $6.55 per hour on July 1, 2008.

LOUISIANA

Child labor. The State child labor statutes were amended to provide for the employment, under certain conditions, of minors 12 and 13 years of age. Minors under 14 years may be employed if all of the following conditions are met: (1) the minor must be at least 12 years of age; (2) the minor's parent or legal guardian is an owner or partner in the business in which the minor is employed; (3) the minor shall work only under the direct supervision of the parent or legal guardian who owns or is a partner in the business; (4) all of the protections afforded to minors between 14 and 15 years of age shall be afforded to minors 12 and 13 years of age; and (5) the minor obtains an employment certificate pursuant to State law.

Drug and alcohol testing. The State amended statutes concerning the provisions for drug testing of certain public employees by certain public employers of parishes and municipalities. The legislation modifies the following definitions, among others: "public vehicle," to include any motor vehicle, watercraft, aircraft, or rail vehicle owned or controlled by the State or by a local governmental subdivision that has adopted an ordinance; and "public employer," to mean the State and any local governmental subdivision that has adopted any ordinance, provided that the subdivision is a public employer for that purpose. Legislation was enacted that amended the provisions for drug testing at refining or chemical-manufacturing facilities to allow certain people involved in construction, maintenance, or manufacturing to reduce or modify the initial cutoff level of 50 nanograms per millimeter for marijuana testing. This amendment won't apply to any person, firm, or company engaged or employed in the exploration, drilling, or production of oil or gas in the State or its territorial waters.

Equal employment opportunity. The State's Revised Statutes were amended to add a section that allows no interruption in the prescriptive time requirement because the plaintiff failed to give the appropriate amount of time pursuant to an upcoming discrimination case. Currently, Section C of the Statute specifies that a plaintiff who believes that he or she has been discriminated against and who intends to pursue court action must give the person who has allegedly discriminated written notice of this fact at least 30 days before initiating court action. The notice should detail the alleged discrimination, and both parties shall make a good-faith effort to resolve the dispute prior to initiating court action. The new Section D stipulates that the prescriptive period for the case shall be one year, but can be suspended during the pendency of any administrative review or investigation of the claim conducted by the Federal Equal Employment Opportunity Commission or the State Commission on Human Rights. However, no suspension of the 1-year prescriptive period shall last longer than six months, and the prescriptive period shall not be interrupted for failure to give the appropriate written notice even if there are other investigations pending.

Overtime. The Governor of the State implemented an Executive order that suspends Federal regulations pertaining to hours of service for drivers of utility service vehicles operated by utilities that are engaged solely in intrastate commerce and are regulated by the Louisiana Public Service Commission or the city of New Orleans. This order is active under the rules of State Proclamation No. 51 BJ 2008, which declares Louisiana to be in a state of emergency as a result of forecasted hurricane activity that threatens the lives and property of the citizens of the State. The order will remain effective until amended, modified, terminated, or rescinded by the Governor or until terminated by the operation of the law.

Whistleblower. The whistleblower protections provided for public employees in the State were amended. Any public employee who reports, to a person or entity of competent authority or jurisdiction, information that the employee reasonably believes indicates a violation of any law, of any order, rule, or regulation issued in accordance with law, or of any other alleged acts of impropriety related to the scope or duties of public employment or public office within any branch or other political subdivision of State government shall be free from discipline, reprisal, or threats of discipline or reprisal by the public employer for reporting such acts of alleged impropriety. No supervisor, agency head, or any other employee with authority to hire, fire, or discipline employees, and no elected official, shall subject to reprisal or threaten to subject to reprisal any public employee because of the employee's efforts to disclose such acts of alleged impropriety. If any public employee is suspended, demoted, dismissed, or threatened with suspension, demotion, or dismissal, as an act of reprisal for reporting an alleged act of impropriety in violation of State statute, the employee shall report such action to the State Board of Ethics.

Worker privacy. Trust companies were added to the list of financial institutions, such as banks, savings and loan associations, or credit unions, that may provide, to any other such financial institution, a written employment reference that may include information reported to Federal banking regulators. Where written employment references contain such information, and where a copy of the written employment reference is sent to the last known address of the employee in question, a bank, savings and loan association, trust company, or credit union shall not be liable for providing such an employment reference unless the information provided is false and the financial institution providing the information does so with knowledge and malice.

MAINE

Family issues. The State definition of "family medical leave" under State requirement for such leave was amended. "Family medical leave" is now defined as leave requested by an employee for (1) a serious health condition of the employee, (2) the birth of the employee's child, (3) the placement of a child 16 years or younger with the employee in connection with the employee's adoption of the child, or (4) a serious health condition of a child, a domestic partner's child, a parent's domestic partner, or a sibling or spouse. The definition of "sibling" was also clarified to mean "an employee's sibling who is jointly responsible with the employee for each other's common welfare as evidenced by joint living arrangements and joint financial arrangements."

Human trafficking. The State Revised Statutes regarding human trafficking were amended. A "human trafficking offense" is now defined as kidnapping or criminal restraint when the crime involves either (1) restraining a person by destroying, concealing, removing, confiscating, or possessing any actual or purported passport or other immigration document, or any other actual or purported government identification document, of the other person or (2) using any scheme, plan, or pattern intended to cause a person to believe that if he or she does not perform certain labor or services, including prostitution, then the person will suffer serious harm or restraint. In addition, the amended statutes now allow a trafficked person to bring a civil action for damages, compensatory damages, punitive damages, injunctive relief, any combination of those conditions, or any other appropriate relief. A prevailing plaintiff also is entitled to an award of attorneys' fees and costs. Actions brought pursuant to this section of the State statute must be commenced within ten years of the date on which the trafficked person was freed from the trafficking situation. The statute of limitations is tolled for an incompetent or minor plaintiff even if a guardian *ad litem* has been appointed. A defendant is stopped from asserting a defense of the statute of limitations if the trafficked person did not file before the expiration of the statute of limitations due to (1) conduct by the defendant inducing the plaintiff to delay the filing of the action or preventing the plaintiff from filing the action or (2) threats made by the defendant that caused duress to the plaintiff.

Minimum wage. Effective October 1, 2008, the State minimum hourly wage was increased to $7.25 per hour. An additional increase, to $7.50 per hour, is scheduled for October 1, 2009. On September 30, 2009, and on September 30 of each year thereafter, the State Department of Labor shall calculate an adjusted minimum-wage rate to maintain employee purchasing power. The adjusted minimum-wage rate must be calculated to the nearest cent on the basis of the Consumer Price Index for Urban Wage Earners and Clerical Workers (CPI-W) or a successor index, as calculated by the U.S. Department of Labor, for the 12 months prior to each September 1. Each adjusted minimum-wage rate so calculated takes effect January 1 of the next year. An employer may consider tips as part of the wages of a service employee, but such a tip credit may not exceed $3.00 per hour. An employer is liable to an employee for any amount of unpaid minimum wages. When a judgment is rendered in favor of any employee in any action brought to recover unpaid wages, such judgment must include among such wages an amount equal to the combined cost of liquidated damages, the cost of the suit (including reasonable attorneys' fees), and a civil penalty of not less than $1,000 or more than $10,000, 90 percent of which civil penalty must be paid to the State. On October 1 of each year, beginning October 1, 2008, the minimum and maximum civil penalties must be adjusted by the State Department of Labor to reflect changes in the CPI-W or a successor index, as calculated by the U.S. Department of Labor.

Worker privacy. State Public Law 2005, c.381, Section 3, was amended to further protect the personal contact information records of public employees. Personal contact information is considered confidential, and the term means "home address, home phone number, home facsimile number, e-mail address, cellular phone, and pager number." Elected officials are not considered public employees under the amendment. Notwithstanding any other provision of law, complaints and investigative files that relate to court and judicial security are confidential; however, they can be disseminated to another criminal justice agency. Applications, resumes, and letters and notes of reference, other than those letters and notes of reference expressly submitted in confidence, pertaining to an applicant who has been hired are public records after the applicant is hired, except for the personal contact information. Upon the request of the employing agency, the State director of the Bureau of HR shall make the determination as to whether the release of certain personal information not otherwise protected by law is permissible. The records and proceedings of the State agency-operated technology centers are public, except for (a) any record obtained or developed by a technology center prior to the receipt of a written application or proposal in a form acceptable to the center for assistance from the center; (b) any record pertaining to an application or proposal that has been received, unless that record is confidential under another provision of the law; (c) a peer review, analysis, or other document related to the evaluation of a grant application or proposal; and (d) a record that the individual or center requests to be designated confidential and that the center determines contains proprietary information which, if released, would be considered competitively harmful and could impair the center's ability to get other proposals or similar necessary information in the future. Data submitted and deemed confidential by the Administrator of the U.S. Environmental Protection Agency may not be available for public inspection. A person who intentionally or knowingly discloses confidential information in violation of this section commits a Class E crime.

MARYLAND

Department of labor. The enforcement authority of the State commissioner of labor and industry has been expanded. The commissioner may now initiate an investigation of a complaint that an employment agency has failed to submit a penal bond as required by statute. If, after investigation, the commissioner finds that the employment agency has failed to submit the required penal bond, the commissioner shall give written notice that requires the agency to complete certain actions within 15 days of receipt of the notice. The employment agency must (1) submit the bond or (2) show written cause why the agency is not required to comply with the statute. If the employment agency complies with the requirement to submit a bond or otherwise submits a timely response, the commissioner may (1) terminate proceedings against the agency or (2) schedule a hearing and, by certified mail, give the agency written notice of the date, place, and time of the hearing. If the agency fails to comply with a lawful order of the commissioner or fails to submit a timely response, the commissioner may impose a civil money penalty of not less than $500 and not more than $1,000 for each failure to comply with the order or failure to submit a timely report. If, after a hearing, the commissioner finds that the employment agency has violated the provisions of the statute, the commissioner may impose a civil penalty of not less than $500 and not more than $1,000 for each violation.

Equal employment opportunity. Section 11–B of the State Human Relations Commission section of the State Annotated Code was amended to cover civil actions resulting from alleged discriminatory acts and the constraints for processing such actions. Within 180 days of the timely filing of a complaint or administrative charge alleging a discriminatory act, the complainant may bring a civil action against the respondent. If the civil action is filed no more than two years after the occurrence of the alleged act of discrimination, the filing shall serve to automatically terminate any proceeding before the commission that is based on the underlying administrative complaint and any amendments thereto. If a payment of compensatory damages is awarded to the complainant for future pecuniary losses, emotional pain, suffering, inconvenience, mental anguish, loss of enjoyment of life, and other nonpecuniary losses, the amount of damages awarded may not exceed (1) $50,000 if the respondent employs not fewer than 15 and not more than 100 employees, (2) $100,000 if the respondent employs not fewer than 101 and not more than 200 employees, (3) $200,000 if the respondent employs not fewer than 201 and not more than 500 employees, and (4) $300,000 if the respondent employs not fewer than 501 employees, in each of 20 or more calendar weeks in the current or preceding calendar year. The court may not inform the jury of the limitations imposed on compensatory and punitive damages, and if back pay is awarded, interim earnings or amounts earnable with reasonable diligence by the person(s) discriminated against shall operate to reduce the back pay otherwise allowable. If the State has sufficient money available at the time an award is made, the State shall pay the award as soon as practicable within 20 days after the award is final. If insufficient monies exist at the time of the award, the affected State unit shall report this fact to the State comptroller, who shall keep an accounting of all outstanding awards and report that accounting annually to the Governor, who shall include in the State budget sufficient funds to pay all awards made against the State under this section of the State code.

Minimum wage. Because of requirements included in legislation that was previously enacted, the State minimum wage was increased to $6.55 per hour on July 24, 2008.

Miscellaneous. The State enacted legislation to establish paid-work-based learning programs in which arrangements are made between schools and employers to provide students certain structured employer-supervised learning. The legislation allows a credit against the State income tax and the tax on insurance premiums for wages paid to each student under an approved paid-work-based learning program. Students must work 200 or more hours before an employer is eligible to claim a tax credit, which cannot exceed $1,500 per student. Further, the legislation defines a "student" as "a person at least 16 years old, but younger than 23, or who reaches the age of 23 while participating in an approved paid-work-based learning program, and who is enrolled in a public or private secondary or postsecondary school in the State."

Time off. The definitions pertinent to the State's Flexible Leave Act were expanded to provide clarification to employers and employees by defining the nature of the leave to be used and how it is to be accounted for, and, in accordance with any terms of a collective-bargaining agreement or employment policy, to prohibit an employer from taking certain actions against an employee for filing a complaint, testifying against or assisting in a certain action, and failing to comply with other provisions related to the State Flexible Leave Act. The relevant new definitions are as follows: (a) an "employer" is a person who employs 15 or more individuals and is engaged in a business, industry, profession, trade, or other enterprise in the State; (b) a person's "immediate family" includes a child, spouse, and parent; and (c) "leave with pay" includes sick leave, vacation time, and compensatory time and is time away from work for which an employee receives compensation. These amendments refer to employers who provide leave with pay under a collective-bargaining agreement or employment policy. An employee may use leave with pay for the illness of the employee's immediate family. An employee may only use leave with pay that has been earned and may designate the type and amount of leave with pay to be used. If the terms of a collective-bargaining agreement or employment policy provide a leave-with-pay benefit that is equal to or greater than the benefit provided by this act, the collective-bargaining agreement or employment policy prevails. An employer may not discharge, demote, suspend, discipline, otherwise discriminate against, or threaten to take any actions against an employee who files a complaint against, testifies against, or assists in an action brought against the employer for a violation of this act. These specifications regarding leave with pay don't affect leave granted under the Federal Family and Medical Leave Act of 1993 and went into effect on October 1, 2008.

Worker privacy. The authorization for data collection and reporting requirements by the State commissioner of labor and industry concerning labor and employment pay disparity data has been amended. The commissioner may now collect and analyze data concerning the racial classification of employees and the gender of employees so that the data may be used to study pay disparity issues. The commissioner shall report to the State general assembly on or before October 1, 2013, regarding the analysis of the data collected and analyzed. The requirement took effect on October 1, 2008, and shall remain effective for a period of five years and three months. At the end of December 31, 2013, with no further action required by the general assembly, the requirement shall cease.

MICHIGAN

Independent contractor. Employers in the State and elsewhere too often misclassify individuals they hire as independent contractors, even when those individuals should legally be classified as employees. In doing so, the employer may be violating a number of legal obligations under State and Federal labor, employment, and tax laws. A State Executive order created the State Interagency Task Force on Employee Misclassification as an advisory body within the State Department of Labor and Economic Growth. The task force shall examine and evaluate existing employee misclassification enforcement mechanisms in the State and other jurisdictions and shall make recommendations for more effective enforcement mechanisms. The task force also shall (1) create a system for sharing information; (2) establish a protocol through which individual task force member agencies may refer relevant matters to other member agencies for assessment of potential liability under other relevant authority; (3) identify barriers to information sharing; (4) facilitate the pooling, focusing, and targeting of investigative resources; (5) develop strategies for systematically investigating employee misclassification; (6) establish joint investigatory strategies and enforcement teams where applicable; and (7) provide assistance to workers who have been exploited by employee misclassification. In addition, the task force shall work at increasing public awareness of employee misclassification and shall establish procedures for soliciting referrals or information from the public, including through a phone hot line. Finally, the task force shall issue a report to the Governor on July 1 of each year, detailing its accomplishments, identifying any administrative or legal barriers that might impede its effective operation, and recommending executive or legislative measures to improve enforcement of employee misclassification.

Minimum wage. Because of requirements included in previously enacted legislation, the State minimum wage was increased to $7.40 per hour on July 1, 2008.

MINNESOTA

Immigrant protection. The State Governor ordered that measures be implemented to ensure that all newly hired executive branch employees are legally eligible to work. As a result, the State commissioner of administration will implement procedures to ensure that State contracts in excess of $50,000 are awarded to vendors that are in compliance with Federal employment verification laws. Those procedures will include (1) developing language for State contracts which certifies that the vendor and any of its subcontractors are complying with the Immigration Reform and Control Act of 1986 in relation to employees performing work in the United States and that the vendor and its subcontractors are not knowingly employing persons in violation of U.S. immigration laws; (2) requiring that, as of the date on which services on behalf of the State will be performed, vendors and any of their subcontractors will have implemented or will be in the process of implementing the e-verify program for all newly hired employees who will perform work on behalf of the State; and (3) developing language for State contracts that allows the State to terminate the contract or debar the vendor (or both) if the commissioner determines that the vendor or the subcontractor within control of the vendor has knowingly employed ineligible workers in violation of the Federal immigration laws. To the extent consistent with State law, the State commissioner of employment and economic development will establish procedures for recipients of business subsidies to certify their compliance with the Immigration Reform and Control Act in relation to employees performing work in the United States. Illegal immigration and criminal activity related to illegal immigration are serious problems for the State. Local, State, and Federal authorities need to work on a cooperative basis to combat criminal activity. The Immigration and Customs Enforcement (ICE) of the Federal Department of Homeland Security has developed programs to allow State and local law enforcement officials to work cooperatively with Federal officials. The State Governor directed the State commissioners of public safety, corrections, and commerce to take appropriate actions and enter into the necessary agreements to work cooperatively as part of the Agreement of Cooperation in Communities to Enhance Safety and Security program. This agreement will allow immigration cross-designation (pursuant to section 287(g) of the Federal Immigration and Nationality Act, as well as allow a select number of State law enforcement officers working with ICE to assist ICE in enforcing Federal customs laws as part of the ICE task force operations relating to narcotics smuggling; money laundering; human smuggling and trafficking; perpetrating fraud; and targeting, dismantling, and seizing illicit proceeds from criminal companies that exploit the immigration process through identity theft and fraud.

Worker privacy. The State Statutes 2007 Supplement, Section 325E.59, was amended by the inclusion of a clarification of the activities that may not be performed by a person or entity, not including a government entity. The selling of Social Security numbers obtained from individuals in the course of business is now prohibited. However, if the release of such numbers is incidental to a larger transaction and is necessary to identify the individual in order to accomplish a legitimate business purpose, or if the release is for the purpose of marketing, then the release does not constitute selling. Social Security numbers may be included in applications and forms sent by mail, including documents sent as part of an application or enrollment process; documents that seek to establish, amend, or terminate an account, a contract, or a policy; and documents that seek to confirm the accuracy of the Social Security number. The number may not be included on the outside of a mailing or in the bulk mailing of a credit card solicitation offer. Access must be restricted so that only an agency's employees, agents, or contractors who require access to records containing the number in order to perform their job duties are able to obtain the information.

MISSISSIPPI

Immigrant protection. The legislature declared that it is a compelling public interest of the State to discourage illegal immigration by requiring all agencies within the State to cooperate fully with Federal immigration authorities in the enforcement of Federal immigration laws. Thus, the State Employment Protection Act was enacted. The act requires employers in the State to hire only legal citizens or legal aliens of the United States. Every employer shall register with and utilize the e-verify system to verify the Federal employment authorization status of all newly hired employees. It shall be a discriminatory practice for an employer to discharge an employee working in the State who is a citizen or permanent resident alien of the United States while retaining an employee who the employing entity knows, or reasonably should have known, is an unauthorized alien hired after July 1, 2008, and who is working in a job category that requires equal skill, effort, and responsibility, and that is performed under similar working conditions, as the job category held by the discharged employee. An employing entity that, on the date of the discharge in question, was enrolled in and used the e-verify system to verify the employment eligibility of its employees in the State after July 1, 2008, shall be exempt from liability, investigation, or suit arising from any action under the act. Employers who violate the provisions of the act shall be subject to the cancellation of any State or public contract, resulting in ineligibility, for up to three years, for any State or public contract; the loss, for up to one year, of any license, permit, certificate, or other document granted to the employer by any agency department or government entity for the right to do business in the State; or both.

Inmate labor. The State Code of 1972 concerning the employment of county-housed State inmates or of county prisoners was amended. It is now lawful for the State, a county within the State, or a municipality of the State to provide prisoners for public-service work for churches according to criteria approved by the State Department of Corrections.

MISSOURI

Independent contractor. Legislation was enacted that authorized the State attorney general (1) to investigate any alleged or suspected violations of an employer's knowingly misclassifying a worker and the employer's failure to claim that worker and (2) to seek an injunction prohibiting the employer from engaging in such conduct. The State shall have the burden of proving that the employer misclassified the worker. If it is found that an employer knowingly misclassified a worker, the court may enter a judgment in favor of the State and award penalties in the amount of $50 per day per misclassified worker, up to a maximum of $50,000. In awarding State contracts in excess of $5,000, businesses must reaffirm their enrollment in a Federal work authorization program, with employers working in connection with the services contracted. Employers must be able to verify the employment eligibility of every employee in the employer's hire whose employment commences after the employer enrolls in the work authorization program. General contractors and subcontractors won't be held liable. The legislation also deems it unlawful for the purposes of trafficking to knowingly transport, move, or attempt to transport, within the State, any alien who is not lawfully present in the United States.

Minimum wage. As a result of legislation enacted in a previous year in which the State minimum wage was indexed to inflation, the State minimum wage was increased to $7.05 per hour on January 1, 2009.

Worker privacy. In new legislation, the State mandates that employers are not allowed to require any employee to have a personal identification microchip implanted into his or her person for any reason. Employers who violate this mandate will be found guilty of a class A misdemeanor. The legislation also prohibits an employer from terminating an employee who has been activated to a national disaster by the Federal Emergency Management Agency and, as a result, has been absent from or late to work. Employees should make a reasonable effort to notify their employers that they may be absent from or late to work due to an emergency.

MONTANA

Minimum wage. The State minimum wage was increased to $6.55 per hour on July 24, 2008, thus matching the Federal minimum wage. As a result of legislation that was enacted in a previous year in which the State minimum wage was indexed to inflation, the State minimum wage was increased again, to $6.90 per hour, on January 1, 2009.

NEBRASKA

Minimum wage. Because of requirements included in legislation previously enacted, the State minimum wage was increased to $6.55 per hour on July 24, 2008.

Time off. The State legislature also adopted the Volunteer Emergency Responders Job Protection Act. Under the Act, employees acting as volunteer emergency responders shall make a reasonable effort to notify their employers that they may be absent from or report late to their place of employment in order to respond to an emergency. No employer shall terminate or take any other disciplinary action against any employee who is a volunteer emergency responder if such employee is absent from or reports late to his or her place of employment in order to respond to an emergency prior to the time the employee is to report to the place of employment. However, an employer may subtract from an employee's earned wages an amount of pay the employee would have earned during the time the employee was away from the place of employment acting as a volunteer responding to an emergency. At an employer's request, an employee acting as a volunteer emergency responder who is absent from or reports late to the place of employment in order to respond to an emergency shall provide the employer, within seven days of such request, a written statement, signed by the individual in charge of the volunteer department or some other authorized person, that includes appropriate information about the date and time of the emergency in which the employee participated as a volunteer. An employee who is wrongfully terminated or against whom any disciplinary action is taken in violation of the act shall be immediately reinstated to his or her former position without any reduction in wages, seniority, or other benefits and shall receive any lost wages or other benefits, if applicable, during any period for which such termination or other disciplinary action was in effect. An action to enforce the act may be brought by the employee.

NEW HAMPSHIRE

Child labor. Legislation was enacted to clarify the conditions and requirements for persons who are 16 and 17 years of age to train and be employed as firefighters. The legislation places limits on youth training and employment, including the following: (1) no youth under the age of 16 shall be employed or permitted to work in firefighting, except when the youth is enrolled in an explorer program approved by the State Department of Labor; (2) when any youth is employed or permitted to work in support of firefighting, fire companies must follow Federal orders regulating youth employment in hazardous occupations at all times and in all places; (3) the supervisory person responsible for following the youth requirements must be the chief authority of the fire company or his or her designee; (4) youths won't be employed at any task or duty in support of firefighting if they have not completed the required training; and (5) the rules adopted by the commissioner of labor must be followed by fire companies when employing or permitting 16- or 17-year-old youths to work in support of firefighting. In addition, the legislation sets minimum training requirements for youths working in support of firefighting and requires an identification card to be issued upon completion of training.

Minimum wage. Because of requirements included in legislation that was previously enacted, the State minimum wage was increased to $7.25 per hour on September 1, 2008.

Overtime. The State clarified the regular rate of compensation for an employee. The rate is one-fortieth of the weekly remuneration of delivery drivers or sales merchandisers covered under the provisions of the Fair Labor Standards Act. Exceptions will be made for those employees who are exempt under provisions of the Act.

NEW JERSEY

Equal employment opportunity. Legislation was enacted that made it unlawful to discriminate against employees because of their religious practices. Employers may not impose upon a person, as a condition of obtaining or retaining employment, including opportunities for promotion, advancement, or transfers, any terms or conditions that would require the person to violate or forego a sincerely held religious practice or observance, including, but not limited to, the observance of any particular day or days or any portion thereof as a Sabbath or other holy day in accordance with the requirements of the religion or the religious belief. This condition is applicable unless the employer is able to demonstrate that it is unable to reasonably accommodate the employee's religious observance or practice without undue hardship on the conduct of the employer's business. The enacted legislation does not affect the ability of the employer to require employees to adhere to reasonable workplace appearance, grooming, and dress standards not precluded by other provisions of State or Federal law, except that the employer shall allow an employee to appear, groom, and dress consistently with the employee's gender identity or expression.

Family issues. The State's temporary disability insurance provisions were extended to provide temporary disability leave benefits for workers caring for sick family members or for newborn or newly adopted children. Qualified workers will be entitled to receive six weeks of temporary disability leave benefits when providing care certified to be necessary for a family member suffering a serious health condition as defined by State statute. Employees are required to give at least 30 days' prior notice, except when unforeseeable circumstances prevent such notice. When possible, employees also should schedule the leave in a manner that minimizes any disruption in employer operations and should give 15 days' prior notice for leave that is intermittent. Employees are required to take benefits provided under the bill concurrently with any unpaid leave taken under the State Family Leave Act (P.L. 1989) or the Family and Medical Leave Act of 1993 (Pub.L.103–3). The legislation provides that the collection of an assessment on employees to pay for family temporary disability leave benefits commence on January 1, 2009, and that the payment of family leave benefits commence on July 1, 2009. During 2009, the bill will raise revenues necessary to pay the benefits through an assessment of 0.09 percent of the portion of each worker's wages subject to temporary disability leave taxes. In 2010 and subsequent years, the rate will be 0.12 percent. The funds raised thereby would be deposited into an account to be used only for family leave benefits and their administration, including the cost of an outreach program to eligible employees and the cost of issuing annual reports on the use of the benefits. In addition, the legislation increases the penalties for misrepresentations, fraud, and other violations regarding the family temporary disability benefit program established by the bill. Penalties for knowingly making a false statement or knowingly failing to disclose a material fact in order to improperly obtain benefits or avoid paying benefits or taxes are increased from $20 to $250 per statement or nondisclosure. Penalties for other willful violations of the law are increased from $50 to $500, and additional penalties for violations with intent to defraud the program are increased from no less than $250 to no more than $1,000.

Miscellaneous. The State Senate memorialized the Congress of the United States to enact legislation requiring the annual publication of a list of companies outsourcing jobs to other countries. Such a requirement would raise public awareness and allow State and local governments to prepare initiatives targeted toward keeping companies from outsourcing critical U.S. jobs.

Plant closing. The State Revised Statutes concerning pre-notification of certain plant closings, transfers, and mass layoffs were amended. The amendment affects employers who employ 100 or more full-time employees for not less than 60 days or for the period required pursuant to the Federal Worker Adjustment and Retraining Act or pursuant to any amendment thereto, whichever is longer. Before the first termination of employment occurs in connection with a termination or transfer of plant operations or a mass layoff, such employers must provide notification of the termination or transfer of operations or the mass layoff to the State commissioner of labor and workforce development, the chief elected official of the municipality in which the establishment is located, each employee whose employment is to be terminated, and any collective-bargaining units of employees in the establishment.

Prevailing wage. The State Economic Development Authority shall adopt rules and regulations requiring that workers employed in the performance of construction contracts, including contracts for millwork fabrication under the authority of financial assistance by the State, be paid at a rate not less than the prevailing-wage rate. This requirement also shall apply to the performance of any contract to construct, renovate, or otherwise prepare a facility for operations necessary for the receipt of authorized State financial assistance, unless the work is performed on a facility owned by a landlord of the entity receiving the assistance and less than 55 percent of the facility is leased by the entity at the time of the contract and under any agreement to subsequently lease the facility. The prevailing wage rate shall be the rate determined by the State commissioner of labor and workforce development. The prevailing wage shall not be paid for construction commencing more than two years after an entity has executed a commitment letter regarding authorized financial assistance with the State and the first payment or other provision of the assistance is received. When a public utility in the State is undergoing construction of some kind, the classification "construction" will refer to construction, reconstruction, installation, demolition, restoration, or alteration of facilities of the public utility. This classification shall not include operational work such as flagging, plowing snow, managing vegetation in and around utility rights-of-way, marking out boundaries or roads, performing janitorial services, landscaping, surveying leaks, performing meter work, and making miscellaneous repairs. Any construction contractor contracting with a public utility to engage in construction work on that utility shall employ, on the site, only employees who have successfully completed safety training certified by the Occupational Safety and Health Administration and required for work to be performed on that site. Any employee employed by a construction contractor to work on a public utility shall be paid the wage rate for that employee's craft or trade, as determined by the State commissioner of labor and workforce development pursuant to the provisions of the State Prevailing Wage Act. A construction contractor who is regulated under the provisions of Title 48 of the State Revised Statutes and is found by the commissioner to be in violation of this statute shall be subject to the provisions that apply to an employer for violation of the public law.

Time off. At present, a leave of absence with pay is given to every police office or firefighter who is a duly authorized representative of certain specified companies to attend any State or national convention of the company. The leave of absence is for the duration of the convention, with a reasonable time allowed for travel to and from the affair. New legislation now includes the following companies as well: the State Patrolmen's Benevolent Association, Inc.; Fraternal Order of Police; Firemen's Mutual Benevolent Association; Fire Fighters Association of New Jersey; and State Association of Chiefs of Police. Also included are any corrections officer who is a member of the Italian American Police Society, any affiliate of the International Association of Black Professional Firefighters, and the National Association of Hispanic Firefighters. Upon request, a certificate of attendance shall be submitted by the representative who is attending the convention. At no time shall a person holding any office, position, or employment other than for a fixed term or period under the government of the State, under the government of any county, municipality, school district, or other political subdivision of the State, or under any board, body, agency, or commission of the State or any county, municipality, or school district thereof be laid off from employment if such person has been on a military leave of absence for active service in the Armed Forces of the United States in time of war or emergency. If the employer's circumstances have so changed for reasons of economy or efficiency or for some other, related reason as to make it impossible or unreasonable for such person who entered service in time of war or other emergency to resume the office, position, or employment held prior to entry into such service, the employer shall restore the person to a position of like seniority, status, and pay, or, if requested by the person, to any position available for which the person is able and qualified to perform the duties. Such person shall not be entitled to layoff protection if the person voluntarily continues military service beyond the time that he or she is eligible to be released from the service.

Wages paid. When a contract between a principal and a sales representative to solicit orders is terminated, the commissions and other compensation earned as a result of the representative relationship, but remaining unpaid, shall become due and payable within 30 days of the date the contract is terminated or within 30 days of the date commissions are due, whichever is later. A sales representative shall receive commissions on goods ordered up to and including the last day of the contract, even if such goods are accepted by the principal, delivered, and paid for after the end of the agreement. The commissions shall become due and payable within 30 days after payment would have been due under the contract if the contract had not been terminated. A principal who violates or fails to comply with the provisions of this act shall be liable to the sales representative for all amounts due, for exemplary damages in an amount three times the amount of commissions owed to the sales representative, for all attorneys' fees actually and reasonably incurred by the sales representative in any action pursued, and for all court costs. In case of any court action, should the court determine that the action against the principal is frivolous, the sales representative shall be liable to the principal for all attorneys' fees and assorted costs incurred.

Workplace security. Under an amendment to the State Public Law, no employee of a public utility who is in possession of any identification badge, as provided for by the State Public Law, shall loan, allow, or permit any other person to use or display such identification badge; in case of the loss of any such badge, the employee shall notify the public utility forthwith of such loss and the circumstances surrounding the same. Any employee who shall display or use the identification badge of a public-utility employee for the purpose of deceiving any person as to his or her identity shall be guilty of a crime of the fourth degree, punishable by imprisonment for up to 18 months, a fine of $10,000, or both. Persons who knowingly sell, offer or expose for sale, or otherwise transfer, or who possess with the intent to sell, offer or expose for sale, or otherwise transfer, a document, printed form, or other writing that falsely purports to be a public-utility employee identification badge required under provisions of the State Public Law and that could be used as a means of verifying a person's identity as a public-utility employee is guilty of a crime in the second degree. The State Waterfront Commission Act was amended in order to clarify the grounds for denial of license applications and revocation of licenses, as well as to provide for the postponement of certain hearings. The commission has the authority to deny an application for a license or registration for a variety of reasons, including association with a person who has been identified by a Federal, State, or local law enforcement agency as a member or an associate of an organized crime group, a terrorist group, or a career offender cartel. The amended act defines a terrorist group as either (1) a group associated or affiliated with, or funded in whole or in part by, an organization designated as a terrorist company by the U.S. Secretary of State in accordance with Section 219 of the Immigration and Nationality Act, as amended from time to time, or (2) any other company that assists, funds, or engages in crimes or acts of terrorism as defined in the laws of the United States, of the State of New Jersey, or of the State of New York. A person whose permit, license, or registration has been temporarily suspended may, at any time, demand that the commission conduct a hearing as provided for in the act. Upon failure of the commission to commence a hearing or render a determination within the time limits prescribed by the act, the temporary suspension of the permittee, licensee, or registrant shall immediately terminate. Notwithstanding other provisions of the act, if a Federal, State, or local law enforcement agency or prosecutor's office shall request the suspension or deferment of any hearing on the ground that such a hearing would obstruct or prejudice an investigation or prosecution, the commission may, in its discretion, postpone or defer such hearing for a certain length of time or indefinitely. Any action by the commission to postpone a hearing shall be subject to immediate judicial review as provided within the contents of this act.

NEW MEXICO

Inmate labor. Research has shown that obtaining gainful employment for a person released from prison is a key factor in rehabilitation, reducing recidivism, and ensuring the safety and security of the State's citizens. Further, these individuals encounter many barriers when they seek employment or a lawful trade, occupation, or profession. The legislators of the State House of Representatives resolved that each State agency cooperate with the State Department of Workforce Solutions and the task force formed in 2007 to serve as a catalyst for helping to remove barriers to employment and to comply with all the provisions of the State Criminal Offender Employment Act.

Minimum wage. An amendment to the State Minimum Wage Act changed the definitions of "employer" and "employee" to exclude State and political subdivisions from all parts of the act except that section which sets the minimum wage. The amendment applies only to the provisions for governing how overtime is calculated and does not exclude State and local governments from having to pay the minimum wage, which rose to $7.50 per hour on January 1, 2009.

NEW YORK

Agriculture. The State private housing finance law was amended to offer assistance for the improvement of existing housing for farm workers by providing advances to local loan administrators to make loans to agricultural producers in order to construct or improve nonconforming farm worker housing. Under the amended section of the law, agricultural producers are defined as those persons who produce food by the tillage of the soil or who raise, shear, feed, or manage animals or other dairying processes.

Department of labor. The duties of the State commissioner of labor relating to the promulgation of rules and regulations regarding the employment and education of child performers were amended. The commissioner shall promulgate such rules and regulations as shall be necessary and proper to effectuate the purposes of State statutes, including, but not limited to, the promulgation of regulations determining the hours and conditions of work necessary to safeguard the health, education, morals, and general welfare of child performers.

Health care overtime. Regularly scheduled work hours shall refer to those hours a nurse has agreed to work and is normally scheduled to work pursuant to the budgeted hours allocated to the nurse's position by the employer. If no such allocation system exists, some other measure generally used by the employer to determine when an employee is minimally supposed to work that is consistent with the collective-bargaining agreement shall be used. On call time cannot be used as a substitute for mandatory overtime, and no employer shall require a nurse to work more than that nurse's regularly scheduled work hours. A nurse can be called to service in the case of a natural health care disaster that unexpectedly affects the county in which the nurse is employed or any contiguous county and increases the need for health care personnel. A Federal, State or county declaration of emergency may be used to call personnel to extra service, provided that a good-faith effort has been made to have overtime covered on a voluntary basis. An ongoing medical or surgical procedure in which a nurse is actively involved and whose continued presence through the completion of the procedure is needed is a reason to demand that a nurse stay on the job and not risk abandoning the patient. Also, the refusal of a licensed practical nurse or a registered professional nurse to work beyond regularly scheduled hours shall not solely constitute patient abandonment or neglect.

Plant closing. As part of the amended State Worker Adjustment and Retraining Notification Act, and as a result of relocation or consolidation of part or all of an employer's business, the employer is required to give notice of any impending mass layoff, relocation, or employment loss. A plant closing is a permanent or temporary shutdown of a single site of employment or of one or more facilities or operating units within a single site of employment. The employer is required to give at least a 90-day notification to the affected employees and their representatives. Such notice is not required if the employment loss is necessitated by a physical calamity or an act of terrorism or war. The mailing of a notice to an employee's last known address by either first-class or certified mail or the inclusion of a notice in an employee's paycheck shall be considered an acceptable method for fulfilling the employer's obligation to give appropriate notice to affected employees.

Prevailing wage. Legislation was enacted that amended the labor law and general municipal law of the State relating to guaranteeing payment of prevailing wages to the workers of the State. Any person contracting with the State, with a public-benefit company, with a municipal company, or with a commission appointed pursuant to law and who shall require more than eight hours' work for a day's labor, unless otherwise permitted by law, is guilty of a misdemeanor and, upon conviction thereof, shall be punished in accordance with the penal law for each offense. Notwithstanding the foregoing, the department of jurisdiction may release, to third parties who weren't themselves involved in the violations, monies due and owing on the contract or subcontract that have not been withheld for the sole purpose of satisfying the contractor's or subcontractor's obligations under the contract or subcontract. Every contract for a public-works project shall contain a term stating that the filing of payrolls in a manner consistent with State law is a condition precedent to payment of any sums due and owing to any person for work done on the project. The department of jurisdiction is defined as the department of the State, board, or officer in the State, or the particular law, whose duty it is to prepare or direct the preparation of the plans and specifications for a public-works project. Each department of jurisdiction shall designate, in writing, an individual employed by such department as the person responsible for the receipt, collection, and review for facial validity of payrolls. Finally, any person or company that conspires to prevent competitive bidding on a contract for public work or purchase that is advertised for bidding shall be guilty of a misdemeanor under the law. The State labor law and general municipal law relating to guaranteeing payment of prevailing wages to workers in the State were amended. Any person participating in a public-works project in the capacity of a contractor or subcontractor and who willfully fails to pay or provide the prevailing wage rate for wages or supplements owed shall be guilty of a Class A misdemeanor when such failure results in underpayments that, in the aggregate amount to all workers employed by such person, results in an amount due of less than $25,000; shall be guilty of a Class E felony when the amount due is greater than $25,000; shall be guilty of a Class D felony when the amount due is greater than $100,000; and shall be guilty of a Class C felony when the amount due is greater than $500,000. Any person convicted of a second such offense within five years shall disgorge profits and shall not be entitled to receive any monies due and owing on the contract or subcontract, nor shall any officer, agent, or employee of the department of jurisdiction or its financial officer pay to such person any such monies without the written approval of the department fiscal officer or without a court order by a court of competent jurisdiction. Contractors and subcontractors shall keep original payrolls or transcripts thereof, subscribed and sworn to or affirmed by the aforementioned department fiscal officer as true under the penalties of perjury. If the contractor or subcontractor maintains no regular place of business in the State, and if the amount of the contract is in excess of $25,000, such payrolls shall be kept on the site of the work. Any person who willfully fails to file such payroll records with the department of jurisdiction shall be guilty of a Class E felony. In addition, any person who fails to file such payroll records within the time specified by law shall be subject to a civil penalty of up to $5,000 per day. Utility companies and their contractors and subcontractors who are required to use or open a street as a condition of issuance of a permit must agree that none but competent workers who are skilled in the work required of them shall be employed for those positions. Further, the prevailing scale of union wages shall be the prevailing wage for the similar titles established by the fiscal officer of the utility and its contractors and subcontractors. The department fiscal officer also has the responsibility of keeping original payroll records or transcripts, subscribed and sworn to or affirmed by him or her as true under the penalty of perjury. The records shall include the names and addresses of each employee, laborer, or mechanic and, for each of them, shall show the hours and days worked, the occupations worked, the hourly wage rates paid, and the supplements paid or provided.

Time off. The State labor law relating to employers permitting a leave of absence for blood donation granted to certain employees was amended. The law now requires an employer, at its option, to (1) grant three hours' leave of absence in any 12-month period to an employee who seeks to donate blood or (2) allow its employees, without using any accumulated leave time, to donate blood during work hours at least two times per year at a convenient time and place set by the employer. Condition (2) includes allowing an employee to participate in a blood drive at the employee's place of employment.

Worker privacy. Among the amendments to the State's executive, general-business, public-officers, and penal and criminal procedure law were changes to the labor law to protect the identity of the employee and any personal identifying information. An employer now may not publicly post or display an employee's Social Security number, visibly print a Social Security number in files with unrestricted access, or communicate an employee's personal identifying information to the general public. Personal identifying information shall include one's Social Security number, home address or phone number, personal electronic mail address, Internet identification name or password, parent's surname prior to marriage, and drivers' license number. The Social Security number shall not be used as an identification number for any occupational licensing. The commissioner may impose a civil penalty of up to $500 on any employer for knowingly violating this law.

NORTH CAROLINA

Minimum wage. Because of requirements included in legislation enacted earlier, the State minimum wage was increased to $6.55 on July 24, 2008.

Whistleblower. The State added agricultural workers to those protected against discrimination and retaliation in the workplace by employers if the employee files a complaint; initiates an inquiry, investigation, inspection, proceeding, or action; or testifies against or provides information to any person.

NORTH DAKOTA

Minimum wage. Because of requirements included in previously enacted legislation, the State minimum wage was increased to $6.55 per hour on July 24, 2008.

OHIO

Minimum wage. As a result of legislation that was enacted in a previous year in which the State minimum wage was indexed to inflation, the State minimum wage was increased to $7.30 per hour on January 1, 2009.

OKLAHOMA

Minimum wage. Because of requirements included in previously enacted legislation, the State minimum wage was increased to $6.55 per hour on July 24, 2008.

Unfair labor practice. The State legislature created the State Freedom of Conscience Act, which prohibits employers from discriminating against certain persons for refusing to perform specified acts on the basis of certain of their beliefs. Employers shall not discriminate against employees or prospective employees by refusing to reasonably accommodate a religious observance or practice of the employee or prospective employee, unless the employer can demonstrate that the accommodation would pose an undue hardship on the program, enterprise, or business of the employer in certain circumstances. No health care facility, school, or employer shall discriminate against any person with regard to admission; hiring or firing; tenure; terms, conditions, or privileges of employment; student status; or staff status on grounds that the person refuses or states an intention to refuse, whether or not in writing, to participate in an activity specified by statute if the refusal is based on religious or moral precepts.

OREGON

Minimum wage. As a result of legislation that was enacted in a previous year in which the State minimum wage was indexed to inflation, the State minimum wage was increased to $8.40 per hour on January 1, 2009.

Wages paid. The State Revised Statutes were amended to exclude from the definition of the term "employment" those services provided in conjunction with skiing activities or events for a nonprofit employing unit by a person who receives no remuneration other than ski passes for the services provided. The amended statute also redefined the term "employee" to exclude those individuals who receive no wage other than ski passes or other noncash remuneration for performing volunteer ski-patrol activities or ski-area program activities sponsored by a ski-area operator or by a nonprofit company or company. In addition, the redefinition of the term "employee" now excludes any individual who is registered with the National Ski Patrol or a similar nonprofit ski-patrol company as a nonprofessional ski patroller and who receives no wage other than passes authorizing access to, and use of, a ski area for performing ski-patrol services, including, but not limited to, services related to preserving the safety of, and providing information to, skiers or snowboarders.

Worker privacy. The scope of public records exempted from disclosure was expanded to include records of the home address and home phone number of any public-safety officer listed in the records of the State Department of Public Safety Standards and Training if said officer requests such an exemption.

PENNSYLVANIA

Overtime health care. Individuals who, as a condition of employment, have agreed to be available to return to the place of employment on short notice if the need arises shall do so in the event of an unforeseeable declared national, State, or municipal emergency that is unpredictable or unavoidable and that will substantially affect the provision of or the need for health care services. The employer must make reasonable efforts (1) to seek persons who will volunteer to work extra time from all available qualified staff working at the time of the unforeseeable emergency, (2) to contact all qualified employees who have made themselves available to work extra time, (3) to seek the use of per diem staff, or (4) to seek personnel from a contracted temporary agency. The health care facility shall neither require an employee to work in excess of an agreed-upon predetermined and regularly scheduled daily work shift nor prevent an employee from voluntarily accepting work in excess of these limitations. An employee who refuses to accept overtime shall not be subjected to discrimination, dismissal, discharge, or any other employment decision adverse to the employee. The State Department of Labor and Industry may levy an administrative fine on a health care facility or employer that violates this regulation, and the fine shall be not less than $100 or more than $1,000 for each violation.

PUERTO RICO

Discharge. Legislation was enacted to discourage the incidence of employee discharge without just cause and to provide discharged employees with some resources that would enable them to make a reasonable transition to a new workplace. The allowance for compensation and progressive indemnity for discharge without good cause shall be computed on the basis of the highest number of regular working hours of the employee during any period of 30 consecutive calendar days within the year immediately preceding the discharge. Employees who are discharged due to technological changes or re-company or due to the total or partial ceasing of operations of an enterprise are excluded from the compensation called for by the legislation.

Equal employment opportunity. The Commonwealth law concerning equal employment opportunity was amended to ensure that neither employers nor their establishments perform any discriminatory act. If such an act of discrimination should be committed, the entity performing the discrimination will be charged with a misdemeanor and will receive a fine of not more than $5,000, 90 days' incarceration, or both.

Wages paid. Legislation was enacted to permit employers to deduct or withhold part of the salary earned by an employee when the employee authorizes the employer, in writing, to deduct an amount from the wages due as a contribution, gift, or donation to the fundraising campaigns of the University of Puerto Rico.

RHODE ISLAND

Prevailing wage. All general contractors and subcontractors who perform work on any public-works contract awarded by the State and valued at $1,000,000 or more shall employ apprentices for the performance of the contract. The number of apprentices shall comply with the apprentice-to-journeyman ratio for each trade approved by the apprenticeship council of the State Department of Labor and Training.

Time off. The State General Laws were amended by the legislative addition of the State Military Family Relief Act. Employers in the State who employ between 15 and 50 employees shall provide up to 15 days of unpaid family military leave to an employee during the time Federal or State orders are in effect. Any employer in the State who employs more than 50 employees shall provide up to 30 days of unpaid family military leave during the time Federal or State orders are in effect. The employee shall give at least 14 days of notice of the intended date upon which such leave will commence if the leave consists of five or more consecutive workdays. Employees taking less than five consecutive days shall give the employer advance notice as is practicable. Whenever possible, the employee shall consult with the employer to schedule the leave so as not to unduly disrupt the operations of the employer. An employee shall not take such leave unless he or she has exhausted all accrued vacation leave, personal leave, compensatory leave, and any other leave that may be granted, with the exception of sick leave and disability leave. Employers shall not interfere with, restrain, or deny an employee's exercise of or attempt to exercise the right to such leave under the law. Employers shall not discharge, fine, suspend, expel, discipline, or discriminate in any manner against any employee who exercises his or her right under the law.

SOUTH CAROLINA

Immigrant protection. The State Code of Laws was amended to enact the State Illegal Immigration Reform Act, requiring that every agency or political subdivision of the State verify the lawful presence of any person 18 years or older who has applied for State or local public benefits or public employment. On or after January 1, 2009, every public employer shall register and participate in the Federal work authorization program to verify the authorization of all new employees. No contract will be let with a public employer unless the contractor and all levels of subcontractors agree to register and participate in the Federal work authorization program. Alternatively, the contractors and subcontractors may utilize another route to verify employees—for example, by executing an affidavit that the person is a U.S. citizen or an authorized alien. Individuals who possess a valid State driver's license or an identification card issued by the State Department of Motor Vehicles, or who are eligible to obtain either one, may be employed. If the individual has a valid driver's license or identification card from another State, the licensing requirements must be deemed to be as strict as South Carolina's. The Web site of the State Department of Motor Vehicles shall publish a list of States whose licensing requirements are at least as strict as those of South Carolina. The employer is compliant with the act if appropriate documentation is supplied in good faith and the contractor certifies that the employer is compliant, in which case neither of them may be sanctioned or subject to any civil or administrative action for employing an individual not authorized for employment in the United States. A person who knowingly makes or files any false, fictitious, or fraudulent document is guilty of a felony and, upon conviction, must be fined within the discretion of the court, imprisoned for not more than five years, or both. A Memorandum of Understanding between the State Law Enforcement Division and the U.S. Department of Justice or Department of Homeland Security will be instituted covering the enforcement, detention, and deportation of unlawful aliens and the training of State and local law enforcement officials.

SOUTH DAKOTA

Minimum wage. Because of requirements included in previously enacted legislation, the State minimum wage was increased to $6.55 per hour on July 24, 2008.

TENNESSEE

Child labor. An exception to the restrictions on the employment of minors between the ages of 14 and 16 years has been established. The general employment restrictions on minors would not apply to a minor 14 years or older who is a student enrolled in a course of study and training in a cooperative's career and technical training program, including a work experience and career exploration program, that is approved by the State Department of Education and that complies with Federal law. The student learner must be employed under a written agreement, a copy of which must be retained in the employer's personnel records.

Drug and alcohol testing. The State Code Annotated was amended to include considerations concerning drug testing performed on childcare employees. All persons or entities operating a childcare agency shall now establish drug-testing policies for employees, directors, licensees, and operators providing services under contract or for remuneration and who have direct contact with a child in the care of the agency. The policy shall specify how testing should be completed and shall provide for immediate and effective enforcement action in the event of a positive drug test. The policy shall be made available to all persons upon their initial employment, and its provisions must be satisfied prior to the employee's engaging in any transportation services. Drug testing is determinative if there is suspicion of drug usage by agency personnel and if there are events that may give rise to reasonable suspicion that employees are engaged in the illegal use of drugs. Among such events are a deterioration in job performance or changes in personal traits or characteristics; a reported observation of the individual's behavior in the work environment; changes in personal behavior not attributable to other factors; involvement in or contribution to an accident in which the use of drugs is reasonably suspected, regardless of whether the accident involves actual injury; and an alleged violation of, or conviction for a violation of, criminal drug law statutes involving illegal or prescription drugs. The agency shall maintain drug-testing results for five years, and the results shall be made immediately available to the State Department of Human Services. Individuals who are to be tested must pay the appropriate fees necessary to obtain a drug test pursuant to the agency's policies. Drug-testing results obtained under this act are confidential and may be disclosed only for purposes of enforcement. Childcare agencies failing to comply with the regulation may be denied a license or a license renewal, and ultimately the license can be suspended or revoked. The act becomes effective July 1, 2009.

Human trafficking. The State Code Annotated was amended by the addition of the State Human Trafficking Act of 2007. The amended legislation created Class B felony trafficking offenses for activities in which a person knowingly subjects another person to, or maintains another person in, labor or sexual servitude or knowingly recruits, entices, harbors, transports, provides, or obtains, by any means, another person for the purpose of labor or sexual servitude. The offense of involuntary labor servitude is committed if the person knowingly subjects, or attempts to subject, another person to forced labor by (1) causing or threatening to cause physical harm to any person, (2) physically restraining or threatening to physically restrain any person, (3) abusing or threatening to abuse the law or legal process, (4) knowingly destroying, concealing, removing, confiscating, or possessing any actual or purported government identification, including immigration documents, or any other actual or purported government identification document, of any person, or (5) using blackmail or using or threatening to cause financial harm for the purpose of exercising financial control over any person. The commission of an act of involuntary servitude is a Class C felony. A Class C felony for trafficking of persons occurs when a person knowingly (1) recruits, entices, harbors, transports, provides, or obtains, by any means (or attempts to do so), another person, intending or knowing that the person will be subjected to involuntary servitude or (2) benefits financially or by receiving anything of value from participation in an involuntary-servitude venture that has engaged in an act described in this paragraph as involuntary labor servitude.

Time off. The State Code Annotated relative was amended with regard to time off for volunteer firefighters. As amended, the code permits any employee who is an active volunteer firefighter to leave work in order to respond to fire calls during the employee's regular hours of employment, without loss of pay or any accumulated vacation time, sick leave, or earned overtime. Such employee may be permitted to take off the next scheduled work period within 12 hours following his or her response as a vacation day or sick leave day without loss of pay if the employee assisted in fighting the fire for more than five hours. If the employee is not entitled to such time off, the employee may be permitted to take off the work period in question without pay. The employer may require the employee to submit a written statement from the chief of the volunteer fire department verifying that the employee responded to a fire or was on call and specifying the date, time, and duration of the response.

Worker privacy. State code now prohibits the disclosure of home addresses, dates of birth, phone numbers, bank account information, Social Security numbers, and driver's license information (unless operating a vehicle is part of the employee's job description or duties) of State and local government employees, including law enforcement officers and the family members of such exempted individuals. The State Department of Labor and Workforce Development is required to maintain the confidentiality of the identity of any agency officer, employee, or entity filing a complaint regarding the employment of illegal aliens. However, such information may be discovered by a subpoena from a court of record. In addition, the department commissioner or the commissioner's designee shall inform the person against whom a complaint is made that such person may request the name of the complainant or, if the complaint is filed by an agency or entity, the name of the person who caused the complaint to be filed. If such person requests such name, the commissioner or the commissioner's designee shall provide the name requested.

TEXAS

Minimum wage. Because of requirements included in previously enacted legislation, the State minimum wage was increased to $6.55 per hour on July 24, 2008.

UTAH

Human trafficking. Legislation was enacted that criminalized human trafficking and human smuggling. Human smuggling is defined as the transportation or procurement of transportation of one or more persons by an individual who knows or has reason to know that the person or persons transported or to be transported are not (1) U.S. citizens, (2) permanent resident aliens, or (3) otherwise lawfully in the State or entitled to be in the State. An individual commits human trafficking for forced labor or forced sexual exploitation by recruiting, harboring, transporting, or obtaining a person through the use of force, fraud, or coercion by various means, and the activity is considered a second-degree felony, except when it is deemed to be aggravated in nature. Such human trafficking includes forced labor in industrial areas, sweatshops, households, agricultural enterprises, and any other workplace. Human smuggling of one or more human beings for profit or for a commercial purpose is a third-degree felony, except when it is considered aggravated in nature. The activity is considered aggravated in nature if (1) it involves the death of or serious bodily injury to the victim; (2) it involves more than ten victims in a single episode; (3) it involves a victim who is held against his or her will for more than 180 days; or (4) the victim is younger than 18 years and, if the activity is smuggling, the victim is not accompanied by a family member who is 18 years or older. Aggravated offenses are considered first-degree felonies.

Immigrant protections. Legislation was enacted that contains provisions related to the immigration status of individuals within the State. A number of those provisions deal with employment issues. Effective July 1, 2009, a public employer may not enter into a contract with a contractor for the physical performance of services within the State unless the contractor registers and participates in the e-verify system of the Department of Homeland Security to verify the work eligibility status of the contractor's new employees who are employed within the State. Contractors shall register and participate in the e-verify system in order to enter into a contract with a public employer. The contractor is responsible for verifying the employment status of only new employees who work under its supervision or direction, and not those who work for another contractor or subcontractor, except as provided under State law. Each contractor or subcontractor who works under or for another contractor shall certify to the main contractor by affidavit that the contractor or subcontractor has verified, through the e-verify system, the employment status of each of its new employees. It is unlawful for an employing entity in the State to discharge an employee working in the State who is a U.S. citizen or permanent resident alien and replace the employee with, or have the employee's duties assumed by, an employee who (1) the employing entity knows or reasonably should have known is an unauthorized alien hired on or after July 1, 2009, and (2) is working in the State in a job category that requires skill, effort, and responsibility equal to, and that is performed under working conditions similar to, those of the job category held by the discharged employee. An employing entity that, on the date of discharge in question, is enrolled in and using its e-verify system to verify the employment eligibility of its employees in the State who are hired after July 1, 2009, is exempt from liability, investigation, or lawsuit arising from an action under this law.

Independent contractors. The State legislature enacted the State Independent Database Act, which modifies State provisions related to commerce. The act, created by the Independent Contractor Enforcement Council within the State Department of Commerce, allows an independent contractor database designed by the council to be accessed by one or more specified agencies, the State attorney general, and the Department of Public Safety and will become effective no later than July 1, 2009. It is expected that the database will (1) reduce costs to the State resulting from misclassification of workers as independent contractors; (2) extend outreach and education efforts regarding the nature and requirements of independent contractors' status; (3) promote efficient and effective information sharing among the member agencies; and (4) be coordinated with the State Uninsured Motorist Identification Database. The database will be used by accessing agencies to identify when a person (1) holds him- or herself out as an independent contractor or (2) engages in the performance of work as an independent contractor not subject to an employer's control. The database shall include a process to compare the information against that found in the State Uninsured Motorist Identification Database, at least on a monthly basis, in order to (1) identify a person who may be misclassified as an independent contractor and (2) promote compliance with State and Federal laws related to withholding taxes and making payments for Social Security, Medicare, and unemployment insurance, thereby preventing insurance fraud and ensuring payment of overtime and minimum wages.

Minimum wage. Because of requirements included in legislation previously enacted, the State minimum wage was increased to $6.55 per hour on July 24, 2008.

Worker privacy. Legislation was adopted that amended the Government Records Access and Management Act to add protected status to certain information if the information is properly classified by a governmental entity. Information containing the name, home address, work addresses, and phone numbers of an individual engaged in, or providing goods or services for, medical or scientific research that is conducted within the State system of higher education and that uses animals is protected from disclosure under the act if the release of such information would jeopardize the life or safety of an individual.

VERMONT

Minimum wage. As a result of legislation enacted in a previous year in which the State minimum wage was indexed to inflation, the State minimum wage was increased to $8.06 per hour on January 1, 2009.

Time off. Employees shall have the right to take unpaid leave from employment for the purpose of attending a town meeting, provided that they notify their employers at least seven days prior to the date of the meeting. An employer shall not penalize the employee for exercising the right provided by the State Statutes Annotated. State law relating to rights provided to nursing mothers in the workplace was amended. Employers of employees who continue to be nursing mothers for three years after the birth of a child shall provide reasonable time, either compensated or uncompensated, throughout the day for the employee to express breast milk for her nursing child. The employer has sole discretion regarding the decision to provide compensated time, unless the issue has been moderated by a collective-bargaining agreement. In addition, the employer shall provide appropriate private space, other than a bathroom, for such purpose. An employer may be exempted from this requirement if providing time or an appropriate private space for expressing breast milk would substantially disrupt the employer's operations. An employer shall not retaliate or discriminate against an employee who exercises the aforesaid right. An employer who violates the provisions described shall be assessed a civil penalty of not more than $100 for each violation.

Whistleblower. The rights of whistleblowers, as defined in the State Statutes Annotated, were amended. A State employee employed as a trustee and servant of the people shall now be free to report (in good faith and with candor) waste, fraud, abuse of authority, violations of law, or a threat to the health of employees, the public, or persons under the care of the State without fear of reprisal, intimidation, or retaliation. Retaliatory action includes any adverse performance or disciplinary action, including discharge, suspension, reprimand, demotion, denial of promotion, the imposition of a warning period regarding the employee's performance, and involuntary transfer or reassignment, that is given in retaliation for the State employee's involvement in a protected activity as enumerated by the statute. In addition, no entity shall prohibit a State employee from engaging in discussions with a member of the State General Assembly or from testifying before a legislative committee, provided that no confidential information is divulged and that the employee is not speaking on behalf of an entity of the State government. There shall be no retaliatory action as a result of the employee's provision of information to a legislator or legislative committee. No protections, however, apply to statements provided that constitute hate speech or threats of violence against a person. The employee has a right to seek remedies should an action be taken against him or her; however, if the claim is filed with the State Labor Relations Board, it may not also be brought before the Superior Court, but if it is filed with the Superior Court, the claim may not appear before any other process available to the employee. The grievance shall be brought to the Superior Court within 180 days of the date of the alleged retaliatory action. Through the Superior Court, the employee may be reinstated to the same position, seniority, and work location held prior to the retaliatory action, as well as to the same back pay, lost wages, benefits, and other remuneration. In the event of a showing of a willful and egregious violation of this legislation, the employee may be granted an amount up to the amount of back pay, in addition to the actual back pay and other compensatory damages, including interest on back pay, appropriate injunctive relief, and reasonable costs and attorneys' fees.

VIRGINIA

Child labor. The State Code was amended and now prohibits a minor who is under 18 years of age from being employed, or suffered or permitted to work, as a driver of school buses.

Immigrant protections. The State Code regarding the involuntary termination of corporate existence was amended. The existence of a company may now be terminated involuntarily by order of the State Company Commission when it finds that the company has been convicted of a violation of eight U.S.C. Section 1342A(f), as amended, for actions of its officers and directors constituting a pattern or practice of employing unauthorized aliens in the Commonwealth. Any company convicted of such an offense shall immediately report such conviction to the commission and file with the commission an authenticated copy of the judgment or record of conviction. Certificates revoked for such cause shall be ineligible for reentry for a period of not less than one year. The same penalty may be invoked against foreign companies, a business trust, or a limited-liability company convicted of such a violation.

Inmate labor. The circuit court of any county or city may allow persons confined in the county or city jail who are awaiting disposition of, or serving sentences imposed for, misdemeanors or felonies to work on a voluntary basis on State, county, city, or town property or any property owned by a nonprofit company that is organized and operated exclusively for charitable or social welfare purposes and is exempt from taxation under U.S. Code 501(c)(3). These individuals also may work on private property that is part of a community improvement project sponsored by a locality or that has structures which are found to be public nuisances, provided that the court has reviewed and approved the project for such purposes and permits the prisoners to work on such project or any private property utilized by a nonprofit company that is, again, exempt from taxation under U.S. Code 501(c)(3).

Minimum wage. Because of requirements included in legislation previously enacted, the State minimum wage was increased to $6.55 per hour on July 24, 2008.

Off-site work. The State has established the State Office of Telework Promotion and Broadband Assistance in the office of the State secretary of technology. The goals of the office are to encourage teleworking as a family-friendly, business-friendly public policy that promotes workplace efficiency and reduces strain on transportation infrastructure. The office shall work with public and private entities to develop widespread access to broadband services and shall promote and encourage the use of telework alternatives for public and private employees, including, but not limited to, appropriate policy and legislative initiatives. The State Code was amended in order to redefine the term "telecommuting." It is now defined as "a work arrangement in which supervisors direct or permit employees to perform their usual job duties away from their central workplaces at least 1 day per week and in accordance with work agreements." The State Code relating to State agency employee commuting policies was amended. The State has now set a goal to have each State agency, with the exception of the Department of State Police, have not less than 20 percent of its eligible workforce telecommuting by January 1, 2010.

Worker privacy. Legislation was enacted that added a Freedom of Information Act exemption for investigator notes and for other correspondence and information with respect to an active investigation conducted by or for the State Board of Education and related to the denial, suspension, or revocation of teaching licenses. The legislation does not prohibit the disclosure of records to a local school board or division superintendent for the purpose of permitting such board or superintendent to consider or to take personnel action with regard to the employee. Records of completed investigations shall be disclosed in a form that does not reveal the identity of charging parties, persons supplying the information, or other individuals involved in the investigation. If an investigation fails to support a complaint or does not lead to corrective action, the identity of the person who was the subject of the complaint may be released only with the consent of that person.

WASHINGTON

Minimum wage. As a result of legislation enacted in a previous year in which the State minimum wage was indexed to inflation, the State minimum wage was increased to $8.55 per hour on January 1, 2009.

Time off. The State Revised Code allowing unpaid leaves of absence for the needs of military personnel was amended. Every employee of the State or of any county, city, or other political subdivision thereof who is a member of the State National Guard; of the Army, Navy, Air Force, Coast Guard, or Marine Corps Reserve of the United States; or of any organized Reserve or Armed Forces of the United States shall be entitled to, and shall be granted, military leave of absence from his or her employment for a period not exceeding 21 days during each year, beginning October 1 and ending September 30. Such military leave of absence shall be in addition to any vacation or sick leave to which the employee might otherwise be entitled and shall not involve any loss of efficiency rating, privileges, or pay. During the period of military leave, the employee shall receive his or her normal pay from the State, county, city, or other political subdivision.

Workplace violence. The State Revised Code relating to increasing the safety and economic security of victims of acts of domestic violence, sexual assault, or stalking was amended. An employee may now take reasonable leave from work, intermittent leave, or leave on a reduced leave schedule, with or without pay, to (1) seek legal or law enforcement assistance, including, but not limited to, preparing for or participating in any civil or criminal legal proceeding related to or derived from the aforementioned acts, in order to ensure the health and safety of the employee or the employee's family members; (2) seek treatment by a health care provider for physical or mental injuries caused by said acts or to attend to health care treatment for a victim who is the employee's family member; (3) obtain, or assist a family member in obtaining, services from a domestic violence shelter, rape crisis center, or other social services program for relief from said acts; (4) obtain, or assist a family member in obtaining, mental health counseling related to an incident of said acts in which the employee or the employee's family member was a victim thereof; or (5) participate in safety planning, temporarily or permanently relocate, or take other actions to increase the safety of the employee or the employee's family members from future such acts. As a condition of taking leave for such purposes, the employee shall provide the employer with advance notice of the employee's intention to take leave. The timing of the notice shall be consistent with the employer's stated policy for requesting such leave, if the employer has such a policy. When advance notice cannot be given because of an emergency or unforeseen circumstances, the employee or his or her designee must give notice to the employer no later than the end of the first day the employee takes such leave. The employer may require that the leave requests be supported by verification that the employee or employee's family member is a victim of domestic violence, sexual assault, or stalking, or that the leave was taken for one of the five reasons listed in this section.

WEST VIRGINIA

Drug and alcohol testing. The State Alcohol and Drug-Free Workplace Act was created to require public-improvement contractors to have and implement a drug-free workplace program which requires that drug and alcohol testing be conducted by the contractor. Public funds of the State or of any of its political subdivisions may not be expended, unless the contractor that was awarded the contract has implemented a drug-free workplace policy and shall have provided a sworn statement in writing, under penalties of perjury, that it maintains a valid drug-free workplace policy. The contract shall provide for its cancellation by the awarding authority if (1) the contractor fails to implement the drug-free workplace policy; (2) the contractor fails to provide implementation information on said policy at the request of the authority or the State Division of Labor; or (3) the contractor provides false information to the awarding authority. Among the requirements of a drug-free workplace policy are that (1) pre-employment drug testing be conducted on all employees and (2) random drug testing be conducted annually on at least 10 percent of the contractor's employees who perform safety-sensitive duties. Violations of the State law pertaining to a drug-free workplace policy shall result in the following consequences: (1) for a first offense, upon conviction, the party is guilty of a misdemeanor and fined not more than $1,000; (2) for a second offense, upon conviction, the party is guilty of a misdemeanor and fined not less than $1,000 and not more than $5,000; for a third and subsequent offense, upon conviction, the party is guilty of a misdemeanor and fined not less than $5,000 and not more than $25,000. In addition, for a third offense and subsequent offenses, the contractor shall be excluded from bidding on any additional public-improvement projects for a period of one year.

Minimum wage. Licensees operating charitable bingo games and charitable raffles may pay a salary, the minimum of which is the Federal minimum wage and the maximum of which is not more than 120 percent of the Federal or State minimum wage, whichever is applicable, to operators of games or raffles who are either (1) active members of the licensee's company who have been active members in good standing for at least two years prior to the date of the filing of the application for the license or for renewal of the same or (2) employees of the licensee's company or its authorized auxiliary company who are residents of the State, who are residents of a bordering State if the county of residence is contiguous to the county where the bingo or charitable operation is conducted, or who reside within 35 miles of the county where the bingo operation is conducted. Wages paid to concession-stand workers at these functions may not exceed more than 120 percent of the Federal minimum wage or the State minimum wage, whichever is applicable. Because of requirements included in legislation previously enacted, the State minimum wage was increased to $7.25 per hour on July 1, 2008.

Wages paid. Employers are now permitted to pay the wages that are due employees via the utilization of a payroll card and a payroll card account. Such payment is to be done by deposit or electronic transfer of immediately available funds in a federally insured depository institution that is directly or indirectly established through an employer and to which electronic fund transfers of the employee's wages, salary, commissions, or other compensation are made on a recurring basis. Such payment of employee compensation must be agreed upon in writing by the person, firm, or company that is compensating the employee and the person who is being compensated.

WISCONSIN

Prevailing wage. On January 1, 2008, the prevailing-wage thresholds for coverage under the State prevailing-wage laws for State and municipal contracts were administratively changed from $216,000 to $221,000 for contracts in which more than one trade is involved and from $43,000 to $45,000 for contracts in which a single trade is involved. On January 1, 2009, these amounts were administratively changed to $234,000 for contracts in which more than one trade is involved and to $48,000 for contracts in which a single trade is involved.

PART THREE

REMAIN PERSONALLY CREDIBLE

*"The reputation of thousand years may be determined
by the conduct of one hour."*

—**Japanese proverb**

CHAPTER 12

MAKE SURE YOU ARE NOT PART OF THE PROBLEM

It is your responsibility as a credible activist to make sure that no managers or leaders, or you yourself, are part of the problems discussed in Part One–ever! To be a part of the solution, you'll need to influence leadership and others with company power to side with you on this issue. Use the HR Tool entitled "Sample Memo to Influence Leadership about Shared Compliance Responsibilities," at the end of the chapter, on page 199, to convince management that legal and ethical compliance should be shared. Taken as a whole, the memos in the chapter provide a general way to reinforce what we've been saying about the importance of legal compliance.

ADDRESSING A COLLEAGUE'S ISSUES ABOUT NOT TAKING COMPLIANCE ISSUES SERIOUSLY

At times it's not just the leadership who are lax about compliance; it's our colleagues at the management level across the organization as well. The HR Tool entitled "Sample Memo to a Colleague about Shared Compliance Responsibilities," on pages 199–200, shows how this might be handled.

USE YOUR AUTHORITY WISELY

Make sure you have a sufficient amount of self-awareness to realize your own feelings when you exercise any authority you may have in the workplace. Unfortunately, many people with authority in any position are often unaware of their own experiences of authority and their own use or abuse of authority, and thus we wind up with police officers who may become physically or sexually abusive or governors who abuse their authority to try to have someone fired for personal reasons.

HR professionals must be aware of the horn and halo effects which are perceived by many employees. Unfortunately, many employees have had negative experiences with HR professionals and are fearful of them and expect to have more negative experiences with them. Conversely, some employees wrongly think that HR can rescue them from whatever workplace problem they may be having. If it is appropriate, ethical, and legal, HR should be able to assist employees with any workplace difficulty; however, if the employee has violated a policy or law, HR can do little to help them avoid consequences.

Avoid Abusing Your Authority. An example of abusing your authority would be if you are aware that someone is fearful of you and you play on that fear to make your job easier, coerce a response or choice the employee has, or create fear when there wasn't any by making false statements about how much authority you do have. For example, if you don't have the authority to fire an employee on your own because it is a decision that must be made by attorneys or higher-level management, you would not want to tell an employee that you do have this complete authority in order to create fear of you. There are rarely benefits to having employees fear you. There are much greater benefits when employees can trust the HR professional.

Avoid Failing to Use Your Authority When You Need To. If you see or observe inappropriate behavior such as put-downs or bullying or harassment, it is your professional and ethical duty to address that behavior. It is probably best to address the behavior with the offending person in private as quickly as possible. Simply interrupt whatever is happening, say, "Joe, I'd like to meet with you briefly right now," and then tell Joe that he has either violated a policy and what it is and why or that he is very close to violating a policy and you need him to understand that. It is important to document that you had this discussion with Joe, and depending on your relationship with Joe and his behavioral history, you might want to have a witness in the room with you when you speak to him. You may also want to follow up with an e-mail to Joe, which can serve as documentation of the discussion as well as a communication with him to ensure that he understands what was said and what he must change about his behavior. Certainly, Joe's supervisor should be copied on this either directly or the e-mail should be forwarded.

It is very important to apply this use of authority consistently. For example, if you respond this way to Joe, but then you see similar behavior from another employee with whom you might be friendly or whom you like very much, you still must respond in the same way. You cannot say to yourself, "Well, that's just Cindy. She doesn't mean it in a bad way, and besides, everyone is laughing." You have a responsibility to address the behavior just as you did with Jim or anyone else who might exhibit that behavior.

The EQi and EQ360 are statistically valid emotional intelligence (EI) assessments that can be taken with someone who is certified in administering them and can be extremely useful self-awareness tools. With the EQi, you rate yourself on various aspects of EI, such as empathy, assertion, flexibility, and self-awareness. With the EQ360, you have others rate you on an almost identical list of qualities. It is helpful to compare one's self-evaluation to the average of a group of people who know you well. The wonderful thing about EI is that unlike our IQ, which does not change too much over the course of our lives, we can further develop our EQ and improve as long as we focus attention on doing so. See Part Six for definitions of EI skills.

Observe the culture of your company and see how others at your level and above handle misunderstandings, conflict, collaboration, anger and other emotions, frustration, and so on. Unless you see a lot of dysfunctional behavior or their behavior would be uncomfortable for you to emulate, do try to handle things as they do, so you assimilate into the company culture. If you are unable to do that or you feel that the culture is dysfunctional and needs to change, consider ways that you can handle things differently that won't be too threatening for them. Remember to make only small changes at a time; people can have rather large, unpleasant reactions to big changes, and you don't want your good intentions to influence the company culture positively to backfire.

Be aware of pitfalls such as abuse of authority. One woman observed an administrative-level employee tell an intern that she had brought the wrong kind of disposable cups into a company celebration. The truth is, it did not matter what kind of cups were there. This employee did not like this intern and had a personal need to exert power over someone. This behavior had been demonstrated many times before but not stopped by anyone, so she chose to do it yet again. Whether this was an unconscious action or not does not really matter. HR professionals must be aware of such personal feelings of being powerless if they exist, so they don't unwittingly abuse their authority and harm relationships with others.

Generally, people who abuse power do so regularly and need to have this behavior brought to their attention as part of the process of stopping it. It can become a form of bullying and harassment. It is best to speak to the employee, tell him or her what you observe, and ask for a behavioral change. Their supervisors should also be spoken to so there is a united front. If their supervisor does not see this issue as you do, you'll want to provide him or her with credible research in this area from organizational psychology and emotional intelligence academic sources, as well as with any resources from SHRM.

Be vigilant about the tendency of some supervisors to deny that anyone in their own department might have any imperfection at all or that these kinds of issues are at all important. These supervisors will probably call this kind of incident an example of a "personality conflict" or say that the offended/bullied party is being oversensitive. Be firm and discuss the previously observed behavior of the employee with the abuse problem, and if the supervisor is unmoved, ask that he or she maintain an open mind and watch for certain behaviors from this employee. Because abuse of power is a significant risk factor for workplace violence, this is not something you should ever back down on. Be persuasive, credible, and persistent on this issue.

AVOID BEING COMPETITIVE

Do notice if you are competitive. This goes back to the Seinfeld joke. When people are competitive instead of collaborative with each other, it's usually about an issue of power and ego. It's a power struggle that is usually unnecessary. When people feel threatened or jealous, they can become competitive. The importance of being "right" and wanting to be "right" about something can also drive competitive behavior. Many divorces happen over who is "right." Abuse often happens over who is "right." Being right is about power. Anger is a display of power that one feels entitled to because he or she is concerned power may be slipping away to someone else, particularly if the other person shows that he or she knows something different or new or "right."

If HR is new to an organization, other colleagues who previously handled HR issues may feel threatened or become territorial. Additionally, lawyers can at times become unnecessarily competitive with HR professionals and try to incite sparring contests over HR technical knowledge. This can lead to the marginalization of HR out of a lack of emotional self-awareness of competitiveness from those who resent that HR has technical compliance knowledge they do not have. The best way to handle this is to continue to be as pleasant as possible and continue to invite cooperation instead of competitiveness. With people who are stuck in this kind of dynamic, you will need to always have proof of research you've done on recommendations you make, as you will likely be challenged.

HUMOR GUIDELINES

The HR Tool entitled "Healing Humor Guidelines," on page 200, are from *Laughing Matters* by Joel Goodman. These useful guidelines can be presented to employees during orientation as part of a focus on corporate culture, they can be rolled out to all employees as a monthly theme, or they can even be made into enforced policy. The benefits of making policy around humor are great. We know that not all employees have the same understanding of what is and is not appropriate humor for the workplace. We also know that when policies are clearly presented and enforced, employees will take them seriously.

By implementing a policy that uses healthy humor, you create a firewall that forces employees to stop short of inappropriate behavior before they approach the danger zone of EEO issues. Doing so also makes employees feel confident that they can work in an environment of dignity, respect, and security. As we know, such an environment contributes to productivity, effectiveness, and equanimity. Also consider distributing a memo, as shown in the HR Tool entitled "Sample Memo on Healthy Humor," on page 201, to encourage this culture.

TECHNOLOGY AWARENESS ALL HR PROFESSIONALS AND MANAGERS SHOULD HAVE

Using all caps in the entirety of an e-mail is construed as "yelling." Most people know this by now. Using all caps to emphasize a word or phrase, however, is not considered yelling and is considered emphasis—unless there is an exclamation point after it and it is in an e-mail message as opposed to an announcement or presentation. So make sure you are not typing in all caps.

Poor spelling and grammar should not be used by an HR person. Actually, everyone should carefully proofread their writing, but the sad reality is that many people, even those with high school and college degrees, don't have an understanding of correct spelling or grammar. An HR person is an office worker and must be able to spell well and use grammar properly. Spelling correctly extends to people's names as well. Do pay attention to these things.

Here are some e-mail tips and usage guidelines for more effective messages.

》》 WHO?

- Make sure you send the e-mail only to those persons who need to receive it.
- Be sure to copy those who need to be copied.
- Keep in mind what kind of issue it is. Does it go to your supervisor? Accounting? HR? Many departments? All managers? All staff?

- If you are ever unsure of what kinds of e-mails your supervisor, coworkers, and management staff want or need, simply ask them.
- If you receive an e-mail you think you should not have received or you wish you had not received, send a quick response to the sender or make a quick phone call and leave a voice mail and *nicely* let the sender know. The communication is enough; no need to lecture or add anything else. A quick e-mail might read, "I don't need the communication, only _____ does. Thank you."

PURPOSE OF COMMUNICATION/SUBJECT FIELD

Make sure your subject field accurately describes your e-mail topic. Good formats are as follows:

- Report Attached—Date of Report
- Approval Requested for _____
- Clarification Needed on _____
- _____ (Simply, the topic, if above don't apply)

In addition:

- Be sure that when you reply to messages, if the subject changes to something else, that you change the subject field.
- If your e-mail reply now contains another topic, be sure that you adjust the subject field to include the new subject within the message.
- Try to limit yourself to one subject per e-mail, unless it is a report.

LANGUAGE

When requesting approval, clarification, information, or action on something, use formal language as opposed to casual or conversational language. When giving direction, clarification, or making an announcement, use formal language as opposed to casual or conversational language as well, unless your corporate culture is specifically and officially more relaxed about any of these.

CLARITY

- When replying, include the entire e-mail to which you are responding or pertinent parts of it as part of your response; this allows both you and the user to maintain a complete record of the interaction.
- Try to be as clear as possible.
- Keep the emotional tone as clear as possible.
- Words can help: excited, concerned, thrilled, confused, hopeful, uncomfortable, and so on.
- The e-mail should be able to stand on its own. Make sure all necessary information is in one place, so if it needs to be pulled up in a month or two, all the important information is there.

SUBJECT FIELDS

- Be sure that when you reply to messages, if the subject changes to something else, that you change the subject field.
- If your e-mail reply now contains another topic, be sure that you adjust the subject field to include the new subject within the message.
- Try to limit yourself to one subject per e-mail, unless it is a report.

PROOFREAD

- Proofread and spell-check your message before you send it.
- Pretend you are the recipient reading it and make sure your intention would be clear to that individual.
- Make changes to your message if you catch something that could be misunderstood, lacks clarity, or has sarcasm.

RESPONSE WANTED

- End messages with "No Reply Needed" if applicable.
- End messages with "REPLY NEEDED BY: _____"
- Note what kind of reply you need and from whom:
  - Action Taken by _____ (date)
  - Approval Given by _____ (date)
  - Clarification Given by _____ (date)
- If you want the recipient to call you on the phone to discuss the matter further when he or she is free, say so. Or, call him or her on the phone.

MISUNDERSTANDINGS

If you are offended, feel that you have been dealt with rudely or unfairly, or are somehow exasperated, you should

- Handle it on your own using sound conflict resolution skills.
- Inform the person you think there may be a misunderstanding or conflict to be resolved.
- Call or e-mail the person back and try to work it out over the phone or in person.
- Open up discussion with the other person to try to locate the source of his or her frustration and see what you can do to alleviate it.
- Unify the two of you and show that you are confident you can both work out whatever the conflict is.
- Call HR for help with formulating a response, to brainstorm, or for assistance.

If you sense that a misunderstanding or conflict is brewing in an e-mail communication, either call the person, speak to them in person, or e-mail him or her again, and *nicely* say, "I want to make sure I'm being clear. What I mean is . . . " Clarify what you need, want, and mean.

URGENCY

If your message is urgent:

- Use the Priority flag
- Clearly state what kind of response you need
- State BY WHEN—Give a date.

If your message is not urgent, say so. This helps recipients prioritize their other work and when they will reply to you.

TEMPLATES

If individuals or departments in your company request the use of templates when receiving messages, use them whenever you can.

TECHNICAL STUFF

- Update your e-mail list after staff changes and keep the Internet Technology (IT) department informed of such changes.
- Create groups for frequent communications that go to several people at once, for instance, managers, staff at your office location, and so on.
- Never delete old messages; you never know when they will be of use to you.
- Print out any important messages to keep on file, just in case.

ADDITIONAL TIPS

- Make "I" Statements, such as, "When I read this e-mail, I thought it meant _____.
- Reality-test your perceptions, consider that you may have misunderstood something, and give the other person the benefit of the doubt: Did you understand the message? Did you misunderstand the message?
- Speak for yourself and what you thought the communication meant: Did you mean that?
- Regardless of whether you understood or misunderstood the message, focus on the message even if the delivery of the message was unprofessional, harassing, bullying, or otherwise problematic. Deal with the delivery style of the message later if at all possible.
- Even when only one person in a communication that goes badly approaches the communication in this way, there is the potential for all involved to learn something by communicating well about it using NVC, EI, and sound conflict resolution skills.

E-MAIL DON'Ts

In addition to the many tips and suggestions above, here are some e-mail pitfalls you'll want to avoid:

- *Sarcasm.* Remember, without the information we get from face-to-face communications—tone, facial expression, body language, and so on—the use of e-mail sarcasm can easily contribute to misunderstandings and hurt feelings.
- *Multiple issues.* Avoid addressing too many topics in one e-mail, unless it is a report.
- *Unnecessary recipients.* Try not to include persons in an e-mail if they don't need to get the communication. If you need clarification from other staff on what they should get, ask.
- *Rudeness.* Don't be rude or unpleasant in e-mails. If you are feeling disappointed, upset, confused, or angry, you can say so using the word to describe how you feel; that is sufficient. There is no need for rudeness or unpleasantness.
- *Blame.* Don't blame others for e-mail misunderstandings. Blame is rarely useful. Even if you feel someone else is wrong, approach the misunderstanding as a learning experience for all involved, and use your best conflict resolution skills when communicating about the issue.
- *Emoticons.* Smiley faces and other text art are unprofessional, a waste of time, and somewhat adolescent. Unless you work in a culture where the use of emoticons is encouraged (perhaps a company that makes or sells emoticons), using them is not a good idea.
- *Abbreviations or acronyms.* At least the first time you use them, you should spell out abbreviations and acronyms, especially if the person you're communicating with is unfamiliar with the meanings. Non-HR people who are in any position above or below you in the company may not know the difference between FMLA and FLSA. So spell it out the first time, and put the abbreviation or acronym in parentheses after the first mention of it. Then you may use the acronym.
- *Too long or too short e-mails.* Ensure that your message is clear, concise, and only includes what is necessary and includes all that is necessary. Proofread your e-mails before you hit Send, get a second opinion if you need assistance proofreading your own work, and take a business-writing course if you need help with length, clarity, grammar, or how to communicate effectively in writing.
- *Not responding to e-mail or voice mail.* This is just rude, unless you're out sick or on vacation. Most professionals work with e-mail and voice mail software that allows them to change to their outgoing messages on both e-mail and phones to let those who contact them know that they are away and when they'll be back, whom to contact in the interim, and what to do if there is an emergency. Make sure you use this feature, and ask for help from your IT department if you need assistance in learning how to use these tools. Otherwise, not responding to e-mails or voice mails is a bad habit one should never get into. As the HR professional, you are there to serve those with whom you work whether they are employees or colleagues. One way in which you do this is to be responsive. This is true of any professional in any department, but it is particularly true for HR professionals.

See the HR Tool entitled "Sample Memo via E-mail," on page 201, for an example.

TELEPHONE DON'Ts

Long before e-mail, workers regularly picked up the phone and called each other. Speaking to another human is still part of the daily workplace experience, and when done poorly, it is a good way to lose credibility. Avoid these two poor phone habits:

- *Shouting on the phone.* There is no reason to shout on the phone. People who do this at work either work in an organization culture where this is accepted and/or encouraged (like the stock market) or they are carrying over behaviors they learned as children into the workplace and are probably causing a great deal of discomfort for those around them and for those at whom they yell.
- *Hanging up on people.* Similarly, this is a behavior people learn in their childhood years as a way of dealing with something unpleasant, and I cannot think of any company culture that would accept or encourage this behavior. Even if someone is having a very bad day, this is not a behavior that should be used at work. If you encounter this behavior, make a note that this person may not have the best self-control skills and that you will need to be careful in how you interact with this person. This is an amount of stress for you, even when this person is being pleasant, because you know that at any given moment, this person can suddenly and without warning lose control of him- or herself and engage in some other form of aggressive behavior that lacks self-control. The important thing is to make sure that as an HR professional, you are not engaging in this behavior yourself.

DON'T WASTE OTHERS' TIME!
IS THIS REALLY THE RIGHT TIME TO TELL A STORY?

How many times have you been on your way to the restroom after having just sat through a long meeting or phone call only to have someone approach you and say, "I really need to speak with you now"? Take care of your physical needs first. Unless the person is in extreme crisis, say that you will make yourself available and be able to give him or her your full attention after you've visited the restroom.

If you are the person who needs to speak to someone or wants to speak to someone, ask yourself if you are catching that person after a long meeting, on his or her way to the restroom, at lunchtime, just before an important meeting, or at an otherwise obviously bad time. Pay attention to these things. It is a very good awareness to have. In addition, once you are in someone's office talking the pressing issue, always assume that person is busy. We are all busy. Ask the person if they have *xx* minutes. Have a sense of how much time you need to talk to someone, give an accurate estimate of how much time you need, and stick within those time parameters whenever possible.

You can also use this skill in reverse when others come to your office. Try to gauge how much time you have available to give them. Know your day. Know your schedule. Know this person. Will this person cut to the chase and be concise? Will this person meander into an unrelated long story about her grandfather and how he used to take her fishing and what life lessons he taught her? Will this person ask to talk about one thing but wind up talking about many more things? Let people know, "I want to give you my full attention, but I can only give you 20 minutes today unless it's a serious complaint or a safety issue or an emergency." Knowing what kind of time you can give is an important part of managing your time and letting others know what to expect.

Knowing the difference between wanting to talk to someone and needing to talk to someone is also very important. If it is not imperative, consider the time of day, what is happening in the company meeting or event-wise, and consider that person's schedule if you know anything about it. Be prepared to send an e-mail instead of having a discussion if the person is not available. Be prepared to have to wait a day or two before having the discussion. We should be able to relax to an extent when we are talking with colleagues, and we shouldn't have to treat every discussion as an executive presentation; however, if you get into the habit of having awareness of others' time, schedule, and environment, you will be appreciated for this.

Learn to read people. Learn to notice the signs of someone fidgeting or looking at his or her computer or tuning you out. It may be that the person has a time constraint but doesn't know how to tell you. Be considerate and always ask if people have time to meet or talk if your meeting with them is unscheduled.

DO I KNOW THIS PERSON WELL ENOUGH TO TELL HIM OR HER THIS?

Some workplaces have the kind of culture where everyone tells everyone everything. Some do not. Some are in between. You can determine your own personal boundaries around this issue for yourself, regardless of what the rest of the workplace culture is. Be aware also that as an HR professional, you are setting an example for others, as are other leadership positions. Know that your behavior will be modeled, whatever you decide.

APPROPRIATE PEOPLE TO TALK TO ABOUT PERSONAL PROBLEMS AT WORK

Although HR professionals occasionally need the assistance of an HR professional just as any employee would, this is a very sensitive area depending on how your HR practice is being received. Someone may be trustworthy one month but not the next. Do be careful whom you share personal issues with at work, and whenever, try to talk to people outside of your workplace about personal issues.

READ YOUR EMPLOYEE HANDBOOK AND UNDERSTAND IT

Make sure you are included in employee handbook revisions and make sure that your handbook explicitly states that the handbook is not an employment contract and that employment is at-will. Handbooks that do not explicitly state this can be argued as evidence that an employment contract existed when it actually was not meant to have existed. If you aren't involved in revising it, do read it carefully, research what you're uncertain of, and provide feedback on the handbook to your leadership.

Don't bother trying to memorize it; like employment laws, it will always change. Your policies will change, state and federal laws will change, and the workplace will change. It's always best to look something up, read it, and be certain you're giving an employee correct information. If anything is unclear, get clarification from legal or elsewhere before communicating with employees. Follow all procedures properly, and document that you've followed them properly. E-mails confirming conversations are excellent ways to accomplish this; then everyone remains clear.

Collect all employee handbook receipt confirmations or give new employees deadlines by which they must return these to you. Putting a reminder on the shared networked calendar can help. Or you can assign this collection task to your assistant or intern to ensure there is a system in place to always collect and file these. Be sure the employee has had a chance to read the entire handbook and ask any questions.

If there are ever revisions to your employee handbook, these should be collaborative efforts among HR, legal, leadership, and finance. Be sure that the form employees sign has a place for their printed name as well, as many signatures are completely illegible. Be sure there is also a line for the date. This form should be immediately filed in the employee's file, as it may be needed if there is ever a violation of policy in the future or if an employee claims he or she was not aware of a policy.

It is unrealistic to expect employees to remember every detail of every policy, however, which is why they are given a handbook. The company intranet should also contain the latest version of your employee handbook as well as user-friendly ways for employees to search the handbook for terms or policies about which they may have questions.

You can get all the information on SHRM and other HR Web sites regarding what policies need to be in your handbook. Keep in mind that while getting the information is easy, employment laws are almost always changing and revising the employee handbook is very time-consuming. The greater challenge is to determine collaboratively with your leadership what kind of company culture you intend to build and how you'll accomplish that via policies, training, reinforcement, and leadership modeling and full support. Hopefully, this book will help both you and your leadership make insightful decisions about company culture and how you plan to influence, shape, and mandate it. Corporations do have the power to mandate their cultures. The question is, will they do it and will they walk the walk?

HR TOOLS

SAMPLE MEMO TO INFLUENCE LEADERSHIP ABOUT SHARED COMPLIANCE RESPONSIBILITIES

On letterhead, in interoffice memo format, or via e-mail

To: Your Supervisor(s)
(Include any others on this list to whom this memo should be addressed.)

From: Your Name

Date:

Re.: Shared Compliance Responsibilities

Given that we share legal and ethical compliance responsibilities, I recommend that we consider implementing a decision-making protocol for any HR issue that requires input from multiple perspectives, such as from HR, Legal, Leadership, and/or Finance.

Such a protocol would include technical assistance consultation from no-cost government or SHRM resources to ensure the use of current and correct information, build consensus, and prevent costly errors. There are a number of no-cost governmental accurate technical assistance resources available to us. I will forward those to you regularly as needed.

Additionally, I recommend that any of us involved in decisions related to discipline, demotion, probation, termination, or the investigation of harassment, discrimination, or retaliation complaints attend formal training on these issues. I will follow this memo up with a list of quality upcoming available trainings in our area and/or via webinar.

We share a strong commitment to prevent liability exposure for (Company) and for ourselves personally. We also share a strong commitment to the consistent application of all (Company)'s policies as well as compliance with all relevant city, state, and federal laws related to employment and an awareness of the importance of precedent in our decision-making processes.

SAMPLE MEMO TO A COLLEAGUE ABOUT SHARED COMPLIANCE RESPONSIBILITIES

On letterhead, in interoffice memo format, or via e-mail

To: Your Colleague(s)
(Include any others on this list to whom this memo should be addressed.)

From: Your Name

Date:

Re.: Shared Compliance Responsibilities

Given that as supervisors we share legal and ethical compliance responsibilities, I recommend that we consider implementing a decision-making protocol for any HR issue that requires input from multiple perspectives, such as from HR, Legal, Leadership, Operations, Safety and Health, and/or Finance. (List any other relevant departments.)

Such a protocol would include technical assistance consultation from no-cost government or SHRM resources to ensure the use of current and correct information, build consensus, and prevent costly errors. There are a number of no-cost governmental accurate technical assistance resources available to us. I will forward links and other relevant information to you regularly as needed.

Additionally, I recommend that any of us involved in decisions related to discipline, demotion, probation, termination, safety and health, or the investigation of harassment, discrimination, or retaliation complaints attend formal training on these issues. I will follow this memo up with a list of quality upcoming available trainings in our area and/or via webinar.

We share a strong commitment to prevent liability exposure for (Company) and for ourselves personally. We also share a strong commitment to the consistent application of all (Company)'s policies as well as compliance with all relevant city, state, and federal laws related to employment and an awareness of the importance of precedent in our decision-making processes.

HEALING HUMOR GUIDELINES

Laughing **with** Others	Laughing **at** People, Feelings, or Issues
Going for the jocular vein	Going for the jugular vein
Caring	Contempt
Put up	Put down
Empathy	Lack of sensitivity
Brings people closer	Divides people
Involves people in the fun	Excludes people
Making the choice to be the "butt"	Having no choice in being the "butt"
Builds confidence	Destroys self-esteem
Invites people	Offends people
Leads to positive repartee	Leads to one-downsmanship cycle
Can involve laughing at yourself	Always involves laughing at others
Supportive	Sarcastic
Facilitate or focusing	Distracting

SAMPLE MEMO ON HEALTHY HUMOR

On letterhead, in interoffice memo format, or via e-mail

To: Your Supervisor

From: Your Name

Date:

Re.: Recommendation Regarding "Healthy Humor" Policy

I recommend that (Company) implement a "Healthy Humor" Policy by mandating an annual hour-long training for all staff and presenting a written policy, along with the attached chart by Joel Goodman, Ph.D. I would be happy to design and present this training, which would simply explain the differences between each example of healthy and unhealthy humor and elaborate upon the many ways in which unhealthy humor is destructive at the workplace. I can provide you with a training draft for review within two weeks if you have no objections.

The benefits of implementing a policy around healthy humor using guidelines such as these are that a firewall is created that forces employees to stop short of inappropriate behavior before they even approach the danger zone of EEO issues and that employees feel confident that they can work in an environment of dignity, respect, and security. As we know, such an environment contributes to productivity, effectiveness, and equanimity.

We also know from research in the emotional intelligence field that both emotions and conflict can be highly contagious and that unhealthy humor will only encourage the spread of destructive emotions and lateral conflict among employees, which ultimately adversely affects communication, collaboration, cooperation, teamwork, and efficiency.

This policy would also support a code of conduct and an anti-bullying policy, thus reinforcing a psychologically, emotionally, and physically safe workplace for all employees.

I look forward to rolling out this important improvement to (Company)'s corporate culture and I would appreciate your support to ensure that this important new policy is consistently and soundly enforced.

SAMPLE MEMO VIA E-MAIL

To: HR Assistant (Person's Name)

From: Your Name

Date:

Re.: Acronyms in Communications with Company Staff

Please keep in mind that most (Company) staff don't understand the many acronyms for HR technical terms as we do. Please be sure to spell out the acronym the first time you use it in any communication with an employee.

Thank you,

Your Name

Title

CHAPTER 13

CONFLICT RESOLUTION

Learning sound methods of conflict resolution may be very different from what we learned in our homes growing up, but what is important to know is that conflict among humans is inevitable, and there are decades of research that have given us proven methods of conflict resolution that we know work. Isn't that great news? The solutions are there, if we want them. Approach it like learning a new language, learning to use new software, or learning to play a musical instrument; it can be done.

Being willing to learn conflict resolution skills requires being open to challenging your thoughts and feelings. We know our brains sometimes lie to us. We know primal brain can hijack rational brain. We know we sometimes are capable of not thinking completely rationally, of being mistaken, or of jumping to conclusions. We also know that our primal brain can affect our thoughts and that our thoughts affect our feelings and vice versa. Again, good news! We can help ourselves respond differently than 2-year-olds, 12-year-olds, or 16-year-olds when we have conflicts at work or anywhere. Practicing sound conflict resolution outside of work is good practice and generally good for us as professionals and as people. Given how much time we spend at work and with our colleagues, it's a good idea for conflict resolution training to be mandatory for all staff and to embed the use of sound conflict resolution skills into the culture of the organization. This is just another way to increase the potential for joy and decrease the potential for sadness, fear, disgust, and anger at work. This also serves to prevent bullying, harassment, discrimination, and retaliation.

For an example of how you might persuade your supervisor about the importance of conflict resolution training, see the HR Tool entitled "Sample Memo Requesting Training for Yourself and Others," at the end of the chapter, on page 210.

BECOME TRAINED OR CERTIFIED AS A MEDIATOR

Mediation training is excellent for HR professionals, as it can only enhance your employee relations, communication, leadership, managerial, and training skills. Many different levels and types of mediation training are offered throughout the United States and the world. Generally, when looking for a quality training, you'll want to learn whether or not the training program is approved and endorsed by the HR Certification Institute (HRCI). Another way to tell if a particular mediation training is of high quality is to check whether you can earn continuing legal education (CLE) credits by completing it. It is also important that any mediation training also provide you with ethical guidelines. In addition, before calling yourself a mediator, you should check whether your state has professional mediation certification guidelines or requirements.

The New York State Dispute Resolution Association (NYSDRA) has a pilot mediation certification program in anticipation of New York State at some point requiring professional certification in order to call oneself or practice as a mediator. The link to these guidelines is http://www.nysdra.org/userfiles/file/ethics_standards.pdf.[1] These guidelines may change occasionally, so whether you are referencing NYSDRA ethical standards or those of other mediation organizations, be sure to be on their list for revision updates. Additionally, these professional ethical guidelines will serve you well should you wish to include any of them in a contract you enter into with external mediators or other kinds of consultants.

If your company is small, it often makes sense to bring external consultants into the workplace, particularly for issues concerning mediation. When everyone knows everyone else, it is extremely difficult, if not impossible, for anyone at the company to approach staff conflict with the kind of objectivity a neutral third party can bring. However, when selecting external consultants, be extremely careful regarding their qualifications and ethical standards. Particularly when using mediators or organization development consultants, you must ensure that there are no conflicts of interest, that the consultants' qualifications are sufficient, that the consultants abide by a code of professional ethics of some kind, and that the consultants have sufficient understanding of relevant employment laws. Ask the consultants if they have such a code that is either specific to their industry or state guidelines, or if they have chosen one to present to clients and by which they intend to abide.

If you have consultants conducting any kind of survey assessment, be sure to clearly delineate who owns the results of the survey or other measurement assessment. There have been well-meaning HR professionals who have retained OD firms to conduct quite costly employee surveys of thousands of employees only to have an organizational leader determine that they dislike the actual results of the survey and choose to release their own false "results" to the employees. For this reason, it is important that any contract with consultants disallows this kind of unethical hijacking of important OD interventions by someone in the company who has the power to do so. If you suspect your company may include someone on staff capable of this action, you need to discuss this frankly with your consultant before even retaining him or her to be certain that the consultant will now allow this and will make this very clear in the contract.

For your own internal ground rules for a facilitated discussion, please see the HR Tool entitled "Sample Ground Rules for a Facilitated Discussion," on pages 210–211. A facilitated discussion is much simpler than mediation, but it can still accomplish a great deal, even in a small company where everyone knows everyone else. The key to success is that all parties follow an agreed-upon, sound process, such as the model presented on the following pages. You will want to be sure to have at least some conflict resolution and mediation training before attempting to facilitate a conflict between two people. If you cannot find a quality mediation program or if you don't have the budget or time to devote to a quality mediation program, then a course at your local college or business training center should be sufficient for conflicts that are not complex, entrenched, or extreme in any way.

Learning Nonviolent Communication (NVC) and Emotional Intelligence (EI) skills will only help your conflict resolution and mediation abilities. Influence corporate culture by using reminder posters, monthly themes (see the HR Tool entitled "Sample Monthly Theme:

Conflict Resolution Month," on pages 211–213, and training (mandatory, if possible), whenever possible. You want to do all you can to positively influence the workplace environment. However, again, the most powerful tool in cultural change is demonstrated leadership support and participation. Positive emotions and behaviors can also be contagious, so the more you can model these effective and constructive communication, conflict, and true leadership abilities, the more others are likely to model them also.

The discomfort that can occur internally as we learn that the way we've previously done or viewed something can be done in a better way needs only to be temporary. Different people have different experiences with this. Discovering a more constructive way to do something doesn't need to turn into a self-berating feeling about how you operated in the past. This can be difficult for leaders and is why arrogance is considered another recipe for disaster in organizations.

Within open systems learning organizations, the minds of leaders, HR professionals, and other executives must also be open within that system. Any discomfort that comes with learning and adjusting to more productive methods should be viewed as the hard work for which leaders are compensated.

SOUND CONFLICT RESOLUTION TRAINING

Many excellent training programs on conflict resolution and mediation skills are available that serve HR professionals well. How does an HR professional know which to choose? Your choice will often depend on factors such as budget, timing, location, and schedule. Your choice will also depend on where you think you are in terms of level of knowledge right now. Where do you go from where you are now? Have you had at least one conflict resolution training program in college or graduate school? Have you attended a conflict resolution training program elsewhere? Do you have training videos or DVDs at your office for staff (and yourself) to watch? When choosing a training program, it is best to go for the highest-quality program you can afford, which is not always the most costly.

Bernadette Poole-Tracy, Ed.D., has done masterful work on the cost of unresolved conflict. What better way to influence your leadership regarding the crucial (and often invisible) positive impact of having all staff fully educated in and practicing sound conflict resolution methods as part of the company culture? Poole-Tracy partnered with NYSDRA and offered a brilliant training to HR/OD executives and ADR professionals simultaneously. Her multidisciplinary approach is among the highest quality training programs that exist.

Multidisciplinary training is often the very best. In the modern workplace, the conflict bone is connected to the emotion bone, the emotion bone is connected to the performance evaluation bone, the performance evaluation bone is connected to the managerial skills bone, the managerial skills bone is connected to the corporate governance bone, the corporate governance bone is connected to the compliance bone, the compliance bone is connected to the profit/efficiency bone, and so on.

Of course, you must consider the learning capabilities of your staff, but hopefully, you are fully capable of understanding the simple yet profoundly true concepts Poole-Tracy presents in her research. Poole-Tracy is both a researcher and a practitioner, and that is often what lays the foundation for an excellent trainer. Her passion for her work only makes this training program even more influential. If only every workplace, government, and educational leaders were required to attend this training. Her explanation of the cost of unresolved conflict in companies is shown in the HR Tool entitled "Economic Reality of Unresolved Conflict," on page 213.

In the HR Tool entitled Alternative Dispute Resolution Fit within Organizational Development Dynamics" on page 213, Poole-Tracy discusses her interdisciplinary dispute resolution model.

Poole-Tracy's conceptual and practical exercises can be applied to examine how clear staff roles are, how they can be more clear, and how that can contribute to a positive chain reaction leading to innovation, lowered costs, greater productivity, improved goal accomplishment, and improved teamwork and conflict resolution. Make a list of 5 to 10 ways in which you can begin to do this now in your company.

SELF-ASSESSMENT

When conducting a self-assessment or an assessment of another's behavior, you want to be sure to use a sound method. The HR Tool entitled "Checklist for Self and Others' Behavioral Assessment," on pages 214–216, examines a number of relevant issues that affect people's emotions and behaviors. These are important to consider if we want to fully understand someone. We can use this to better understand ourselves, as well.

DEFER TO AUTHORITY APPROPRIATELY AND RESPECTFULLY—UNLESS . . .

Draft parameters of autonomy and obtain supervisor input and approval. Update and discuss this as needed with your supervisor so there is clarity about your role. Do treat your leadership, all colleagues, and employees with respect. When disagreeing or raising potential issues, do so respectfully. If you sense resistance, competition, exclusion, or a stubborn digging in of heels, allow those reactions and then just wait. You've sent your memo or verbally raised a concern. The call will always be yours as to how far to go in trying to influence leaders who are resistant to what works best or who believe they are not violating the law even though you've proven to them that they are or will be. Keeping the lines around authority very clear is crucial for your own sanity and professional well-being. The HR Tool entitled "Sample Parameters of Autonomy for an HR Director for a Small Company," on pages 216–217, can be very helpful and can be modified as needed.

The HR Tool entitled "Sample Protocol for Supervisor/Staff Issues," on pages 217–218, can be used to let supervisors know when and why you would like them to involve and consult with HR.

If you do find your recommendations for legal compliance being repeatedly vetoed, you may want to consider the following sections on anonymous memos and formal external complaints. Consider this carefully before taking any action to be sure you're prepared for any possible outcome.

WHEN ANONYMOUS MEMOS AND/OR FORMAL EXTERNAL COMPLAINTS ARE APPROPRIATE

There may be times when anonymous memos might be appropriate or formal external complaints may be necessary. Some companies encourage forms of anonymous communication, understanding that certain issues feel risky or frightening for employees to raise. The suggestion box is one form of invited anonymous communication that many companies use and benefit from. In addition, 360-feedback forms are sometimes used anonymously, and many companies also benefit from such performance evaluation or company survey tools. Companies with excellent outcomes also frequently use anonymous surveys measuring morale, compensation and benefits, or other aspects of the workplace.

At times employees and the HR professional might find the anonymous memo to be helpful. This would be a last resort for those employees and HR professionals who believe that they will be retaliated against if they raise certain issues. An anonymous memo can be sent to the head of a company, a board of directors, a board of trustees, a group of shareholders, a group of stakeholders, or the chair of a board, or to law enforcement and government entities such as the attorney general, an inspector general, the FBI, the governor's office, or any other relevant office or agency that is willing to accept anonymous complaints. Again, agencies and offices such as those listed generally do accept anonymous complaints because they understand that people are often aware of wrongdoing and are reasonably fearful of having their name attached to reporting it.

Retaliation is a very real issue in the workplace, and it can be difficult to prove. Most of the time persons who report wrongdoing anonymously don't seek any form of credit by reporting it; they simply just want the wrongdoing to stop. They want their workplace to function properly and in full legal compliance. When it is not safe to address such issues directly, professionally, and graciously in the workplace in a way that won't jeopardize your job, it makes complete sense to submit a written complaint. What you must remember is that if you are reporting any detail to which you are the only person who is privy, you will probably be suspected of having filed the complaint and you may still experience retaliation. You will have to be extra careful after filing an anonymous complaint and you will want to take precautions outlined in the HR Tool entitled "Checklist: Precautions to Take When Preparing Anonymous Memos and Formal External Complaints," on pages 218–219.

WHAT CAN HAPPEN FROM ONE OR MANY ANONYMOUS MEMOS

Many times, there is a group of people who work together who do trust each other and who have noticed the same kinds of things that are disturbing enough to them that they decide to take action. Frequently, these people won't consider their suggestion boxes or directly talking to their bosses about their concerns to be effective or safe. Frequently, employees have tried to communicate with their bosses on matters that deeply concern them; however, they have felt that their concerns were ignored, denied, or simply not addressed effectively.

Groups of employees will often choose to send many anonymous complaints to an investigative or shareholder body all at once. With each person writing an anonymous complaint from his or her perspective, the hope of the group is that the recipient of these letters will understand that the problem is very serious and affects many employees. The recipient will also understand that the letters have been sent anonymously because there is fear about communicating these things directly in the workplace. Any agency or entity that welcomes anonymous complaints does so for a reason and knows why offering this option to employees is necessary.

Care must be taken when anonymous letters are sent to an individual or a group that does not solicit such letters, such as a board of directors, board of trustees, or other shareholder or stakeholder group. There may not be an understanding among those group members as to why anonymous letters are being sent at all or why these issues are not just being handled within the workplace. There may not be an effective response from such a group, as it is generally not their role to handle such matters and they don't have a mechanism or process set up to respond to getting anonymous letters. Therefore, again, this approach has some risks and should only be used in the direst of circumstances when there are no other options.

Sending formal complaints to external agencies from individuals and groups may also help, depending on what the issues are. The HR Tool entitled "Sample Letter (Nonanonymous Version): Formal External Complaints," on pages 219–220 can be sent with or without names on it. However, if you do not put your name on it, it becomes difficult to include the first important paragraph in which whistleblower protection and protection from retaliation is requested.

ADDRESSING PERSONAL HABITS

Hygiene and grooming do matter. Sometimes there are people at work with whom you wish you could talk directly about certain personal hygiene and grooming habits, but you don't dare do so. Sometimes, as an HR professional, you are called upon to do this often unpleasant and uncomfortable task. Always consider the possibility of health and/or disability issues before addressing a seeming appearance or hygiene (or performance) issue with an employee. To be prudent, check with the Job Accommodation Network (http://www.jan.wvu.edu/) first or call them to speak to a specialist.

There are various things that most people have to deal with in relation to their bodies that are best done in the privacy of a restroom or at home. Be sure you're doing them privately and/or at home.

An example is a lady who would sometimes floss her teeth in her office while sitting at her desk, even though her position required that her door be open, as many employees had to come see her for various reasons throughout the day. She would sometimes stop flossing as soon as someone walked in, but she would sometimes continue flossing.

A second example is a man who picked his nose in the privacy of his own office, but, again, there were many reasons for employees to come in and visit him. He had been caught with his finger up his nose more than once, and there were now rumors spreading about his personal habits, which made people wary of shaking his hand or borrowing pens and other items from him.

You should, of course, make sure your own personal habits are acceptable. In addition, make sure you understand your company's dress code and abide by it. If there is a medical condition that inhibits this, you will want to consider documenting this and asking for some accommodation. Many people do not realize that for a good portion of the population, colognes and perfumes can cause asthma attacks, allergic reactions, migraine headaches, nausea, dizziness, and other chemical sensitivity reactions. These are very serious, and it is recommended that workplaces adopt scent-free policies. There is more information about this at the Job Accommodation Network at http://www.jan.wvu.edu/.

Jewelry in the workplace can be a safety hazard, depending on the work environment. Otherwise, there are more and more "appearance" issues arising in legislative efforts and court cases regarding unusual piercings, tattoos, and other unconventional types of adornment. The HR professional wants to know what the company rules are where he or she is and wants to follow them as long as they are sound and legally compliant.

Also, be aware of gender, racial, and cultural discrimination. Many black men have difficulty shaving their beards and can develop skin conditions, so it is not always acceptable to demand that men be clean-shaven. Additionally, many religions consider the male beard to be sacred and important. Among women, office standards of acceptable appearance should not demand criteria that are impossible or problematic for women of certain racial, age, cultural, ability, or religious backgrounds. High heels may be problematic for someone's feet. Makeup may be against someone's religion. Hairstyle requirements must be doable for all races. For some women, facial piercings are also a sacred religious ornament. And it goes without saying that in general, potentially embarrassing, natural, involuntary biological responses should not be the topic of reprimand.

A REFRESHER COURSE IN WORKPLACE MANNERS

Basic manners apply to the workplace at all times. The challenge is, not everyone was taught the same basic manners. This is another reason to have a code of conduct for employees to follow. A monthly theme on manners is a good idea, too, emphasizing the importance of greeting coworkers in the morning, saying please and thank you, and generally being helpful and courteous. Following are some helpful euphemisms:

- Instead of saying "She went to the bathroom," say "She stepped away from her desk."
- Instead of saying "He got fired," say "He's no longer with the company."
- Instead of saying "Our leadership team is fighting over the issue right now," say "We're still reviewing the documents."

Having manners even while under stress is a skill to cultivate. Emotional intelligence training and practice as well as NVC training and practice can help with this enormously and are particularly helpful for HR professionals in stressful situations. Acknowledging mistakes is a part of being polite, as much as part of being honest and having integrity. This need not shift blame onto someone else who did not make the mistake.

Being able to acknowledge that we've made a mistake is another aspect of emotional intelligence that can be further developed both individually and within the corporate culture. There is great importance in corporate leadership being able to honestly acknowledge errors. Whatever behavior leaders exhibit will trickle down eventually, whether it's wearing shorts to the office, acknowledging an error, making an inappropriate joke, or apologizing for missing a meeting. Tylenol, JetBlue, and President Obama have all set excellent professional examples of how acknowledging an error can transform the whole error into something better, whether it's better safety measures for pill bottles, improved customer service, or inviting two men of different races to resolve a potentially explosive conflict and deconstruct a misunderstanding in a cordial and relaxed manner. This is what leaders are paid for.

Leadership always sets the tone. If HR or anyone else begins admitting errors in a culture where there are serious consequences rather than a transformative learning experience, admitting errors is unlikely to continue in that culture. The danger in such a culture is that learning rarely occurs because employees are too afraid and errors continue to happen and be hidden.

WHAT DO YOU NEED TO UNLEARN AND WHAT DO YOU NEED TO LEARN REGARDING UNEXAMINED BIAS?

Make yourself aware of any personal biases you may have before you are made aware of them in a memo you don't want to receive. We must be aware of biases we may have, favorable or unfavorable, about race or ethnicity, gender, age, ability or disability, religious beliefs, armed forces status, marital status, sexual preferences, and so on. In many states, we must be aware of any biases we have related to sexual orientation in terms of others who may be heterosexual, homosexual, transgender, or bisexual. The point of making sure we have these awarenesses relates to workplace-appropriate behavior, awareness of privilege, and the ability to understand why these are considered "protected classes" if we do not already. See the HR Tool entitled "Checklist of Resources for Self-Development and Self-Examination," on pages 220, for ways to assess your own emotional intelligence.

HR TOOLS

SAMPLE MEMO REQUESTING TRAINING FOR YOURSELF AND OTHERS

On letterhead, in interoffice memo format, or via e-mail

To: Your Supervisor
(Include any others on this list to whom this memo should be addressed.)

From: Your Name

Date:

Re.:   Request for NYSDRA Workplace Conflict Management Training for all Managerial Staff

I request that all (Company) management staff attend the NY State Dispute Resolution's (NYSDRA) Workplace Conflict Management Training as their schedules allow, or that (Company) retains NYSDRA to bring this excellent training to (Company).

This training does not just teach conflict resolution and introductory mediation skills; this training teaches the four distinct types of conflicts that affect workplaces and what can be done to prevent and effectively handle them, and also addresses common dysfunctional beliefs about conflict in general.

The training also addresses constructive and destructive responses to workplace conflict, as well as how the organizational power and roles of those involved in a conflict have significant influence upon how the conflict will be handled, which is very significant for managers and leaders to be aware of.

This training addresses group conflict, interpersonal conflict, the costs of unresolved conflict, and successful options for conflict resolution. This training would serve to prevent bullying, harassment, discrimination, retaliation, workplace violence, and entrenched costly unresolved conflict that can easily spread from individuals to groups.

I believe this training would be enormously helpful to (Company)'s staff among managers, with managers and their staff, and that it could eventually be taught to all staff.

I have attached a copy of the materials from my attendance at this training last week.

SAMPLE GROUND RULES FOR A FACILITATED DISCUSSION

☐ One person speaks at a time and identifies the issues that are important for him or her to discuss as well as what he or she views the conflict to be.

- ☐ Each person should also be prepared with some ideas for solutions to the problem.
- ☐ Listen to what others say about the situation as well as how they felt about it and what they thought about it.
- ☐ If you have something you feel you must say, make a note and wait your turn.
- ☐ PLEASE DON'T INTERRUPT. Each person has a right to be heard completely. You will get your turn.
- ☐ Work hard to understand what the other person is saying even if you need to take notes.
- ☐ Remember that when we are very emotional, our IQ can temporarily drop 10 to 20 points, so be aware that you may be misunderstanding something if you are extremely emotional about the conflict.
- ☐ Be prepared to explain the other person's point of view if you are asked to do so.
- ☐ Be prepared to explain your feelings, thoughts, and needs.
- ☐ Be prepared to try to understand the other person's feelings, thoughts, and needs both now and in relation to any previous interchange you may be discussing.
- ☐ Be prepared to consider that you may have been mistaken about something, have been missing information, or may have made an incorrect assumption.
- ☐ Follow the instructions of the facilitator/mediator.
- ☐ Be aware of time limits.
- ☐ Be willing to make some adjustments in your behavior if any are requested.
- ☐ Be ready to request behavioral changes from the other person:
  - More of something
  - Less of something
  - Something entirely new or instead of something

SAMPLE MONTHLY THEME: CONFLICT RESOLUTION MONTH

DOs

INFORMING

- ☐ Use a respectful tone.
- ☐ Use "I" statements.
- ☐ State your needs.
- ☐ Use calm delivery.
- ☐ Be polite.
- ☐ Share information.
- ☐ Collaborate well with others.

OPENING

☐ Use respectful tones.

☐ Politely ask questions.

☐ LISTEN!

☐ Say "tell me more about . . ."

☐ Or say "help me understand . . ."

UNITING

☐ Use a respectful tone.

☐ Use "we" statements: "I'm sure *we* can come to an agreement about this after *we* listen to each other" or "*We*'ll find a way to work this out."

DON'Ts

ATTACKING

☐ Yelling

☐ Sarcasm

☐ Gossip

☐ Being competitive

EVADING

☐ Avoidance (unless it's a necessary cooling off period that isn't forever)

☐ Not responding

☐ Not showing up

☐ "Forgetting"

Sometimes evasion can serve as a "cooling-down" period, which can be constructive; however, it should be clearly stated: "I really want to discuss this with you, but I need a cooling-off period. How about tomorrow at 4 p.m.?"

REMEMBER

☐ It is possible to disagree in an agreeable manner.

☐ Pay attention to tone of voice, choice of words, respect for others, and loudness.

☐ Conflict is normal and can be a positive thing, if dealt with constructively.

☐ All people have conflicts, misunderstandings, disagreements, and miscommunications. What matters is how we handle them.

☐ Tone and amount of respect used can affect the words we speak. Try this sentence with different tones and see:

- "I need the information by the end of this week."
- "Can I have the information by the end of this week?"

ECONOMIC REALITY OF UNRESOLVED CONFLICT

- ☐ Unresolved Conflict Increases
- ☐ Work Avoidance Increases
- ☐ Productivity Decreases
- ☐ Accidents and Workers' Compensation Costs Increase
- ☐ Sickness and Health Insurance Costs Increase
- ☐ Absenteeism and Production/Service Costs Increase
- ☐ Forced Layoffs and Unemployment Insurance Increase
- ☐ Experienced Employees Decrease
- ☐ Training Costs Increase
- ☐ Legal Suits and Litigation Costs: Increase, while Revenues Decrease

ALTERNATIVE DISPUTE RESOLUTION FIT WITHIN ORGANIZATIONAL DEVELOPMENT DYNAMICS

Organizational Development (OD) Concepts/Alternative Dispute Resolution (ADR) Impact

Goals: Statement of the Common Focus

Role Clarity (RC): Willingness to Work Together to Achieve Goals

Roles: Clarity of What Each Person Does In Relation to Others

RC: Ability to Work Effectively with Unit Team Members & Input-Output Company Units

Procedures: Documentation of How Work is Done

Role Clarity: Awareness of Opportunities for Process Improvements

Relationships: Patterns of Interpersonal Behavior

RC: Willingness to Share Ideas—leads to—Innovation

RC: Ability to Work Cooperatively—leads to—Increased Productivity

Result: Trust in Peers and Company Leaders—leads to—Vision Realization

CHECKLIST FOR SELF AND OTHERS'
BEHAVIORAL ASSESSMENT

(This can be modified to be used as an anonymous staff survey.)

☐ Is there any rater-bias being experienced by you or someone else in any current relevant situation that might be affecting the behavior of anyone in the workplace system?

☐ Is there any unexamined bias concerning EEO categories that needs to be observed, considered, expressed, explored, and discussed?

☐ Is any training needed?

☐ Are you aware of the emotions currently being experienced by you or others in any current relevant situation that might be affecting the behavior of anyone in the workplace system?

☐ What needs are related to the emotions that currently exist in you or others in the workplace system? Are these needs being met or not? Why or why not? How can these needs be met either in or outside of the workplace system?

☐ What thoughts and ideas do you and others have about any current relevant situation in the workplace system?

☐ What do you think others are experiencing in terms of observations of you, experiences of you, thoughts about you, feelings about you, and things they need from you in the workplace system?

☐ Do you have any requests of anyone in the workplace system? Can you make those requests? Why or why not? Can someone else help you make those requests? Why or why not? Who might be available to help you make these requests, if anyone?

☐ Are there any emotional intelligence skills that you can further develop to help you handle the current situation better?

☐ If there is or has been a conflict, how have you responded? Have you acknowledged that there is a conflict?

☐ Have you been willing to discuss the conflict? Have you made resolving the conflict a priority?

☐ Have you considered what, if anything, you may have done, said, not done, or not said to contribute to the conflict, even if you contributed unwittingly?

☐ Have you been following the company (and/or SHRM for HR professionals) code of conduct? How can you follow it in an improved manner? What aspects of it can you focus on in your thoughts and feelings about any current workplace situations?

☐ How are you functioning in the system that is the workplace?

☐ How open or closed would you say the workplace system is? Why? What might improve this?

☐ Are you open to feedback and information?

☐ Are you willing to consider the feelings and needs of others? Are you aware of your own feelings and needs?

☐ Are you functioning within your role in the organization? Are there any aspects of your or anyone else's role that need to be discussed, clarified, learned about, or agreed upon?

☐ Are there any role issues related to you or anyone else in the system that are affecting you and/or others related to any issue within the system right now?

☐ Are there any in-group/out-group issues that are being contributed to by issues concerning role confusion or role-disagreement?

☐ Are there any diversity issues affecting how people in the workplace system experience in-groups or out-groups?

☐ Are there any diversity issues affecting you and/or others in the company at this time? Are there any subtle patterns around diversity that the company should take note of and consider addressing?

☐ Are any conflicts being affected by diversity issues, even if only in very subtle ways? Can this be discussed in the company, or is this an "undiscussable"? Is there any way to raise any "undiscussables" about diversity that currently exist in the workplace?

☐ Are there any diversity issues that you can see that are affecting you or your behavior or those of others in the current workplace situation?

☐ Are there any diversity issues that are contributing to in-group/out-group issues? Are there any diversity issues that are contributing to legal compliance concerns or issues?

☐ Are there any diversity issues that are creating feelings of anger, disgust, fear, or surprise for anyone in the workplace system? If so, how can HR address these emotional reactions? Alternatively, are these emotional reactions "undiscussables" in some way?

☐ Are there any current in-groups and out-groups?

☐ If so, what are these? Are there in-groups and out-groups based on any diversity issues? If so, what are those? Are there in-group/out-group issues that relate to "undiscussables"?

☐ Are you experiencing being in an in-group or an out-group right now in relation to anything happening currently in the workplace system?

☐ Are you functioning within legal and ethical compliance requirements? Is anyone in the workplace system not doing so? How are each of these affecting the workplace system?

☐ Is there agreement or disagreement regarding specifics related to legal and ethical compliance issues?

☐ Is there anything related to this that is affecting you or anyone else right now in the workplace system?

- [ ] Do any of these issues have to do with any current in-group/out-group issues? Do any of these issues have to do with diversity issues? Do any of these issues have to do with legal and/or ethical compliance issues?

- [ ] Are there any gaps between company policies and practices? Are these gaps being addressed? Have you or has anyone else in the workplace system raised these issues? Are these "undiscussables," or can they be discussed?

- [ ] Self-check: how are you doing? What are your goals for now, the next six months, the next year, and the next five years? How does that help you decide about now?

- [ ] How can you best accomplish your work goals now? How can you best get what you need in your current workplace environment? Who can provide assistance to you?

SAMPLE PARAMETERS OF AUTONOMY FOR AN HR DIRECTOR FOR A SMALL COMPANY
Recommended HR Autonomy Parameters at (Company)

HR seeks approval from leadership for:

- [ ] Creation of new positions or departments
- [ ] Elimination of positions or departments
- [ ] Compensation adjustments
- [ ] Probationary discipline of any staff member
- [ ] Any discipline of a member of senior staff (including documented verbal warning)
- [ ] Selection for certain positions (e.g., others as identified by supervisor)
- [ ] Termination of any staff.

HR will make recommendations to and consult collaboratively with leadership on:

- [ ] Benefits enhancements
- [ ] Employee manual adjustments (also consult with Finance, Legal, and any other pertinent departments).
- [ ] Recommend promotion, termination, and job design adjustments
- [ ] Written policy and procedure
- [ ] Strategic planning for OD and change
- [ ] Communications to staff about challenging company/staffing situations
- [ ] Rewards and recognition other than compensation or benefits
- [ ] Company program development
- [ ] Any incident involving an employee and the media
- [ ] Emergency response plan

HR is empowered to act independently regarding:

- ☐ Recruitment, selection, and placement for most existing positions
- ☐ Benefits comparisons
- ☐ Troubleshooting and resolving conflict
- ☐ Mediation of conflict
- ☐ Delivering multidirectional feedback throughout company
- ☐ Safety and health training and equipment issues
- ☐ Training-needs assessments
- ☐ Training creation and delivery
- ☐ Implementation of performance management system (i.e. self-assessments, managerial assessments, coaching, performance evaluations, discipline)
- ☐ Clarifying approved policy to employees
- ☐ Assessment of strategic staffing
- ☐ Company assessment instruments for all staff for anonymous/collective feedback delivery
- ☐ Needs assessment and delivery of managerial trainings
- ☐ EEO training delivery
- ☐ Individual and group trainings as needed
- ☐ Employee relations and confidential problem resolution
- ☐ Internal incident reporting with managers, workers' compensation.
- ☐ Recruitment of seasonal staff and unpaid interns

HR will always inform leadership of:

- ☐ Unlawful harassment, discrimination, or retaliation complaints
- ☐ Injuries on the job
- ☐ Complaints of bullying
- ☐ Threats
- ☐ Violence

SAMPLE PROTOCOL FOR SUPERVISOR/ STAFF ISSUES

- ☐ Verbal warnings can be handled by Supervisors with copies of documentation to HR, though consultation with HR is available and preferred.
- ☐ Supervisors should handle written warnings in consultation and collaboration with HR. HR will consult Legal if needed.

- ☐ Supervisors should handle probationary actions in consultation and collaboration with HR.

- ☐ HR will brief the designated Legal contact on probationary actions before they take place, and Legal will determine the extent to which they will be involved. Executive Leadership will be briefed before any probation or termination is decided.

- ☐ Supervisors should handle crisis suspensions or concerns about potential employee violence in consultation with HR.

- ☐ HR will brief the designated Legal contact on crisis suspensions before they take place, and Legal will determine the extent to which they will be involved. Executive Leadership will be briefed before the action, whenever possible.

- ☐ Termination will always require a review of the employee file by HR and the designated Legal contact, a discussion with the Supervisor, and a briefing of Executive Leadership.

- ☐ If Supervisor, HR, Legal, and Executive Leadership agree upon a course of action, termination will occur after HR and Legal have collaborated on the termination letter and terms of termination.

- ☐ If there is disagreement regarding whether or not to terminate or the terms of termination among Supervisor, HR, Legal, and/or members of Executive Leadership, a meeting will be called, involving Supervisor, HR, Legal representative, and a member of Executive Leadership.

- ☐ Most termination meetings will take place with HR and one other person present, either the Supervisor, a member of Legal, or a member of Executive Leadership in one of the conference rooms. All persons present during terminations will be briefed on appropriate termination behavior and reminded of (Company)'s policies related to termination: privacy issues, reference policy, nondisparagement, and so on.

CHECKLIST: PRECAUTIONS TO TAKE WHEN PREPARING ANONYMOUS MEMOS AND FORMAL EXTERNAL COMPLAINTS

- ☐ Don't prepare or print the complaint on your work computer.
- ☐ Don't research the office you are complaining to on your work computer, unless you would normally do so in the course of your work.
- ☐ Don't call the office you are complaining to from your office phone, unless you might do so during the course of your work.
- ☐ Don't use your work e-mail to file a complaint.
- ☐ Don't use a work fax machine to file a complaint.

- ☐ Don't discuss your complaint with anyone at work unless you are absolutely 500 percent certain you can trust him or her, and even then, think twice about telling anyone.

- ☐ Realize that when you file a complaint anonymously, it may take the investigating body longer to look into the matter and they won't be able to follow up with you, so you may never know to what extent an investigation has been undertaken and what results, if any, came of any investigation.

- ☐ Avoid getting your fingerprints on the letter, envelope, or stamps.

SAMPLE LETTER (NONANONYMOUS VERSION): FORMAL EXTERNAL COMPLAINTS

On letterhead (if possible, but not necessary)

Date:

Name and Address of Person/Commission/Agency to Whom You Are Complaining

To Whom It May Concern: [Individual(s) or Commission to which you are complaining]

First and foremost, I am/we are requesting whistleblower protection inasmuch as it applies to me/us at the city, state, and/or federal level for myself (and others if relevant) for making this/these complaint(s). I/we are also requesting any other protections against retaliation to which this complaint may entitle me/us.

I am/we are a current (and/or former) employee(s) of (Company), and I/we implore you to initiate an official, prompt, sound, and impartial investigation into issues concerning (choose one as many as apply: unethical, unlawful, retaliatory, conflicts of interest, financial mismanagement, harassment and discrimination, unsafe working conditions, public health and safety issues, environmental illegalities, etc.).

I/we have enclosed copies of evidence for your review with a cover sheet identifying each piece of evidence and explaining its relevance and my/our concerns.

(Only include this statement if it is true): I/we have communicated our concerns regarding these issues with (Company)'s leadership; however, these problems have not been remediated.

(Only include this statement if it is true): I/we are being (or have been) retaliated against, and I/we do fear that I/we will be wrongfully terminated in retaliation for having raised these issues. I/we implore you to contact (Company)'s leadership and order a freeze on all employee terminations until the conclusion of an official, prompt, sound, and impartial investigation. We are also concerned about incriminating evidence being removed from main system computer, BlackBerry, and other servers, and I/we ask that a forensic investigation of all (Company)'s servers be conducted as well.

If your office is unable to assist me/us with this/these complaint(s), or if these complaints do not fall within the jurisdiction of your office, please direct me/us to the appropriate place to bring these complaints as soon as possible.

My/our complete contact information (address, e-mail, phones) is below.

Thank you.

Sincerely yours,

Type and Sign Name(s)

Include full contact information for all complainants.

CHECKLIST OF RESOURCES FOR SELF-DEVELOPMENT AND SELF-EXAMINATION

☐ Learn Nonviolent Communication from a Certified NVC Trainer or join a local NVC practice group led by a trained NVC group leader.

☐ Have your emotional intelligence measured by a Certified EI Practitioner using either the EQi, the EQ360, or the MSCEIT (Mayer-Salovey-Caruso Emotional Intelligence Test) EI measurement tools. The companies Six Seconds and Collaborative Growth also have excellent EI measurement tools.

☐ Attend as many high-quality conflict resolution and/or mediation trainings you can.

☐ Attend diversity learning groups often offered by local university psychology, I/O psychology, or HR/OD academic programs. The Unitarian Universalist Church also often offers high-quality diversity learning programs as well. To look for one near you, visit http://www.uua.org.

☐ Always keep in mind that you are free to believe what you wish, but behaviorally and verbally, you must check it at the door. That is what you agreed to when you accepted your job.

PART FOUR

THE CREDIBLE ACTIVIST ADDS OD AND EI VALUE TO THE WORKPLACE

"To know what is right and not do it is the worst cowardice."

—Confucius

CHAPTER 14

WHAT MATTERS? ACCURATELY DISCERNING MUSCLE FROM FAT

When we ask "What matters?" we're asking HR credible activists and executive leadership what matters to the company and to the employees. Here are some correct responses:

- The company functions as efficiently, safely, and profitably as possible while also being compliant with all required laws.
- Leadership understands how to value employees and support efficiency, safety, and profitability in a way that is clear and workable for everyone through established practices and processes.
- Employees feel valued by the company and are motivated to do their best work.
- Unnecessary costs are intentionally avoided, and there are systems in place designed to avoid and address them.

Think about your company and ask yourself if these basics are in place. Unless you have intentionally created a system that ensures these outcomes, chances are they are not. By systemically implementing the crucial linchpins of corporate competitive governance, you will enjoy these outcomes and you will boost profits and efficient use of resources. The first step is to discern the muscle from the fat in your company. To begin, we start at the top.

SEPARATING MUSCLE FROM FAT

9 to 5, *Norma Rae*, *The Insider*, *Erin Brockovich*, *Office Space*, *The Grapes of Wrath*, *The Office*, *Silkwood* and *Serpico*. You don't want a movie or a television series like any of these blockbusters made about, or based on, your company. You also don't want employees to blog negatively about your company. And you certainly don't want the expense and embarrassment of being in violation of the seeming alphabet soup of laws with which you must comply: FLSA, FMLA, ADA, ADEA, ERISA, Title VII, EPA, FCA, EPPA (Employee Polygraph Protection Act), OSHA, NLRA, COBRA, HIPAA, USERRA, WARN, and so on. This book does not provide legal advice; however, OD has taught us how to remain legally compliant while also remaining efficient, productive, and profitable. What makes a company wind up as the focus of scandal, public disdain, or costly lawsuits and fines? Fat.

What is fat and what is muscle? Fat is anything that prevents, diminishes, or destroys what matters. Muscle is anything that promotes, propels, and supports what matters. All leaders and managers are human and may not always be able to accurately assess what is fat and what is muscle. Humans make errors regularly. Organization development theory and practice help us discern accurately between fat and muscle. The crucial linchpins of competitive corporate governance presented here will guide you to implement a corporate infrastructure that will automatically prevent fat and increase muscle.

Here is only one example of the value of knowing the difference between fat and muscle: In 1998, Blue Cross Blue Shield Illinois pleaded guilty to eight felony counts and paid $144 million after admitting it concealed evidence of poor performance in processing Medicare claims for the federal government. The company admitted it was guilty of conspiracy to obstruct a federal audit and of obstruction of a federal audit. It also falsified and destroyed documents.

In order for Blue Cross Blue Shield Illinois to have engaged in practices deemed felonies, many people had to approve those practices. Who came up with the ideas to defraud the government in the first place? Who supported and approved those ideas? Who believed that breaking the law was worth risking having to plead guilty to eight felony counts? Any employee who believes that legal risk is worth it is fat. Any employee, regardless of executive authority, who approves that risk, is fat—not muscle. Any employee who wishes to stop such practices is muscle. However, most employees who wish to stop illegal practices are afraid to come forward. How are you, as the HR leader and credible activist of your company, going to ensure that you know who is the fat and who is the muscle? How will you encourage employees who are aware of risk and liability to come forward?

In these challenging times, workplace leaders and HR credible activists need to know how to strategically supersize the muscle and downsize the fat in their workforces and operations. To survive now and remain sustainably competitive, business leaders need to look beyond the seemingly obvious cost-cutting measures of the past. The world has changed. The OD field has taught us that there is a direct link between competitive corporate governance and profits.

We now know how to do this from an OD perspective, which unsurprisingly mirrors those areas that are now scrutinized by prudent investors. There is often ultimately a direct relationship between governance and profits. Quality is more important than quantity, and cutting back does not have to mean extreme suffering. In fact, this economic downtown is an opportunity for businesses to become more efficient, more effective, and more profitable. Yes, more profitable. Implementing crucial changes in operations to ensure safety, legal compliance, efficiency, competence, and improved processes *will* save money and increase profit and productivity.

Can you afford risking convictions in civil court, criminal court or the court of public opinion? Think about these examples. Which aspects of your corporate governance might be the fat and which might be the muscle? As you consider the questions in the paragraph that follows, think of answers regarding your own company as well as the companies that have been in the news because of fraud allegations.

Who is responsible in the company for hiring and ensuring there are no citizenship issues either regarding legal eligibility to work in the United States or regarding discrimination and harassment based on citizenship? What would happen if an employee came forward and went to you or a member of your staff to say that he or she believed that the company was taking a big risk regarding citizenship issues? How would that person be responded to? In what way are you as a leader responsible for this? How do your current policies and practices support competitive corporate governance? Are there any gaps between your policies and practices? As an HR credible activist, how can you influence the necessary decision and policy makers in your company to ensure that all of the stakeholders of the company are protected by competitive corporate governance practices and operating in all ways within legal and ethical compliance?

Who is responsible for safety compliance and required safety processes and training? What would happen if a concerned employee came to you or a member of your staff to say that he or she believed that there might be safety risks or not enough safety training? How would that person be responded to? In what way are you as a leader responsible for this? How do your current policies and practices support competitive corporate governance? Are there any gaps between your policies and practices? As an HR credible activist, how can you influence the necessary decision and policy makers in your company to ensure that all of the stakeholders of the company are protected by competitive corporate governance practices and operating in all ways within legal and ethical compliance?

Who is responsible for ensuring compliance with the FLSA? What would happen if a concerned employee came to you or a member of your staff to say that he or she believed that there might be problems with employees not being paid properly for the hours they had worked? How would that person be responded to? Who is responsible for anything related to FLSA compliance? In what way are you as a leader responsible for this? How do your current policies and practices support competitive corporate governance? Are there any gaps between your policies and practices? As an HR credible activist, how can you influence the necessary decision and policy makers in your company to ensure that all of the stakeholders of the company are protected by competitive corporate governance practices and operating in all ways within legal and ethical compliance?

Who is responsible for ensuring the safe disposal of all chemicals, emissions, and materials? What would happen if a concerned employee came to you or a member of your staff to say that he or she believed that there might be illegal dumping of chemicals or materials? How would that person be responded to? Who is responsible for anything related to legal disposal of hazardous waste? In what way are you as a leader responsible for this? How do your current policies and practices support competitive corporate governance? Are there any gaps between your policies and practices? As an HR credible activist, how can you influence the necessary decision and policy makers in your company to ensure that all of the stakeholders of the company are protected by competitive corporate governance practices and operating in all ways within legal and ethical compliance?

Who is responsible for administering FMLA properly and for training managers to be compliant with FMLA? What would happen if a concerned employee came to you or a member of your staff to say that he or she believed that an employee was being harassed or discriminated against or retaliated against for needing Family Medical Leave? How would that person be responded to? Who is responsible for anything related to FMLA compliance? In what way are you as a leader responsible for this? How do your current policies and practices support competitive corporate governance? Are there any gaps between your policies and practices? As an HR credible activist, how can you influence the necessary decision and policy makers in your company to ensure that all of the stakeholders of the company are protected by competitive corporate governance practices and operating in all ways within legal and ethical compliance?

How are "internal whistleblowers" responded to? What mechanisms are in place to welcome and receive communications from concerned employees? How are "internal whistleblowers" treated after they come forward? What kind of retaliation-prevention training is in place for all managers and executives? What is the corporate response to an employee concern regarding public safety? In what way are you as a leader responsible for this? How do your current policies and practices support competitive corporate governance? Are there any gaps between your policies and practices? As an HR credible activist, how can you influence the necessary decision and policy makers in your company to ensure that all of the stakeholders of the company are protected by competitive corporate governance practices and operating in all ways within legal and ethical compliance?

How does your company prevent fraud? What is in place systemically? How might a concerned employee come forward with suspicions of fraud? How might your company respond to that employee? Who is responsible for preventing fraud? In what way are you as a leader responsible for this? How do your current policies and practices support competitive corporate governance? Are there any gaps between your policies and practices? As an HR credible activist, how can you influence the necessary decision and policy makers in your company to ensure that all of the stakeholders of the company are protected by competitive corporate governance practices and operating in all ways within legal and ethical compliance?

As you consider the answers to these questions regarding your company's corporate governance practices, ask yourself how at risk your company might be for winding up in the headlines. Find out how many charges or claims exist against your company historically.

You don't want to be the HR director or vice president for the next Enron. There is no justification or reason for costly, preventable errors. Compliance violations, safety violations, harassment and discrimination lawsuits, fraudulent activity, false claims cases, accounting scandals, and financial mismanagement are all extremely costly, but most important is that they are preventable. Anything that is preventable and costly is fat. Anything that prevents unnecessary cost is muscle. The most perceptive workplace leaders and HR credible activists will implement competitive corporate governance in order to survive and thrive in this recession and beyond.

More and more companies of every stripe are retaining the services of firms that encourage employees to come forward with knowledge of liability risk. Government agencies have inspector generals, the U.S. Attorneys' Office, the FBI, and attorney generals at their disposal for public employees to report noncompliance of any kind. Increasingly, perceptive leaders demand the implementation of formal processes and internal controls to ensure sound reporting, investigating, tracking of, and responding to violations. In addition, many companies recognize the need to prevent retaliation against employees who come forward by implementing strict and protective policies. Internal controls and processes are no longer considered by smart leaders to be invisible and insignificant. How things are done or not done can make or break a company. Perhaps most poignantly, the seemingly insignificant events that ultimately result in huge plaintiff awards, government fines, and/or CEO perp walks also significantly contribute to the condition of the current economy.

Irresponsible corporate governance and noncompliance—whether detected and punished or not—ultimately contribute to preventable wrongful termination lawsuits, preventable EEO lawsuits, governmental regulatory fines, individual bankruptcies, shareholder losses, unemployment, underemployment, disability, pension and retirement fund decimation, demotions, loss of health care, increased use of government-funded social services, increased violent crime, homelessness, psychosocial problems for children and families, defaulted mortgages, and early death. Those things are bad enough. When headlines such as "Big Three Auto CEOs Flew Private Jets to Ask for Taxpayer Money" are printed, concerns about mismanagement, fraud, and waste consume all Americans, not just workplace leaders. The court of public opinion will influence profits. The more corporate mismanagement results in taxpayer money being spent, the more impossible it becomes to even attempt to justify it and to justify not having prevented it.

The following sections redefine outdated concepts of corporate muscle and fat in a way that keeps pace with the twenty-first-century realities of globalization. Most importantly, HR credible activists and business leaders who realize the value of strategic governance based in proven OD practices are ahead of the competition in every way. The cost-saving linchpins presented throughout will ensure sustainable profitability. Concrete governance strategies are necessary in order to build an organization infrastructure that prevents costly noncompliance and garners employee loyalty in the event that determined outliers succeed in breaking through procedural firewalls. The crucial linchpins in competitive governance strategies are outlined later in this chapter.

CUT UNNECESSARY COSTS

The list of unnecessary costs below is not just a list of things to be delegated and then ignored. We've all heard the phrase "it comes from the top," and in business success, nothing could be truer. Leaders must take these risks seriously even after they delegate them to competent employees by supporting robust internal systems that prevent them.

Each of these is an example of systemic corporate dysfunction, which operates like a disease that can decimate a business, whether it is a small dry-cleaning operation in the suburbs, a family-run winery in the country, or a large multibillion-dollar international company in a city. Each of these has been the root cause of countless lawsuits and fines for many companies whose leadership did not recognize the costly significance of them.

One thing we have learned in OD in the real world is that each of these often causes another and another and all, or nearly all, of these plague another until a company simultaneously experiences layers and layers of interconnected dysfunction.

1. Inefficiency and financial mismanagement
2. Incompetence
3. Nepotism/rater-bias in performance evaluation
4. Unresolved conflict
5. Harassment/bullying/discrimination/retaliation
6. Inconsistent application of policies
7. Fraud and other illegal activity
8. Refusal to share power appropriately
9. Closed systems—not welcoming or responding to employee feedback
10. Workplace illness and injury

The bad news is that if there is not intentional planning to create systems to avoid these workplace dysfunctions, they will almost inevitably happen. This is not because human beings or groups are inherently malevolent, but because the workplace is a unique environment directly linked to the survival of modern human beings. Moreover, absent a corporate culture that clearly instructs employees and groups of employees in how to handle the inevitability of conflict, competition, role confusion, and misunderstandings, dysfunction is extremely likely. The good news is we can prevent this by implementing the linchpins of competitive corporate governance.

To whatever extent any company of any size truly implements the linchpins of competitive corporate governance, that is the extent the company will be successful. Conversely, to whatever extent any company or company does not implement the linchpins of competitive corporate governance, that is the extent to which it will experience dysfunction in the form of lawsuits, regulatory fines, high turnover, low morale, employee complaints, inefficiency, and a greater risk for workplace violence and workplace injuries and illnesses. Your company will be at much greater risk for being legally noncompliant, and your highly paid executive staff will spend very costly hours cleaning up the messes caused by these problems.

The good news is that there are proven preventative solutions to each of these, and we have also learned that these solutions often lead to other solutions until an organization is functioning optimally with sound, effective processes and systems in place. Behavior is contagious; we will implement systems so that you can use this to your advantage.

One of the biggest unnecessary costs is workplace injuries. Work with your workers' compensation insurance carrier's representative and ask if the carrier will provide free, brief safety and accident-prevention trainings to your staff with the promise of lowering your workers' compensation insurance rates on your policy as much as they can. Refer to the HR Tool entitled "Checklist of Safety Training Programs," on pages 229–234, at the end of the chapter for some ideas for what kinds of training your staff might need. You can also learn what kinds of safety training your staff may need by simply reviewing all of the workplace injury paperwork that is on file at your company. After you've read this chapter, make a list of 5 to 10 other things you can do in your company to cut unnecessary costs. Brainstorm with your colleagues, your staff, and your leadership.

ADDRESS WORKPLACE CULTURE

To what extent is your workplace culture an open or closed system? Does the workplace support a learning culture? Are compliance issues considered to be genuinely important or necessary evils? How are employees who raise concerns responded to? Does it matter who the employee raising the concern is? What three words would employees use right now to describe your workplace culture? Would employees at different levels use vastly different words? Open systems and learning cultures are crucial to preventing conflict, preventing compliance violations, preventing injury, and preventing lawsuits.

The budget is flat, hot, and crowded, too. When salaries cannot be raised, there is the concept of velvet handcuffs. Google, Walgreen's, Ben and Jerry's, SAS Institute, and some other companies have figured this out. There are inexpensive ways to create an efficient and profitable work culture that employees enjoy and to which they happily and easily remain loyal. Creating this kind of corporate culture prevents liability exposure and increases profitability by saving time and money.

We've already discussed culture and defined it extensively. Now it's time to see in which areas your leadership is willing to collaborate with you to build a sustainable, healthy, safe, profitable, and compliant workplace culture. Make a list of 5 to 10 things you can do to improve your workplace culture over the next 6 to 12 months. Choose from the following:

- Mandatory EEO/SHP/Safety training
- 360-degree feedback
- Leadership training
- EI training
- NVC training
- Conflict resolution training and policies
- Anti-bullying policies
- Healthy humor policies
- Mandated mediation or ADR processes
- Improved supervisory training
- Compliance training
- Internal feedback mechanisms
- Team-building exercises

SOUND INTERNAL COMPLAINT AND INVESTIGATION PROCEDURES

To conduct your own internal EEO/SHP training, you should familiarize yourself with all the necessary content, research and purchase DVDs or videos that you are comfortable using as training tools, be prepared to answer any questions, have copies of your company's harassment and complaint policies and procedures for all attendees, have a sign-in sheet, and have a list of what kinds of protected classes are protected in your city and state (these vary in different cities and states). You should also have a sheet defining what "the workplace" means.

Other than mandatory training programs, what other ways can you get staff interested in learning more about EEO/SHP issues? Think of 5 to 10 ways you can increase awareness of all employees' responsibilities to keep the workplace compliant with these important laws. Here are some ideas from which to choose. Check how your leadership and staff feel about them.

- Posters
- Monthly themes
- Focus groups (voluntary)
- More in-depth, focused diversity trainings
- Staff film screenings on Friday afternoons that deal with true stories of diversity, discrimination, harassment, workplace violence, bullying, or retaliation

HR TOOL

CHECKLIST OF SAFETY TRAINING PROGRAMS

BEHAVIOR-BASED SAFETY/ EMPLOYEE SAFETY MOTIVATION

☐ Accidents In General

☐ High Impact Workplace Safety

☐ Human Behavior and Reducing Unsafe Acts

BUILDING MAINTENANCE

☐ Mold Awareness

CHEMICAL/GLASSES

☐ Battery Safety

☐ Carbon Monoxide Poisoning

☐ Basic Principles of Safely Handling Chemicals

☐ Compressed Gas Cylinders

☐ Compressed Gases: Safe Handling

☐ Using Chemicals in Confined Spaces

☐ Eyewash Stations and Safety Showers

☐ Fueling a Machine

☐ Handling Gas Cylinders

CONSTRUCTION

☐ Back Care (Public Agencies/Construction)

☐ Chains and Safety

☐ Confined Spaces: Non-Entry Rescue

☐ Hydro-Blasting Safety

☐ Personal Fall Protection

☐ Traffic Control/Flagger Safety

☐ Trenching Safety

DRIVING SAFETY

☐ Buckle Up for Safety

☐ Defensive Driving

☐ Route Safety and Safe Driving Technique

- ☐ Safe Winter Driving
- ☐ Truck Safety
- ☐ Traffic Safety

ELECTRIC SAFETY

- ☐ Electrical Maintenance
- ☐ Fire Protection/Electrical Safety
- ☐ Shock Hazards and Power Tools
- ☐ Power Line Safety

ERGONOMICS

- ☐ Carpal Tunnel Syndrome

GENERAL SAFETY

- ☐ First Aid Kits

HAND SAFETY

- ☐ Amputation Injuries
- ☐ Hand Protection
- ☐ Hand Safety

HAZARD COMMUNICATION

- ☐ Chemical/Waste spills
- ☐ Basic Principles of Safely Handling Chemicals
- ☐ Using Chemicals in Confined Spaces
- ☐ Eyewash Stations and Safety Chemicals
- ☐ Hazard Communication for Office Personnel
- ☐ Hazard Communications for Janitors/Custodians
- ☐ Hazard Materials and Leaks, Drips, and Spills
- ☐ Cleanup
- ☐ HazCom Training for Employees
- ☐ Role of the First Responder
- ☐ Restaurant Hazard Communication "Right to Know"

HEALTH CARE

- ☐ Elements of Back Care/Health Care
- ☐ Ergonomics: Safe Patient Transfer

- ☐ Fire Safety for Health-Care Facilities
- ☐ General Safety for Home Health Providers
- ☐ Hazard Communication Standard (Home Health Care)
- ☐ Health-Care Violence
- ☐ How to Prevent Slips and Falls (Health Care)
- ☐ Infection Prevention and Control for Home Health Care
- ☐ Lifting Patients from Beds
- ☐ Lifting Patients from Wheelchairs
- ☐ Moving and Lifting for the Home Health Care Setting
- ☐ Oxygen Safety for the Home Health Provider
- ☐ Protecting Against Hepatitis B in the Workplace
- ☐ Sanitation and Disinfection in the Health-Care Environment
- ☐ Sanitation in Health-Care Cafeterias

HEARING

- ☐ Hearing Protection
- ☐ Machine Guarding and Conveyers
- ☐ Machine Guarding Responsibilities
- ☐ Machine Safety Guards
- ☐ Machine Safety
- ☐ Personal Protective Equipment

HOTELS

- ☐ Back Safety
- ☐ Bacteria and Disease Control
- ☐ Controlling Exposures to Bloodborne Pathogens
- ☐ In Service Industries
- ☐ Hazard Communications for Janitors/Custodians
- ☐ Hotel Safety
- ☐ Housekeeping Safety (Hotels)
- ☐ Kitchen Safety
- ☐ Safe Lifting

HOUSEKEEPING

- ☐ Bacteria and Disease Control
- ☐ Floor Cleaning Tips

LADDER/SCAFFOLD SAFETY

☐ Ladder Safety

☐ Scaffolds Safety

LANDSCAPING

☐ Groundskeeping Safety

☐ Heat Safety

☐ Power Tools and Machinery Safety

LOCKOUT/TAGOUT

☐ Energy Sources

MACHINE SAFETY

☐ Amputation Injuries

☐ Baler Safety

☐ Fueling a Machine

MANUFACTURING

☐ Amputation Injuries

☐ Back Safety

☐ Employee Safety Orientation (Manufacturing/Warehouse)

☐ Hand Protection and Hand Guarding

☐ Machinery Safety

☐ Personal Protective Equipment Use

MATERIAL HANDLING EQUIPMENT

☐ Crane Safety

☐ Back Safety for Material Handlers

☐ Chains and Safety

☐ Chains, Slings, and Hoist Safety

☐ Electric Pallet Jack

☐ Forklift Loading

☐ Forklift Operator Safety

☐ Materials Handling and Storage (Chemical Drums)

☐ Roll Off Operations and Safety

☐ Safe handling of Wood Pallets

OFFICE SAFETY

- ☐ Egress/Exit Safety
- ☐ Ergonomics
- ☐ Fire Extinguishers
- ☐ Fire Safety: Alert, Aware, Alive
- ☐ Hazard Communication for Office Personnel
- ☐ Preventing Slips, Trips, and Falls
- ☐ Safety Orientation in Office Environments
- ☐ Stay Low, Stay Alive
- ☐ Video Display Terminal Safety
- ☐ Hepatitis B Safety
- ☐ Puncture Wound Prevention and Safety

PERSONAL PROTECTIVE EQUIPMENT

- ☐ Electrical Maintenance
- ☐ Eye Protection
- ☐ Fit Testing/NIOSH Rules
- ☐ Head Protection
- ☐ Hearing Protection
- ☐ Personal Protective Equipment
- ☐ Respirator Safety and Standards

RESPIRATORY SAFETY

- ☐ Carbon Monoxide Poisoning
- ☐ Stairways and Ladders
- ☐ Work Surface Safety

SUBSTANCE ABUSE

- ☐ Cocaine
- ☐ Drug Use and Abuse
- ☐ Recognizing Drug and Alcohol Abuse for Employees
- ☐ Recognizing Drug and Alcohol Abuse for Managers
- ☐ Alcohol at Work

SUPERVISOR TRAINING

- ☐ Conflict Resolution
- ☐ Documentation of Safety Efforts

- ☐ Hazard Recognition
- ☐ How to Develop a Safety Program
- ☐ Safety Committee
- ☐ Safety Tips for New Safety Supervisors
- ☐ Workplace Safely Inspection Checklist

TOOL SAFETY

- ☐ Box Cutter Safety
- ☐ Powered Hand Tool Safety
- ☐ Shock Hazards—Power Tools

WELDING

- ☐ Gas welding safety
- ☐ Safe welding

WORKPLACE VIOLENCE

- ☐ Conflict resolution
- ☐ Sexual harassment: Your rights and responsibilities[1]
- ☐ Workplace violence

CHAPTER 15

FOSTERING FEEDBACK, TRAINING, AND IMPROVED PERFORMANCE MANAGEMENT

Smart performance management is accurate, unbiased, free of attribution error, comprehensive, robust, and multidirectional. It includes multiple raters, approaches job performance issues with curiosity and the benefit of the doubt, regards job performance as one part of a larger workplace system, and always checks for disability, health issues, or challenges, as well as having the necessary tools, time, and training, before evaluating job performance.

In order to achieve smart performance management, anyone evaluating performance must first be trained in all of the above elements of sound assessment. Adults learn best experientially, so training that involves different practices with different ways of rating performance—and is fun—works best. If you are qualified to present such a training program, go for it. If not, bring in an external consultant.

Cornell School of Industrial Labor Relations (ILR) offers excellent training programs, as do many other training providers. Along with training, your company will still need a sound performance management system. Using a reliable 360-degree feedback assessment, along with evaluation of adherence to a company behavioral code and assessment of job description duties, is a good start. There are many options for performance management mechanics and formats, but having supervisors trained in the elements mentioned above is the first and most crucial step no matter which mechanism or format you ultimately use.

SOUND INTERNAL COMPLAINT PROCEDURES

Implementing sound internal complaint procedures begins with leadership, legal, supervisors, and HR/OD genuinely wanting to know if there are any complaints and what those are. This is a crucial piece of culture that must not be glossed over or assumed to be in place. In many companies it is nonexistent, and millions of dollars in unnecessary lawsuits, injuries, and regulatory fines are the result. Do leadership, legal, supervisors, and HR/OD genuinely want to know if there are any complaints and what those are? Do they only want to know if the complaints are from certain employees? Do they only want to know if the complaints are against or not against certain employees? Do they simply not want to know? Does each and every employee in any position in leadership, legal, management, or HR/OD truly and genuinely want to know and want to receive any complaints regardless of whom they come from and whom they're against? Furthermore, is each employee in any of the positions authorized to receive employee complaints properly trained in how to receive, respond, process, and document those complaints? If the answer to any of these questions indicates that there are employees who need training or a shift in perspective, this should be considered an urgent matter to be handled as soon as possible with the full support of leadership.

Regular, high-quality training is necessary for all employees, but especially for managers. Regardless of what your company employee handbook says, what your company policies are, and what your company's stated "values and culture" are, the fact is that employees report to and share experiences with their supervisors and managers. *To employees, those experiences with their supervisors, managers, and other colleagues are the company.* And they are. The law says that the impact upon a person is more important and carries more weight than the intent. That means that someone saying, "But I didn't mean for my joke/words/comment/picture/etc. to be offensive! My intention was not to offend but to joke/laugh/etc." The court and the law do not care about intention; they care about and rightly look at the impact this behavior had on the person whose civil rights were violated. What can we learn from this? The very important lessons in this for all of us are the following:

Corporate culture is crucial. Think about the word culture. If you ever took an Anthropology 101 course in college, you know that one of the definitions used by anthropologists to define culture is that it is a set of answers to questions such as:

What is funny?
What is sad?
What is insulting?
What is socially acceptable?
What is taboo?
What gender roles are there?
What age roles are there?
Are events and milestones acknowledged and/or celebrated?
If so, how, when, why, and for whom? For all people or just certain people?
Who, if anyone, has a dominant role in the culture?
If so, why? What is the history of this?
How does the nondominant part of the culture experience the dominant part?
What disparities exist in the culture as a result of having part of the culture be dominant?
Are there any challenges to this dominance within the culture?
How is conflict handled?
How does cultural dominance influence how conflict is handled?
Is there a concept of "wrongdoing" in the culture?
If so, how is that handled?

Of course, this list of questions goes on, but these are the questions about culture that can be transferred to our understanding of the workplace and can help us determine how our workplace culture can best serve our quest for a corporate governance that is legally compliant.

Willingness from leadership is crucial. A company can have the best employee handbook with the best-written and designed policies in the world, but if the company's leadership is unwilling to comply with these policies in a serious and consistent manner and in all circumstances, that is a serious crack in the dam. Heather Anderson of Leading

Challenges (http://www.leadingchallenges.com) teaches CEOs regularly that they are *in the business of influencing behavior.* We know that most employees will eventually do whatever they see someone with more organizational authority than they have doing—whether it's related to dress code, drug use, sexual jokes, jokes about disabilities, jokes about race, attending meetings late, yelling at staff, or producing shoddy work and cutting corners.

Some of these things are not particularly problematic; some workplace cultures do start all their meetings a bit later than they're scheduled for. That's okay, because it doesn't violate any laws. Some corporate cultures allow casual dress, and that's also okay for the same reason.

Part of addressing willingness includes addressing resistance that may and often does exist. Again this goes back to the Monopoly box joke. Are leaders (and frequently corporate lawyers) willing to acknowledge that a corporate governance that is legally compliant requires certain behaviors, decision-making processes, conflict resolution skills and procedures, awareness, and technical knowledge of them? Are they willing to further acknowledge that they may not always have the technical knowledge required for a situation and that their choices are to either learn that technical knowledge or trust someone else in their organization who does have that technical knowledge? And, further, are they able to trust someone else to have the correct technical knowledge? If yes, why and why that person? If not, why not, and why not that person?

This means being willing to invest in high-quality training programs and to hire qualified people for all positions handling any compliance issues from supervisors to lawyers to HR staff to leadership. This means being willing to terminate the best salesperson if he repeatedly sexually harasses others. This means being willing to tell the VP down the hall with whom the leader may have become very friendly that she must change her behavior, because she is significantly harming the corporate culture and placing the company in danger of legal noncompliance. This means being willing to consult with widely available credible free technical assistance sources and invest in training for themselves and their staff on a regular basis, because the goal is compliance.

ONGOING LEADERSHIP AND EMPLOYEE DEVELOPMENT

Leaders must be connected to the outside world of leadership in some way, whether through an alumni association, an annual meeting of leaders, a professional company, monthly subscriptions to leadership publications, regular training and development, or regular executive coaching. You yourself must continue to develop because you will demand this from your staff, and you will need to know what they're talking about and why it is relevant for your business. You cannot afford to not sharpen the sword.

The ground rules shown in the HR Tool entitled "Sample Basic Management Training," at the end of the chapter, on page 244, can be customized and done internally for any managers or leaders who need to develop basic management, leadership, communication, delegation, and managerial self-awareness skills.

LEADERSHIP SELECTION AND TRAINING

Conflict resolution skills, communication skills, compliance awareness, and emotional intelligence skills are necessary leadership skills. Leaders must walk the talk, demonstrate high EI skills, give praise when deserved, be compliant with all policies, embrace the concept of open systems and transparency, and reject nepotism, personal bias, and abusive behavior. Leaders must also embrace appropriate power sharing with persons whose skills, knowledge, and abilities would benefit the company and whose roles require their involvement. Leaders call abuses what they are and know that if they don't, the abuses will continue. Managers and supervisors are part of leadership and must be trained to understand and adhere to governance strategies for efficiency and behavioral modeling.

SOUND CONFLICT RESOLUTION METHODS AND SKILLS TRAININGS

Leadership, HR, and management must never avoid conflict. Conflict is almost always an opportunity to improve a system, process, hierarchy, or communication. All employees must be trained in conflict resolution; policies and culture must support sound conflict resolution methods. Regardless of what a person's "default conflict system" is, in an open-systems learning culture, conflicts are resolved using sound processes which are known to be effective. Above-average conflict resolution skills must be requirements for any supervisory, managerial, or leadership positions. When leaders model above-average conflict resolution skills for all other employees, the behavioral bar is raised and a major linchpin of culture is firmly placed which prevents the enormous expense of unresolved conflict. Unresolved conflict is significantly costly in terms of quality of work relationships, work productivity, contagion of the conflict spreading to others, and time spent resolving complicated, entrenched conflicts.

The New York State Dispute Resolution Association (NYSDRA) is an example of a training company that offers extremely effective training programs for HR/OD professionals and other executives. NYSDRA's programs go beyond teaching sound conflict resolution methods and skills and strive to integrate salient knowledge about the anatomy of conflict, different kinds of conflict, the cost of unresolved conflict, and tools for effectively handling conflict. In addition, companies like NYSDRA present the highest-quality programs and are invaluable for HR/OD professionals and other management executives because they have highly qualified trainers who are also scholars, researchers, and practitioners working in cutting-edge, multidisciplinary, and interrelated fields. Such companies value the overlap of the fields of alternative dispute resolution, EI, constructive communication, OD, and HR.

For those business executives who realize they don't really have the skills they need to competently and effectively handle the many types of workplace conflict, NYSDRA invites them to network with Alternative Dispute Resolution (ADR) Professionals and with OD trainers, who can train them, coach them, and assist in mediating workplace conflict. NYSDRA offers an unrivaled program in Workplace Conflict Management that teaches the types of workplace conflict that exist, what will likely occur without sound intervention, how conflict escalates, how it deescalates, and how it is often enormously affected by how much company power those involved in the conflict have.

What kind of conflict resolution system do you have in place? How do your executives resolve conflict? Do they? Are employees walking around with grudges against each other, deleteriously affecting the quality of your operation? How much money do you think you are losing because of unresolved conflict in your company? We know that conflict is inevitable. We also know that we have sound methods of resolving conflict productively. We also know that most of us have to be taught these skills in order to carry them out because we aren't born with them. With this in mind, refer to the HR Tool entitled "Sample Conflict Resolution Procedures," on pages 244–245, for one way to approach this issue.

IMPLEMENT EMOTIONAL INTELLIGENCE TRAINING, COACHING, NONVIOLENT COMMUNICATION TRAINING, AND ACCOUNTABILITY AS IMPORTANT CORPORATE CULTURAL VALUES

In order for employees to give their best at work, they need to know at all times, but especially during hard times, that they are physically, financially, and psychologically safe. The workplace culture, policies, leadership, management, handling of conflicts, and processes must communicate these things at every opportunity. There are simple, practical ways to accomplish this. Demanding above-average emotional intelligence (EI) skills from all employees raises the bar for communication, behavior, and conflict resolution. Doing this prevents costly problems that have plagued workplaces and have easily developed into unnecessary lawsuits. How a sexual harassment complaint is handled, how a potentially dangerous safety issue is handled, or how an employee's point that could prevent a disastrous computer glitch is handled are all examples of how emotional intelligence skills can make or break the bank.

How does the emotional intelligence of leadership and any other executives who enjoy the privilege of having great organizational power affect the decisions made by them? How does their emotional intelligence affect their responses to HR calling for legal compliance? How does their emotional intelligence affect their responses to possible EEO claims, actual EEO claims, OSHA citations, employee feedback, employee complaints, HR's concerns about disparate treatment of employees, and conflicts of interest? How does the EI of any workgroup affect their job performance and how well the group functions? How can EI training improve decisions at every level, increase profits, and increase efficiency in your organization?

Nonviolent communication (NVC) training can instill behavioral, communication, and most importantly, improved thought processes in the entire company. As described throughout this book, NVC teaches very simple basic communication skills that start with our feelings and thoughts. In this way, NVC is a perfect training complement to EI and conflict resolution training, as well as any communication or management training. NVC is exemplary in that it is very easy to learn and very efficiently helps individuals and groups get to the core of an issue. Be sure to find a Certified NVC trainer as well as Certified EI trainers.

Reinforcement of these important and fun learning tools through coaching and accountability for the entire organization using a learning organizational approach can and will transform the ugliest and costliest of workplace cultures in as few as 6 to 12 months—as long as quality training is involved with leadership's full support.

Remember, emotions and behavior are contagious. If we do nothing to influence corporate culture, we will almost inevitably wind up with the ugly and costly remnants of unconscious fear, disgust, and anger from individual and group primal-brain instincts, urges, and reactions. However, if we choose training, reinforcement, leadership support, and accountability, corporate culture can and will bloom into a cost-savings mechanism which will be evident once there is sufficient learning, practice, and cultural transformation. Visitors to your company will notice the many good outcomes resulting from using EI, NVC, and sound conflict resolution training programs to produce a culture that uses the best of what our brains have to offer.

SMART PERFORMANCE MANAGEMENT

Eliminate rater-bias and attribution error by using 360-feedback mechanisms, providing necessary management and conflict resolution training programs, clearly identifying what is wanted, and demanding accountability. Understand employees' strengths, give them work they can succeed in completing well, and adjust positions, if necessary, to maximize staff productivity. All employees should know that core communication, collaboration, and behavioral skills are just as important as technical skills. Goals are made clear, coaching and mentoring are regularly available, improvement is supported, and mistakes are learning opportunities. Promotions are based on performance. Titles are based on job descriptions, and there is consistency in application of titles, salaries, and privileges.

What would happen if someone, let's call him person A, did a great job but his supervisor did not like him for whatever reason? What would happen if someone in the same department, person B, did a terrible job, but she had been friends with the supervisor for years? What would happen if one day this supervisor promoted person B but did not promote person A? What would happen if person B was given a large salary increase, but person A was given a much smaller salary increase? How might this impact the company if person B's errors weren't noted but person A's errors were? How might this impact the company if person B's very serious or frequent errors weren't acknowledged, noted, documented, or addressed, but person A's much smaller and/or infrequent or less serious errors were acknowledged, documented, and addressed in performance evaluations as serious matters?

How might this impact the job performance of person A? How might person A's anger impact the operation of the business? Whom might person A discuss this with? How might this impact the entire workforce once employees notice this and discuss it? How might this eventually cause large problems for this company?

Do you have a situation like this anywhere in your company? How would you know if you did? Consider what your liability risk in this situation might be after what you have already read.

Certainly, there are times when performance is problematic and it needs to be addressed. Problematic performance can be anything from needing to acquire a new skill, needing to enhance or master a skill, needing to improve behavior or communication skills, or needing to follow company policies.

When skills are an issue, the company must look at why this person is in this position and how he or she got there. Frequently, HR/OD professionals inherit situations where the wrong person is in the wrong position for a number of reasons. Sometimes you can remediate this and sometimes you cannot. If the owner of the company has his incompetent, harassing, rule-breaking son-in-law in an important position that requires competence, respectful behavior, and visibility, you have a serious problem. Certainly, the credible activist will do what she can to explain to the business owner the many liabilities involved in keeping the son-in-law in that position with his current skill set and behaviors. If the business owner cannot be persuaded to send the son-in-law to needed training programs and demand that he change his behavior immediately—or transfer the son-in-law to the basement library job where he won't be seen, heard, or have any interaction with anyone—you will have a very challenging situation.

As we know from credible EI research, behavior and emotions are very contagious, and emotions linger.[1] Other employees will undoubtedly resent what the son-in-law gets away with, their own behavior will become more lax and more like the son-in-law's behavior, the anger about the special treatment afforded the son-in-law will start pouring in, and the anger over his incompetence versus the competence of the other employees will only add to that anger. Very soon, this poor HR professional will have an angry mob on her hands. Even if there is fear among employees about complaining about the son-in-law, the anger will seethe silently under the surface. Everyone will know about it, but nobody will officially complain or actually speak to HR about it. What will likely happen is there will be anonymous complaints dropped into the suggestion box, there will be stories of injustices blogged about on the Internet, and there may be leaks to the press about what the son-in-law is allowed to get away with.

Hopefully, you haven't inherited too many wrong people placed in the wrong positions, and hopefully if you do need to help a manager handle a performance issue, it is handled with some friendly critical thinking, effective feedback delivery, coaching discussions, and appreciative inquiry.

Frequently, what at first appears to be a performance problem turns out to be only a misunderstanding. As supervisors learn through training and improved corporate culture to become motivating managers who elicit excellent work from their staff members, employee performance will definitely improve. Many times supervisors simply have not clearly communicated to their staff members what they expect from them. In the case of workplaces that have not yet implemented the use of formal job descriptions and regular coaching sessions for supervisors and employees, it is easy for misunderstandings to occur regarding what is expected.

There are many effective ways to manage performance. The HR Tools entitled "Checklist of Characteristics of Great Managers" and "Checklist of Conditions in a Workplace System That Support Excellent Employee Work," on pages 245–246, outline some of these. After perusing the information, you will notice that this issue is not just about whether a particular employee is trying hard enough or is even the "right fit" for the position. It is about an entire workplace system and to what extent that system supports employees in producing their most excellent work.

Before we delve further into characteristics of effective managers, let's look more closely at a couple of terms we've been using throughout the book. First is attribution error, which, as the term implies, occurs when the wrong source is blamed for the error. Say, for example, you order soup, and when the soup arrives, it is cold. You blame the chef, thinking that he didn't cook it long enough; however, the real reason is that the delivery person's bike got a flat tire and he took too long to get the soup to you.

The second term is rater-bias. Rater-bias happens when, for example, the son-in-law mentioned earlier is given all excellent scores on his performance evaluation despite chronic problems with competence, behavior, and interpersonal difficulties. Other employees who are more competent, don't harass others, and don't have problematic interpersonal skills are given lower ratings because they don't have a favorable relationship with the boss.

Other terms that frequently show up in HR/OD training programs are Theory X and Theory Y management styles. First defined by Douglas McGregor at the MIT Sloane School of Management in the 1960s, Theory X easily blames the employee for his or her job performance without looking at any other factors or even considering that there is a workplace system that is contributing to employee performance. This method of job performance assessment is very old-fashioned and easily misses a great deal of important information. This style also frequently makes attribution errors or engages in rater-bias. Theory Y, on the other hand, recognizes that employees are self-motivated, achieve pleasure from their work duties, and can attain a level of self-control. They innately possess problem-solving abilities, but the organization must know how to tap into these abilities. They also possess the desire to perform quality work. See the HR Tools entitled "Checklist of Characteristics of Great Managers" and "Checklist of Conditions in a Workplace System That Support Excellent Employee Job Performance," on pages 245–246, for some ideas on what a great management style involves.

There are times when despite all of the items listed in the HR Tools section being in place, an employee has difficulty performing well. In this case, managers and HR will need to document the steps taken to assist the employee in improving. When this occurs, it's important to guide managers and supervisors through an assessment process that ensures that negative or positive rater-bias, attribution error, personal conflicts of interest, unexamined unlawful discrimination, or misinformation are not interfering in any way with a fair, sound, rational, nondiscriminatory, error-free and bias-free performance evaluation process. This is not always easy, as not all managers or corporate leaders are open to what they see as an unnecessary training and/or an easy process. Credible activists understand the importance of doing their best to convince their leadership of the necessity of such training and processes. See the HR Tool entitled "Sample Performance Management Procedures: Your Map for Coaching and Discipline," on pages 247–248.

Before you convince leadership of the importance of sound managerial assessment skills, you must convince them of the importance of sound managerial communication, delegating, and directing skills. The HR Tool entitled "Sample Training on Delegating, Directing Effectively, and NVC Problem Solving," on pages 248–250, shows a training outline to help managers understand the impact of their words, their tone, their EI, their goals, their expectations, and how clearly they communicate.

The HR Tool entitled "Sample Performance Management Procedures: Your Map for Coaching and Discipline shows a training review, recommended for all managers and especially for new managers, of what and when to document, how to document, and when to consult with HR.

There may be times when disciplining an employee is necessary. If managers and HR are collaborating sufficiently to recruit and select the best-qualified people for their positions; if all employees have sufficient tools, time, and training to succeed in their jobs; and if the corporate culture is one with a solidly and consistently enforced code of conduct and an open system that solicits employee feedback regularly and is positively responsive to this feedback, discipline should be a rare event. However, the HR Tool entitled "Checklist of Six Questions to Ask Yourself before Disciplining an Employee," on pages 250, shows some guidelines to follow before you determine whether to move forward with discipline.

It is also very important to solicit feedback from those who attend any training. The form in the HR Tool entitled "Sample Feedback Sheets," on pages 250–251, can be customized and used to invite feedback on any training programs you design and present.

The HR Tool entitled "Sample Managerial Record-Keeping for Employee Job Performance Tracking," on page 252, is only one example of a tool that can be used when this is needed, after NVC problem-solving and effective feedback delivery.

Hopefully, the appropriate people in the company have control over determining who has the required skills, knowledge, and abilities, as well as corporate cultural attributes required for success during the selection process. (For those who don't have these requirements, there is a simple postcard text, shown in the HR Tool entitled "Sample Postcard to Send to Applicants You Will Not Be Interviewing," on page 265, in Chapter 16.) It is recommended that you have several hundred or thousand of these printed up so you can have your assistant or intern send them out to those candidates who are not scheduled for any interviews.

The HR Tool entitled "Sample Manager's Self-Assessment Tool," on pages 253–254, can teach all managers about giving effective feedback to employees when communicating privately with the goal of discussing job performance goals, perceptions, and any gaps between those two.

Review the HR Tool entitled "Checklist of 2008 General Mills Awards," on pages 254–255, and ask yourself the following questions: How many would your company win? What does this list tell you about General Mills and its internal governance? Clearly, they have all the crucial linchpins in place and are functioning optimally. They are also having an incredibly positive effect on the communities in which they operate.

In contrast, consider some of the other companies we've looked at throughout this book. Consider other companies in the headlines now. Ask yourself how your company's internal corporate governance might be rated if each of your stakeholders were able to rate you—employees, customers, community, investors, board members, and so on. Now, do all you can to influence your leadership to fully support you in collaboratively installing these crucial linchpins so your corporate governance is competitive governance.

HR TOOLS

SAMPLE BASIC MANAGEMENT TRAINING

GROUND RULES

- ☐ Allow the presenter to present the information with no interruptions.
- ☐ If you have a thought or question, note it; there will be specific times to contribute.
- ☐ Participate!
- ☐ Be respectful.
- ☐ Be aware of time limits.
- ☐ Follow instructions.
- ☐ Be willing to learn.

SAMPLE CONFLICT RESOLUTION PROCEDURES

- ☐ These structures are new to all of us.
- ☐ It will take time to develop new habits and ways of working, communicating, and supporting each other to grow, excel, and succeed.
- ☐ We will all be patient with each other if we forget our new procedures.
- ☐ We will all give each other the benefit of the doubt.
- ☐ We will refrain from blaming each other whenever possible.
- ☐ We will gently remind each other of our new procedures for working and communicating.
- ☐ ANY conflict about these new procedures can and should be brought to HR to resolve. HR will be a safe haven for any party having conflict with these new ways of working.
- ☐ HR will gently, without blame, clarify procedures, and redirect the parties to adhere to our new working procedures.
- ☐ This is not about discipline; this is about supporting everyone at (Company) to EXCEL.

Because these procedures are new to us, we may need to check in with each other and remind each other more frequently at first (perhaps even once a day) to make sure we are employing these new ways of working together. It's OKAY. We need to agree that it's okay and it's SAFE to do so.

Gradually, as time goes on, we'll probably do this less and less. However, everyone should feel safe to ask any questions they have if they are unsure of how to proceed with communications or responsibilities.

If we need to revisit and revamp them, we will do so as needed.

Feedback regarding how these procedures serve the three goals is always welcome and should be directed to HR.

The three goals:

☐ All (Company) staff are empowered to succeed and excel at their jobs.

☐ Support the profitable GROWTH of (Company).

☐ All employees support safety, EEO, and total policy compliance with all behavior at all times to ensure a positive working environment for everyone.

CHECKLIST OF CHARACTERISTICS OF GREAT MANAGERS

MSA = Managerial Self-Awareness (Allan H. Church, Ph.D., and Janine Waclowski, Ph.D., lecture, Teachers College, Columbia University, April 2001). MSA-Managers WANT to know how their staff experiences them

☐ Great Managers WANT to develop as much MSA as possible.

☐ Developing MSA means being able to consider that you can manage differently and better!

☐ Developing MSA means wanting to know how to adjust your management style so it's more effective!

☐ Great Managers contribute to a culture of Constructive Feedback Delivery, where it's safe and not threatening to get constructive feedback about how you're doing.

☐ Great Managers give feedback constructively!

☐ Great Managers are a pleasure to work for and with, most of the time!

☐ Great Managers motivate staff to do their best work!

☐ Great Managers model the behavior they want from their staff!

☐ Great Managers develop effective ways of handling conflict!

☐ Great Managers communicate without confusion.

☐ Great Managers make sure their staff have all the tools, time, and training they need to succeed.

☐ Great Managers are mentors, coaches, cheerleaders, and clear communicators.

CHECKLIST OF CONDITIONS IN A WORKPLACE SYSTEM THAT SUPPORT EXCELLENT EMPLOYEE JOB PERFORMANCE

☐ The employee in the position applied for the position because he or she wanted that position and didn't just wind up there through company-force, as a favor to someone, or "by mistake."

☐ The employee in the position was recruited for the position through a job ad that accurately and thoroughly described the position.

☐ The employee in the position has the necessary skills, knowledge, and abilities in order to succeed in the position.

☐ The manager of this employee is well trained in management skills as well as in his or her own management position. The manager understands the difference between Theory X and Theory Y management and has been well trained in interpersonal communication, including some combination of emotional intelligence, NVC, and sound conflict resolution methods. The manager also understands what rater-bias and attribution errors are and consciously avoid these by questioning, fact-checking, and reality-testing his or her perceptions of job performance. The manager actively examines his or her managerial self-awareness by attending internal or external training sessions that address these many crucial management skills in workshops and seminars with other managers in a supportive learning environment where mistakes are considered opportunities for learning and correction.

☐ The employee was interviewed with this position in mind, and the skills, knowledge, and abilities that appeared on the employee's résumé match those exhibited and tested for during the job interview. If certain technical skills are necessary, those were tested for during pre-employment screenings.

☐ If writing is a necessary skill, a writing sample was obtained prior to even considering an interview with this person.

☐ The employee has a clear and up-to-date job description that matches the job ad he or she applied for that has been reviewed with him or her along with their manager on their first day or even during the interview process.

☐ The employee has been given clear guidelines on behaviors expected within the corporate culture, as well as a clearly written employee handbook, a comprehensive orientation, and an opportunity to ask any questions.

☐ The employee has a safe and clean area in which to do his or her work with sufficient tools, time, and training needed.

☐ The employee works with others who are polite, civil, and professional, and who adhere to the requirements of the corporate culture.

SAMPLE PERFORMANCE MANAGEMENT PROCEDURES: YOUR MAP FOR COACHING AND DISCIPLINE

☐ HR is available for consultation with managers on any step in this process.

☐ Be sure all employees reporting to you understand their job descriptions and any codes of conduct.

☐ Remember that as supervisors, we intend to provide tools, training, sufficient time, clear guidance, and encouragement to those we supervise in support of their success.

☐ Point out and discuss any infractions of code of conduct or difficulty performing job functions, and have an informal discussion with the employee to better understand what may be going on. (Use investigative problem solving as a discussion tool to be sure you have all data and are not making an attribution error in assessing job performance.) Feel free to include HR in informal discussions or investigative problem-solving discussions.

☐ Familiarize yourself with Coaching Skills for Supervisors and Managers and Use of critical thinking skills and consult with HR for tips on coaching employees to succeed.

☐ If the same issue continues after a first discussion, inform HR and proceed as follows:

- If it is a conduct issue: move directly to a Verbal Warning. (Consult HR and document with HR.)
- If it is a job performance issue, please have HR present.
- If the same issue continues after a first discussion, inform HR and proceed as follows:
  - ☐ If it is a conduct issue, move directly to a Written Warning. (Must be done with HR.)
  - ☐ If it is a job performance issue, revisit the Coaching guidelines (Schedule with HR.)
- If the same issue continues after a first discussion, inform HR and proceed as follows:
  - ☐ If it is a conduct issue, move directly to Probation (Must be done with HR)
  - ☐ If it is a job performance issue, consult with HR on options (More Coaching, Verbal Warning, Written Warning, Probation, Demotion, Transfer, or Termination with HR.)
- Verbal Warnings:
  - ☐ Consult with HR first, if possible, if not, please inform HR and provide documentation afterwards.
  - ☐ Use the Discipline Form either with HR or give to HR after you document.

- Written Warnings (Should be preceded by a Verbal Warning):
  - ☐ Consult with HR first and provide details for HR to document or provide your own documentation.
  - ☐ Fill out Discipline Form with HR or give to HR after you document. Review Written Warning with HR.
  - ☐ Meet with the Employee Privately to deliver the Written Warning (HR presence important).
- Probation (Should be preceded by both a Verbal Warning and a Written Warning):
  - ☐ Consult with HR and fill out Discipline Form with HR. Review final Probation Memo with HR.
  - ☐ Meet with the Employee Privately to deliver the Probation Memo (HR presence necessary).
- Demotion, Transfer, or Termination* (*Please Consult Termination Instructions for Terminations):
  - ☐ Consult with HR and Review final Demotion, Transfer, or Termination Memo from HR.
  - ☐ Meet with the Employee Privately and with HR to deliver this memo.
- Crisis Suspension (Use for violence, threats, drunkenness, etc. Does not need a Warning):
  - ☐ Instruct Employee to leave (Company) Property and inform the Employee that you will contact him/her following an investigation.
  - ☐ Call Police if necessary.
  - ☐ Document incident including witness accounts.
  - ☐ Inform HR, fill out Discipline Form and supporting documentation if any. Consult with HR.

SAMPLE TRAINING ON DELEGATING, DIRECTING EFFECTIVELY, AND NVC PROBLEM SOLVING

(Approximately 75 minutes for a group of 10 managers, including time for questions)

PART I: DELEGATING AND DIRECTING EFFECTIVELY:

WHAT IS THE DIFFERENCE?

Directing: When the person you direct is a direct extension of you, carrying out your instructions exactly as you've given them (also called micromanaging when taken to an unnecessary and over-detailed extreme.)

Delegating: When you instruct someone to do something within guidelines or parameters. Both people understand that the person carrying out the project will be making decisions on his or her own.

Macro-managing: Trusting the judgment, skills, and experience of the person carrying out the project or task.

IMPORTANT PARTS OF DELEGATING AND DIRECTING

- ☐ Give clear instructions.
- ☐ Written instructions are best. They help us remember when we forget. They keep us and our staff accountable. E-mail is great for this.
- ☐ Check for understanding!

EXERCISE DEMONSTRATION (REQUIRES TWO VOLUNTEERS)

Materials: Flipchart, markers, sponges, Styrofoam plates and cups, paper lunch bags, pads and pens for participants.

Exercise A: Staff pairs up. "Person 1" *directs* "Person 2" to assemble or build something using sponges, Styrofoam plates, Styrofoam cups, and paper lunch bags. Switch and repeat. Check to see how good the instructions were.

What was the outcome?

What was learned?

Exercise B: Switch partners. "Person 1" *delegates* to "Person 2." Check to see how good the instructions were.

What was the outcome?

What was learned?

PART 2: NVC PROBLEM SOLVING

REVIEW HANDOUT ON NVC PROBLEM SOLVING ATTRIBUTION ERROR EXERCISE 1

Close your eyes and picture a man is walking on the sidewalk. Another man is sitting in his car and sees that the man lost his balance and fell down. Another woman is in a store, happens to look out the window, and sees the first man lose his balance and fall down. Open your eyes and write down what you think is going on that caused this man to lose his balance and fell down. What do you think the woman observing thinks? What do you think the man observing thinks?

NVC PROBLEM-SOLVING EXERCISE

"Person 1" directs "Person 2" to assemble or build something using sponges, Styrofoam plates, Styrofoam cups, and paper lunch bags. "Person 3" observes, and then changes the outcome.

Persons 1 and 2 will then use NVC to try to understand what Person 3's feelings and needs were and why the construct was changed as it was.

All group members observe use of Person 1's NVC problem-solving skills.

What was the outcome?

What was learned?

CHECKLIST OF SIX QUESTIONS TO ASK YOURSELF BEFORE DISCIPLINING AN EMPLOYEE

☐ Did the employee clearly understand the rule or policy that was violated?

☐ Did the employee know in advance that such conduct would be subject to disciplinary action?

☐ Was the rule that was violated reasonably related to the safe, efficient, and orderly operation of the company?

☐ Is there substantial evidence that the employee actually did violate the rule?

☐ Is this conduct something that other employees would receive discipline for?

☐ Is the disciplinary action you're planning reasonably related to:

- The seriousness of the offense?

- The employee's record with the company?

- Action taken with other employees who have committed similar offenses?

SAMPLE FEEDBACK SHEETS

To: Your Name (HR)

From: A Manager Who Is Focusing on Being a Great Manager

Date:

Re.:   Feedback on Basic Management Training

Please take a few moments to give me some feedback on today's training. Please fill this out anonymously, and don't put any indication of your identity on this at all. Please place your completed form in my mailbox.

Your honest feedback is invited and welcomed. Your honest feedback will help continually improve the training so that it's more effective.

What would you have wanted more of?

What would you have wanted less of?

What else would you have wanted that wasn't represented?

What topics presented would you like to focus on in future trainings?

Circle the number that best describes how the training seminar was experienced by you in each of the areas listed.

1 means Not at All   9 means Completely

Informative	1	2	3	4	5	6	7	8	9
Fun	1	2	3	4	5	6	7	8	9
Interesting	1	2	3	4	5	6	7	8	9
Important	1	2	3	4	5	6	7	8	9
Valuable	1	2	3	4	5	6	7	8	9
Educational	1	2	3	4	5	6	7	8	9
Confusing	1	2	3	4	5	6	7	8	9
Annoying	1	2	3	4	5	6	7	8	9
A Waste of Time	1	2	3	4	5	6	7	8	9
Unpleasant	1	2	3	4	5	6	7	8	9
Uncomfortable	1	2	3	4	5	6	7	8	9
Boring	1	2	3	4	5	6	7	8	9
Other _____	1	2	3	4	5	6	7	8	9

Any Other Comments:

Feel free to write or type on the back of this form or on additional paper.

Thank you for taking the time to fill this out!

Your feedback is valued!

Please place in HR's mailbox. Don't hand directly to HR.

Thank you.

SAMPLE MANAGERIAL RECORD-KEEPING FOR EMPLOYEE JOB PERFORMANCE TRACKING

Improvement Requested: (date and description)	Any Discussion Notes: What Does Employee Need from Manager to Improve Performance?	Results or Changes in Request, if any:	Comments on Improvement or Not, and Why Not?

SAMPLE MANAGER'S SELF-ASSESSMENT TOOL

Answer each question as honestly as you possibly can. Reflect upon your answers and consider where there is room for improvement. Discuss an improvement plan with specific exercises and goals that you will hold yourself accountable for with either HR or your supervisor.

Name:_____

I have noticed that I've made attribution errors as a Manager:

    Frequently

    Occasionally

    Rarely

    It depends on the employee.

    Never

I tend to operate as a Manager out of Theory X:

    Frequently

    Occasionally

    Rarely

    It depends on the employee.

    Never

I tend to operate as a Manager out of Theory Y:

    Frequently

    Occasionally

    Rarely

    It depends on the employee.

    Never

I would describe my Directing Style as:

    Very clear

    Fairly clear

    It depends on the employee.

    Not sure

    Unclear, lacking in specific direction

I would describe my Disagreement Style as:

Very diplomatic and data-based

Fairly diplomatic and data-based

Not very diplomatic or data-based—it depends on my mood/day.

I can be mean, sarcastic, and emotional when disagreeing at times.

It depends on who I'm disagreeing with.

I would describe my Conflict Style as:

I tend to approach conflict with the goal of finding a win/win solution.

I tend to openly address a conflict and state my perceptions and experience.

I tend to avoid conflicts as much as possible.

I tend to attack or discredit those I'm having a conflict with.

It depends on who I'm having a conflict with.

I would describe my Problem-Solving Style as:

I try to look at all the data available to me and see what all the options are.

I tend to give the other person(s) I'm dealing with the benefit of the doubt.

I tend to think that someone may have done something wrong.

I tend to find someone to blame.

It depends on which employees are involved.

I would describe my Feedback Delivery Style as:

Constructive, helpful, specific, and respectful

Usually constructive, helpful, specific, and respectful

It depends on my mood and what kind of day I'm having.

I tell it like it is; if they don't like it, too bad.

It depends on which employee I'm giving feedback to.

CHECKLIST OF 2008 GENERAL MILLS AWARDS

Best Places to Work, Glassdoor.com

50 Best Places to Intern, *BusinessWeek* magazine

100 Best companies for Working Mothers, *Working Mother* magazine

2008 American Business Ethics Award, Foundation for Financial Service Professionals

Top 10 in National Corporate Reputation Survey (No. 4), Harris Interactive

Best Places to Work in IT (No. 3), *Computerworld*

40 Best companies for Diversity, *Black Enterprise* magazine

World's Most Reputable companies (No. 11, No. 5 in United States), The Reputation Institute, Forbes

World's Most Ethical companies, The Ethisphere Institute

Best companies for Multicultural Women, *Working Mother* magazine

United Kingdom's 50 Best Workplaces, *The Financial Times*

America's Most Admired companies, *Fortune* magazine

Top companies for Executive Women, National Association for Female Executives

Top 50 companies for Diversity, *DiversityInc*

Training Top 100 (No. 7), *Training* magazine

100 Best companies to Work For, *Fortune* magazine

100 Best Corporate Citizens, *Corporate Responsibility Officer* magazine

100 Best companies to Work For, *London Sunday Times* (UK)

CHAPTER 16

JOB DESIGN, SELECTION, AND RECRUITMENT

Have all positions within your organization been analyzed to ensure they are necessary, to know what can be realistically done, and to determine exactly what the requirements must be? What tools, time, and training programs are needed? Is it realistic for job applicants to be qualified, or must we train them ourselves? Consider using inexpensive in-house developed tests collaborated on by supervisors and HR to test applicants for actual skills needed for positions. Clear job descriptions eliminate role confusion and prevent unnecessary conflict and competition, which is ultimately extremely costly. See the HR Tool entitled "Sample Form Required by HR for Position Vacancies or Newly Created Positions," at the end of the chapter, on pages 258–259.

Are your internal stakeholders regarding Fair Labor Standards Act (FLSA) status in agreement before a job is even posted? Job hazard analyses must be done and safety trainings provided as necessary. Every injury must be a learning opportunity for prevention. All employees must be oriented in a manner that leaves them feeling positive about working at your company and clear about what to expect. The value of employee benefits must be calculated so employees appreciate and maximize use of them. See the HR Tool entitled "Sample Orientation Guide," on pages 259–263, which is customizable for any company, for ideas in this area.

⟫ MISSION STATEMENT

Your HR Department should have a mission statement for your company. Here is an example:

> Our HR Department recruits skilled and knowledgeable company team members, assesses and coordinates ongoing training for all staff, and actively contributes to a professional and friendly customer-service based environment that serves all employees and dependents as needed while also serving the larger workplace mission statement.

You may want to use background-checking services for various or all positions in your company, depending on your industry, location, and budget. The HR Tool entitled "Sample Background Checking Company Research Table," on page 263, shows how you can present research on only a small sampling of background screening vendors to the key decision makers at your company.

You'll want to meet with your leadership and legal department to confirm which level of background checking services you'll need for your industry, your company, and perhaps for different positions or locations. Be sure to choose any drug labs for preemployment drug testing carefully or there is a chance of getting false-positive results. Look for a certified drug lab. With background checking companies, you'll want to be very clear on procedures and what you can expect from them in terms of a guarantee of accuracy. You'll also want to note any specific costs for the services offered next to the Y (for yes) in this chart.

Depending on your role, you may have varying roles in the selection of staff. If you're able to do so, recommend using the EQi and/or the EQ360 or the MSCEIT for preemployment tests. This will help you get a better fit for the position, the department, and your workplace culture.

Meet with the department heads of those departments that are recruiting, and ask them how they'd feel about preemployment testing. You should also come to agreement with the department head regarding any interview questions that will be asked of all candidates and remind all others interviewing with you of EEO questions to avoid on interviews, which they will have learned in their supervisory trainings.

You should have ready the various letters for applicants being offered a position as well as for those who will not be going further in the application process. Keep in mind that all applicants should receive the courtesy of a response, even if they are not being offered a position. See the HR Tools entitled "Sample Full-Time Employment Offer Letter," "Sample Postcard to Send to Applicants You Will Not Be Interviewing," "Sample 'Dear Interviewee' Letter #1," and "Sample 'Dear Interviewee' Letter #2," on pages 264–266. Have your IT department set up an automatic reply response for those applicants who apply via e-mail.

HR TOOLS

SAMPLE FORM REQUIRED BY HR FOR POSITION VACANCIES OR NEWLY CREATED POSITIONS

HR needs all of this information so that hire letters and hiring paperwork have accurate information.

Job Title: _____   Department: _____

Name and Title of Supervisor:

_____

Desired Start Date: _____ Budgeted Annual Salary _____
Hourly Rate if Non-Exempt: _____

Approvals Required:

F/T or P/T New Positions: _____

New position requires approval by _____ (customize for your Company)

Replacement F/T or P/T Positions: _____

Required by _____ (customize for your Company)

Seasonal or Paid Internship Positions: _____ (Required by Dept. Head)

Classifications:

Exempt (is not paid overtime under FLSA)

Non-Exempt (is paid overtime under FLSA)

Regular

Temporary

Full-time

Part-time

Seasonal

Unpaid Intern

Paid Intern

1099 Contractor

Health Benefits

No Health Benefits

Waive Introductory Probationary Period:

Justification: _____

Is a driver's license required?   Yes or No

Is a drug test required?   Yes or No

What machines or equipment is the jobholder responsible for operating?

Instructions

Background check required for all new F/T employees.

(This takes at least 10 days. SS number and signed consent form is required.)

(Company) Job Descriptions for new positions due to HR before posting:

Attach to this sheet, when submitting for approval of position.

This form initiates with Supervisor and is then submitted to HR.

SAMPLE ORIENTATION GUIDE

At (Company), we want to provide you with the information you will need to have a pleasant and successful work experience.

Please read through this Orientation Guide on your first day. You will receive a great deal of new information during your first week in your new position, and please read it all as much as you are able to do so. Ask your supervisor or HR any questions you may have. Our philosophy is that there are no silly questions.

We know that you will be absorbing a great deal of new information, and we know that it takes time to fully understand new policies and procedures, so please don't hesitate to ask your supervisor or HR any questions you may have.

Below are some basics you will need to understand.

PAPERWORK AND INTRODUCTIONS

Within your first week of employment at (Company), an orientation will be conducted with your supervisor, members of your department, and HR. All necessary paperwork will be filled out during this time.

You will be expected to present the appropriate ID, and you will also meet with our Payroll Administrator to ensure that you understand how to use our electronic timesheets.

You will collaborate with HR on an e-mail to (Company) staff announcing your position at (Company) and welcoming you.

HIRING PAPERWORK AND EMPLOYEE ID

Your hiring paperwork will be completed with members of the HR department. Please ask any questions you may have.

You MUST provide acceptable identification for the I-9 form within three business days of your start date.

EMPLOYEE HANDBOOK

You will receive a copy of your Employee Handbook on your first day. Please read the entire handbook and see HR when you have finished doing so. HR will have you sign a form indicating that you have read the handbook and that you understand the policies and procedures in it. If you have any questions, please don't hesitate to ask HR or your supervisor. The form you sign indicating that you have read and understand the Employee Handbook is placed in your personnel file along with all of your hiring paperwork.

MANDATORY TRAINING

A member of the HR department will provide you with at least two videos about Equal Employment Opportunity issues and Sexual Harassment Prevention. You may be given other videos or DVDs to watch as well. You are required to watch these videos or DVDs within your first week at (Company) and to sign a form indicating that you understand our policies and procedures regarding harassment. If you have any questions about the videos or DVDs or (Company)'s policies on Equal Employment Opportunity, Sexual Harassment, or procedures for filing a complaint, please speak with the Director of HR of (Company).

E-MAIL

(Company) is very much an e-mail culture. We prefer this for both efficiency and account-ability. Everyone has e-mail, and most announcements regarding changes in policy, holiday schedules, reservations for vehicles, meeting scheduling, and communication about work is done via e-mail. It is very important that staff check their e-mail at the beginning of their day and have it notify them throughout the day.

Conference Rooms are also scheduled using our shared calendar (whichever kind your company uses).

Please see IT if you need a tutorial in using _____ (specific software your company uses).

Please be mindful of e-mail etiquette, and ask HR if you have any questions about this.

Personal e-mails including jokes should be directed to your external (e.g., Yahoo, Hotmail, Gmail, etc.) accounts.

OFFICE LOCATIONS

There are _____ office locations for (Company) staff. (Customize for your company.)

DEPARTMENTS

(Company) has the following Departments in the following locations: (List as per your company.)

The I-9 form must be completed in person with a member of the HR department.

ELECTRONIC SECURITY ID BADGES

New employees, interns, and some volunteers will receive an electronic security ID card. The electronic key provides access to all locked doors to which you have access based on your position in the company. Please note that there is also a computerized printout showing exactly what time and day (Company) passkeys are used on doors and for vehicle keys. Access is only authorized based on a staff member's work needs.

COMPUTERS AND COPIERS

Employees, Interns, and Volunteers will be set up with a computer login, password, and an e-mail account by an IT staff member, as needed. If your work with (Company) does not require use of a computer, this will not be in place. If you have any problems logging in or with your computer, please contact the IT dept via e-mail, by phone, or in person.

Most staff print from their computer to a copier/printer that is nearby their office. Please be sure to take only what you have printed and respect the privacy of others sharing the printers with you.

If your printer/copier needs service, please call or e-mail the IT staff for assistance if you are not sure how to fix the problem.

Internet access is available for company business only. Staff are reminded that the internet Web sites are logged showing exactly what time and day and Web site visited. Streaming audio and Internet radio are not permitted.

KITCHENS

The kitchens at (Company) may be used by all staff. Feel free to bring food and nonalcoholic beverages and store them in the refrigerators or cabinets. Food left in refrigerators will be discarded at the end of each workweek. It is best to label your food and beverages with your name. You may purchase your own office-sized refrigerator on your own if you wish to place this in your office and if there is room.

All (Company) kitchens have a first aid kit either in them or nearby. Please locate this on your first day so you know where to find it.

RESTROOMS

Restrooms are located in each main office.

LENDING LIBRARY

There is a shelf in HR designated for books that staff bring in to donate to the staff library. Staff may also borrow books from the library. These books must be returned.

SMOKING

Smoking is prohibited in private offices, and in all other office areas at (Company).

Employees who wish to smoke must exit the building and go to the designated smoking area outside of (Company)'s office buildings.

DRESS CODE

(Company) permits employees to wear business casual every day. If you have any questions about what this means, please ask HR.

When (Company) employees will be in contact with representatives from other businesses that do not dress in business casual, business attire is expected.

SAFETY

Safety is extremely important at (Company). ANY injury or illness sustained at work MUST be reported immediately to your supervisor and/or HR. HR and/or your supervisor will determine with you together whether medical treatment is required.

There are first aid kits located in or near all (Company) kitchens. Staff are encouraged to familiarize themselves with their contents on their first day. Staff may use these supplies as needed.

THE ENVIRONMENT

(Company) cares about protecting the environment. Please use the recycling bins to recycle paper whenever possible.

Be mindful of not using more gas than is necessary when using company vehicles.

Be mindful of turning your computer screens and office lights off at the end of the day.

PHONE CALLS

Business phone calls may go through the Receptionist. You may reach her or him by pressing (__) on your phone. You may ask to have your calls held or screened, or simply have all calls put through to you.

You may also give out your direct phone number to business callers if you wish. A member of the IT department will be able to tell you what your direct phone number is if it is not already labeled on your desk phone.

Personal phone calls are logged with date and time, and staff may be required to reimburse (Company) if there are excessive personal calls.

Please refer to the frequently updated (Company) Phone List for the phone extensions of all (Company) staff.

Cell phones will be given to employees depending on job function. Lost or broken cell phones resulting from personal abuse or neglect may result in employee reimbursement to (Company).

(COMPANY) VEHICLES

(Company) has a vehicle policy, which you should read on your first day if you will be driving. Only persons whose licenses have been checked and approved by HR may drive (Company) vehicles.

Access to (Company) vehicles is determined by Department Heads and HR. Computerized records are kept regarding who uses which vehicle keys.

Mileage, date, time, and destination must be logged in to each vehicle's logbook.

MAIL

Mailboxes for full-time staff are located in the main office. Be sure to check your mailbox at least once a day.

QUESTIONS

Please ask HR or your supervisor any questions you may have.

WELCOME!

We are pleased that you have joined (Company) Team. Welcome!.

SAMPLE BACKGROUND CHECKING COMPANY RESEARCH TABLE

Services	Background Checking Companies			
	Company 1	2	3	4
Criminal Records	Y	Y	Y	Y
Civil Records	N	Y	N	Y
Social Security Trace	Y	Y	N	Y
Driving Records	Y	Y	N	Y
Education Verification	Y	Y	N	Y
Employment Verification	Y	Y	N	Y
Professional License Verification	Y	Y	Y	Y
Reference Verification	Y	Y	N	Y
Credit Report	Y	Y	N	Y
Drug Testing	Y	Y	N	Y
Sex Offenders Search	Y	Y	Y	Y
Terrorist Search	Y	N	Y	N
Fingerprints	N	N	N	N
Form I-9 Employment Eligibility	Y	Y	N	N
National Wants and Warrants	N	N	N	N
International Services	Y	N	N	N
Additional Fees	nonusage fees per month	N	N	N
Do They Operate in States where we need them?	Y	N	N	Y

SAMPLE FULL-TIME EMPLOYMENT OFFER LETTER

On letterhead and/or via e-mail

Date

Applicant's full name and full home address

Dear Mr./Ms. _____:

We would like to extend to you an offer of full-time, at-will employment at (Company) in our _____ position at the rate of $_____ per year (or, per hour, if a nonexempt position). As a reminder, our dress code is business casual on a daily basis unless there is a special meeting or occasion, which you will be told about in advance.

We would like your start date to be _____. Please arrive by 9:30 a.m. and ask for _____, at the main office of (Company) at (address). (If applicable: We recommend that you use Hopstop.com to learn the best way to get to our offices.)

My assistant, _____, will mail you a hiring package under separate cover including several forms we ask you to review before your first day, if at all possible.

Please do not hesitate to contact either me or _____ with any questions about paperwork, dress code, or anything at all. We can both be reached by phone or e-mail, and our contact information will be included in the benefits package that will be sent to you.

On your first day, after you've finished meeting with _____, s/he will bring you to my office to complete hiring paperwork, review any questions you may have, and participate in an orientation session. You and I will then collaborate on a brief e-mail to the entire company introducing you to the staff.

Again, please don't hesitate to ask us any questions you may have. *Please confirm back to me via e-mail or voice mail that you accept this position.*

Thanks very much and welcome aboard; we all look forward to working with you!

Sincerely yours,

Name

Title

Full Contact Information

www.(Company).com

SAMPLE POSTCARD TO SEND TO APPLICANTS YOU WILL NOT BE INTERVIEWING

Thank you for your interest in (Company).

We appreciate the inclusion of (Company) in your career search. We have received your résumé, and it will be carefully considered. Should there be a position available that matches your credentials with our staffing needs; a member of our team will contact you.

Best wishes in your search for a rewarding position.

Sincerely yours,

The HR and OD Department

(Company)

SAMPLE "DEAR INTERVIEWEE" LETTER #1

On letterhead

Date

Interviewee's Name

Full Address

Dear Mr./Ms. _____:

Thank you very much for interviewing with us for the _____ position recently advertised at (Company).

We have offered the position to another applicant.

However, we genuinely appreciate your interest in (Company), and we wish you great success in your search for a meaningful position.

Sincerely yours,,

Name

Title

Limited or Full Contact Information (your decision)

(Company)

SAMPLE "DEAR INTERVIEWEE" LETTER #2

On letterhead postal mailed and/or via e-mail

Date

Name of Applicant

Address of Applicant

Dear _____:

Thank you for taking the time to meet with us regarding the _____ position available at (Company). We enjoyed meeting you and discussing your qualifications for this position.

We were fortunate to have many well-qualified applicants for this position and met with each of the top applicants. Although you have an impressive background, we have decided to pursue an applicant whose skills, knowledge, abilities, and experience more closely meet our department's needs for that position.

Thank you for your interest in (Company). Please accept our best wishes in your future career endeavors.

Sincerely yours,

HR Person's Name

Title

www.(Company).com

(Company)

PART FIVE

ADDED VALUE

"For the human mind is seldom at stay:
If you do not grow better,
you will most undoubtedly grow worse"

—**Samuel Richardson**

CHAPTER 17

WORKPLACE IMPROVEMENTS

Workplace improvements are no- or low-cost ways that HR working collaboratively with other employees at every level can come up with both general best practices and unique ideas that fit their workplace in order to contribute to joy in the workplace and help lessen sadness, frustration, anger, disgust, or fear in the workplace. Use your imagination and encourage all employees to do so as well.

RECOMMEND A SUGGESTION BOX

Recommending a suggestion box is a way to show that the company values employee suggestions and feedback. By allowing employees to make suggestions and give feedback anonymously at any time, you are also respecting that until there is a certain culture in place for a good six months, it will be hard for employees to trust that their feedback is truly welcome and will not create any form of reprisal. Even with a welcoming culture in place, some employees will still want and need the comfort of anonymity, so it's good to allow that option.

As some of the suggestions made by employees are responded to with actions and changes, employees will begin to experience the workplace in a much more positive way, which will contribute to all aspects of their work improving. See the HR Tool entitled "Sample Memo for Recommending a Suggestion Box," at the end of the chapter, page 275.

RECOMMEND AND IMPLEMENT AN UNPAID INTERNSHIP PROGRAM

You can do this yourself or have your assistant help you with the first steps. First, make a list of all the community colleges, four-year colleges and universities, technical schools, and graduate schools within a 60-mile radius of your workplace. (You can have your assistant, a skilled intern, or volunteer do this or do it on your own.) Then use the HR Tool entitled "Checklist: School Information Gathering for Unpaid Internship Program," on pages 275–276 to have your assistant gather the following information from the schools.

Once you've done this research, you can submit a memo similar to that shown in the HR Tool entitled "Sample Memo Recommending Unpaid Internship Program," on pages 276–277 to your leadership and suggest implementing an unpaid internship program for your company.

Implementing this unpaid internship program will save your company money, increase productivity, build positive rapport with your colleagues, cultivate powerful community relationships, increase your company's value, increase human capital, provide introductory management experience to employees who otherwise would not have it, and provide meaningful learning experiences for eager students.

If you are successful in implementing an internship, it would then be in your (and your company's) best interest to solicit feedback from interns to help you improve your program, as shown in the HR Tools entitled "Sample Internship/Seasonal Employee/Regular Employee Feedback Form" and "Sample Anonymous Unpaid Internship Survey," on pages 277–281.

)) REWARD INTERNS WHEN POSSIBLE

Although college and graduate students apply for internships to gain workplace experience, learn more about a field, or get academic credit, they are still students. Though we compensate them to an extent by mentoring them, if we can give them a company t-shirt or tote bag, a free lunch on their last day, a small stipend toward transportation costs, or a small cash reward to recognize their hard work, as with employees, this kind of recognition goes a long way. See the HR Tools entitled "Sample Memo Regarding Rewarding Interns" and "Sample (Company) Intern of the Month Nomination Form," on pages 282–283.

RECOMMEND PARAMETERS OF AUTONOMY FOR YOURSELF AND OTHER KEY STAFF

Recommending parameters of autonomy for yourself to your supervisor is an excellent way to ensure that there is clarity regarding your role in the organization. When you begin, you may use your job ad or job description to clarify with your supervisor what actions you are empowered to make on your own, what actions you need to consult with someone else on (and who for which actions), and what actions you need permission for first.

This is a very simple formula that can prevent a great deal of confusion, frustration, and conflict. Your supervisor will probably be thrilled that you brought this to him or her and may ask your colleagues to do this as well. If he or she doesn't do this, you can still raise this idea to your colleagues as well as to your staff. Reviewing these periodically as the company grows or changes can result in important discussions, communications, ideas, and shifts in responsibility that reflect your professional growth as well as that of your staff and colleagues.

RECOMMEND A REASONABLY RELAXED CASUAL DRESS CODE FOR MOST DAYS

Most people would love to work at Google. Why? No suits! Instead, there is a relaxed atmosphere while people are also working very hard, being productive, and having a good time. Following are some of the many good reasons to support a casual dress code:

- Employees who are comfortable produce better work.
- Employees who are comfortable are happier.
- Happier employees have fewer conflicts.

- Dry cleaning can be expensive and inconvenient.
- Weight gain due to pregnancy or aging is more comfortable in casual clothing.
- Sneakers and flatter shoes are healthier for feet.
- Pantyhose are uncomfortable and not particularly healthy for women's bodies.
- Men often complain that ties are uncomfortable and pointless.
- Less dry-cleaned clothing is good for the environment.
- Employees will save money on clothing and laundry and will be grateful and more productive.

Refer to the HR Tool entitled "Sample Memo for Recommending a Reasonably Relaxed Dress Code for Most Days," on page 284.

RECOMMEND A FLEXIBLE SCHEDULE POLICY (FLEXTIME)

Just like the casual dress code policy, flextime is a policy that employees value greatly and costs the company nothing. Employees do need assistance in balancing work and life. There are child-care, elder-care, personal health, finance, and spousal/partner issues that come up regularly for all employees. When they know there is some flexibility for them, they will go the extra mile for the company, when the company needs that from them. See the HR Tool entitled "Sample Flextime Memo," on pages 285–286

RECOMMEND A LIMITED COMP-TIME POLICY FOR EXEMPT STAFF

Frequently, exempt staff put in long hours, but we know they're not eligible for overtime pay. Many companies have created a compensation-time, or comp-time, policy to give back some of that time to those employees, since they essentially worked unpaid hours.

The example shown in the HR Tool entitled "Sample Comp Time Policy," on pages 286–287, can, of course, be customized for your needs.

RECOMMENDATIONS FOR LOWERING CORPORATE HEALTH CARE COSTS

HR can implement wellness programs by publicizing weekly or monthly health tips from one of the many HR e-zines that send such tips for free. HR can also recommend hiring a chef to make healthy lunches for employees on a daily or weekly basis.

HR should already be helping employees understand and maximize their health benefits. HR can also recommend that the company provide up to three or five hours of paid time off for preventative tests once annually.

Recommend a workplace bullying prevention policy, a conduct policy, and a mandatory conflict resolution policy to ensure that your company is a mentally, emotionally, and psychologically healthy workplace.

Start a lunchtime or after-work walking group nearby.

Implement a scent-free policy and educate employees about chemical sensitivities and asthmatic and migraine reactions to strong perfumes, colognes, soaps, air "fresheners", and cleansers.

Send out monthly informational themes on health issues such as obesity, sleep apnea, heart health, diet, exercise, dental, vision, mental health, and other issues of concern to your staff.

Remove the candy and soda vending machines, and order organic fruits and vegetables from a local farmer. Instead of the budget that is usually spent on coffee, tea, creamer, sugar, and milk, consider buying fruits and vegetables for all staff to eat whenever they are at work.

If you have the room, your staff can grow vegetables right there at work in a workplace garden.

Educate staff on the impact healthier eating has on their dental, mental, and physical health. Ask your healthcare, dental, and vision providers if they provide informational newsletters that can be e-mailed to staff on a regular basis.

RECOMMEND A BEHAVIORAL AND/OR ETHICAL CODE OF CONDUCT

A behavioral code of conduct only works if it is abided by and enforced. Since we've already discussed emotions and behavior at length throughout the book, we won't discuss it further here. Just refer to the HR Tool entitled "Sample Behavioral and Ethical Code of Conduct," on pages 287–288, as a refresher. You may also, of course, customize this form for your own company.

RECOMMEND GREENING YOUR OFFICE

Greening your office is another great way to make work more enjoyable and purposeful for employees. If they know they can bring their expired batteries and old printer cartridges to work where they'll be disposed of or recycled responsibly, that is one less errand for them to do outside of work. If they know they're contributing to an improved environment at work, they will experience the company as that much of a better place to be. See the HR Tool entitled "Sample Checklist for Greening Your Office," on page 288.

RECOMMEND REGULAR INTERDEPARTMENTAL RATINGS

When all departments know that they are all each others' internal customers, their posture toward each other can change—especially if they know they will be evaluated on how well they interact with other colleagues and departments. Having a standard assessment form that all members of departments can fill out about all other departmental performance is one way to do it. Another way to do it is to only have department heads rate each other, which may or may not be practical. You can experiment with what will work best for your company. It's a good idea to have a meeting with all department heads to let them know you'll be implementing this feedback system and that you'd like their ideas on how to do it. They will be more likely to cooperate and buy into it if you allow them to participate in the creation of the system. The HR Tool entitled "Sample Checklist for Departmental Internal Customer Service," on pages 288–289, lists important elements that different departments should be able to deliver to each other and assess each other on. This can be used for departments as a whole, for the department head, or for every member of a department to get a more accurate measure of how each department is performing.

RECOMMEND EMOTIONAL INTELLIGENCE TRAINING FOR ALL STAFF OR ALL MANAGERS

Emotional intelligence training for every single staff member is ideal; however, not all companies can afford that. Still, with so many instances of workplace violence in the news, many companies might ask if they can afford *not* to do these trainings for every employee. The EQi, EQ360, and the MSCEIT are statistically valid measures of emotional intelligence. Certified trainers are all over the world.

After a self-test and perhaps an EQ360 assessment of those who know the testee, employees who are lucky enough to be exposed to these measures can establish self-selected goals which they can handle privately or report to their managers, however the company chooses to handle this process. It is generally recommended to work on three EI subscale skills at a time over a period of 6 to 12 months.

There are many EI consultants available. Check for testimonials from their clients, and research well before you choose one. MHS, Collaborate Growth, and Six Seconds are excellent sources for high-quality EI training. See the HR Tool entitled "Sample Memo Announcing EI Assessment and Training," on page 289, for one way to announce an EI initiative.

RECOMMEND MONTHLY E-MAIL THEMES FROM HR TO INFLUENCE CULTURE

The HR Tool entitled "Sample List of Monthly Themes for Experiential Learning: Communication Skills," on pages 289–290, shows a list of possible monthly themes for a company just beginning to make the positive cultural changes recommended by the credible activist. These examples largely focus on intra- and interpersonal issues, as well as communication, conflict resolution, and emotional intelligence skills. However, monthly themes can also focus on employee benefits to help employees better understand and maximize their use. Other examples include "Focus on Vision Plan Month," "Focus on Dental Plan Month," "Focus on Retirement Month," "Focus on the Employee Assistance Program Month," and so on. You can plan these in advance and schedule them when you know you'll be able to bring in a representative from these benefit plans for staff presentations or individual consultations.

Other monthly themes can be about state or federally mandated programs that are often confusing to employees, such as "FMLA Awareness" Month, "ADA and JAN Awareness Month, "Workplace Safety" Month, "Workplace Violence Prevention" Month, "Drug-Free Workplace" Month, and others. Government resources such as the Department of Labor (DOL), Job Accommodation Network (JAN), or your state DOL will often send out e-mails announcing their own versions. Keep an eye out for these, as you may be able to get great e-mails, posters, and other free promotional and informational materials to use for monthly themes.

RECOMMEND A COMPANY INTRANET TO ASSIST EMPLOYEES MORE EFFICIENTLY

An intranet can make HR's job much easier. Employees can have a 24-hour self-service tool that is faster than manually flipping through an employee handbook looking for the right policy because they can do an electronic search to find the information they need within seconds.

The entire current version of the company's Employee Handbook should be posted in a read-only form and in a way that makes it searchable for terms. In addition, forms that can be downloaded and information that is usually updated annually such as paid holidays and insurance plans and costs should be made available in an easy-to-use format. Any time a policy or handbook is updated, a company-wide announcement must be made. New employees should be given training on how to use the intranet, and employees should also be given a handy "how-to" card or magnet to keep nearby so they can follow simple directions if they've forgotten their training. The intranet should also have instructions posted on it that appear when it is opened, and it should be as user-friendly as possible, keeping in mind that not all employee positions require computer skills but that all employees should be able to easily use the intranet. Make sure that your IT department or any consultant who designs your intranet understands this.

If you have staff members who don't speak English or speak it well, you'll want a translated version of your intranet as well, and you'll have to ensure that the translation is accurate. This may require the services of a bilingual HR person or other manager or those of a consultant. You might be lucky enough to recruit an unpaid intern from either the United States or another country who is bilingual and can do this task very well.

You will also want to see if your IT department or an external vendor can connect an HR Information System (HRIS) to your intranet that will allow employees to independently and directly update changes to their addresses, phone numbers, emergency contact information, and beneficiaries, and that can link to external sites such as company health, vision, dental, retirement, deferred compensation, disability, and life insurance plans. This helps with efficiency, saves paper, saves time, protects privacy better, and can help eliminate human inputting errors.

The HR Tool entitled "Sample Intranet Posting: Calendar of Paid Holidays for Employees," on page 290, shows examples of the kinds of information you'll want to disseminate to staff annually as well as keep posted and updated as needed on your intranet.

RECOMMEND HR MEDIA MATERIALS TO HELP STAFF UNDERSTAND POLICIES

Have business cards, postcards, bookmarks, and magnets made to help staff keep important information handy. Business cards are great to make for both employees and their dependents to have at home, in their wallets, at work, in the glove compartment of their car, or in their purses to bring to visits with medical providers so they can always have their policy number, group number, toll-free number of the insurer, and any other necessary information with them.

Magnets come in different sizes and can help welcome new employees and explain "What HR Can Do For You." Larger magnets can be used to remind managers of their responsibilities to HR during the hiring, separation, or other processes that might be changing or recently changed. Smaller magnets are also good for providing separation information to departing employees that includes the toll-free numbers they may need for various benefits, for unemployment insurance, for retirement information, or for your office if questions arise.

RECOMMEND INTERDEPARTMENTAL FEEDBACK AND RESPONSIBILITY CLARIFICATIONS TO PROMOTE COLLABORATION AND PREVENT DYSFUNCTION

Each department head should make one list for his or her department and every other department listing what his or her department's responsibilities to the other departments are and what those other department's responsibilities to his or her department are. Therefore, if there are seven other departments, each department head will make a total of seven lists.

If a responsibility is shared with more than one department, it will be listed for each department with which it is shared. Under each responsibility, the department heads will list what their related departmental tasks are in order to meet the responsibility. This should be created and reviewed with all departmental staff for a complete view of what gets done and what is needed so that nothing is missed. This also helps in the creation of accurate job descriptions.

When every department has done this, every collaborated task should be documented. Whenever there is disagreement among departments regarding how collaborations need to happen or what individual departmental responsibilities are, these should be discussed openly and with respect so that agreement can be achieved. This is the kind of conflict that when approached with sound conflict resolution skills and developed emotional intelligence skills can result in clarity, trust, and innovation.

HR TOOLS

SAMPLE MEMO FOR RECOMMENDING A SUGGESTION BOX

On letterhead, in interoffice memo format, or via e-mail

To: Your Supervisor

(Include any others on this list to whom this memo should be addressed.)

From: Your Name

Date:

Re.:   Recommendation to Install and Announce Suggestion Boxes for Employees to Use Anonymously

I would like to suggest that (Company) install suggestion boxes in each location where employees regularly gather, such as the lunchroom, the time clock area, or the kitchens.

This will give employees an opportunity to make suggestions for (Company) without having to identify themselves, which includes employees in a way that allows them to be comfortable but still know that their ideas and suggestions for (Company) are welcomed and invited.

I can regularly collect any suggestions and relay them to leadership in my (choose which you use: weekly/biweekly/monthly/quarterly) reports. I can also comment on the suggestions if you would like and let you know if I believe the suggestion is one (Company) would benefit from pursuing.

Unless you have an objection, I will draft a memo announcing this new initiative that will solicit and welcome employee feedback and contribute to an optimally functional workplace.

CHECKLIST: SCHOOL INFORMATION GATHERING FOR UNPAID INTERNSHIP PROGRAM

Full name of school:

_____

Complete address of school:

_____

Contact name and office name for internship program—if they have one (if they don't have one, get the same information for career services or student services)

_____

Complete phone, e-mail, and fax information for those offices listed above that will allow you to regularly send them internship openings and opportunities:

_____

Names of departments the school has that correspond to departments you have in your company:

_____

Does the school allow students to earn academic credit for the unpaid internships they complete? ____

If so, are there hours required by the school and if so, how many? ____

Does the school have its own evaluation forms they want you to use if the student is getting academic credit for the internship? ____

Does the school or departments at the school or student advisor require your résumé or the résumé of the staff person who will be supervising them prior to considering your company as an appropriate internship site? ____

Does the school or department at the school or student advisor require a site visit to your company prior to considering your company as an appropriate internship site? ____

SAMPLE MEMO RECOMMENDING AN UNPAID INTERNSHIP PROGRAM

On letterhead, in interoffice memo format, or via e-mail

To: Your Supervisor

From: Your Name

Date:

Re.: Proposed Unpaid Internship Program for (Company)

I propose that (Company) implement the unpaid internship program I have outlined below. Each of our ___(number of departments you have that could use an unpaid intern) could use an unpaid intern during the _____ times of the year (or you may want to say year-round, depending on your industry and company).

The initial investment in training the unpaid interns will prove to have been worthy once the many small projects that department Heads need completed are handled well because of the diligent work of eager students who are excited to have an opportunity to join the work world and be able to list their internship at (Company) on their résumés.

Most interns will work at least 20 hours per week for at least 10 weeks. Any department heads who believe their department would benefit from having a part-time employee at no cost can let me know what kind of skills they require in a prospective intern. If I am able to connect with agencies that place foreign students in unpaid internships, we may be able to host unpaid interns who work 40 hours per week for 3 to 18 months, depending on the student. These agencies handle all immigration and housing issues for these foreign students.

Department heads would just need to e-mail me 4 to 10 bullet points indicating the kinds of tasks they would have interns work on; I will then insert those into a basic ad I will blast e-mail to our list of _____ schools within a 60-mile radius of (Company).

I have already spoken with contacts at the schools, and I predict that implementing this project could save (Company) approximately $ _____ a year in labor costs, assuming each intern would be doing the work of an employee earning $10 an hour and each department had at least one intern per year. Interns will not be in any position where there is the possibility of getting physically hurt, as they are not covered by (Company)'s workers' compensation insurance, though I recommend that we have our unpaid interns sign the same waiver we ask volunteers to sign.

Please let me know if you have any thoughts, concerns, or objections regarding (Company) beginning an unpaid internship program.

SAMPLE INTERNSHIP/SEASONAL EMPLOYEE/ REGULAR EMPLOYEE FEEDBACK FORM

(Note: This form can also be modified and used for seasonal employees or for welcoming feedback from employees who are completing a three- or six-month introductory period. The supervisor should not be the only one able to provide feedback on a new employee's work experience; the new employee should also be welcomed to provide feedback.)

I would have wanted MORE of:

_____

_____

I would have wanted LESS of:

_____

_____

I also would have wanted SOMETHING ELSE, which is:

_____

_____

My supervisor gave clear instructions: (no) 1 2 3 4 5 (yes)

My supervisor was respectful towards me: (no) 1 2 3 4 5 (yes)

Other (Company) employees were respectful towards me: (no) 1 2 3 4 5 (yes)

(Company)'s workplace felt and was a physically safe place to work: (no) 1 2 3 4 5 (yes)

I learned important skills during my internship: (no) 1 2 3 4 5 (yes)

I would do this same internship again if I knew what it would be like: (no) 1 2 3 4 5 (yes)

My supervisor was able to acknowledge when he or she made errors: (no) 1 2 3 4 5 (yes)

My supervisor rated my job performance fairly and accurately: (no) 1 2 3 4 5 (yes)

My supervisor managed his or her frustration levels very well: (no) 1 2 3 4 5 (yes)

My supervisor taught me a great deal: (no) 1 2 3 4 5 (yes)

I met many or all of my learning objectives during this internship: (no) 1 2 3 4 5 (yes)

If I had the opportunity to work with my supervisor again, I would: (no) 1 2 3 4 5 (yes)

My supervisor gave me clear instructions for my work tasks: (no) 1 2 3 4 5 (yes)

If I had questions, my supervisor was receptive, polite, and helpful: (no) 1 2 3 4 5 (yes)

My supervisor adheres to (Company)'s policies in the handbook: (no) 1 2 3 4 5 (yes)

My supervisor treated other employees with respect: (no) 1 2 3 4 5 (yes)

My supervisor welcomed any concerns or complaints I had: (no) 1 2 3 4 5 (yes)

My supervisor handled any concerns/complaints I had appropriately: (no) 1 2 3 4 5 (yes)

I had the tools, time, and training I needed to succeed in my work: (no) 1 2 3 4 5 (yes)

My supervisor has very good conflict resolution skills: (no) 1 2 3 4 5 (yes)

My supervisor has very good communication skills: (no) 1 2 3 4 5 (yes)

My internship duties were exactly what I was told they would be: (no) 1 2 3 4 5 (yes)

The corporate culture of (Company) is one I enjoyed and felt good in: (no) 1 2 3 4 5 (yes)

My supervisor told me when I did a good job: (no) 1 2 3 4 5 (yes)

If my supervisor had to correct me or my work, it was done politely: (no) 1 2 3 4 5 (yes)

My supervisor gave me and others the same respect and fairness: (no) 1 2 3 4 5 (yes)

My supervisor was easy to work for and with: (no) 1 2 3 4 5 (yes)

My supervisor was difficult to work for and with: (no) 1 2 3 4 5 (yes)

While I worked at (Company), I noticed many employee injuries: (no) 1 2 3 4 5 (yes)

In my opinion, most employees at (Company) are treated fairly: (no) 1 2 3 4 5 (yes)

In my opinion, only some employees at (Company) are treated fairly: (no) 1 2 3 4 5 (yes)

In my opinion, there are some employees at (Company) who are rude: (no) 1 2 3 4 5 (yes)

I thought that humor at (Company) was healthy for all involved: (no) 1 2 3 4 5 (yes)

I believe humor at (Company) was a form of bullying or harassment: (no) 1 2 3 4 5 (yes)

I had all the technological tools to perform my duties well: (no) 1 2 3 4 5 (yes)

If I was in charge of the department I worked in, I would: (please explain)

_____

_____

If I was in charge of this organization, I would: (please explain)

_____

_____

I would like to attach additional sheets of paper to elaborate on some of my answers above:

Thank you: (print and sign full name and date).

SAMPLE ANONYMOUS UNPAID INTERNSHIP SURVEY

Please answer the following questions and remain in contact with us so we may follow your career! Feel free to add comments indicating why you chose a response right after that response.

PUTTING YOUR NAME ON THIS IS OPTIONAL.

YOU MAY REMAIN ANONYMOUS IF YOU WISH TO DO SO.

Please feel free to write on the back and/or attach additional sheets of paper. Please type or write legibly.

Your feedback and experiences are extremely valued and important to (Company).

Thank you.

How would you rate your overall (Company) Internship experience?

___Wonderful _____

___Very Good _____

___Okay _____

___Not So Great _____

___Bad _____

How would you rate your compensation at (Company) for your internship?

___Wonderful _____

___Very Good _____

___Okay _____

___Not So Great _____

___Bad _____

___Not applicable

How would you rate your immediate Intern or Seasonal Supervisor(s)? (if applicable)

___Wonderful _____

___Very Good _____

___Okay _____

___Not So Great _____

___Bad _____

___Not applicable

How would you rate your (Company) Staff Supervisor(s)?

___Wonderful _____

___Very Good _____

___Okay _____

___Not So Great _____

___Bad _____

How would you rate your orientation? (Please choose as many as apply and be specific with reasons.)

___Wonderful _____

___Very Good _____

___Okay _____

___Not So Great _____

___Bad _____

How would you rate the other staff at (Company)? (Please choose as many as apply and be specific with reasons.)

___Wonderful   _____

___Very Good   _____

___Okay   _____

___Not So Great _____

___Bad   _____

How would you rate your working conditions at (Company)? (Please choose as many as apply and be specific with reasons.)

___Wonderful   _____

___Very Good   _____

___Okay   _____

___Not So Great _____

___Bad   _____

How would you rate your job duties as an intern? (Please choose as many as apply and be specific with reasons.)

___Wonderful   _____

___Very Good   _____

___Okay   _____

___Not So Great _____

___Bad   _____

Given the opportunity, would you want to intern here again? Why or why not?

_____

_____

Would you recommend to a friend to look into Internships at (Company)? Why or why not?

_____

_____

Any other feedback you'd like to give us about our Internship Program? Feel free to write on the back of this sheet and/or add additional sheets of paper. Please indicate supervisor names when rating them on this form. Thanks!

SAMPLE MEMO REGARDING REWARDING INTERNS

On letterhead, in interoffice memo format, or via e-mail

To: Your Supervisor

(Include any others on this list to whom this memo should be addressed.)

From: Your Name

Date:

Re.:   Recommendation to Reward Unpaid Interns with Recognition Awards

I would like to suggest that (Company) reward unpaid interns with lunch with their supervisor paid for by (Company) and a (Company) t-shirt at the end of their internships.

I would also like to suggest a recognition program in which each month, (Company) staff can nominate an unpaid intern to be "Intern of the Month" and be rewarded with $25 from (Company).

Rewarding our unpaid interns is a way for (Company) to show its appreciation for the hard work and dedication they provide. This initiative will also contribute to a workplace culture that acknowledges and appreciates those with whom we work.

I have attached a draft nomination form as well as a draft form for approval of the $25 reward, which I will forward to Finance for approval.

Unless you have an objection, I will draft a memo announcing this new initiative to all staff.

SAMPLE (COMPANY) INTERN OF THE MONTH NOMINATION FORM

(Note: This can also be used for Employee of the Month, Employee of the Quarter, or Employee of the Year, though increasing the reward amount and discussing accompanying tax issues with payroll is recommended.)

I would like to nominate _____ as (Company)'s Intern of the Month.

If an intern has gone beyond the "Call of Duty" in aiding a fellow employee, customer, vendor, the public, or someone else, please describe the situation. (This means above and beyond "normal" internship duties.)

_____

_____

If an intern has handled an extraordinarily difficult or frustrating situation (within job duties) with exemplary professionalism and tact, please describe the situation.

_____

_____

If an intern has overseen and/or completed a project that greatly improved the environment, morale, or working conditions for coworkers, and/or customers, please explain how things have improved and who has benefited.

_____

_____

Please be very detailed in your descriptions. Your nomination does need to go into sufficient detail regarding why an intern deserves this honor.

_____

_____

This is an honor to be bestowed upon unpaid interns by fellow employees; please do not nominate yourself. There may be times when there is no Intern of the Month due to number and/or quality of submissions received.

Thank you for participating in this important Exceptional Intern recognition program!

Nominated by: _____

Date _____

When you have completed this form, place in the HR Director's Mailbox or e-mail it to _____.

Please submit nominations by the 25th of each month.

Please call the HR Director with any questions.

(Company)'s Intern of the Month will be announced each month by HR.

Thank you!

SAMPLE MEMO FOR RECOMMENDING A REASONABLY RELAXED DRESS CODE FOR MOST DAYS

On letterhead, in interoffice memo format, or via e-mail

To: Your Supervisor

(Include any others on this list to whom this memo should be addressed.)

From: Your Name

Date:

Re: Recommendation to Implement a Defined, Relaxed Dress Code for Most Days

I would like to suggest that (Company) implement a defined yet relaxed dress code for (Company) employees for most days. The exception would be for any formal (Company) events, while representing (Company) at certain specified events, or with certain clients whether at (Company) offices or elsewhere.

This will give employees a benefit they will greatly appreciate that costs (Company) nothing. Employees who are physically comfortable produce better quality work and are happier, thereby providing them with more energy for solving difficult challenges. Employees who are physically comfortable are less likely to be on edge, and are therefore less likely to become involved in conflicts based on misunderstandings. Employees who are physically comfortable think more clearly and perform better.

Allowing t-shirts, neat jeans, and sneakers as long as they are clean, not inappropriately revealing, not ripped, and don't have anything potentially offensive written on them is a policy that will save employees money on dry-cleaning bills, save them time, lessen the likelihood of employee lateness, and keep them physically comfortable while they're at work. This can also be publicized as a "greener workplace policy" or a "healthy workplace policy."

Most sneakers are much healthier for the human foot than any formal work shoe. Additionally, traditional dry-cleaning methods have been reported to have a deleterious effect on the environment as well as on human health. Allowing employees to avoid "formal" office attire is like giving them a small raise, encouraging improved employee health and, as a result, lowers health insurance bills, and supports a healthier environment.

Employees will greatly appreciate this benefit, which will increase their loyalty to (Company) and cause them to perform better and be more invested in their positions and work at (Company).

Unless you have an objection, I will draft a memo announcing this new initiative that will allow employees to be more physically comfortable as well as happier at (Company).

SAMPLE FLEXTIME MEMO

Via e-mail or in interoffice memo format

To: All Staff

From: _____, HR

Date:

Re.:   Flextime

We are pleased to announce a new Flextime Policy for (Company)!

Please see the policy guidelines below and let me know if you have any questions.

Flextime may be used by both exempt and non-exempt staff.

Employee requests must be submitted via the Time Away form and MUST be approved by employee's supervisor and HR.

Flextime can be requested by staff to address temporary and occasional personal situations (work/life balance issues) by any staff member, regardless of hourly/salaried status.

Flextime can also be requested by supervisors via e-mail, copied to HR, to address scheduling or changing work needs.

A minimum of 160 hours must be worked in a single month, and the request must be approved by a supervisor before it is taken. (You may customize this to your company.)

Staff may request a shift in his or her start time for a temporary period of time as needed (e.g., for regular MD visits or other reasons). This request must be approved by a supervisor. Medical provider notes may be requested by HR, and FMLA may be discussed as needed.

If emergency circumstances create lateness or absences that can be made up on another day during the same pay period, flextime can be implemented, with supervisor approval, and without use of the Time Away form or notation of "flex" on the timesheet.

Flextime can be requested either by an employee or by a supervisor. For example, a supervisor may ask an employee to work on a weekend day and take other time off.

A staff member's request should be in writing via the Time Away form to a supervisor unless it was unplanned and emergent, and then reviewed by HR.

A manager's request for an employee to change his or her schedule should be put in writing via e-mail and copied to HR. Employee response should also be copied to HR and payroll. Any private health information (PHI) or specific health information (SHI) will be redacted or XXXX'd out by HR before the information is passed on in accordance with HIPAA.

Employee Flextime requests can be applied to whole days as well as partial days and are always at the discretion of supervisors (core workdays remain—insert your company's core hours—for most staff). In addition, a supervisor may request that an employee substitute a weekend day for a weekday on a case-by-case basis.

Flextime is limited in terms of usage:

Flextime should be used WITHIN a single pay period *whenever possible*.

If a weekend day is substituted for a weekday, at a supervisor's request, the number of hours worked should be noted on the timesheet under the day actually worked, and "flex" should be noted on the weekday.

With the approval of a supervisor and HR, flextime may extend beyond one month. The employee submits a Time Away form to the supervisor, which is reviewed by HR. The employee notes the days that are being requested, as "flex," as compensation additional hours worked.

Employee must use the Time Away form and get approval from the supervisor. The approved form will be forwarded to HR for inclusion in the employee file. HR will forward this form to Payroll.

A copy of the timesheet for the period during which the hours in excess of 80 hours were worked must be signed and submitted prior to usage.

SAMPLE COMP TIME POLICY

Via e-mail or in interoffice memo format

To: Exempt Staff Only

From: _____, HR

Date:

Re.:   Comp Time Policy

For exempt staff only. Any hours worked in excess of 80 hours per pay period can be taken as time off *with prior approval from supervisor* at a rate of one hour for one hour of the hours worked in excess of 80 hours. No more than 80 hours can be taken consecutively, and comp time hours must be used within 12 months of having earned them; otherwise, they expire.

Requests for usage of comp time hours should be made using the Time Away form, requesting a "comp" for specific days, and the employee must also attach a copy of the timesheet for the period during which the hours in excess of 80 hours were worked. ONLY signed, approved Comp Time requests, submitted prior to usage, are authorized to be taken as comp time. Nonauthorized absences can result in usage of vacation time and/or docking of paychecks.

Records of hours in excess of 80 hours per pay period can be kept either by Department Heads or by HR, whichever is preferred by the Department Head, and these records must be forwarded to payroll.

Comp time *is not payable* upon termination, resignation, or retirement. Comp time may be used only as described above.

Comp time only applies to time worked that is mandated by supervisor. Comp time does NOT apply to time that an employee chooses to arrive at work early or stay late for personal reasons, without prior supervisory approval.

Lunch hours at (Company) are unpaid and do not count as time towards total hours worked or comp time.

A maximum of (XX) hours of comp time may be earned in a single pay period.

All requests are REQUESTS and can be denied or approved by a supervisor and/or by HR.

Comp Time is limited in terms of usage:

Comp Time should be used WITHIN a single month *whenever possible*.

Employee must use the Time Away form and get approval from the supervisor. The approved form will be forwarded to HR for inclusion in the employee file. HR will forward this form to payroll.

A copy of the timesheet for a weekly period during which the hours in excess of 40 hours were worked must be signed by supervisors and submitted to HR or payroll for approval prior to usage of comp time.

SAMPLE BEHAVIORAL AND ETHICAL CODE OF CONDUCT

- ☐ We do not gossip.
- ☐ We use "healthy humor" and have annual mandatory trainings regarding it.
- ☐ We have a zero tolerance policy for any EEO harassment, discrimination, or retaliation.
- ☐ We have a zero tolerance policy toward violence or threats of violence in our workplace.
- ☐ We have a zero tolerance policy toward any type of bullying behavior including spreading rumors, intentionally damaging anyone's personal or professional reputations, or refusal to resolve conflicts using sound conflict resolution methods. .
- ☐ We require all employees to attend a mandatory conflict resolution training sessions annually.
- ☐ We require all employees to practice and use sound conflict resolution skills whenever necessary and to ask HR or their supervisor for assistance if needed.
- ☐ All employees are required to report any EEO violations and/or conduct violations they observe, overhear, or become aware of through direct experience. All supervisors are required to report those they know of through direct experience or if someone reports direct experience to the supervisor.
- ☐ No sexual material of any kind is allowed on computers, cell phones, bulletin boards, in photo frames, on clothing, on voice mail, or on PDAs.
- ☐ No disparate treatment of any employee is allowed for any reason whatsoever.
- ☐ We require that employees have acute awareness of any conflicts of interest at work.

- ☐ We require emotional intelligence and NVC training for all employees every six months. Employees at every level are encouraged to ask questions and ask for assistance if needed. This is a learning organization.
- ☐ We require EEO/SHP/ and workplace violence prevention training annually.
- ☐ Our workplace is a drug-free and weapon-free workplace.
- ☐ We value and welcome diversity: we celebrate our differences.
- ☐ We value our company as a learning organization.
- ☐ We acknowledge the mistakes we make and endeavor to learn from them.

SAMPLE CHECKLIST FOR GREENING YOUR OFFICE

- ☐ Have employees bring their own reusable utensils.
- ☐ Install a dishwasher for reusable plates and mugs.
- ☐ Do not purchase disposable plates, cups, or cutlery anymore.
- ☐ Provide employees with limited paid time off to do environmental volunteer work.
- ☐ Use only energy-efficient lightbulbs and lights.
- ☐ Encourage your staff to use reusable water bottles.
- ☐ Stop purchasing individual bottles of water.
- ☐ Ask employees for their ideas on greening the office.
- ☐ Encourage car-pooling and the use of mass transit, biking, or walking to work.
- ☐ Allow telecommuting when possible to save on the impact of commuting.
- ☐ Develop paperless communication and tracking systems whenever possible.
- ☐ Implement recycling programs at work for glass, plastic, aluminum, batteries, printer cartridges, and paper.
- ☐ Relax your dress code so employees will use traditional dry-cleaning less and purchase less synthetic materials.

SAMPLE CHECKLIST FOR DEPARTMENTAL INTERNAL CUSTOMER SERVICE

Rate each department on a scale of 1–10 with 10 being best.

Name of Department above:

Collaboration Skills	1	2	3	4	5	6	7	8	9	10
Responsiveness	1	2	3	4	5	6	7	8	9	10
Helpfulness	1	2	3	4	5	6	7	8	9	10
Cooperation	1	2	3	4	5	6	7	8	9	10

Providing Timely Information	1	2	3	4	5	6	7	8	9	10
Respectfulness	1	2	3	4	5	6	7	8	9	10
Following Procedures	1	2	3	4	5	6	7	8	9	10

(Add Other Core Skills Depending on Your Industry)

SAMPLE MEMO ANNOUNCING EI ASSESSMENT AND TRAINING

To: All Staff

From: _____,HR

Date:

Re.:   Emotional Intelligence (EI) Training Initiative

I'm excited to announce that (Company) will be bringing in a Certified Emotional Intelligence Consultant, who will meet with us as a group and then individually.

We will each take a short EI self-test. In about two weeks, we'll meet with our consultant again and discuss our results privately. We will then each choose 3 of the 15 EI subscale skills to focus on improving over the next year.

Please give the consultant your full cooperation, and don't hesitate to come to me with any questions or concerns. I do believe this will be an exciting process for us all.

SAMPLE LIST OF MONTHLY THEMES FOR EXPERIENTIAL LEARNING: COMMUNICATION SKILLS

1. "Conflict Resolution Practice" Month:
   - ☐ I'm having a conflict with the situation of _____, and I'd like to let you know _____.
   - ☐ I'm having a conflict with the situation of _____, and I'd like to ask you more about _____.
   - ☐ I'm having a conflict with the situation of _____, and I'd like to see how we can share our ideas and come to an agreement about handling it.

2. "Respectful Workplace" Month

3. "Emphasis on Improved Fairness" Month: Being aware of negative or positive bias

4. "Focus on Positive Feedback" Month

5. "Benefit of the Doubt" Month:
   - ☐ "I'd like to learn more about how you're handling _____ and why it's being handled in this way."

6. "Learn and Practice NVC" Month:

   ☐ "When you do _____, I notice that the result is _____. I'd like to suggest: _____, but first I'd like to hear from you about your experience."

7. "Perhaps I Misunderstood" Month: It's okay to make mistakes and admit them.

8. "Improved Reporting Skills" Month: Give reporting tips list.

9. "Super-Clarity" Month: A focus on verbal, written, and e-mail communication.

10. "Everyone You Communicate with Is Your Favorite Person" Month

11. "If I Was In Charge of This Company" Month: Let the staff recommendations flow!

SAMPLE INTRANET POSTING: CALENDAR OF PAID HOLIDAYS FOR EMPLOYEES

Month	Legal Holiday
January	New Year's Day
	Dr. Martin Luther King, Jr. Day
February	Lincoln's Birthday
	Washington's Birthday
May	Memorial Day
July	Independence Day
September	Labor Day
October	Columbus Day
November	Election Day
	Veterans' Day
	Thanksgiving Day
December	Christmas Day

These holidays will be automatically programmed into our company's networked shared calendars. Any special policies or wage and hour laws regarding overtime pay, holiday pay, floating holidays, or other unusual circumstances will include information regarding these issues in the notation on the company calendar.

If you have any questions, please contact _____ in HR at _____ or consult your employee handbook.

Thank you.

CHAPTER 18

ADDITIONAL FORMS AND LETTERS

ACCEPTING RESIGNATIONS

When employees do depart, depending on the circumstances, HR is often responsible for planning any type of farewell gathering in the office. It's a good idea to first ask the departing employee if he or she wants a farewell party; the person might not. If they do, you'll then want to ask what kind of food or dessert he or she would like. (Of course, there are cases such as a termination as a result of a disciplinary action where a farewell party is not at all appropriate.)

Exit interviews, termination paperwork, retirement paperwork, transfer paperwork, resignation letters, and extended sick leave all require an amount of sensitivity to the person who is leaving, whose feelings should be the focus regardless of the circumstances. Always do your best to handle these matters with composure. See the HR Tool entitled "Sample Letter: Accepting a Resignation Letter with Outgoing Separation Information Included," at the end of the chapter, on pages 294–295, for one way of doing so.

DISCIPLINARY ACTION

If the person is leaving as a result of a disciplinary action, the necessary paperwork must also be completed and on file. See the HR Tool entitled "Attendance/Incident Tracking Documentation Form," on pages 295–296.

Disciplinary action can be unpleasant but it is necessary at times. You'll want to be prepared and be sure to have the employee file and all the necessary information and forms on file for when you plan one of these meetings. You'll also want to be aware that these can be unpredictable. With some employees, you may want another manager there with you as a witness or as a safety measure. With some employees, you may want security nearby but not obviously so. In some meetings, you'll want to have tissues available if someone begins to cry. You will also need to be prepared for employees who contest the discipline and in that case you'll need time to continue to meet with that employee and to be prepared to ask the employee for a written response to the discipline. Depending on what your discipline policies are and what the issue is, you may or may not allow the employee to prepare his or her rebuttal there and then. If a serious offense has been alleged, you may need to suspend the employee with or without pay and ask him or her to complete such a rebuttal at home, off the premises of the office.

COMPLAINTS OF DISCRIMINATION AND INTERNAL COMPLAINT PAPERWORK

If the employee feels he or she has been the target of unlawful discrimination, harassment, or retaliation, the matter must be handled with the utmost sensitivity, professionalism, and attention to detail. Your company must have specific guidelines in the employee handbook that address exactly how complaints are to be submitted, to whom, when, in what format, and within what time frame from the alleged violation. Additionally, those staff members charged with receiving or reviewing such complaints must have high-quality training to ensure they competently and knowledgeably handle these very sensitive and important duties.

Not having clear procedures or high-quality training in place can ultimately be very expensive if such complaints are mishandled.

There should also be a clear investigation policy including high-quality training for any staff member charged with any investigative responsibilities. Employees and managers should also receive regular annual training on all of these policies and procedures so that there is clear understanding regarding such situations and how they will be handled. All new employees must also be oriented on all of this information, which should also be covered in detail in the employee handbook.

At times, qualified, third-party investigators who are more neutral and unbiased than those working in the organization daily should be brought in if there are ever potential conflicts of interest that would require any investigative staff to recuse themselves from investigations of complaints.

See the HR Tools entitled "Sample (Company) Internal EEO Complaint Form," and "Sample Letter to EEOC in Washington, D.C.," on pages 296–298.

Although EEO complaints can be given verbally or in writing under the law, it is a best practice to have a standard form that is given to any employee who makes an EEO complaint and to ask that employee to provide all of the details in written format in his or her own words. This prevents any misunderstandings or errors in the event that someone else writes down a complaint that is given verbally. However, there will be employees who cannot due to illness, disability, or language barriers write their own complaints and in that case, you'll need to transcribe their verbal account to you verbatim and ask them to read it over or read it to them so they can make corrections to any errors you may have made in your transcription. The HR Tool entitled "Sample (Company) Internal EEO Complaint Form" can be customized to your organization's needs.

When receiving a complaint it is important to reserve judgment and say something like "I am sorry you had this experience. If this is all accurate, then it does appear that there may have been a violation of policy." You want to be very careful to not believe or disbelieve anything that is told to you and to not verbally indicate any belief or disbelief. Nothing is known for sure until after a sound, thorough, and impartial investigation is concluded.

At the same time, you do want to be comforting, welcoming, and appreciative to the employee who has brought this complaint to your attention. You should thank the employee for coming forward and making the complaint and you should reiterate that it is the policy of the workplace to not tolerate retaliation in any form. Make it known to the employee that if he or she believes retaliation is happening or has happened, that he or she must immediately inform HR, preferably in writing.

You will need to keep a confidential EEO complaint log. Nonprofit companies, educational institutions, research institutions, and government entities are particularly going to want to do this, as many grant applications will require this information as part of their applications. Grantors of large sums of money want to ensure that their money will be funding a meaningful project and not somehow contribute to the legal costs involved in responding to or defending against allegations of wrongdoing in the EEO area. However, all companies, even those that are for-profit, should keep a log of this kind in case there are any future investigations that ask to see data on this topic going back many years to look into whether or not there have been any patterns of EEO noncompliance and how your company has chosen to handle these.

The HR Tool entitled "Sample (Company) Internal EEO Complaint Log," on pages 298–299, shows a simple and useful format you may use to keep track of not only all EEO complaints that are made but also any inappropriate behavior concerning EEO issues that has been noted by any member of the management team (which is their responsibility as well as HR's), and to help you keep track of every document related to the issue.

TRAINING

We have discussed the importance of meaningful training sessions throughout the book. The HR Tool entitled "Sample Acknowledgement of Receipt of EEO/Sexual Harassment Prevention Training," on pages 299–300, shows a form to use to keep track of employees receiving EEO/Sexual Harassment Prevention Training. The HR Tool entitled "Sample Training Sign-In Sheet," on page 300, shows a simple form to use to keep track of those who attend.

BENEFITS

Keeping track of benefits and health-care plans is an important function of HR. The HR Tools entitled "Sample (Company) Health Plan Benefits Comparison Chart" and "Sample Benefits Form/List," on pages 301–304, will help you keep this information at your fingertips so that you can readily answer interviewees' and employees' queries on these matters. Additionally, each year when there is open enrollment for benefits changes, you'll want to be able to clearly let all employees know via e-mail what is changing and how.

You'll also want to make it easy for all HR staff to have the correct information to give employees when they ask about benefits. Be sure that the entire HR department clearly understands how to answer employee benefits questions and who to go to for help if there is confusion.

HR TOOLS

SAMPLE LETTER: ACCEPTING A RESIGNATION LETTER WITH OUTGOING SEPARATION INFORMATION INCLUDED

On Company letterhead

Date

Full Name

Full Address

Dear Mr. / Ms._____:

This letter formally acknowledges your resignation from (Company) effective (date). This is effective as per your letter dated (date of their resignation letter), which will remain in your employee file.

Please meet with HR for an Exit Interview at your earliest convenience.

You will receive your final commission and/or paycheck no later than four weeks after your date of departure. Your final paycheck will be mailed to you or direct deposited in your account on the next payroll cycle.

This letter is also to inform you about the federal program entitled COBRA, the Consolidated Omnibus Budget Reconciliation Act of 1985.

Under COBRA, you have the opportunity to continue health-care coverage at your own expense after ending your employment with (Company). From the date of this letter, you will have 60 days to decide whether you wish to continue health-care coverage under COBRA. If you don't contact us within 60 days, we will assume that you have declined COBRA continuation coverage. There may be an additional administrative fee payable to (Company) if you choose this option.

In addition, if you have made contributions to your retirement plan, you may access information regarding your personal plan by contacting _____ Investments, Retirement Plan Service Center, P.O. Box (XXXXX), (City), (State), (12345-6789), or you may contact them at (1-800-555-5555). If you wish to obtain further documentation regarding your retirement funds from (Company), you may call _____.

If you have any questions, please don't hesitate to call or e-mail me. Please know that everyone at (Company) wishes you well.

Sincerely yours,

Your Name

Your HR title

CC: Payroll

Resigning employee's supervisor

Anyone else in HR who needs a copy

Employee file

IT—if they need to disable network access security if applicable

ATTENDANCE/INCIDENT TRACKING DOCUMENTATION FORM

EMPLOYEE INFORMATION

Name of Employee:

Employee's Job Title:

Supervisor:

INCIDENT INFORMATION

Date/Time of Incident:

Location of Incident:

Description of Incident:

Witnesses:

Was this incident in violation of a company policy?

Yes   No

If yes, specify which policy and how the incident violated it.

ACTION TAKEN

What action will be taken relating to this incident?

Verbal Warning

Written Warning

Probationary Period for at least three months

Transfer

Demotion

Crisis Suspension

Termination

Other:

_____

Has the concern about the employee's actions been explained to the employee?

_____

Did the employee offer any explanation for the conduct? If so, what was it?

_____

(Employee can write here and can use additional pages, if desired.)

_____

_____

_____

Signature of Supervisor: _____ Date

Signature of Employee: _____ Date

Signature of HR Director: _____ Date

SAMPLE (COMPANY) INTERNAL EEO COMPLAINT FORM

(Company) takes complaints of discrimination, harassment, and retaliation very seriously. You have indicated that you have experienced unlawful discrimination or harassment as an employee of (Company).

(Company) thanks you for coming forward with your concerns and assures you that a complete and fair investigation will take place with as much confidentiality as is possible.

If you have any questions, please feel free to ask your HR Director.

It is required that you fill out these forms. Please feel free to type or write on additional sheets of paper and attach them to this form.

Please write legibly and be as specific as you possibly can with dates, times, and days of the week. Please also identify any witnesses to the behavior you are reporting. Thank you.

Please identify the person(s) who has discriminated against, harassed you, or retaliated against you at (Company):

_____

_____

_____

Please describe the events which concern you:

_____

_____

_____

_____

_____

_____

(Feel free to attach separate sheets of paper.)

Please describe any previous or subsequent events which concern you:

_____

_____

_____

_____

_____

_____

(Feel free to attach separate sheets of paper.)

Sign and Print your full name   Date

Page 2

EEO Complaint form

Please note that the person(s) alleged to have discriminated against or harassed you will be asked to provide his/her version of events as part of a formal investigation.

Signed statements from any witnesses will be collected.

Retaliation against a person who makes such a complaint is unlawful. Please notify your supervisor or the HR Director immediately if you feel that you are experiencing retaliation from the person whom you have made a formal complaint about.

Name

Title

Company

SAMPLE LETTER TO EEOC IN WASHINGTON, D.C.

On Company Letterhead

Date

To Whom It May Concern:

(Company) is a (choose one: governmental/not-for-profit/for-profit) entity. There has never been an HR department here at (Company)—or—I am the new HR Director at (Company), and I have found no evidence in the files of any prior EEO-1 or EEO-4 reports having been submitted by (Company). To my knowledge, we have not received any forms from you sampling us to provide a report.

I began my position here at (Company) on _____ (date), and I have just recently been able to obtain the information necessary to complete this report.

I understand that we will prepare these reports annually. Will we need to merely keep them on file or will we need to send them in? Please advise.

I understand that at any point, the Commission may inform us via postal mail as to which years it may have us report as a sampling. We have (number) full-time employees, approx-imately (number) part-time employees, and (number) of seasonal employees, which totals (number) employees in any given previous year. (If true: we also have a volunteer/unpaid internship program.)

Please contact me with any questions or concerns. You may call me at the number below or e-mail me at _____.

I appreciate your kind assistance.

Best regards,

Name

Title

Complete Contact information

(Company) Web site

SAMPLE (COMPANY) INTERNAL EEO COMPLAINT LOG

For every EEO complaint received by HR or any Manager AND for any inappropriate behavior observed by any management, HR, legal, or leadership employee:

Date:

Allegation(s):

Position of complainant(s):

Investigation conducted by:

Investigation begun on: (date) and ended on (date)

Confidential file location:

Copies of investigation findings in all involved employee files: YES NO

(If no, explanation required)

Disposition:

SAMPLE ACKNOWLEDGEMENT OF RECEIPT OF EEO/SEXUAL HARASSMENT PREVENTION TRAINING

I have attended (Company)'s EEO/Sexual Harassment Prevention Training on _____ (date), and I also have received copies of (Company)'s Employee Handbook which includes (Company)'s policies regarding Equal Employment Opportunity and Harassment, including Sexual Harassment. This handbook also includes a complaint procedure.

I understand what harassment is and that employees should not engage in any harassing or discriminatory behavior towards others in the workplace.

I understand what I should do if I feel or believe that I am being harassed, discriminated against, or retaliated against; and I understand those to whom and how I may make complaints either verbally, via e-mail, via private fax, or in writing.

I understand that I will not be retaliated against for reporting harassment or assisting in a harassment investigation. I understand what retaliation is and is not from the training we had, and I will raise any questions I have with HR, my supervisor, or other appropriate staff.

I also understand that I cannot be retaliated against for participating in any workplace EEO investigation or for complaining that I have observed unlawful harassment, discrimination, or retaliation by any other staff member(s).

I also understand that if I am found to have engaged in any harassment or discrimination of any employee, I may be disciplined, demoted, suspended, or terminated upon the conclusion of a sound, prompt, and thorough investigation.

If I am a manager or if I am ever promoted to a management position, I clearly understand that observing my own and others' behavior regarding EEO/SHP issues is one of my most important duties and that if I ever observe or overhear any violation of (Company)'s EEO or SHP policy, I am required to report this immediately to HR/OD or another member of Senior Management who is authorized to accept EEO/SHP complaints.

I understand that if I am ever in a management or supervisory position, my failure to handle any known EEO/SHP violation appropriately can result in my own discipline, demotion, suspension, and/or termination upon the conclusion of a sound, prompt, and thorough investigation.

_____   _____

                            Signature   Date

PRINT Name: _____

SAMPLE TRAINING SIGN-IN SHEET

For _____ TRAINING

(Customizable for any kind of training, mandatory or not)

Attendance Sheet for Date:_____

                    Print Name   Sign Name

Print Name	Sign Name
_____	_____
_____	_____
_____	_____
_____	_____
_____	_____
_____	_____
_____	_____
_____	_____
_____	_____
_____	_____
_____	_____
_____	_____
_____	_____
_____	_____
_____	_____

SAMPLE (COMPANY) HEALTH PLAN BENEFITS COMPARISON CHART

Rates for (year)	Health Plan Option 1	Health Plan Option 2
Phone #	Toll free #	Toll free #
Web Address	Web site address	Web site address
Employee Cost Per Pay Period: **Individual** **Couple** **Family**	$____ $____ $____	$____ $____ $____
Office Visit Co-payments	$____ /visit	$____ / visit
Specialist's Office Visits Co-payments	$____ /visit	$____ / visit
Emergency Room Visit Co-payments	$____ /visit	$____ / visit
Outpatient Mental Health Co-payments **Inpatient** **Max. 30 days** **No Co-payments**	No co-payment for max. ____ visits. First call member services at toll-free number for authorization.	$____ / visit Unlimited visits when medically necessary. No referral required. Must first call toll-free number for pre-authorization.
Chiropractor Co-payments and benefit terms:	$____ /visit No referral required. Only ____ visits allowed per calendar year	$____ / visit Must call toll-free number first (provide #). No visit limit per calendar year.
Prescription Drugs Co-payments:	**Retail: 30-day supply** $____ **Mail Order: 90-day supply** $____ Co-pays reduced by ____% when utilizing insurance company mail-order service. (Subject to Drug formulary: this means what the plan will pay for.)	**Retail: 30-day supply:** $____ generic, $____ brand-name, $____ for non-preferred brand-name drugs **Retail: 31–90-day supply:** $____ generic, $____ preferred brand-name, $____ non-preferred brand-name drugs **Mail Service: 31–90 day supply:** $____ generic, $____ preferred brand-name, $____ for non-preferred brand-name drugs

Plan Highlights	Provides a 24-hour Nurse Line 1-800-555-5555 Open formulary/Some medicines require prior authorization. **Special Cancer Centers:** Paid in full coverage for cancer-related expenses for approved treatment centers and a lifetime maximum travel allowance of $_____ for cancer treatment. Hospital Benefits through Empire Blue Cross Blue Shield No co-payment for Radiation, Anesthesia, Pathology, Dialysis, or Chemotherapy $_____ lifetime allowance for infertility treatments External Mastectomy prostheses covered in full per calendar year	
Counties served:	Available worldwide	
Vision $_____ per pay-period for employee $_____ for couple $_____ for family	Web site Toll-free number See Web site for plan details.	
Dental $_____ per pay-period for employee $_____ for couple $_____ for family	Web site Toll-free number See Web site for plan details.	

SAMPLE BENEFITS FORM/LIST

REQUIRED	Retirement Plan for (Company)	Must contribute ____% of gross salary.
REQUIRED	Workers' Compensation Coverage	Employee covered for protection from loss of income and medical expenses incurred in the event of a work-related injury/accident. No cost to employee.
OPTIONAL	Health Insurance—Pre-tax Insurance Premium Payments	Enables eligible employees to pay for health insurance premiums on a pre-tax basis. 3 Options: List each plan and provide information on costs and services offered by each.
OPTIONAL	Supplemental Health Insurance	Personal Cancer Plan Personal Accident Plan Personal Disability Income Protector Life Insurance
OPTIONAL	Dental Insurance	No cost to (Company) staff (after six months)
OPTIONAL	Vision Care	No cost to (Company) staff (after six months)
OPTIONAL	Health Club Membership	Eligible employees are allowed to cash in up to (X) sick days per year for the purpose of paying for a health club membership.
OPTIONAL	Life Insurance Company Accidental Death and Dismemberment Insurance Short and Long-Term Disability Insurance Plan Basic Life Insurance	1st day of Hire 1st Day of Hire 1st Day of Hire 1st Day of Hire
OPTIONAL	Flex Time Policy	As Needed with Supervisor and HR approval
OPTIONAL	Flexible Benefit Plan	1st day of Hire/Change of Life Event/Open Enrollment.

OPTIONAL	Dependent Care Assistance Plan Name of Dependent—	Enables eligible employees to pay for child or other dependent care expenses on a pre-tax basis through payroll deductions.
OPTIONAL	Direct Deposit	(Company) employees are eligible after successful completion of introductory period.
OPTIONAL	A Certain Bank	Membership in this credit union requires a letter from HR to verify (Company) employment. See www.bankwebsite.com for more information.
OPTIONAL	Another Bank	Free checking with direct deposit.
OPTIONAL	Tuition Assistance Program	(Company) employees are eligible after completion of one year of service.
OPTIONAL	Continuing Education Program	(Company) employees are eligible after successful completion of introductory period.
OPTIONAL	Professional Membership/ Association Fees	(Company) staff are eligible upon 1st day of hire.
OPTIONAL	Deferred Compensation Plan	Employees are eligible at any time.
OPTIONAL	Transportation Assistance Benefit Program	(Company) employees are eligible after successful completion of introductory period. Beginning (year) the maximum pre-tax for transit allotment is $____ per pay cycle.
OPTIONAL	Employee Assistance Plan	(Company) employees are eligible at any time. No cost to employees or their dependents.

PART SIX

RESOURCES FOR HR PROFESSIONALS AT EVERY LEVEL

*"Work joyfully and peacefully,
knowing that right thoughts and right efforts
will inevitably bring about right results."*

—**James Allen**

CHAPTER 19

RESOURCES AND MISCELLANEOUS TIPS

RECOGNIZE THAT HR CAN OFTEN BE EMOTIONAL WORK

Recognizing that HR can often be emotional work and requires a certain amount of self-care and clear boundaries is important. Following are three things to keep in mind that will help you maintain perspective:

- Be careful about mixing work with friendships.
- Always practice clear boundaries with work friends.
- Learn from your mistakes.

You are probably going to make mistakes. Try to only make small mistakes, like typos or forgetting to send an attachment with an e-mail. Depending on the culture of your company and your own personal ability to acknowledge your own mistakes, you will have different feelings about how to address the mistakes you make. One thing is for sure: the way you handle others' mistakes will most certainly influence how they handle your mistakes. (Of course, both their own personalities and the culture of the workplace will figure into how different people respond to your mistakes as well.)

Your standing in the company will also have an impact on how any mistakes you may make or your "judgment" of situations and issues are received. If your company is a learning organization with an open system of communicating, learning, and improving, then chances are your mistakes will be responded to with forgiveness, understanding, and encouragement to do better the next time. If you're working in an organization that is adverse to change and likes to blame people—or likes to blame certain people—you can expect some harsh responses to mistakes. If this is the case, you want to be certain to document not only your own mistakes and how they're responded to but also mistakes made by others and how those are responded to—or not.

There are dysfunctional workplace cultures in which there is an "in-group" composed of people who are seemingly or actually immune from any acknowledgment of their errors and any consequences for their errors, while other employees in the "out-group" will have their errors acknowledged and will have consequences. This is a grave mistake that company leaders make in allowing this kind of culture to exist, and it ultimately will harm the company even if it takes years for things to fall apart. If you find yourself in an organization like this, you'll have a choice to make about how to respond according to your own goals and needs at the time.

See the HR Tool entitled "Checklist of Recommended Reading for the Credible Activist" at the end of the chapter, on page 320, for some sources to educate yourself on how to deal with situations the credible activist faces.

UNDERSTAND THE "HORN EFFECT" AND "HALO EFFECT" WITH WHICH MANY HR PROFESSIONALS COPE

The Horn Effect and Halo Effect are self-explanatory. They refer to the predetermined conclusions we draw about various people (and they about us) for whatever reason. They can be positive or negative predeterminations, but they are not based on a full experience or appreciation of the person. You may have a Halo Effect with people if they feel they can relate to you because you're similar to them in terms of age, gender, nationality, culture, language, educational level, sexual orientation, or any other reason. Other people might have a Horn Effect experience of you for the very same reasons, and it may be because you're different than them in certain ways and this causes a "primal brain" reaction, or it might be that you are very similar to them or one of their family members they just can't stand and so they react negatively to you.

It's important to understand the basics of this idea, as you will probably encounter this, but you shouldn't let it get to you or wonder what you did to make someone almost always or always react negatively to you. When you are certain that you are being kind, respectful, and professional with others and they still respond negatively to you, it is them, not you.

There may be times if you are a new HR person in an organization that has resistance to changes you'd like to implement when others may try to bait you with the intention of discrediting your call for improved conflict resolution or communication skills. These are tests. Remain as calm and professional as you can, and remember this is not about you. However, you should document these instances in case they evolve into a bullying or harassment situation.

When you do encounter people who are resistant to the positive changes you hope to implement, kill them with kindness, have good intentions, and then let it go. Some people are so afraid of change that they will oppose you at every opportunity, as you are now a symbol of the changes you hope to implement. Do your best to not take it personally.

SHRM AND LOCAL CHAPTER OR STATE SHRM MEMBERSHIP

The Society for Human Resource Management (SHRM) is your best resource for almost every HR matter. You'll want your company to pay for your annual membership, and you'll want to stay on top of that to make sure it's renewed annually. Even if your company doesn't have a large HR budget and you cannot attend the many excellent conferences SHRM sponsors annually, you'll want to receive their e-mails and read updates on changes in laws that are coming or have occurred. You'll want to utilize their excellent research and assistance request services, which can and will save you time and money. You'll want to utilize their many useful toolkits on every topic from creating the best orientation program for your company to how to handle different types of FMLA leave to what your many options are in terms of creating wellness programs.

SHRM can also provide excellent support in terms of communicating with other HR professionals who may share the same challenges you do. SHRM can provide support when you have questions, can provide information when you need to persuade someone that your recommendation is the best way to handle something, and can help you post and look for other HR jobs.

SHRM has more than 225,000 individual members in over 125 countries, and has a network of more than 575 affiliated chapters in the United States, as well as offices in China and India. SHRM members are encouraged to continually learn, read, and attend training programs and constantly contribute toward improving their workplaces. SHRM is particularly helpful for HR/OD professionals who are solo practitioners.

SHRM also hosts several annual conferences open to members and nonmembers, including:

- SHRM Annual Conference and Exposition
- SHRM Staffing Management Conference and Exposition
- SHRM Employment Law and Legislative Conference and Exposition
- SHRM Global Conference and Exposition
- SHRM Strategic HR Conference and Exposition
- SHRM Diversity Conference and Exposition
- SHRM State Conferences

Additionally, SHRM has many newsletters you will automatically receive with your membership that will keep you updated on legislative changes well before they happen. The only criticism many HR professionals have of SHRM is that they will often send e-mails telling you to support or not support a certain legislative initiative.

Most states have their own HR chapters that are independent of SHRM and may offer various benefits and networking opportunities for a nominal membership fee; however, these are generally not as useful as SHRM. These state HR companies usually offer networking and training events, speakers, and social events. If you want to establish yourself as a speaker, this is one way to begin. If you have the budget, it's a very good idea to support these companies and to have people physically nearby to consult with if that appeals to you more than the e-mail, fax, and phone contact with SHRM representatives.

VARIOUS HR AND/OR OD WEB SITES

You'll want to be on the e-mail lists of every possible HR and OD e-zine and Web site so that you don't miss a thing. See the HR Tool entitled "Checklist of Sites to Which You'll Want to Subscribe," on pages 320–321.

YOUR ALUMNI ASSOCIATION FOR HR/OD DEPARTMENTS AND LOCAL COLLEGES AND UNIVERSITIES

Your previous university may have networking events and lectures or training and development events for HR and OD professionals that may prove to be helpful in terms of having colleagues in the HR/OD field to talk with and to learn from, and from whom to get support.

Check to see if any local colleges and universities have lecture series, courses you can audit, training programs that are relevant, or SHRM chapters you can network within.

EEOC, STATE AND CITY DIVISIONS OF HUMAN RIGHTS, OSHA, STATE DOL, DOSH

The Equal Employment Opportunity Commission (EEOC) offers technical assistance, training, publications, and media materials, which can be purchased. There is free online assistance at www.eeoc.gov.

State Department of Safety and Health (DOSH) sites often provide high-quality free or low-cost training programs on a number of workplace safety issues for local employees at every level. For example, NYS DOSH offers free courses in OSHA Log Reporting Requirements, Workplace Violence Prevention, Respiratory Protection, Ergonomics in the Workplace, Job Hazard Analysis, OSHA 10-Hour Construction Course, Safety for Youth Workers, and more.

Occupational Safety and Health Administration (OSHA) information can be found at www.osha.gov. OSHA can provide helpful information to prepare for natural disasters, epidemics, and other emergencies. You can draft a company emergency plan from their safety materials, which http://www.jan.wvu.edu/ also has.

You will want to visit your state Division of Human Rights Web site and familiarize yourself with their complaint procedures. Sometimes they are available to provide workplace educational presentations or have printed materials that you may order for a fee. This is a good resource and should be viewed as a partner in the commitment to legal compliance in the workplace.

Many workplaces are choosing to include in their employee handbooks the contact information for both their state Division of Human Rights and the Equal Employment Opportunity Commission. Companies that do this tend to have very good complaint reception and processing mechanisms in place.

Visit the Web site of your city Division of Human Rights, utilize their technical assistance, understand their procedures, and learn if they provide any training programs for a fee or at no cost. They may also be able to provide brochures and posters for your workplace if you ask.

AMERICANS WITH DISABILITIES ACT TECHNICAL ASSISTANCE HOTLINES AND JOB ACCOMMODATION NETWORK

The Job Accommodation Network (http://www.jan.wvu.edu/) is an excellent resource for any HR professional seeking to learn about or expand accommodations for employees with disabilities. With the recent expansion and clarification of the Americans with Disabilities Act (and the ADAAA) and the EEOC's definitions of "retaliation," it is important to educate yourself, all managers, and your leadership about accommodations that are available for a variety of short- and long-term disabilities.

For companies that choose to value diversity and seek out persons with disabilities to hire, there is Just One Break, (http://www.justonebreak.com/), which is part of a national company that has a Web site posting the résumés of professionals with disabilities that are only visible to member-employers. The Job Accommodation Network is an excellent guide for conducting your HR role in a legally compliant manner and can assist you in educating those in your company who need improved understanding of your company's legal compliance responsibilities when handling any of the following:

- Disabilities
- Workers' compensation injuries and illnesses
- Disability accommodation requests from employees
- Responding to disability accommodation requests from employees
- Your own disability accommodation request
- Determining what is a "reasonable accommodation"
- Ideas for different kinds of reasonable accommodations
- Dealing with issues of "light duty" or temporary disabilities
- Pregnancy
- Determining whether something is or is not a "disability"
- Your company's compliance responsibilities under ADA and ADAAA

WHISTLEBLOWER PROTECTION LAWS

There are many whistleblower protection laws and they often change, so you must always do your research. OSHA whistleblower information can be found at www.osha.gov. A complete index of U.S. whistleblower laws can be found at http://famguardian.org/Subjects/Discrimination/EmplmntDiscr/WhistleblowerLaws.htm.[1]

YOUR STATE INSPECTOR GENERAL'S OFFICE

You will want to go to the Web site of your state Inspector General's office and see exactly who and what is under their jurisdiction before you invest time, effort, and energy into submitting a complaint to this office. You will also want to ask whether your identity will be protected before you make a complaint, and if so, how. You should ask for something in writing that promises there will be no leaks of any kind to those about whom you are complaining.

Most state Inspector General's offices will only address issues of financial fraud, though many say they will also address issues of harassment, discrimination, financial mismanagement, and retaliation. Be sure you carefully read all instructions on your state Inspector General's office Web site and follow all directions, including using any complaint forms, procedures, formats, or other specific presentation methods.

This is also true if your state government has complaint processes available to you for state or private employment, such as your state Comptroller's Office, Ethics Commission, Attorney General's Office, Governor's Office, Governor's Counsel's Office, state Consumer Fraud Office, or any other options available to you on your state government's Web site.

ANTI-WORKPLACE-BULLYING GROUPS

Several groups are focused on addressing workplace bullying and making it unlawful. In the United States, this movement has several dedicated leaders including Gary Namie, Ph.D., and Ruth Namie, Ph.D., among others.[2] In addition, several states have strong grassroots movements that lobby their state legislators with the goal of making workplace bullying unlawful in the United States as it is in nearly every other industrialized democracy. Such groups include New York Healthy Workplace Advocates,[3] among many others.

ALTERNATIVE DISPUTE RESOLUTION GROUPS

There are many alternative dispute resolution (ADR) groups all over the United States and in other countries. There are also many excellent think tanks, academic programs, research labs, and for-profit consulting firms that handle ADR on a daily business as their main focus. Do look for organizations that have ethical standards, quality-training programs, and continuing practical and academic inquiry, such as New York State Dispute Resolution Association (NYSDRA).[4]

TAXPAYERS AGAINST FRAUD

Per Taxpayers Against Fraud's Web site:

> TAF's mission is both activist and educational. Established in 1986, TAF serves to: (1) Inform and educate the general public, the legal community, government officials, the media, and other interested groups about the False Claims Act and its *qui tam* provisions; (2) Contribute to understanding of the Act's nature, workings, and critical importance to the public interest; (3) Vigorously defend against any attempts to repeal or weaken the Act; (4) Facilitate meritorious *qui tam* suits; (5) Advance public and government support for *qui tam*; (6) Document the public policy value and the intellectual and legal foundation of the Act, and its *qui tam* provisions in particular.
>
> TAF works directly with *qui tam* plaintiffs and their attorneys to develop and successfully litigate *qui tam* cases. When a prospective *qui tam* plaintiff brings information about fraud against the Government to TAF, the information is evaluated to determine whether it appears to support a meritorious FCA case. TAF treats all such contacts as confidential. In furtherance of its mission, TAF has sometimes served as a co-plaintiff or supported FCA cases in other ways.
>
> To further assist *qui tam* plaintiffs, TAF has established a *Qui Tam* Plaintiff Loan Program. Qualified applicants can receive low interest loans secured by the prospective recoveries in their *qui tam* cases.
>
> As part of its public outreach, TAF promotes and disseminates information concerning the False Claims Act and *qui tam*. TAF publishes the *False Claims Act and Qui Tam Quarterly Review*, which provides an overview of case decisions, settlements, and other developments under the Act. TAF maintains a comprehensive FCA library, open to the public by appointment, and their Web site keeps the press, public and

legal professionals up to date on False Claims Act developments. In addition, TAF has established an information network to assist counsel in their efforts to provide effective representation to *qui tam* plaintiffs.

TAF also files *amicus* briefs on important legal and policy issues in FCA cases, writes articles about the Act and *qui tam,* and has provided testimony to Congress. On a regular basis, TAF responds to inquiries from journalists and government officials as well as the general public. TAF holds regular conferences for relators' counsel, and also publishes reports from time to time about various aspects of the FCA. TAF is based in Washington, D.C., where a staff of attorneys and other professionals is available to assist anyone interested in the False Claims Act and *qui tam.*

For more information about the False Claims Act or TAF, or if you are interested in pursuing a *qui tam* lawsuit, call TAF at 202-296-4826 or 1-800-US-FALSE (1-800-873-2573). *Note:* TAF has extensive expertise in the False Claims Act and *qui tam*, but it is not a law firm and does not represent outside clients or provide legal advice.[5]

NATIONAL WHISTLEBLOWER CENTER

Per the NWC Web site: "The National Whistleblowers Center (NWC) is an advocacy company with a 20-year history of protecting the right of individuals to speak out about wrongdoing in the workplace without fear of retaliation. Since 1988, NWC has supported whistleblowers in the courts and before Congress, achieving victories for environmental protection, nuclear safety, government ethics and corporate accountability. NWC also sponsors several educational and assistance programs, including an online resource center on whistleblower rights, a speakers bureau of national experts and former whistleblowers, and a national attorney referral service run by the NWC's sister group the National Whistleblower Legal Defense and Education Fund (NWLDEF). The National Whistleblowers Center is a non-partisan, non-profit company based in Washington, D.C.[6]

NATIONAL EMPLOYMENT LAWYERS ASSOCIATION

Per the National Employment Lawyers Association: "The National Employment Lawyers Association (NELA) advances employee rights and serves lawyers who advocate for equality and justice in the American workplace."

NELA's vision is that "workers will be paid at least a living wage in an environment free of discrimination, harassment, retaliation, and capricious employment decisions; employers will fulfill their promises to provide retirement, health, and other benefits; workers' safety and livelihood won't be compromised for the sake of corporate profit and interests; and individuals will have effective legal representation to enforce their rights to a fair and just workplace, adequate remedies, and a right to trial by jury.

"NELA is the [United States'] largest professional company that is exclusively comprised of lawyers who represent individual employees in cases involving employment discrimination and other employment-related matters. NELA and its 68 state and local affiliates have more than 3000 members."[7]

LINKEDIN TOOLS

LinkedIn is an important tool for many aspects of HR/OD work. It is a great way to keep your résumé public and updated. Recruiters often use LinkedIn when recruiting. It is a reliable and efficient way to remain in contact with your many professional connections even when they or you change jobs.[8]

LinkedIn is where you can connect with those with whom you work both at your company and externally. These are important contacts for networking, support, expert questions and answers, industry polls, groups that can help your career and provide support during stressful times, and staying on top of the latest HR/OD news.

USEFUL LINKEDIN CONNECTIONS

LinkedIn is a truly excellent professional networking site on which you can post your résumé, training, education, current projects, groups you belong to, interests, and more. You can have a blog, create polls, add PowerPoint presentations, store documents, and share all of these with whomever you choose to connect with on LinkedIn. You may also recommend those with whom you have worked and have others post recommendations of your work.

You should join groups that interest you on LinkedIn, connect with anyone you meet and have a positive experience with at conferences, trainings, lectures, workshops, networking events, workplace events, alumni events, at former companies for whom you have worked, and at your current company. This is like having a permanent Rolodex you never have to physically bring with you or worry about misplacing.

Use LinkedIn to link to:

- Anyone with whom you work and have a productive and positive working relationship
- Recruiters
- School internship contacts
- Former interns
- Former supervisors and coworkers
- People you meet at conferences, seminars, meetings, and trainings
- Former professors
- Former classmates
- Alumna of your undergraduate and graduate schools working in your field or in related fields
- Government contacts you have had over the years
- Trainers and seminar or conference leaders and organizers with whom you've had good rapport
- Mentors and mentees
- Family members whose work you know and recommend
- Friends whose work you know and recommend
- Contacts for your company's disability, health, dental, vision, mental health, workers' compensation, background check, long-term care insurance, banking, death benefits, and any other contacts for benefits for your former and current companies with whom you have good working relationships

- Consultants, trainers, and vendors of HR/OD products, even if you weren't able to use their services but have had enough contact with them to know that you'd like to work with them if you could

Many HR/OD professionals use LinkedIn as a recruitment tool, as hundreds of thousands of people from all over the world post their résumés or seek jobs there. If you are job hunting or want to post a job on LinkedIn, you can make that known and do so at no cost. LinkedIn is growing daily and is an excellent way to get information, ask or reply to questions, post polls, post job ads, or announce your own desire for a new position elsewhere.

LinkedIn is also a way to join existing groups or form new groups related to a particular challenge in your industry or geographical area.

You may also create your own LinkedIn Groups and spread the word to get others to join if there is something about which you are passionate. The HR/OD Credible Activist Group on LinkedIn (http://www.linkedin.com/groups?gid=2057398&trk=hb_side_g) is growing every day. By now, you should fully understand what it takes to be a credible activist. If you are committed to being one, please join this group on LinkedIn!

CONSIDER GETTING YOURSELF A CERTIFIED COACH

A coach can help you get from where you are to where you want to be with almost any goal, large or small. Examples of a small goal might be that you want to speak up more in meetings but you lack the confidence to do so or that you don't feel your comments are really welcome but you want to find an effective way to speak up anyway. On the other hand, your goals may be larger and more complex, such as you want to get more training and specialize in an area of HR or move to another location, state, or nation. A good coach can help you with these kinds of goals.

Talane Miedaner's book *Coach Yourself to Success* is an excellent resource for anyone who is unfamiliar with coaching or who wants coaching but cannot afford or commit to hiring a coach at this point.[9]

YOUR RÉSUMÉ

CAREER OBJECTIVE

You will want to tailor your résumé and cover letter to each position you seek to an extent, yet always make sure it is truthful. Here are some examples of good career objectives:

- To lead an HR department that delivers excellent internal customer service to all employees and models respectful behavior, alignment with company goals, and compliance with all relevant employment laws.
- To contribute to an HR department that serves all employees consistently while supporting the company's goals and ensuring compliance with all relevant employment laws.

- To direct an HR department with a focus on employee relations, benefits improvement, legal compliance, respectful workplace initiatives, increased conflict resolution and communication straining, and a contribution to a workplace culture of dignity and respect.

I recommend always inserting something about "supporting legal compliance with relevant employment laws" to ensure that you are rejected by those companies who don't intend to be legally compliant and who really don't want an HR professional—or anyone—pointing out when a company has compliance responsibilities they are not meeting or are at risk of not meeting. You will be better off not working at such an organization.

As mentioned throughout the book, HR professionals must not settle for companies that disregard their compliance responsibilities and must be very careful to screen them out as unacceptable places to work. Working in such an environment will only prove to be nightmarish and a source of unbearable stress. Talk to other HR professionals and ask them about their experiences in workplaces that don't value their legal compliance responsibilities. You will hear stories of lies, mistrust, cover-ups, documents and e-mails that somehow "disappear," lawsuits, EEO and OSHA charges, investigations, sloppy investigations and possibly arrests, huge monetary losses, extremely poor workplace morale, bad publicity, and an HR person who is considering other fields.

)) TRAINING AND FORMAL EDUCATION

You'll want to list your training and formal education at the beginning of your résumé. Putting the dates of degrees earned is not necessary, though you will want to indicate either on your résumé, in your cover letter, or verbally in your interview how many years of relevant experience you have for this position. You will also want to list all of the relevant training programs you have taken, from workplace safety training to soft-skills communication or conflict resolution training to nuts-and-bolts training, such as how to administer intermittent FMLA leave or handle disability claims. Be sure to list the name of the training, the city in which you attended the training, and who or what company presented the training. Listing the year you attended the training is a good idea, but not necessary. A number of training companies offer webinars so you never have to leave your office.

In addition, volunteer work is a very good thing to list as long as it is something that makes you look good and doesn't make your interviewer think you'll allow such work to somehow take precedence over the job you may soon have with them. For example, being a volunteer with the Big Brothers Big Sisters Foundation (http://www.bbbsfoundation.org) is something that looks great on a résumé. However, being a volunteer person who camps out in a tree for a week or a month at a time will make your interviewer question if you'll be around to perform the job.

Of course, only list things that are actually true. Review your résumé carefully before you send it out. You may have volunteered at the local homeless shelter seven years ago when you last updated your résumé, and if you are no longer doing that volunteer work, you may keep it on your résumé and list the years during which you did that volunteer work and make it clear in doing so that you are no longer volunteering there.

You'll want to limit the amount of volunteer work you list, again, so your prospective employer doesn't wonder when you'll be sleeping so you can perform your possible future job there in an excellent manner!

Unless you are required to disclose all of your external activities as with certain government positions, avoid listing volunteer work that is political in nature unless you are applying for a position that will appreciate that particular volunteering. Be ready to discuss any volunteer experience you list on your résumé.

PUBLIC SPEAKING

If you want to stretch your skills and give back to the schools in your local community, agreeing to do speaking engagements for college or graduate school HR/OD students is a great way to challenge yourself. Reach out to local schools that have HR/OD departments and ask if they have student SHRM chapters who may benefit from having a speaker on a certain HR/OD topic. Make sure you are in agreement with the group or organizer regarding what the topic should be, the length of the presentation, and how many students will be there. Bring handouts for the students and encourage an interactive discussion at the end of your presentation. If you have implemented an unpaid internship program, bring your business cards and some internship descriptions so the students can consider applying. Cultivate relationships with any faculty involved with the student chapter who are supportive and have a realistic understanding of the challenges HR professionals often face. Be sure to list any volunteer speaking engagements on your résumé.

MENTORING

If you have been part of a mentoring program either as a mentor or as a mentee, this is good to list. If you developed the mentoring program, that is even better. Mentoring can be around specific skills such as conflict resolution, communication, writing well, or time management. It can also be a general grooming process to help some workers be more efficient, professional, polished, poised, and competent. Be ready to discuss any experience you list on your résumé, including this one. If you were mentored by someone famous for something positive or related in some way to the job for which you are applying, by all means list that person's name.

NONVIOLENT COMMUNICATION TRAINING

Consider reading the book *Nonviolent Communication: A Language of Life* by Marshall Rosenberg, Ph.D.[10] Also, consider taking a course to learn this "language" or completing the online course if you don't have a certified trainer near you. It is also possible to continue in-depth study of NVC, and in the future, you might want to become certified so that you can present trainings in your workplace or elsewhere. NVC is a simple yet extremely effective set of communication skills to learn and practice with family, friends, partners, and in the workplace.

NVC can help managers and all employees become more aware of communication skills that are effective and those that are ineffective. Once we bring awareness to how we communicate and are able to observe other behavioral options (which we see modeled by those with authority in the workplace), it becomes easier and even fun to change our communication methods and try new ones to see how they work. When employees begin to use more effective communication methods such as NVC, workplaces have less conflict, more collaboration, fewer complaints, more teamwork, greater instances of good citizenship behavior, and healthier and happier employees who tend to be more productive.

NVC is particularly useful to help diffuse conflict situations and efficiently get to solutions. NVC helps people focus on:

- Their observations
- Their feelings
- Their needs
- Their requests

It's an incredibly simple yet effective formula for communications in the workplace whether they are tense or not. With practice, this kind of communication can begin to feel more natural and can prove to be extremely effective, especially when whole groups learn and utilize it together. If you are the only person using NVC, it will be more of a challenge; however, it can still help you and others reach consensus and agreement while cutting through any feelings that may exist and are obstacles to resolution. NVC can be particularly helpful when language or cultural barriers exist that create obstacles to clear communication or that contribute to frequent misunderstandings. Keep in mind that even two people of similar age, race, and ethnicity can have "cultural" differences that result in misunderstandings.

Additionally, we know from emotional intelligence research that all people of every culture have the very same nonverbal facial expressions for the five basic emotions of fear, joy, anger, sadness, and disgust. For this reason, NVC is an excellent training to undertake if you work or wish to work in global HR and to encourage among workplaces that have diversity of language and culture.

According to the NYCNVC Web site, "Nonviolent Communication (NVC) strengthens our ability to understand and respond compassionately to others and to ourselves. It guides us to reframe how we express ourselves and hear others by focusing our consciousness on what we are observing, feeling, needing, and requesting. By practicing NVC, we can hear our own needs and those of others with a depth of understanding that gives us the ability to transcend conflict. When we focus on needs and values, rather than diagnosing and judging, the world looks different and becomes different. When we focus on needs and values, rather than diagnosing and judging, the world looks different and becomes different."[11]

CCP, CEBS, PHR, SPHR: FORMS OF HR CERTIFICATION AVAILABLE TO HR PROFESSIONALS

CCP stands for Certified Compensation Professional (CCP®), and is recognized as a mark of expertise and excellence in all areas of compensation. CEBS stand for Certified Employee Benefits Specialist. The HR Certification Institute (HRCI) offers four certifications for HR professionals:[12]

- PHR® (Professional in Human Resources)
- SPHR® (Senior Professional in Human Resources)
- GPHR® (Global Professional in Human Resources)
- PHR-CA® and SPHR-CA® (PHR with state certification in California and SPHR with state certification in California).

MANAGING HR ASSISTANTS AND INTERNS

Tell your staff clearly what you expect of them. For interns, it might be the following tasks: Get my mail daily, tell me when you go to lunch, call or e-mail if you'll be out, and check your e-mail from me daily to learn your tasks for the day.

You'll also want to ask your staff to tell you their goals; learn what interests them, what they want more training in, and how they'd like to grow and develop. Give your unpaid interns large empty binders and let them make copies of interesting training materials, checklists, or templates that will help them in their future careers.

Be sure to solicit feedback from your staff regularly, whether it is in individual or group meetings. Be sensitive to their health, family, and other needs. Be sure to give them tasks to do when you are on vacation. Have them make HR as user-friendly as possible for employees by making informational packets for policies that often confuse employees, such as FMLA, UI, WC, Maternity leave, STD, LTD, and COBRA. Keep this information organized and easily accessible to employees.

Do treat your assistant(s) and/or intern(s) and all other staff with respect and dignity. Realize that there will come a day when you will need to depend on them for something and on that day, in that moment, you will want their utmost support and loyalty. These are relationships like any others, and they require deposits into the bank of goodwill by all involved.

Try not to give them unreasonable work deadlines. Remember what it was like when you were an assistant. Do your best to give clear instructions, preferably written or e-mailed so there is no question about what was communicated. Be as clear as possible.

Review job descriptions as needed so there is no confusion about who is responsible for what. Be kind and considerate when he or she is ill or has family stresses. Don't share confidential information with staff who are not approved to receive it just because they are in the HR department. Be sure your assistant(s) and intern(s) have all the tools, time, and training they need in order to do excellent work. Solicit their feedback regularly about what else they may need in order to produce excellent work, about any ideas they have for your department, and about any feedback they have about working with you. When you welcome feedback and welcome it regularly, your staff will believe that you truly want it and will feel safer giving it to you. Of course, you must then respond well to the feedback, consider it fairly, and give credit for good ideas wherever it is due. Do review their performance regularly and invite their ideas and feedback as much as possible on internal processes that affect their jobs, their work with you, and the procedures of the department. Do give praise when it is deserved.

Do *not* yell at, berate, or otherwise disrespect your staff. Don't take out anger or frustration on them or otherwise displace any emotions onto them simply because they are available. Don't deny them any rights to any policies or procedures that are available to any other employee, and similarly, don't extend any special privileges to them because they work in HR. Don't have a posture of mistrust toward them unless there is good reason to, and don't expect any more of them than you would expect your boss to expect from you. Don't be unreasonable if mistakes are made, and remember that all employees, including you, make mistakes occasionally. Don't document petty mistakes and make a bigger deal out of them than is necessary.

PRIORITIZATION

Use the following checklist to help prioritize your work:

- Understand which projects you have that are higher priorities.
- Meet deadlines.
- Do the work well and be thorough.
- Take notes.
- Know what you're supposed to know.
- Ask questions.
- Ask for more time or help if you need it.
- Make sure there are checks and balances.
- Stay on top of changing policies and procedures.
- Double-check your work and sometimes triple-check it; ask your assistant to help you.
- Keep daily lists of priorities.

Use an annual HR calendar for your HR department and your company; this will let staff know when to expect open benefits enrollment, certain mandatory trainings, or the company picnic. The HR Tool entitled "Sample HR Annual Calendar," on pages 321–324 shows one example. This can, of course, be customized to fit your own needs.

THE MOST VALUABLE HUMAN RESOURCE OF ALL— YOU!

Please share your credible activist workplace experiences with me so I can share them with others. Please also visit my Web site at www.LoveAndWorkCoach.com, and stay tuned to my EQ Blog on Emotional Intelligence at work, in the family, in relationships, and with friends.

And here's to every HR professional positively influencing their leadership toward legal compliance and a healthy and productive corporate culture!

Challenging workplace experiences inspire courage, endurance, and integrity. When we look back on labor history, we are often appalled by various events. What will our reaction be when we look back on this time? What is your story? Please share it with me.

HR TOOLS

CHECKLIST OF RECOMMENDED READING FOR THE CREDIBLE ACTIVIST

Coach Yourself to Success: 101 Tips from a Personal Coach for Reaching Your Goals at Work and in Life by Talane Miedaner (New York: McGraw-Hill, 2000).

Designing and Using Organizational Surveys by Allan H. Church, Ph.D., and Janine Waclawski, Ph.D. (Gower Publishers, Limited Pub. Date: 09/01/1998).

The Emotionally Intelligent Manager: How to Develop and Use the Four Key Emotional Skills of Leadership by David Caruso, Ph.D., and Peter Salovey (Hoboken, NJ: Jossey-Bass, 2004).

The EQ Edge: Emotional Intelligence and Your Success, 2nd ed. by Steven Stein and Howard Book (Hoboken, NJ: Jossey-Bass, 2006).

Nonviolent Communication: A Language of Life, 2nd ed. by Marshall Rosenberg, Ph.D. (Encinitas, CA: PuddleDancer Press, 2003).

The Seven Habits of Highly Effective People, 15th anniv. ed. by Stephen Covey (New York: Free Press, 2004).

The Surprising Purpose of Anger: Beyond Anger Management: Finding the Gift by Marshall Rosenberg, Ph.D. (Encinitas, CA: PuddleDancer Press, 2005).

The Thin Book of Naming Elephants: How to Surface Undiscussables for Greater Organizational Success Naming Elephants by Sue Annis Hammond and Andrea B. Mayfield (Bend, OR: Thin Book Publishing Co., 2004).

We Can Work It Out: Resolving Conflicts Peacefully and Powerfully by Marshall Rosenberg, Ph.D. (Encinitas, CA: PuddleDancer Press, 2004).

When Anger Scares You: How to Overcome Your Fear of Conflict and Express Your Anger in Healthy Ways by John Lynch (Oakland, CA: New Harbinger Publications, 2004).

CHECKLIST OF SITES TO WHICH YOU'LL WANT TO SUBSCRIBE

BLR (Business and Legal Resources): http://www.blr.com

BusinessWatch Network: http://www.BusinessWatchNetwork.com

Chief Learning Officer magazine: http://www.clomedia.com

Council on Education: http://www.counciloned.com

HRGuru: http://www.HRGuru.com

HRHero: http://www.HRHero.com

HR Resource: http://www.HRResource.com

Human Capital Media (HCM): http://www.humancapitalmedia.com

Job Accommodation Network (JAN): http://www.jan.wvu.edu/

Leader Connections: http://www.leaderconnections.com

Organisation for Economic Co-operation and Development: http://www.oecd.org

Partners in Leadership: http://www.ozprinciple.org

Professional and Organizational Development Network in Higher Education:
    http://www.podnetwork.org

Sandler Assoc.: http://www.sandlerassoc.com

Talent Management: http://www.talentmgt.com

Thought Leaders: http://www.thoughtleaders.com

Training Advisor Inc.: http://www.TrainingAdvisorinc.com

U.S. Department of Labor: http://www.dol.gov

VolunteerMatch: http://www.volunteermatch.org

Workforce Management: http://www.workforce.com

Workplace Issues Today, Cornell University, ILR:
    http://www.ilr.cornell.edu/library/research/worldOfWorkNews/wit

SAMPLE HR ANNUAL CALENDAR

January: Issue holiday schedule

Propose changes to Employee Handbook to leadership and legal

Review Job descriptions for changes with Supervisors and check FLSA status

Announce monthly theme

Mandatory Safety Training

Mandatory Emotional Intelligence Training

Remind Supervisory staff about:

    Coaching

    Investigative problem solving

    When to consult with HR

    Importance of documentation

February: Review Spring/Summer Seasonal Employee budget

Begin Performance Evaluation meetings with deadlines of April 1

Review Intern/Seasonal Staff Manuals and make changes

Review Intern and Seasonal Staff Hiring packages

Post OSHA stats: February 1 to end of April

Begin recruitment for seasonal spring/summer positions

EAP informational meetings: optional, information disseminated to staff

Mandatory EEO/SHP Training

Mandatory EEO/SHP Training for Managers

Announce monthly theme about tax and personal accounting issues

March: Post Seasonal position ads

Announce Employee of the Quarter

Review posting compliance in all employee posting locations

Announce "Take Your Child to Work Day" in April

Mandatory Conflict Resolution Training

Mandatory Supervisory Training: Avoiding Rater-Bias/Attribution Errors

Announce monthly theme

April: Mandatory Revised Employee Handbook Training

Begin interviewing Seasonal Staff

Begin Directors' and Officers' Liability Insurance Renewal

Fax forms to all Directors and Officers for return to HR

Assemble all application attachments

Begin preparing EEO-1 or EEO-4 report

Remind Supervisory staff about use of coaching and problem solving

Incident Report/Mandatory Safety Trainings

Announce monthly theme

May: Hire and orient Seasonal Staff

Announce Intern/Seasonal Employee of the Month

Mandatory NVC (Nonviolent Communication) Training

Plan and Schedule Employee Appreciation Picnic/BBQ

Prepare for Annual Workers' Comp Safety Walk-through

Announce monthly theme

June: Mandatory Safety Training

Continue Seasonal Make-up Orientation

Announce Intern/Seasonal Employee of the Month

Announce Employee of the Quarter

Get approval to renew dental/vision benefits contracts

Make sure SHRM and other professional memberships are paid

Inquire about COLA (cost of living) annual increases, bonuses, and commissions for the FY (financial year)

Announce monthly theme

July: Announce Intern/Seasonal Employee of the Month

Ask employees which cultural holidays are important to them to be recognized at work

Performance Evaluations with Seasonal Staff as needed

Remind Supervisory staff about use of coaching and problem solving

Plan Managers or All-Staff team-buildings

Announce monthly theme

August: Announce Intern/Seasonal Employee of the Month

Plan and Schedule Employee Appreciation BBQ

Exit interviews with departing interns/seasonals

Collect exiting seasonal employee contact information

Prepare for workers' comp audit

Plan Intern farewell BBQ (check Jewish holidays and work around)

Meet with Department heads re: unpaid internship recruitment

Announce monthly theme

September: Announce Employee of the Quarter

Announce Intern/Seasonal Employee of the Month

Prepare for Financial Planning week/Bank visits for staff

Prep for Workers' Comp Audit with Finance

Prepare for Health Benefits Open Enrollment

Announce monthly theme

October: Announce Open Enrollment for Benefits Changes

Update rates on Health Plan Comparison Information Chart for Staff

Update changes to health plan information

Financial Planning Week

Prepare for cash-in of vacation time

Train or Remind Supervisory staff about use of coaching and problem solving

Announce monthly theme

November: Issue _____ policies with any updates

Plan and schedule Holiday Party

Plan and schedule in-office Holiday Potluck Luncheon

Plan and schedule optional Secret-Santa game

Open Enrollment for health benefits changes

Supplemental Insurance Plan Open Enrollment

Announce monthly theme

December: Send out responsible drinking memo to staff re. holiday party

Send out Employee of the Quarter form

Send out Employee of the Year form

In-house Defensive Driving course

Holiday Party

Finalize employee health benefits changes

Send out annual injury memo to all staff soliciting injury/illness reports HR is unaware of

Announce monthly themes

Ongoing: Handling employee relations issues

Responding to suggestions

Responding to complaints and grievances

Providing training options to supervisors and staff

Meeting with supervisors and staff

Mediating conflict

Dispute resolution

Providing assistance

Providing benefits information and assistance

Planning and administering discipline when needed

Consulting with supervisors on coaching

Consulting with supervisors on discipline

Handling Workers' Compensation paperwork as needed

Handling Short- and Long-Term Disability paperwork as needed

Handling FMLA paperwork as needed

Providing various communications, safety, management, conflict resolution and other training programs, as needed

Consulting with supervisors regarding discipline, probation, and termination

Administering terminations as needed, etc.

Researching trainings

Attending trainings

Recruitment as needed

Orientation and onboarding as needed

NOTES

CHAPTER 1

1. Tim V. Eaton and Michael D. Akers, "Whistleblowing and Good Governance: Policies for Universities, Government Entities, and Nonprofit Organizations," *The CPA Journal* (June 2007), http://www.nysscpa .org/cpajournal/2007/607/essentials/p58.htm.
2. BNET, http://www.bnet.com.
3. U.S. Equal Employment Opportunity Commission, *Compliance Manual*, Section 8, Chapter II, Part B: Opposition and Part C: Participation, http://www.eeoc.gov/policy/docs/retal.html
4. U.S. Equal Employment Opportunity Commission, http://www.eeoc.gov/policy/docs/retal.html
5. Annabelle Gurwitch, *Fired!* (Shout Factory Theatre, DVD, 2006).
6. Henry L. Thompson (lecture, International Conference on Emotional Intelligence, Toronto, Canada, June 29–30, 2009). (Used with permission.)

CHAPTER 2

1. J. D. Mayer, M. T. DiPaolo, and P. Salovey. "Perceiving Affective Content in Ambiguous Visual Stimuli: A Component of Emotional Intelligence," *Journal of Personality Assessment* 54 (1990): 772–781.
2. Henry L. Thompson, "Catastrophic Leadership Failure" (lecture, International Conference on Emotional Intelligence, Toronto, Canada, June 29–30, 2009). (Used with permission.)
3. Heather Amberg Anderson, "From Skeptics to Champions: Tools to Excite Executives into Investing in EQ Development" (lecture, International Conference on Emotional Intelligence, Toronto, Canada, June 29–30, 2009).
4. David Caruso, EI Skills Group: "Ability Model of Emotional Intelligence" (International Conference on Emotional Intelligence, Toronto, Canada, June 30, 2009).
5. BusinessDictionary.com, s.v. "reasonable person," http://www.businessdictionary.com.
6. TheFreeDictionary.com, s.v. "reasonable person standard," http://legal-dictionary.thefreedictionary .com/Reasonable + person + standard.
7. Bernadette Poole-Tracy, "Economic Reality of Unresolved Conflict" (NYSDRA, New York, September 2007. (Used with permission.)

CHAPTER 3

1. Henry L. Thompson, "Catastrophic Leadership Failure" (lecture, International Conference on Emotional Intelligence, Chicago, 2008). (Used with permission.)
2. SHRM Code of Ethics, SHRM Web site, November 16, 2007, http://www.shrm.org/about/Pages/code-of-ethics.aspx. (Used with permission.)
3. Bruce W. Tuckman, "Developmental Sequence in Small Groups," *Psychological Bulletin* 63 (1965): 384–399.

CHAPTER 4

1. EEOC, s.v. "Mediation" http://www.eeoc.gov/eeoc/mediation/ada-parties.cfm
2. Ibid.
3. Occupational Safety and Health Administration, http://www.osha.gov.

4. Job Accommodation Network, http://www.jan.wvu.edu.
5. Ibid.
6. Ibid.
7. Ibid.

CHAPTER 5

1. U.S. Department of Labor, Wage, and Hour Division, http://www.dol.gov/esa/contacts/state_of.htm.
2. Ibid.
3. U.S. Department of Labor, Wage and Hour Division, "Revised Final Regulations Under the Family and Medical Leave Act (RIN 1215-AB35), http://www.dol.gov/whd/fmla/finalrule.htm.

CHAPTER 6

1. U.S. Department of Labor, Occupational Safety and Health Administration, "The Whistleblower Protection Program," http://www.osha.gov/dep/oia/whistleblower/consumer-product-industry-employees.html.

CHAPTER 7

1. Workplace Fairness, "Resources," http://www.workplacefairness.org/resources. (Used with permission.)

CHAPTER 8

1. U.S. Department of Labor, Occupational Safety & Health Administration, "Workplace Violence: OSHA Standards," http://www.osha.gov/SLTC/workplaceviolence/standards.html.
2. National Institute for Occupational Safety and Health, "Occupational Violence, http://www.cdc.gov/niosh/topics/violence.
3. Federal Bureau of Investigation, "Violence in the Workplace: Preventing It; Managing It," http://www.fbi.gov/page2/march04/violence030104.htm (PDF: http://www.fbi.gov/publications/violence.pdf).
4. Ibid.
5. National Institute of Occupational Safety and Health.
6. Washington State Department of Labor and Industries, "Workplace Violence," http://www.lni.wa.gov/Safety/Research/OccHealth/WorkVio/default.asp#Bullying (PDF: http://www.lni.wa.gov/Safety/Research/Files/Bullying.pdf).
7. Ibid.
8. Workplace Bullying Institute, http://www.workplacebullying.org.
9. Washington State Department of Labor and Industries, "Workplace Violence," http://www.lni.wa.gov/Safety/Research/OccHealth/WorkVio/default.asp#Bullying (PDF: http://www.lni.wa.gov/Safety/Research/Files/Bullying.pdf).
10. Peterson, Beverly, "There Oughta Be a Law" Web page, http://nojobisworththis.com, 2009.
11. National Labor Relations Board, "What is the National Labor Relations Act," http://www.nlrb.gov/Workplace_Rights/i_am_new_to_this_website/what_is_the_national_labor_relations_act.aspx.
12. Michael Lotito, "HR Plays Important Role in Keeping Unions 'Irrelevant'" Annual Conference for the Society for Human Resource Management (SHRM), New Orleans, LA, June 28–July 1, 2009. (Used with permission.)
13. Washington State Department of Labor and Industries, "Workplace Violence," http://www.lni.wa.gov/Safety/Research/OccHealth/WorkVio/default.asp#Bullying (PDF: http:lni.wa.gov/Safety/Research/Files/Bullying.pdf).
14. Ibid.
15. Ibid.

CHAPTER 9

1. Job Accommodation Network, http://www.jan.wvu.edu.
2. U.S. Department of Labor, Bureau of Labor Statistics, "Employment Situation of Veterans Summary," http://www.bls.gov/news.release/vet.nr0.htm.
3. U.S. Department of Labor, Office of Compliance Assistance Policy, Compliance Assistance—Worker Adjustment and Retraining Notification Act (WARN)—Preamble to the 1989 Final Rule, http://www.dol.gov/compliance/laws/comp-warn-regs.htm.
4. Job Accommodation Network, http://www.jan.wvu.edu.
5. Ibid.
6. U.S. Department of Labor, Employment Standards Administration, Office of Federal Contract Compliance Programs, http://www.dol.gov/ofccp/aboutof.html.
7. U.S. Department of Labor, Bureau of Labor Statistics, "Employment Situation of Veterans Summary," http://www.bls.gov/news.release/vet.nr0.htm.
8. U.S. Department of Labor, Office of Compliance Assistance Policy, "The Employee Retirement Income Security Act (ERISA)," http://www.dol.gov/dol/topic/health-plans/erisa.htm.
9. http://www.dol.gov/compliance/laws/comp-ina.htm.
10. Ibid.
11. Ibid.

CHAPTER 10

1. U.S. Department of Labor, Bureau of Labor Statistics, "Definitions of Health Insurance Terms," http://www.bls.gov/ncs/ebs/sp/healthterms.pdf. The BLS document, in turn, cites the following sources:

SURVEY DEFINITIONS
The Medical Expenditure Panel Survey definitions (AHRQ)
The National Employer Health Insurance Survey definitions (NCHS)

DEFINITIONS FROM OTHER FEDERAL AGENCIES AND SURVEYS
The Current Population Survey (BLS/Census)
ERISA-related definitions (from PWBA)

GLOSSARIES AND INFORMATIONAL PAPERS FROM WEB SITES
OPM's Federal Employees Health Benefit Plans (glossary and specific plan booklets), Blue Cross/Blue Shield, The National Center for Policy Analysis, and The Health Insurance Association of America.

PUBLICATIONS
Employee Benefit Plans: A Glossary of Terms, 9th ed., 1997, Judith A. Sankey, editor, International Foundation of Employee Benefit Plans.
Fundamentals of Employee Benefit Programs, 4th ed.
"Managed Care Plans and Managed Care Features: Data from the EBS to the NCS,"
Cathy A. Baker and Iris S. Díaz, Compensation and Working Conditions, Spring 2001
EBRI Notes Vol. 16, no. 7, July 1995
HIPAA Source Book
U.S. Department of Labor, Bureau of Labor Statistics. Health Insurance Terms, http://www.bls.gov/ncs/ebs/sp/healthterms.pdf
Personal communications with staff from some of the data sources cited above were used as well.

CHAPTER 11

1. John J. Fitzpatrick, Jr., James L. Perine, and Bridget Dutton, "State Labor Legislation Enacted in 2008," *Monthly Labor Review Online* (January 2009), http://www.bls.gov/opub/mlr/2009/01/art1full.pdf.

CHAPTER 12

1. Joel Goodman, The Humor Project, http://www.humorproject.com/. (Used with permission.)

CHAPTER 13

1. The New York State Dispute Resolution Association Ethics and Standards Committee, "NYSDRA Mediator Standards of Practice," (New York: NYSDRA, 2005), http://www.nysdra.org/userfiles/file/ethics_standards.pdf.
2. Bernadette Poole-Tracy, "Economic Reality of Unresolved Conflict," (New York: NYSDRA, September 2007). (Used with permission.)
3. Ibid.

CHAPTER 14

1. Just a pet peeve of many HR professionals: Don't call it "sexual harassment training"; we aren't training people in how to successfully sexually harass others. It is SHP training—sexual harassment *prevention* training. We are hoping to train them in knowledge that will prevent them from sexually harassing anyone.

CHAPTER 15

1. David Caruso, Ph.D., IEI Conference, (Toronto, Canada: IEIC, June 30, 2009).

CHAPTER 19

1. Whistleblower Laws.com, http://whistleblowerlaws.com/index.php.
2. Workplace Bullying Institute, http://www.workplacebullying.org.
3. New York Healthy Workplace Advocates, http://www.nyhwa.org.
4. New York State Dispute Resolution Association, Inc. (NYSDRA), http://www.nysdra.org.
5. Taxpayers Against Fraud Education Fund, The False Claims Act Legal Center, "About TAF," http:// www.taf.org/abouttaf.htm. (Used with permission.)
6. National Whistleblowers Center (NWC), http://www.whistleblowers.org. (Used with permission.)
7. National Employment Lawyers Association (NELA), http://www.nela.org/NELA/#. (Used with permission.)
8. LinkedIn Web site, http://www.LinkedIn.com.
9. Talane Miedaner, *Coach Yourself to Success.* (New York: McGraw-Hill, 2000).
10. Marshall Rosenberg, *Nonviolent Communication: A Language of Life*, (Encinitas, CA: PuddleDancer Press, 2003).
11. The New York Center for Nonviolent Communication, "What Is NVC?" http://nycnvc.org/aboutnvc.htm.
12. HR Certification Institute, "Overview and Benefits," http://www.hrci.org/certification/ov/.

INDEX

Locators in **bold** indicate HR Tools.

Organizational Development (OD), xiv, 29
  (*See also* Human resources (HR);
    specific topics)
Orientation guide, 256, **259–263**
Overtime
  FLSA, 74, **78**
  legislation, 143, 158, 167, 171, 175

PACE formula for memos, 60
Paid holidays, 273, **290**
Pennsylvania legislation, 175
Performance management
  internal complaint procedures, 235–237
  leadership/employee development, 237–238,
    244
  smart, 240–243, **245–255**
  [*See also* Conflict resolution; Emotional
    intelligence (EI); Nonviolent Communication
    (NVC)]
Perine, James L., 135
Personal hygiene, 207–208
Peterson, Beverly, 105
Physician-hospital company (PHO), 131–132
Plant closing legislation, 143–144, 168, 172
Point-of-service (POS) plan, 131–132
Policy application, inconsistent, 89–92, **95–100**
Poole-Tracy, Bernadette, 204–205
Preadmission certification, managed care, 132
Preadmission testing, managed care, 132
Preferred provider company (PPO) plan,
    131–132
Premium/premium equivalent, 133
Prevailing wage legislative action, 138–139, 144,
    153, 168–169, 172–173, 176, 185
Primary care physician (PCP), 133
Prioritization checklist, 319
Privacy of workers, legislative action, 140–143,
    146, 148, 151–154, 156, 158–160, 162,
    164–165, 173, 175, 179–181, 183
Problem-solving abilities, improving, 94
Product safety, 79–80, **86–87**
Professional development, SHRM Code of Ethics,
    36
Profits and HR/OD, 7
Protected activity, EEOC, 4–6, 51
Public safety, 79–84, **85–87**

Public speaking, on résumé, 316
Puerto Rico legislation, 175–176

Qui tam fraud provisions, 81–82, 84, 311

Rater bias, 240, 242
Reading lists, 320
Reality testing, improving, 94
"Reasonable person standard," 18
Record-keeping, 52–53, **60–63,** 70, 243, **252,** 291,
    295–296
Recruitment (*see* Job design, selection, and
    recruitment)
Reference tools, 320–324
Reinsurance, 133
Relator, fraud reporting, 84, **87–88**
Resignations, accepting, 291, **294–295**
Resilience, and emotional intelligence, 14
Resources
  annual HR calendar, 321–324
  conflict resolution, 209, **220**
  governmental resources, 309
  recommended reading, 320
  Web sites, 320–321
Résumé development, 314–316
Retaliation protection
  ADA/ADAAA, **66–67**
  CPSA/CPSIA, 79–80, **86–87**
  EEO/EEOC, 3–6, 49–51, **62–63**
  fraud reporting, 84, **87–88**
  OSHA, **63–64,** 310
  personal protective steps, 91, **99–100**
  state legislation, 158, 173–174, 181–182
Rhode Island legislation, 139–140, 176
Rosenberg, Marshall, 316

Safety
  public safety, 79–84, **85–87**
  workplace, **67–69,** 227, **229–234**
Salovey, Peter, 13
School information, internship program,
    275–276
Searchable Online Accommodation Resource
    (SOAR), 56
Second surgical opinion, managed care, 132
Seinfeld (TV program), 6